Charles Campion's London restaurant guide 2009

Written and edited by
Charles Campion

Additional research by Jan Leary

P

PROFILE BOOKS

This edition first published in Great Britain in 2008 by
Profile Books Ltd
3A Exmouth House
Pine Street
Exmouth Market
London EC1R 0JH
www.profilebooks.com

A CIP catalogue record for this book is available from the British Library.

ISBN 978 1 84668 143 1

Text design by Sue Lamble
Typeset in Humanist 777 by MacGuru Ltd
info@macguru.org.uk

Printed and bound in Italy by Legoprint S.p.A., Lavis, Trento

The publisher and author have made every effort to ensure that the information in *Charles Campion's London Restaurant Guide* is accurate and up to date, but they can accept no responsibility for any loss, injury or inconvenience sustained as a result of information or advice contained in the guide.

The maps used in this guide are based originally on the 1939 Bartholomew atlas, revised with the assistance of copyright-free material provided by Alan Collinson Design and checked extensively on foot. Subsequent revisions courtesy of Lovell Johns Ltd, Oxford, and David Haslam Publishing. Further revised and extended by ML Design London using Bacon's *Atlas of London* 1948 and out-of-copyright OS 1:25,000 sheets plus checking on foot. Maps © ML Design 2008.

A big thank you

Once again it falls to me to thank Gonzalez Byass for their whole-hearted support and everyone at Profile Books for their tireless endeavour. Tio Pepe occupies a unique position in the affections of many gastronauts as a extremely versatile stimulator of the appetite – whether you're talking curry or consommé! And without Tio Pepe's generous backing (coupled with a welcome, and almost saintly, lack of interference) this book would never have got written. So saying, the team at Profile must also take credit for putting up with all the alarms, excursions and last-minute crises that are always part of writing a restaurant guide. In particular I would like to thank Paul Forty for project management; Kate Griffin at Profile; Fiona Screen for copy editing; Jan Leary for telephone research; and Martin Lubikowski of ML Design for work on the mapping.

Charles Campion

About the author

Charles Campion is an award-winning food writer and restaurant reviewer. He is a past winner of the Glenfiddich 'Restaurant Writer of the Year' award, and has written about restaurants in the *London Evening Standard* for over a decade. He also contributes to various radio and TV food programmes, as well as a long list of magazines. He has written a number of cookery books including *The Real Greek at Home*, which he wrote with chef Theodore Kyriakou, and *Food from Fire*, a book of barbecue recipes which was published by Mitchell Beazley in 2006. Before becoming a food writer, Charles worked in a succession of London ad agencies and had a spell as chef-proprietor of a hotel and restaurant in darkest Derbyshire.

Help us update

We've tried to ensure that this book is as up to date and accurate as possible. However, London's restaurant scene is in constant flux: chefs change jobs; restaurants are bought and sold; menus change. There will probably be a few references in this guide that are out of date even as this book is printed – and standards, of course, go up and down. If you feel there are places we've underrated or over praised, or others we've unjustly omitted, please let us know: comments or corrections are much appreciated.

Please address letters to:
Charles Campion
c/o Profile Books
3a Exmouth House
Pine Street
London EC1R 0JH

Or send your comments via email to
Charles@CharlesCampion.com

Foreword
by Tom Parker Bowles

Charles Campion is a serious eater. And that is meant as a high compliment. There is no man who knows more about the London eating scene in its every guise. And he's always the first port of call for advice on the fieriest Pakistani lamb chops, the most silken dim sum pastry or the finest laksa soup. That's not to say he knows nothing of the starrier Michelin establishments. Far from it, as he's equally at home in Le Gavroche or The Square and in the lino-floored kebab houses of the city's more far-flung boroughs. But Charles is a man dedicated to treading the byways and backwaters of the capital, searching out restaurants and dishes that most of us would wander right past. He's not dazzled by multi-million pound refits and extravagant marketing campaigns, and refuses to be blinded by hype. His sole concern is good food, and that what's makes this guide so superior to any of its rivals. His knowledge, experience and love of all food shine through in every line: armed with this book, you need nothing more than a healthy appetite to find the very best of London eating.

Introduction

This is the third edition of my *London Restaurant Guide* and it is the largest ever. The London restaurant scene is in a state of continual flux as restaurants open, change their menus, refurbish their décor and then, all too often, crash and burn. The 2009 edition includes over 75 completely new entries, but every single page has been painstakingly updated to reflect changing prices, opening times and menus. If you were to include in the tally each of the multiple branches we list for some restaurants, the total number of eating places in the guide would nudge the 600 mark, but we prefer to stick with 'over 400'. Anyone who has lived or worked in London knows that while it may seem like one big city to the outsider, it is really a series of villages, each with their own character, their own restaurants and their own secrets. If you're a Londoner you are probably pretty familiar with the restaurants that are close to where you live, but keeping tabs on the whole of the West End or the far-flung suburbs is a full-time job and one made more difficult by the way that restaurants open and close with lightning speed – and that's where this guide comes in. Given the above, it's therefore strange that almost every other restaurant guide assumes that 'what to eat' is your starting point when you want to go out. It shouldn't be – eating out is much more often about 'where to eat'. If you're meeting friends in Chiswick your best options might be French or Modern British; in Wembley or Tooting they might be Indian. But you also want to know about that oddball great restaurant, too, whether it's an interesting newcomer like Urban Turban on Westbourne Grove; a new gastro-pub like The Carpenters Arms in Hammersmith; or a City newcomer like The Mercer on Threadneedle Street. This book divides London into five geographic sections – Central; City & East; North; South; West – and then breaks these down into neighbourhoods. With restaurants arranged alphabetically in each neighbourhood section, it's your key to eating well across the whole city.

Something for everyone

This guide reviews restaurants for every possible occasion, from grabbing a bite to pushing the boat out. It also covers many different kinds of food – some sixty cuisines in all. In reality, we cover even more, since for simplicity we have used 'Indian' and 'Chinese' as catch-all terms. The reviews also keep faith with original menu spellings of dishes, so you'll find satays, satehs and satés – all of which will probably taste much the same – so you will certainly find some apparent inconsistencies.

All recommended

Another important thing to note about the restaurants selected and reviewed in this book is that they are all recommended – none has been included simply to make up the numbers.

Prices, websites and credit cards

Every review in this book gives an indication of the prices of starters, mains, sides, desserts, set meals, the lowest-priced bottle of wine... in fact everything you need to form a clear picture of how expensive the restaurant will be. At some time in the Guide's life these prices will become out of date, but they were all as accurate as we could make them when the book left for the printer. Even in the uncertain world of restaurants, when prices rise or prices fall, everyone tends to move together. If the prices make it appear that one restaurant is twice as expensive as another, that situation is likely to prevail. Websites are particularly fickle; they were accurate when we went to press, but it only takes a restaurant to change internet provider and all bets are off. Opening hours and days are given in every review, as are details of any service charge and the credit cards accepted. Where reviews specify that restaurants accept 'all major credit cards', that means at least AmEx, MasterCard and Visa. Acceptance of Visa and MasterCard usually means Switch and Delta, too; we've tried to pinpoint any exceptions, but if you're relying on one particular card it's always best to check with the restaurant when you book.

Access

You will also see that the entries for some restaurants display the wheelchair symbol. As provision for the disabled varies wildly, this must be something of a catch-all, so when an entry has the symbol it means that the restaurant has *some* facilities specifically for disabled diners – that may be a lift, or ramps, or converted loos. It is always best to check exactly what's what before setting out, all restaurants should be keen to help.

It just remains to wish you 'happy eating', and enjoy the Guide

Charles Campion

THIS YEAR THE BEST MONTH TO EAT OUT IS OCTOBER!

This October a 'Restaurants Against Hunger' campaign from humanitarian charity **Action Against Hunger** is encouraging diners to 'Fight hunger: Eat out'. To coincide with UN World Food Day on 16 October 2008, more than 500 chefs and restaurateurs up and down the country will be joining forces for a month of tasty fundraising.

Importantly, the emphasis of 'Restaurants Against Hunger' is on pleasure, not guilt. Simply pop along to a local eatery that supports the campaign to enjoy a great meal, and by doing so help people in some of the world's poorest countries to feed their families. Restaurants taking part choose how they fundraise, whether by making a donation to the charity for every sale of a specially created dish, asking diners to leave a little extra with the bill, or hosting a special event.

To find out which of the restaurants in this guide are supporting the scheme, log on to www.restaurantsagainsthunger.org – and if you have bought this book after October 2008, please don't feel left out: you can make a donation at www.aahuk.org

Registered UK charity no. 1047501

Top picks

We've all got favourites. But to make matters even more confusing, we dedicated eaters-out can be fickle as tastes and fashions change. I would happily eat out at any restaurant listed in this book, and none has been included just to make up the numbers – but only a fool would claim that he was completely unbiased! Here are some Top Picks: six of the best in each category!

Best newcomers

Best Chinese

Best for high style

Best for a meat feast

Best for haute cuisine

Best cheapies

Best tapas

Best for affordable wines

Best for lovers of fish

Best 'high street' Indian

Best wild cards

The centre

Bloomsbury and Fitzrovia

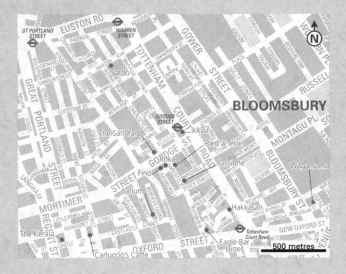

Carluccio's Caffe

8 Market Place, W1 ■ 020 7636 2228

⊖ Oxford Circus

🍽 Italian

🕐 Mon to Fri 07.30–23.00; Sat 09.00–23.00; Sun 09.00–22.30

🖰 www.carluccios.com

🗗 all major credit cards ■ 10% optional service added for parties of 8 or more

££ starters £3.95–£9.95 ■ mains £6.75–£13.95 ■ sides £2.25
■ desserts £2.85–£8.25 ■ lowest bottle price £11.95

✪ Italian shopping, eating and drinking

Branches of Carluccio's Caffe are now springing up almost as fast as Antonio Carluccio's beloved porcini. These are extremely busy restaurants, which means that there is usually a great atmosphere, but the downside is the likelihood of a queue at peak times. The front of the premises is a delicatessen-cum-shop, the mid-section is a bar and the rear is a café-restaurant. Commendable effort has been made to incorporate all that is admirable about continental coffee shops: Carluccio's is open throughout the day, proper meals are available at all hours, the coffee is notably good and children are welcome. There are always a couple of good soups on the main menu, such as zuppa di funghi con pancetta. Look for sound antipasti – as well as deli-counter items there are specialities like the Sicilian dish arancini di riso, which are crisp, deep-fried rice balls filled with mozzarella or ragù. There's also a selection of well-made salads. Main courses range from pasta dishes – penne alla Luganica; tortellini; ravioli – to fegato Veneziana, which is calves' liver and balsamic onions, or a respectable steak and chips. Puds major in ice cream (gelati artiginali) and include the magnificent 'Affogato' – strong coffee over vanilla ice cream. For a restaurant serving such large numbers of customers, the cooking is pretty decent and the service is efficient enough to cope. The dishes are well seasoned and the prices are fair.

→ For branches, see index or website

Eagle Bar Diner

3–5 Rathbone Place, W1 ■ 020 7637 1418

⊖ Tottenham Court Road

🍽 North American

🕐 Mon to Wed 12.00–23.00; Thurs & Fri 12.00–01.00; Sat 10.00–01.00; Sun 11.00–18.00

🖰 www.eaglebardiner.co.uk

🖰 all major credit cards except AmEx ■ 10% optional service added for parties of 6 or more

££ breakfast £3.95–£6.95 ■ mains £4–£13.50 ■ sides £1.50–£5 ■ desserts £4–£4.50 ■ lowest bottle price £12.95

✪ Anyone for a 6oz ostrich and cranberry burger?

Unsurprisingly, the Eagle Bar Diner is both a bar and a diner. It's a modern-looking sort of place with the booths for diners on a slightly raised platform. The bar is purposeful and its large size gives a clue as to how busy it gets. The room is comfortable and service is informal – an agreeably grown-up sort of diner. The menu sticks to tried and trusted diner fare: Caesar salad, to which you can add grilled chicken or grilled king prawns; an American breakfast – short-stack pancakes, or Belgian waffles with bacon and maple syrup; or pasta dishes and sandwiches – hot salt brisket with Dijon mustard and pickles. There are hot dogs and a few American mains, such as Jambalaya or New York strip loin. But the burgers take centre stage here. They are large and sassy, and if you plan on taking a bite out of one you'll need jaws that gape like an anaconda's. An 8oz ground-topside burger comes with good accompaniments and is accurately cooked. You'll need spuds, so choose from a variety of styles: hash browns, Eagle mash, cheesy fries, hand-cut fat chips, or skinny chips. The fat chips are good. The speciality burgers range from the Intshe, made with ostrich and cranberry, to the Golden Hog (wild boar and apples) or the Dundee – a burger made from crocodile, chicken and pineapple. Puds are sticky: brownie served warm with ice cream; New York baked cheesecake; or carrot cake.

Fino

33 Charlotte Street, W1 ■ 020 7813 8010

⊖ Goodge Street

🍴 Spanish/tapas

🕐 Mon to Fri 12.00–14.30 & 18.00–22.30; Sat 18.00–22.30

🛒 all major credit cards except AmEx ■ 12.5% optional service added

££ tapas £1.20–£17.50 ■ mains £6.50–£15.50 ■ sides £3–£9.50
■ desserts £3–£10.20 ■ lowest bottle price £17

✪ Authentic Spanish food, authentic London setting

Say tapas, and the mind makes an involuntary leap towards cool, tiled, old-fashioned Iberia. Fino approaches the same Spanish virtues, but from a different angle. There's a stylish bar for drinking on the mezzanine and a bar for eating tapas while sat along the front of the open kitchen downstairs. The dining room is large and airy. There's a good range of classic tapas dishes and some items fresh from the plancha (a no-frills grill). Start with some pan con tomate, a tomatoey, garlicky bread. Add arroz negro, a very delicious squid-ink risotto. Then try crisp-fried squid, delicious with a squeeze of lemon. The croquetas are good – filled with ham, or piquillo peppers. From the meat section there are milk-fed lamb cutlets, which are impossibly small, tender and with good gravy; and some shoulder of jamón Jabuga – top stuff, melting in the mouth, with an amazing silky texture and gentle richness. From the plancha you could choose tuna with sun-dried tomatoes, clams, cod Bilbaina, squid, or sardines. In keeping with the smartness of the surroundings, the wine list is priced on the merciless side, although there are several interesting sherries that are worth investigation. If you cannot face the responsibility of ordering ask for advice, as there are sometimes specials that are not listed on the main menu. Fino offers an elegant and sophisticated Spanish restaurant with slick service and prices to match.

Hakkasan

8 Hanway Place, W1 ■ 020 7927 7000   &

⊖ Tottenham Court Road

🍽 Chinese/dim sum

🕐 Mon to Fri 12.00–15.00 & 18.00–24.00; Sat 12.00–16.00 & 18.00–24.00; Sun 12.00–16.00 & 18.00–23.00; bar open Mon to Wed to 01.00; Thurs to Sat to 03.00; Sun to 00.30

🗗 all major credit cards ■ 13.5% optional service added

££ dim sum lunch only £3–£9.50 ■ starters £5.50–£80
■ mains £9.50–£68 ■ rice & noodles £1.50–£10.90
■ desserts £6–£13.50 ■ lowest bottle price £24

✪ Super slick, super cooking, super bills

Hakkasan is a very superior kind of Chinese restaurant. The décor is slick (as you would expect when the design budget was a reputed £3 million) and the double-smart cocktail bar is consistently and fashionably crammed. Top-name designers from the worlds of film and fashion have given their all, and this is a stylish and elegant place. The food is novel, well presented, fresh, delicious and, in strangely justifiable fashion, expensive. The starters are called 'small eats' and do not shy away from expensive luxury ingredients. The three-style vegetarian roll teams a mooli spring roll with a bean curd puff and a yam roll. Marinated abalone with corn-fed chicken and jelly fish cannot be many people's idea of a 'small eat'. Or there is grilled Shanghai dumpling. The main dishes are innovative and delicious. Try pan-fried silver cod with XO sauce, or the stir-fry scallop with eryngi mushroom and lily bulb. There's also jasmine-tea smoked chicken and sweet-and-sour organic pork with pomegranate; steamed lotus-leaf wrapped corn-fed poussin with luffa melon; or braised ribeye Waygu beef with Chinese spice. By way of a staple, add the stir-fry glass vermicelli, which enlivens noodles with chicken, crabmeat and fried shallots. The dim sum (served only at lunchtime) are not cheap, but they are very good – prawn puff and sesame prawn toast are exceptional. Whisper it: 'You'll be hard pushed to find dim sum this good in Chinatown'.

Ikkyu

67a Tottenham Court Road, W1 ■ 020 7636 9280

⊖ Goodge Street

🍴 Japanese/sushi

🕐 Mon to Fri 12.00–14.30 & 18.00–21.30; Sat & Sun 18.00–21.30

🖪 Mastercard, Visa, AmEx; no Switch or cheques ■ 10% optional service added at dinner only

££ sushi/nigiri £2–£12.50 ■ sashimi £4.50–£13.50
  ■ dishes £6.50–£13.50 ■ rice/noodles 80p–£3.50
  ■ desserts £2.20–£3.50 ■ set meals £4.90–£9.60
  ■ lowest bottle price £11; small sake £2.60; shoucho £3.90

✪ Small, shabby and authentic Japanese restaurant

First you will have to find Ikkyu – it is hidden at the bottom of a non-descript stairway with an entrance on Tottenham Court Road. Ikkyu is busy, basic and full of people eating reliable Japanese food at sensible prices – all of which makes it a good match for any popular neighbourhood restaurant in Tokyo. It is an engaging place, quite obviously tailored to Japanese customers. But don't worry, the strangeness of the welcome comes over as politeness, and you won't feel completely stranded. Nigiri sushi is good here and is priced by the piece: tuna, salmon, mackerel, cuttlefish. Or there's sashimi, which runs all the way from mackerel to sea urchin eggs. Alternatively, start with soba – delicious cold brown noodles. Then allow yourself a selection of yakitori, either a portion of assorted yakitori, or a mix and match selection from tongue, heart, liver, gizzard and chicken skin. You will need many skewers of the grilled chicken skin, which is implausibly delicious. Moving on to the main dishes, an order of fried leeks with pork brings a bunch of long, onion-flavoured greens strewn with morsels of grilled pork. Whatever the green element is, it is certainly not leeks. Or there's grilled aubergine, or rolled five vegetables with shrimp, which is like a Swiss roll made with egg and vegetable with a core of prawn. Only the very adventurous will try a shouchu and soda; shouchu is a clear spirit that tastes like – clear spirit.

The Kerala

15 Great Castle Street, W1 ■ 020 7580 2125

⊖ Oxford Circus

🍽 Indian

🕐 Mon to Sat 12.00–15.00 & 17.30–23.00; Sun 12.30–15.00 &
17.30–20.00

🗄 all major credit cards ■ 12.5% optional service added

££ starters £3.35–£5.35 ■ mains £4.65–£8.95 ■ sides £1.20–£6.25
■ desserts £3.35–£4.35 ■ lunch buffet £10.95
■ lowest bottle price £13.50

⭐ Authentic Keralan food, high on hospitality, low on price

This is a straightforward family business and one that takes a
genuine pride in home cooking. At the end of the 1980s Shirref's
wine bar was taken over by David Tharakan, who added a short
menu of pub food favourites. The big changes came nearly a decade
later when David's wife Millie took over the kitchen and changed the
menu. Shirref's started to offer Keralan home cooking, with well-
judged, well-spiced dishes at bargain-basement prices. Since then The
Kerala restaurant has gone from strength to strength and achieved
a certain notoriety for the great-value lunch deals. To start with, you
must order a platoon of simple things: cashew nut pakoda; potato
bonda; lamb samosa; chicken liver masala; mussels ularthu. These
are honest dishes, simply presented and at a price that encourages
experimentation. Thereafter, the menu is divided into a number of
sections: Syrian Christian specialities from Kerala; coastal seafood
dishes; Malabar biryanis; vegetable curries; and special dosas. From
the first, try erachi olathiathu, a splendid dry curry of lamb with
coconut. From the second, try meen and mango vevichathu, which
is kingfish cooked with the sharpness of green mango. From the
biryanis, how about chemmin biryani, prawns cooked with basmati
rice? Avial is a mixed vegetable curry with yogurt and coconut. The
breads are fascinating – try the lacy and delicate appams made from
steamed rice-flour. Look out for the 'lunch buffet' too – a bargain
feast worth noting.

Passione

10 Charlotte Street, W1 ■ 020 7636 2833

⊖ Goodge Street

▮◉▮ Italian

🕐 Mon to Fri 12.30–14.15 & 19.00–22.15; Sat 19.00–22.15

🖱 www.passione.co.uk

🖅 all major credit cards ■ 12.5% optional service added

££ antipasti £12.50–£15 ■ pasta & risotti £11.50–£15.50
■ mains £19–£26.50 ■ sides £5.50–£7.50 ■ desserts £7
■ lowest bottle price £14.50

⚙ Telly chef Gennaro Contaldo's real passion

Gennaro Contaldo may have been eclipsed in the fame stakes by his protégé Jamie Oliver, but he still cooks delicious and simple food. Simplicity, an unpretentious feel to the place, seasonal ingredients and talent in the kitchen are the main springs of Passione. You owe it to yourself to have four courses. The menu changes daily and there is a constant procession of specials. Among the antipasti, there's zuppa di cecci, con gremolata di rosmarino – chickpea soup with rosemary; and carpaccio di manzo con carciofi – beef carpaccio with artichokes. Then there are pasta and risotti, which are available in two portion sizes. Try papardelle con ragù di mare (seafood sauce) or, when the tangy wild sorrel is in season, risotto con accetosella. Mains are rich and satisfying: orata con endiva belga salsina di miele e aceto bianco is sea bream with endives and a honey and vinegar sauce; melanzane al forno ripiene di provolone is a rich dish of aubergines and cheese; coniglio con rosmarino e patate saltate is rabbit with rosemary and sauté potatoes. The service is slick here; this is a place where they understand the art of running a comfortable restaurant. Puddings are serious stuff, though it has to be said that the delicious gelato Passione, a swirl of zesty limoncello ice with a splash of wild strawberry folded into it, is for all the world a grown-up's raspberry ripple.

Pied à Terre

34 Charlotte Street, W1 ■ 020 7636 1178

⊖ Goodge Street/Tottenham Court Road

🍽 French

🕐 Mon to Fri 12.15–14.30 & 18.15–23.00; Sat 18.15–23.00

🖰 www.pied-a-terre.co.uk

🖃 all major credit cards ■ 12.5% optional service added

££ du jour lunch £24.50 (2 courses) & £30 (3 courses)
■ à la carte £49.50 (2 courses) & £60 (3 courses) ■ desserts £10.50
■ tasting menu £80 & £122 (with wine) ■ lowest bottle price £18

✪ Heavy hitter, revitalised

It's always difficult for a restaurant to endure a prolonged closure, and at Pied à Terre the trauma started with a fire. Not one of those small flare-ups in the chip pan, but a real raging inferno. Fast forward a year or so and in September 2005 the resto re-opened with a new dining room front and back, a new bar on the first floor, a completely new kitchen and an elegant new private room on the second floor. Following the upheaval things settled down and soon Pied à Terre was back to its silky best. The food is ambitious; dishes are complex both in terms of tastes and textures and in presentation. Service is suave and there is a particularly long and fulsome wine list. The food is very good indeed. Starters may include roast breast of mallard with choucroute; pan-fried scallops with squash and vanilla purée; or pepper seared tuna with chive crushed potatoes. For mains choose from pan-fried zander with a ragout of lentils, snails and root vegetables; assiette of kid with caramelised endive and roast shallot; roast black-leg chicken, lasagne of trompette de la mort, and baby leeks; or roast rabbit saddle with a warm rabbit and foie gras terrine. Desserts are elaborate: bittersweet chocolate tart; macadamia nut mousse and stout ice cream; or a prune and walnut frangipane with ginger ice cream, tea-infused prunes and crystallised ginger. If your bank account flinches at the prospect of a visit, try the du jour menu at lunch. This is top-notch cooking.

Roka

37 Charlotte Street, W1 ■ 020 7580 6464

⊖ Goodge Street/Tottenham Court Road

◉ Japanese

⊕ Mon to Sat 12.00–15.30 & 17.30 to 23.30; Sun 17.30–22.30

⌁ www.rokarestaurant.com

⊟ all major credit cards ■ 12.5% optional service added

££ tempura & kushiage £4.90–£28.90 ■ sashimi & maki
£4.90–£17 ■ robata £4.90–£22.60 ■ roka dishes £3.60–£39.50
■ desserts £4.90–£8.90 ■ set lunch £25 ■ tasting menu £50 & £75
■ lowest bottle price £21; sake from £8.50

⊛ New wave Japanese, Charlotte Street chic

Roka is little sister to style palace Zuma (see p. 69). It has a striking
dining room with one wall entirely taken up with large jars in which
bits and bobs are marinating. The feel of the place is very modern and
very slick, and that is probably how the customers view themselves.
The food here is original and elegant – Roka is well adapted to the
modern trend of 'grazing'. The term 'robata' means cooking on an
open flame or, to cut to the chase, a barbie. The grilled dishes are
good – chicken wings come with sea salt and lime; there are lamb
cutlets with Korean spices. Then there is an array of sashimi and
maki rolls, some of which get quite complex – a cone-shaped roll
made with eel teriyaki, avocado, shiso and sansho pepper, or grilled
salmon belly and skin with cucumber, wasabi and tobiko (flying fish
roe). Or perhaps the rice hot pot with Cornish crab and wasabi, or
the pancake balls filled with prawn and octopus, appeal. Or maybe
a whole lobster tempura? The set lunch options help with decision-
making; all are served with shiro miso soup and home-made pickles:
katsudon is trad pork in breadcrumbs with egg rice and onion;
unadon is teriyaki grilled eel, sansho pepper and red onion. Sake is a
good accompaniment – take advice from the staff. Roka is suave and
somewhat pricey, but the food is good.

The Salt Yard

54 Goodge Street, W1 ▪ 020 7637 0657

⊖ Goodge Street

🍽 Spanish (they say Mediterranean)

🕐 Mon to Fri 12.00–15.00 & 18.00–23.00; Sat 17.00–23.00; bar snacks all day

🖰 www.saltyard.co.uk

🖶 all major credit cards ▪ 12.5% optional service added

££ charcuterie £8–£17 ▪ tapas £3.25–£8.75 ▪ desserts £4.50–£6.50 ▪ cheese selections £6.75–£8.25 ▪ lowest bottle price £14.50

⭐ Considered tapas, serious charcuterie

When is a tapas not a tapas? When it's a miniaturised dish picked from a modern grazing menu, that's when. In 2007 the proprietors opened Dehesa (in Soho, see p. 158), which leans even further towards tapas, so it seems that whether Spanish or not the concept of ordering 'three or so dishes each and sharing' seems to be all the rage. Rather pleasingly, the food is either very simple – a board with a selection of different Spanish charcuterie: salchichón, cabedaza, lomo and chorizo – or quite sophisticated, such as a dish of pot-roast rabbit with gnocchi and black olives. The rabbit is good and comes in a middleweight portion, rather more than you would expect as a tapas. Also good from the meat options are the confit of Gloucester Old Spot pork belly with rosemary cannelini beans, and the morcilla croquetas, which are amazing black pudding rissoles. From the fish choices, the crispy squid with chickpea purée is a winner: good crisp and dry squidlets on a layer of what is very like a hot and savoury houmous. The piquillo peppers filled with salt cod come with a black olive dressing, and you could order pan-fried bream with chargrilled baby leeks. In the veg section you'll find chargrilled peppers and a panzanella salad with buffalo mozzarella. The wine list is carefully chosen. Service is notably efficient – and it needs to be with the dishes coming in waves.

→ For branch, see index or website

Sardo

45 Grafton Way, W1 ■ 020 7387 2521

⊖ Warren Street

|○| Italian/Sardinian

🕛 Mon to Fri 12.00–15.00 & 18.00–23.00; Sat 18.00–23.00

🔗 www.sardo-restaurant.com

🖶 all major credit cards ■ 12.5% optional service added

££ antipasti & primi £7.90–£10.90 ■ secondi £12–£17.50
■ sides £2.90–£7.50 ■ desserts £4.50 ■ lowest bottle price £14

✪ Sardinia's unofficial gastro-ambassador

Romolo Mudu is from Caligari, and he is the proud and ebullient
owner of Sardo. Coupled with plain but fairly uninspired décor, this
may make elderly diners feel that they have wandered into a Soho
trattoria circa 1980. Take heart, for the food is more interesting than
you would expect, particularly the specials. Start with the mosciame
di tonno – air-dried tuna, or the calamari ripieno – baby squid,
stuffed and grilled. As a pasta course perhaps the specials will include
the classic malloreddus, which is hard wheat pasta with tomato
and sausage. Move on to something simple, but impressive, such
as fregola ai gamberi e zucchni. Fregola is a Sardinian pasta that
comes in small enough pieces to take over the role of rice, and here
it is teamed with prawns and courgettes. Or maybe salsiccia Sarda
appeals? The proprietor will happily discuss his brother's recipe for
these home-made sausages, which have a distinctive aniseed tang.
For dessert, go trad Sardinian: sebada is a puff pastry filled with
orange peel and cheese and topped with honey. Or there is a splendid
array of five or six different pecorino cheeses. The wine list includes a
page of reasonably priced Sardinian specialities, and there are some
distinctive, aromatic whites – note the Vermentinas. As well as the
listed specials, it is always worth enquiring about even more special
specials – occasionally this restaurant has the famous mountain
prosciutto made from mutton.

→ For branch, see index or website

Wagamama

4 Streatham Street, WC1 ■ 020 7323 9223

⊖ Tottenham Court Road

🍴 Japanese/Chinese

🕔 Mon to Sat 12.00–23.00; Sun 12.00–22.00

🖱 www.wagamama.com

🖶 all major credit cards ■ no optional service added

££ mains £6.25–£9.25 ■ sides £1.35–£5.90 ■ lowest bottle price £11.75

✪ This is the way of the noodle

Wagamama is as good a canteen as you'll find, serving simple and generally rather good food at very reasonable prices. At regular eating times you'll find yourself in a queue lining the stairway – there are no reservations. When you reach the front, you're seated, your order is punched into a hand-held computer and that spurs the kitchen into action. Dishes arrive when they're cooked, so your party will be served at different times. Most people order a main dish – noodles in soup; fried noodles; or sauce-based noodles – or a rice dish. Side dishes can also be pressed into service as a starter: yasai yakitori is chargrilled chicken with the ever-popular yakitori sauce, while gyoza are delicious fried chicken dumplings. The mains include a splendid chilli beef ramen, slivers of sirloin steak in a vat of soup with vegetables. Also good is the yasai katsu curry, which is boiled rice with a light curry sauce and discs of deep-fried vegetables; and yasai chilli men, a vegetarian 'everything-in' dish with courgette, ginger, mushroom, carrot, peas, tomato, tofu and so on, plus ramen noodles. If this all sounds confusing, that's because it is. To enjoy Wagamama you'll need to go with the flow. As the cod philosophy on the menu would have it, Wagamama is 'Wilfulness or selfishness: selfishness in terms of looking after oneself, looking after oneself in terms of positive eating and positive living'. Now you know.

→ For branches, see index or website

Chinatown and Covent Garden

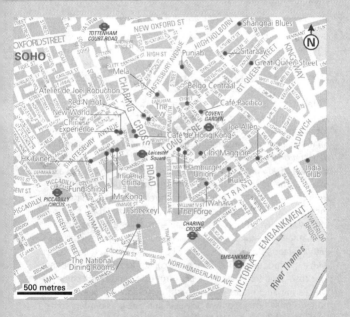

L'Atelier de Joel Robuchon

13–15 West Street, WC2 ■ 020 7010 8600

⊖ Leicester Square/Covent Garden

🍽 French

🕐 Mon to Sat 12.30–15.00 & 17.30–24.00; Sun 12.30–15.00 & 17.30–22.30

🖰 www.joel-robuchon.com

🖥 all major credit cards ■ 12.5% optional service added

££ tasting dishes £9–£20 ■ mains £12–£30 ■ desserts £9
  ■ tasting menu £80 (9 courses & coffee) ■ lowest bottle price £22

✪ French maestro plays new tune on old fiddle

L'Atelier means workroom and there is certainly a great deal of work going on at this moody London outpost of French superstar Joel Robuchon. The dining room is darkly stylish and seems tacked on to the kitchen as an afterthought. 'Les plats en petites portions dégustation' is supposed to head up an array of tapas-sized portions from which you pick three or four – but some are tapas-sized and others at the bottom of the list are more main-course sized. Then from the carte you can choose either entrées or meat and fish, the former starter-sized, the latter main-course sized. Don't try to understand, just pitch in. 'Le tourteau en rouelles d'avocat a l'huile aromatisée' is a sound, small and elegant helping of dressed crab with avocado. 'L'oeuf cocotte' is a wholly successful soft egg topped with a mushroom foam. Ordering 'les cuisses des grenouilles' brings four crisp, fried frog's legs. The pig's trotter is minced and comes with Parmesan on toast – very good. The scallop with seaweed butter is small but good. Two pixy beef and foie gras burgers come with great spiral chips. The lamb chops are very tender. When you get to the puds opt for the café glace – very decent coffee ice cream. Service is attentive, Gallic and slick. Should you get past the wines by the glass and one or two regional wines, the wine list will show no mercy whatsoever. Eating at L'Atelier is good fun and the cooking is very honest and unfussy, but if you get greedy and order extravagantly the bill will bite.

Belgo Centraal

50 Earlham Street, WC2 ■ 020 7813 2233

⊖ Covent Garden

🍴 Belgian

🕐 Mon to Thurs 12.00–23.00; Fri & Sat 12.00–23.30; Sun 12.00–22.30

🕙 www.belgo-restaurants.com

🗄 all major credit cards ■ 12.5% optional service added

££ starters £5.50–£7.65 ■ mains £8.25–£18.95 ■ sides £1.50–£2.75
■ desserts £3.50–£4.50 ■ express lunch (12.00 to 17.00) £5.95
■ lowest bottle price £12.50

✪ Moules frites stronghold

'Name five famous Belgians' is a question made a little easier by
the beer at Belgo. The Belgo group's flagship restaurant is a massive
metal-minimalist cavern accessed by riding down in a scissor-powered
lift. Turn left at the bottom and you enter the restaurant (where
you can book seats); turn right and you get seated in the beer hall,
where diners share tables. With 95 different beers, some at alcoholic
strengths of 8–9 per cent, it's difficult not to be sociable. A kilo of
classic moules marinières served with frites has fresh mussels that
have clearly been cooked then and there. Other options include
classique, with cream and garlic; Provençal, with tomato, herbs and
garlic; or even Green Thai, which comes with a Thai curry sauce. The
non-mussel eater could start with a salade Brabançonne, a warm
salad including bacon, black pudding and duck confit, or the cheese
croquettes, made with Orval beer. Move on to carbonnade Flamande,
beef braised in Geuze beer with apples and plums, and served with
frites. Desserts include, among many others, traditional Belgian
waffles with dark chocolate. Belgo delights in special offers: there's
a good-value set lunch, and a deal called 'beat the clock', where the
prices shift downwards in relation to how early you eat. Beware the
'32 stick' – 32 shot glasses of fruit schnapps and billed as 'great to
share between two!' Take a third person to help you out.

→ For branches, see index or website

Café de Hong Kong

47–49 Charing Cross Road, WC2 ■ 020 7534 9898

⊖ Leicester Square

🍴 Chinese

🕐 Mon to Sat 11.30–23.00; Sun 11.00–22.30

🖬 all major credit cards ■ no service added

££ snacks £2.20–£4.50 ■ mains £5.20–£10 ■ sides £1.80–£4.50
■ rice & noodles £4.20–£6 ■ desserts £2–£2.30

✪ Chinese, Jim, but not as we know it

Café de Hong Kong is an engaging place, bustling along, brightly
coloured, simple and with utilitarian booths. There are two dining
areas – one on the first floor overlooking the Charing Cross Road
and a larger one on the floor above. This place puts a new spin on
the term café culture. It's full of young Chinese people lingering
over spooky soft drinks and eating hearty stuff from large bowls. No
bookings are taken. To say that the menu is eclectic would be selling
it short. How do you fancy 'spaghetti Bolognaise'? You get an oval
dish full of spaghetti, topped with some tomatoey meat sauce and
then cheese, which has been finished in a hot oven. It's OK – the
kind of cooking you would have expected from an Italian trattoria in
about 1980. The menu also offers Russian borscht, pork chop curry, a
luncheon pork and egg sandwich, smoked pigs' trotters in five spice
sauce and some very good meals-in-a-bowl, such as fried noodles
with pork. And to wash it all down? How about sampling one of the
tapioca pearl drinks? A tall glass is filled with crushed ice, various
flavourings and a secret spoonful of 'pearls' – these are chewy, pea-
sized balls of tapioca. You drink your milkshake through a special
large-gauge straw and, as you suck up the drink, the pearls shoot into
your mouth and rattle around, transforming your head into a giant
pinball machine.

Café Pacifico

5 Langley Street, WC2 ■ 020 7379 7728

⊖ Covent Garden

🍴 Mexican

🕐 Mon to Sat 12.00–23.45; Sun 12.00–22.45

🖰 www.cafepacifico-laperla.com

🖶 all major credit cards ■ 12.5% optional service added

££ starters £4.95–£9.95 ■ mains £6.75–£16.95 ■ sides £1.50–£3.50
   ■ desserts £3.95–£4.50 ■ lowest bottle price £14.95

✪ Beware the mescal worm

The salsa is hot at Café Pacifico – in both ways. As you are seated,
a complimentary bowl of searing salsa dip with corn chips is put on
your table. As you eat, hot salsa music gets your fingers tapping.
The atmosphere is relaxed and you're soon in the mood for a cold
beer and the tequila list is a twinkle in your eye   there are over 60
varieties. The menu mixes old-style Californian Mexican and new
Mexican, so while favourites like fajitas, flautas and tacos dominate,
there are also some interesting and unusual dishes. Portions are
generous and spicy, and many main courses come with refried beans
and rice. Try nachos rancheros for starters, and enjoy a huge plate of
corn chips with beans, cheese, guacamole, onions, sour cream and
olives. Excellent for sharing. Taquitos – filled, fried baby tacos – are
good, as are smoked chicken quesadillas – flour tortillas with chicken,
red peppers and avocado salsa. Main courses include degustación
del Pacifico, which includes a bit of almost everything. There's the
chimichanga del mar, a seafood-packed, deep-fried, rolled tortilla;
burrito especial, a flour tortilla filled with cheese, refried beans and
a choice of roast beef, chicken or ground beef and covered with
ranchero sauce; or Cuervo swordfish steak asada, grilled fish with a
tequila and sun-dried tomato salsa. Puds are predictable, but pretty
soon it will be time to explore those rare top-shelf tequilas. Beware.

Chinese Experience
118 Shaftesbury Avenue, W1 ■ 020 7437 0377

⊖ Piccadilly Circus

⭑⭙⭑ Chinese/dim sum

🕐 Mon to Thurs 12.00–23.00; Fri & Sat 12.00–23.30

🕙 www.chineseexperience.com

🗗 all major credit cards ■ 10% optional service added

££ dim sum £2.50–£5.50 ■ starters £2–£8.50 ■ mains £7.50–£20
■ sides £2–£9 ■ desserts £2.50–£5 ■ set menus £17–£23
■ lowest bottle price £12

✪ Bright restaurant, authentic dim sum

This light and seriously busy restaurant on Shaftesbury Avenue
combines slick service with low prices and has the added bonus of
a menu that has not been 'dumbed down'. At lunch there is fierce
competition for tables and the dim sum service is fast and furious.
Cuttlefish cakes are good – chewy and well flavoured; Shanghai
pork buns work well – admirably juicy; the 'BBQ pork pastry' is not
as good as the pork puff at Royal China (see p. 80) or indeed the
venison puff at Yauatcha (see p. 169), but it is pretty good. Prawn
dumplings and scallop dumplings are good. There are also all those
moody dumplings that sound more adventurous and exciting than
they turn out to be, such as ducks' tongues or chicken's feet. What's
best about this place is that it feels modern – square plates and even
square steamers – but prices are still reasonable. The main menu
reflects the feel of the dim sum approach; there are some interesting
dishes like braised pork belly in five-spice sauce; seriously good
noodle dishes; stir-fried lamb with leek Peking-style; or how about
deep-fried prawns with salted egg yolk; or stir-fried prawns with
Chinese tea leaves? Plus there are some intriguing desserts, such as
deep-fried crispy milk, or mango and grapefruit tapioca pearl. An
area at the front of the room is set aside for juice-making, and there
are a number of healthy fruit and vegetable juices on offer.

Clos Maggiore

33 King Street, WC2 ■ 020 7379 9696

⊖ Covent Garden

🍽 French

🕐 Mon to Fri 12.00–14.15 & 17.00–22.45; Sat 17.00–23.00

🌐 www.closmaggiore.com

🔲 all major credit cards ■ 12.5% optional service added

££ starters £6.90–£12.90 ■ mains £14.90–£24.90 ■ sides £3.90–£4.50 ■ desserts £6.50–£7.50 ■ lunch & pre-theatre £19.50 (2 courses) (3 courses Sun 17.00-22.00) ■ dinner £25, £45, & £55 ■ tasting menu £60 (6 courses), £110 with matched wines ■ lowest bottle price £18

⭐ Provençal élan, et haute cuisine pour les Anglais

The proprietors of this restaurant, which was reborn in 2007, haven't actually said that their sights are set on stars, but they have brought over a chef and kitchen brigade from a two-Michelin-star French establishment; they have polished a lengthy wine list that's littered with famous names (and with some jaw-dropping prices); and they have re-designed the restaurant so that it looks like a cross between *Country Living* and a French holiday brochure. Service is remarkably good – slick and attentive. Sitting in the rear part of the dining room where the twigs with everlasting cherry blossom make a canopy under the roof light does lead to a surreal feeling, but the food is compensation enough. The menu is both seasonal and ambitious, while dishes are complicated, multi-textured and rich. Starters may include an etuvée of asparagus and new-season morels with ricotta gnocchi and a sauce made with marc de Gewürztraminer; or a remoulade of Dorset crab with marjoram, pickled cauliflower and brown shrimps, where the contrasting textures work really well. For mains, slow-cooked Cornish cod fillet comes with ricotta and Burgundy snails while braised Charolais beef cheek comes with potato and almond croquette and Hermitage sauce. Puds are elaborate – the tarte Tatin of apples and quince with cinnamon ice cream lingers in the memory. This is a terribly ambitious, and largely successful, French restaurant – we could all do with a few more of those.

The Forge

14 Garrick Street, WC2 ■ 020 7379 1432

◉ Leicester Square

🍽 French

🕐 Mon to Sat 12.00–15.00 & 17.00–24.00; Sun 12.00–23.00

🖯 www.theforgerestaurant.co.uk

🖻 all major credit cards ■ 12.5% optional service added

££ starters £5.50–£10.50 ■ mains £12–£30 ■ sides £3–£4 ■ desserts £6 ■ prix fixe (lunch, 17.00–19.00 & 22.00–24.00) £13.50 (2 courses) & £16.50 (3 courses) ■ lowest bottle price £14.50

✪ Comfortable French restaurant, comfortable French menu

The Forge threw open its doors in early 2007. The dining room is pleasant; comfortable chairs, some room between the tables, light and airy. Service is very impressive – crisp and efficient in a thoroughly Gallic way. There's a voluminous wine list and the advice on navigating its nooks and crannies is friendly and un-pushy. All in all there is much to please the elderly regulars who stroll over from the Garrick Club for a nosebag. The menu works along the same lines – the carte is huge, and unashamedly old-fashioned, with 20 starters, plus 6 dishes that can be small or large, 22 main courses and 12 puddings. It would be virtually impossible to read this menu and not find something appealing. The cooking is traditional but that is really a compliment rather than a criticism. Starters include truffled duck egg and smoked ham hock – very rich and satisfying; omelette aux fines herbes; or devilled lamb kidneys on toasted sourdough. Mains range from honey-glazed confit duck leg with pommes Sarladaise; to baked wild halibut with Puy lentils and jus gras; leg of lamb '7 hours' with pommes fondantes; or a fillet of beef 'bordelaise' with roasted bone marrow. Puds are classical – a pavé au chocolat; a Grand Marnier crème caramel. If you enjoy reduced sauces, and solid and reliable dishes, you will be happy here. And you probably won't mind being labelled old-fashioned.

Fung Shing

15 Lisle Street, WC2 ■ 020 7437 1539

⊖ Leicester Square

🍽 Chinese

🕐 daily 12.00 to 23.30

🖱 www.fungshing.co.uk

🖥 all major credit cards ■ 10% optional service added

££ starters £2–£19 ■ mains £8.50–£75 ■ sides £2–£8.50
   ■ menus £18 & £30pp ■ lowest bottle price £15

✪ Proud Chinatown old-timer

Fung Shing was one of the first restaurants in Chinatown to take cooking seriously. Some decades ago, when the restaurant was still a dowdy little place with a mural on the back wall, Chinatown's number one fish cook, chef Wu, ruled the kitchens. When he died, in 1996, his sous-chef took over. Some commentators suggest that there has been a slight decline in overall standards, but that may be rose-tinted hindsight and the menu is still littered with interesting dishes. To start, ignore the crispy duck with pancakes, which is good but too predictable, and the lobster with noodles. Instead try the steamed scallops with garlic and soy sauce – nowhere does them better. Or spare ribs, barbecued or with chilli and garlic. The prosaically named 'mixed meat with lettuce' is also good, a savoury dish of mince with lettuce-leaf wraps. You could happily order your mains solely from the chef's specials: stewed belly pork with yam in hot pot; crispy spicy eel; roast crispy pigeon; or oysters with bean thread vermicelli in hot pot. Try the perfect Singapore noodles; crispy stuffed baby squids with chilli and garlic; and steamed aubergine with garlic sauce. The Fung Shing has always been classy, but what is unusual, certainly in Chinatown, is the gracious and helpful service. Ask for advice with confidence, although you'll need an unflinching wallet if the recommendation is braised double-boiled shark's fin in hot pot.

Great Queen Street

32 Great Queen Street, WC2 ■ 020 7242 0622

⊖ Covent Garden/Holborn

🍽 British

🕐 Mon 18.00–22.30; Tues to Sat 12.00–14.30 & 18.00–22.00

🖰 all major credit cards except AmEx ■ no service added

££ starters £4.80–£.40 ■ mains £9.40–£22 ■ sides £3.40–£3.80
   ■ desserts £4.80–£5.80 ■ cheese £4 ■ lowest bottle price £12

✪ Brilliant food, brilliant people, brilliant prices

The people who opened this restaurant during April 2007 are no
dummies. It went from 'haven't heard of that one' to hot ticket in
the blink of an eye, and that was despite a few little eccentricities
– such as not putting the name of the resto on the frontage;
doubtless there will be death threats from cabbies. Inside the theme
is 'tamed-gastropub'. Great Queen Street is a sister to The Anchor
& Hope (see p. 186) and we, the most loyal of loyal customers,
are pathetically grateful that here the tables are larger, the chairs
are more comfortable and bookings are taken. The menu changes
twice a day, and dishes slide on and off. The heartbeat of this place
is seasonal British cooking using painstakingly sourced, top-quality
ingredients – and it works. It works very deliciously indeed. An array
of spring starters may include beetroot, goat's curd and mint – a
terrific combo of tastes and textures; brawn – a real belter, savoury,
yielding and toothsome; artichoke vinaigrette; warm duck heart,
bacon and foie gras salad; or crab on toast. Mains range from
Arbroath smokie, cream and chives; to a very, very good hamburger
made with Hereford beef and served on dripping toast with a parsley
salad (the accompanying chips merit three stars). Or how about a
grilled lemon sole with leeks and anchovy butter? Or slow-cooked
Welsh lamb neck served with Dauphinois potato? The latter is very
good indeed, a proper stew with all the flavour you get from the
bones, the Dauphinois offering a creamy counterpoint. Puds include a
flourless chocolate cake; a little lemon pot – a sort of creamy posset;
and a muscat caramel custard. There's a forgiving wine list, and
decent beer.

Hamburger Union

4–6 Garrick Street, WC2 ■ 020 7379 0412

⊖ Leicester Square

🍽 Burgers

🕐 Sun & Mon 11.30–21.30; Tues to Sat 11.30–22.30

🖱 www.hamburgerunion.com

🖶 all major credit cards ■ no service added

££ hamburgers £3.95–£9 ■ sides 95p–£3.95 ■ desserts £2.95
  ■ lowest bottle price £12.95

✪ This resto cares about meat

Rather than getting fancy, purveyors of hamburgers should get real, because with some dishes simpler is always better, and one of those dishes is the hamburger. Everything starts with decent meat and at Hamburger Union the meat comes from organic and free-range herds and is properly hung; the burgers are freshly made on the premises. The restaurant occupies two shop fronts: start on the left where you order, pay and then go on through to the very modernist dining room next door. You take a ticket with you and pop it into the metal stand on your table, so that the waitress can find you when your drinks are ready and your meal is cooked. The menu is short. There are burgers, cheeseburgers, bacon cheeseburgers, some veggie options, and a notable fillet steak. Adherents to the low-carb cult can have their burger 'protein style', which means that the kitchen replaces the bun with a couple of lettuce leaves. The straightforward burger is very good – juicy, and on an Italian-style bun. It is cooked as requested and comes with some red onion, mayo and lettuce. The chips are described on the menu as 'proper chips, never frozen' and that is what they are. There are reasonably priced drinks and a suitably sticky and unctuous malted milk. 'Cocktail shakes' – Baileys, Tia Maria or crème de menthe – are a bit more puzzling and probably best left to experts.

→ For branches, see index or website

HK Diner

22 Wardour Street, WC2 ■ 020 7434 9544

⊖ Piccadilly/Leicester Square

|●| Chinese

⊕ daily 11.00–04.00

🗗 all major credit cards (over £12) ■ 10% optional service added

££ starters £2.50–£9 ■ mains £8.50–£12.50 ■ sides £4.50–£7
■ lowest bottle price £9.50

✪ Modern vibe, modern interior, trad food

HK Diner really is a diner at heart, and the atmosphere has more
in common with American eateries than Chinese restaurants. This a
light, bright, busy, modern sort of place, so if you like your Chinese
restaurants seedy and 'authentic' you will almost certainly walk past.
Yet pre-judging this place would be a major mistake, as the food
is very good. Prices are not cheap, but they are not over-the-top
either, and the prospect of getting decent food very late at night is
a beguiling one. Service is attentive, you don't wait long for food
and the tables turn over at a ferocious pace. The menu offers all the
Cantonese favourites, from very good salt-and-pepper spare ribs to
grilled dumplings and steamed scallops on the half shell. For main
course, deep-fried squid with salt, pepper and garlic is as light, crisp
and un-rubbery as you could wish, or there's steamed crab with
Shao Sing wine. Fried beef with chilli and black bean sauce is rich
and delicious, as is honey-barbecued pork. The Singapore noodle is a
model of its kind. From the vegetable dishes, choose the fried snow
pea shoots with minced garlic – if you love garlic. This is the one dish
to guarantee that even good friends will keep their distance for the
next couple of days. The simple dishes, such as fried noodles with
mixed meat or fried noodle with mixed seafood, always hit the spot.

Imperial China

White Bear Yard, Lisle Street, WC2 ■ 020 7734 3388

⊖ Leicester Square

¶❍¶ Chinese/dim sum

🕛 Mon to Fri 12.00–22.30; Sat & Sun 11.30–22.00

🖰 www.imperial-china.co.uk

🖶 all major credit cards ■ no service added

££ dim sum £2.20–£4.50 ■ starters £2.80–£9.95 ■ mains £6.95–£19.95
■ sides £2–£7.95 ■ desserts £2.95–£3.95 ■ set menus
£14.95–£18.95 ■ lobster feast £28.50 ■ lowest bottle price £12

✪ Large and opulent resto in private backwater

At Imperial China there are various different dining rooms spread
over three floors; some are dedicated to karaoke, and the one on the
ground floor seems to have been modelled on James Bond's idea
of a cocktail bar. It's not often that you see a baby grand piano in a
Chinese restaurant; stranger still to have a pianist tinkling the ivories
while you're the one playing chopsticks. The dim sum here have a
growing reputation – look to the specials where you'll sometimes
find such delights as fried pork and spring onion buns; preserved egg
and sliced fish cheung fun, as well as most of the steadier dim sum
favourites. There is trend here to dumb things down and offer tourist-
friendly dishes like sizzlers and duck in pancakes, but there may be a
few more interesting dishes lurking in the menu, such as lotus root
and straw mushrooms; sliced preserved pork knuckle with jelly fish;
and simple soups such as hot and sour or, encouragingly, 'soup of
the day – Chinese clear soup'. When it comes to main courses, dishes
like salt-baked chicken appeal; as do shredded pork with ginger and
aubergine; stir-fried scallop with lily bud; or deep-fried fillet of eel
with chilli. Imperial China tries to be a grown-up sort of restaurant
and the pricing reflects this ambition, but you may find some
intriguing stuff and, providing you relish the over-the-top styling, it
makes a good option.

India Club

143 Strand, WC2 ■ 020 7836 0650

⊖ Holborn

🍴 Indian

🕒 Mon to Sun 12.00–14.30 & 18.00–22.45

🔖 cash or cheque only ■ no service added

££ starters £2.50–£3.25 ■ mains £6–£8 ■ sides £1–£3 ■ desserts (kulfi) £2.50 ■ lowest bottle price £6

✪ A venerable living fossil

Heed the kindly chilli warning of your waiter. The chilli bhajis are extra-hot green chillies deep fried until crisp – not for novices. When the India Club opened in 1950, the linoleum flooring was probably quite chic. Situated up two flights of stairs, sandwiched between floors of the grandly named Strand Continental Hotel, the Club is an institution. Regulars are in love with the strangely old-fashioned combination of runny curry, low, low prices and time-warp décor. They can be split into two categories: suave Indians from the nearby High Commission, and a miscellany of folk from the BBC World Service down the road in Bush House. The food at the India Club predates any London consciousness of the different spicing of Bengal, Kerala, Rajasthan or Goa. It is Anglo-Indian, essentially, although to palates accustomed to more modern Indian dishes it is something of a symphony to runny sauce. Mughlay chicken is a wing and a drumstick in a rich, brown, oniony gravy, garnished with the two halves of a hard-boiled egg; while scampi curry is runny and brown, with fearless prawns swimming through it. Masala dosa is a well-made crispy pancake with a pleasantly sharp-tasting potato filling; dhal is yellow and – runny. There are good dishes of bhindi or brinjal. The mango chutney is a revelation: thick parings of mango, which are chewy and delicious. Breads – paratha, puris – are good, while the rice is white and comes in clumps.

The Ivy

1 West Street, WC2 ■ 020 7836 4751

⊖ Leicester Square

🍴 British

🕑 daily 12.00–15.00 (Sun 15.30) & 17.30–24.00

🖱 www.caprice-holdings.co.uk

🗄 all major credit cards ■ no service added

££ starters £4.75–£16.75 ■ mains £11.50–£28.50 ■ sides £3.50–£4.75
   ■ desserts £6.75–£8 ■ weekend lunch £26.75
   ■ lowest bottle price £17.75

✪ Lifestyles of the rich and famous

The Ivy is a beautiful, Regency-style restaurant, built in 1928 by
Mario Gallati. The staff, it is said, notice recessions only because they
turn fewer people away. That's no joke: The Ivy is booked solid, and
behaves like a club even if it isn't one. To get a booking, it helps to
proffer the name of at least a B-list celebrity. If your heart is set on a
visit, try booking at off-peak times a couple of months ahead, or at
very short notice, or ask for a table in the bar area. It's also less busy
for weekend lunch – three courses for a bargain price, with valet
parking thrown in. And once you're in? Well, whether you're famous
or not, the staff are charming and un-hurrying and the food is pretty
good. The menu is essentially a brasserie list of comfort food – nice
dishes that combine simplicity with familiarity. You might start with
spiced pumpkin and coconut soup; the risotto of wild mushrooms;
or the eggs Benedict. Then there's deep-fried haddock; grilled pork
sausage; and well-made versions of classic staples such as the Ivy
hamburger with dill pickle; shepherd's pie; and salmon fishcakes.
Even the vegetable section is enlivened with homely delights like
bubble and squeak. For dessert you might turn to chocolate pudding
soufflé; rhubarb fool; or go all Pickwickian and finish with a savoury –
herring roes on toast, or a serious Welsh rarebit.

J. Sheekey

26–32 St Martin's Court, WC2 ■ 020 7240 2565

⊖ Leicester Square

|●| Fish

🕘 Mon to Sat 12.00–15.30 & 17.30–24.00; Sun 12.00–15.30 & 18.00–23.00

⌂ www.caprice-holdings.co.uk

🗗 all major credit cards ■ no service added

££ starters £6.50–£16.75 ■ shellfish/crab/oysters £10.75–£39.50 ■ mains £12.75–£39.50 ■ sides £3.25–£4.75 ■ desserts £6.50–£8.00 ■ weekend lunch £24.75 ■ lowest bottle price £17.75

✪ Fresh fish with flair

Sheekey's is one of a handful of restaurants that had shambled along since the war – World War I. Then, towards the end of the last millennium, it was taken over by the team behind The Ivy and Le Caprice (see p. 29 and p. 127). After a good deal of redesign and refurbishment, it emerged from the builders' clutches as J. Sheekey, with much the same attitudes and style as its senior siblings, but still focused on fish. The cooking is accomplished, the service is first-rate, and the fish is fresh – a good combination. The long menu presents a seductive blend of plain, old-fashioned, classic fish cuisine, such as lemon sole belle meunière, and more modern dishes like whole roast gilthead bream with herbs and olive oil. There are always handwritten dishes on the menu, 'specials' that change weekly. To start with, there are oysters, crabs and shellfish, plus everything from jellied eels and devilled whitebait to seared rare tuna. Main courses, like pan-fried wing of skate with capers and brown butter, or Cornish fish stew with celery heart and garlic mayonnaise, are backed up by classics such as fillet of cod and Sheekey's fish pie. Puddings range from spotted dick with butter and golden syrup to wild strawberry and champagne jelly with Jersey cream. As well as smart wines, there are plenty of options at the cheaper end of the list for sensible drinking.

Joe Allen

13 Exeter Street, WC2 ■ 020 7836 0651

⊖ Covent Garden

🍽 North American

🕐 Mon to Fri 08.00–11.30 (breakfast) & 12.00–24.45; Sat 11.30–23.30; Sun 11.30–23.30

⌂ www.joeallen.co.uk

🖪 all major credit cards ■ 12.5% optional service added for parties over 8

££ breakfast £2.50–£9.50 ■ starters £5–£7.50 ■ mains £9–£19 ■ sides £3.50–£4 ■ desserts £5.50–£8 ■ set lunch & pre-theatre Mon to Fri £15 (2 courses) & £17 (3 courses) ■ brunch Sat & Sun £18.50 (2 courses) & £20.50 (3 courses) ■ lowest bottle price £15 (litre carafe)

✪ American diner for theatrical types

This is the restaurant with a 'secret' hamburger – not listed on the menu, but well worth ordering. By some inexplicable alchemy, Joe Allen continues to be the Covent Garden eatery of choice for the acting profession. It is a dark, resolutely un-trendy place and you get a somewhat refined version of American comfort food. If your heart is set on a Caesar salad, chilli con carne or eggs Benedict, this is the place to come. Joe Allen has a splendid attitude to mealtimes: the à la carte runs all day, so you can have lunch whenever you want. The menu lists a succession of dishes that we are all comfortable with. Starters include spicy Italian sausage hash with poached egg; buffalo mozzarella with caponata and pine nuts; and black bean soup. They are followed by a section described as 'salads/eggs/sandwiches', in which you'll find some of Joe Allen's strengths: the Caesar salad; the roast chicken salad; and eggs Joe Allen, a satisfying combination of poached eggs, potato skins, Hollandaise sauce and spinach. Main courses range from New England lobster roll through barbecue spare ribs with rice, wilted spinach, black-eyed peas and corn muffin to pan-fried calf's liver with mashed potato and grilled bacon. As you would suspect, the dessert offerings provide the kind of serious sugar hit that's in keeping with their affiliation to the USA – go for the brownie, with an extra portion of hot fudge sauce.

Mela

152–156 Shaftesbury Avenue, WC2 ■ 020 7836 8635

⊖ Covent Garden

🍽 Indian

🕐 Mon to Sat 12.00–23.30; Sun 12.00–22.30

🖰 www.melarestaurant.co.uk

🖰 all major credit cards ■ 12.5% optional service added

££ starters £3.50–£5.95 ■ mains £6–£15 ■ sides £1.95–£4.50 ■ desserts
£3.25–£4.50 ■ set lunch £2.95–£5.95 ■ lowest bottle price £10.95

✪ This may be London's best-value set lunch

Mela is a restaurant dedicated to India's regional dishes. Like
its sibling, Chowki (see p. 157), Mela may even have cracked the
great lunch conundrum; Indian restaurateurs find it very difficult to
persuade Londoners to eat curry for lunch, but Mela has managed
by offering really good value. At lunchtime there's a 'Paratha
Pavilion', which offers a variety of delicious set lunches based
around the simple street food of Delhi. Mela has a pleasant modern
dining room and service is slick and friendly. At lunch the set meals
revolve around bread – which may be made from maize, sorghum,
millet, wholewheat flour or chilli- and coriander-flavoured chickpea
flour. The latter is particularly good. It may come with the dhal or
curry of the day, or perhaps with a savoury stuffing. There may be
other breads, too, such as roomalis (large and thin, wholemeal
handkerchief bread); puris (fried chapatis); uttapams (rice-flour
pancakes); and naans. Fortunately, Mela's prices are low enough to
encourage experiment. The main menu makes a real attempt to offer
genuine regional dishes. Starters range from batar khada masala –
quail with ginger and garlic – to lehsooni whitebait. Then tandoor
dishes such as barrah kebab lead on to Hyderabad crab curry, or
methi murg, a rich dish teaming chicken with fenugreek. There is
also an exemplary gosht rogan josh. Mela is a template for a modern
Indian restaurant and it combines good cooking with fair prices.

Mr Kong

21 Lisle Street, WC2 ■ 020 7437 7341

⊖ Leicester Square

🍴 Chinese

🕐 Mon to Sat 12.00–02.45; Sun 12.00–01.45

🖥 www.mrkongrestaurant.com

🗗 all major credit cards ■ 10% optional service added

££ starters £2–£5.50 ■ mains £6–£14.50 ■ sides £2–£12 ■ desserts
£2.90 ■ set lunch & dinner £10–£24 ■ lowest bottle price £9

✪ Late night extra – some moody dishes

Mr Kong re-opened after a thorough refurb early in 2008. This,
the latest refurb of many, was made necessary by a serious fire that
followed hard on the heels of a previous new look. Now all is light,
bright and a rather painful yellow. Thankfully the kitchen at Mr Kong
is back on song. The new menu lists plenty of favourites and the
Chef's Special menu makes a triumphant return, reversing a trend
towards dumbing down that had been creeping in over recent years.
Take it as read that dishes like steamed razor clams with glass noodles
and garlic; braised eel with whole garlic and roast pork; spicy pig's
knuckle with jelly fish; or stuffed bitter melon with minced pork
will be consistently good. A further tip is to look out for 'hot pot'
dishes – these are casseroles that come to the table in clay pots. If
the Chef's Special dishes all sound a bit too obscure, the 'standard'
dishes are also done well and there is plenty here that will please
the less adventurous diner. Portions are generous and prices are
reasonable, even when dishes contain exotic ingredients. Thanks to
accommodating late-night opening hours, Mr Kong is just the place
to assuage the midnight munchies. Should you ever get the urge to
try the deep-fried pig's intestine with spicy salt, this is the place to
do it.

The National Dining Rooms

Sainsbury Wing, National Gallery, Trafalgar Square, WC2

■ 020 7747 2525

⊖ Charing Cross/Leicester Square

🍴 British

🕐 restaurant Thurs to Tues 12.00–15.30; Wed 12.00–15.30 & 17.00–19.15: bakery 10.00–17.30; Wed 10.00–20.30

🖰 www.thenationaldiningrooms.co.uk

🖶 all major credit cards ■ 12.5% optional service added

££ menus £24.50 (2 courses) & £29.50 (3 courses)
■ afternoon tea £12–£20.00 ■ lowest bottle price £14.50

✪ National by name, national by cuisine

The National Dining Rooms are perched on the first floor of the Sainsbury wing and overlook Trafalgar Square. As you come into the dining room there is a large cold cabinet with a very impressive array of British cheeses. The nicest things about the National Dining Rooms are the informal elements: there's an intelligently devised children's menu; you can have a proper afternoon tea with cake stand, scones and all; and there is a magnificent offering of cheese (you get to choose from several fine British cheeses). It's not a cheap place to eat, and the menu is short (which some would say was a blessing!), but this is a centrally located lunch spot, with good views and surprisingly good cooking. What's more, it stands by seasonal British produce – always a good thing. Pitch up and there may be chilled cucumber scented with Dorset crab and mint; a chicken liver pate with home made piccalilli; or eight varieties of Heritage tomatoes with sour cherry vinegar, olive oil and wild herbs. Mains range from Jerusalem artichoke and forest mushroom tart with parsley and lemon; to baked trout with rhubarb compote and minted peas; or Goosnargh chicken breast with wild mushrooms, grapefruit and spelt crumble. The puds will gladden a sugar addict's heart – ice creams with brandy snaps; home-made chocolate truffles; or warm treacle tart with clotted cream. Service with a smile, even when the place is busy.

New World
1 Gerrard Place, W1 ■ 020 7734 0396

⊖ Leicester Square

|⊙| Chinese/dim sum

⊙ daily 11.00–24.00

🗗 all major credit cards ■ no service added

££ dim sum (served until 18.00) £2.20–£2.60 ■ soups £2.70–£9 ■ mains £7.30–£15.50 ■ sides £2.20–£9.50 ■ set menus £10.50–£21.80pp ■ lowest bottle price £10.50

✪ A trolley Grand Prix over several floors

This is one of the largest restaurants in Europe, seating as it does between 400 and 600 people, depending on how many functions are going on at any one time. The menu, a leather-bound tome and nearly twenty pages long, features everything you have ever heard of and quite a lot you haven't. In any case, you don't need it – go for the dim sum, which are served every day from 11.00 until 18.00. The dim sum come round on trolleys. First, catch the eye of a waiter or waitress with a bow tie to order drinks, and then turn to the trolley pushers. The trolleys are themed: one has a lot of barbecued meat; another is packed with ho fun (broad noodles); another with steamed dumplings; another with soups. A good mix would be to take siu mai and har kau from the 'steamers' trolley, then char sui cheung fun – a long roll with pork. Follow this with some deep-fried won ton, little crispy parcels with sweet sauce, or something filling such as char sui pow, steamed doughnuts filled with pork. Or perhaps nor mai gai, a lotus-leaf parcel of glutinous rice and meats. Should you arrive after 18.00, it all becomes a good deal more complicated, as there are literally hundreds of dishes on the main menus. Dim sum trolleys are a great way to introduce small children to Chinese food.

Punjab

80–82 Neal Street, WC2 ■ 020 7836 9787

⊖ Covent Garden

🍽 Indian

🕐 Mon to Sat 12.00–15.00 & 18.00–23.30; Sun 12.00–15.00 & 18.00–22.30

🖰 www.punjab.co.uk

🖶 all major credit cards ■ 10% optional service added

££ starters 75p–£3.90 ■ mains £8.20–£11.50 ■ sides £1.90–£2.90 ■ desserts £2.20–£2.70 ■ lowest bottle price £11.25

✪ One of London's three oldest Indian restaurants

In 1951 Gurbachan Singh Maan moved his fledgling Indian restaurant from the City to take over premises in Neal Street in Covent Garden, his plan being to take advantage of the trade from the nearby Indian High Commission. This strategy worked handsomely. Today, his grandson Sital Singh Maan runs what is the oldest North Indian restaurant in the UK, though one that has always been at the forefront of new developments; in 1962 the Maan family brought over one of the first tandoor ovens to be seen in Britain. Punjabi cuisine offers some interesting, non-standard Indian dishes, so start by ordering from among the less familiar items on the menu – kadu puri, for instance, a sweet and sharp mash of curried pumpkin served on a puri; or aloo tikka, which are described as potato cutlets but arrive as small deep-fried moons on a sea of tangy sauce; or chicken chat, which is diced chicken in rich sauce. To follow, try the acharri gosht, or the acharri murgha. The first is made with lamb, and the second with chicken. The meat is 'pickled' in traditional Punjabi spices. Chicken karahi is good, too – rich and thick – while from the vegetable dishes channa aloo offsets the nutty crunch of chickpeas with the solace of potatoes. Or you could try the benaam macchi tarkari, which is billed as a 'nameless fish curry, speciality of chef'. Nameless, but not tasteless.

Red N Hot

59 Charing Cross Road, WC2 ■ 020 7734 8796

⊖ Leicester Square

⦿ Chinese/Sichuan

🕒 Mon to Thurs & Sun 12.00–23.00; Fri & Sat 12.00–24.00

🖰 www.rednhotgroup.com

🖰 all major credit cards except AmEx ■ 12.5% optional service added

££ appetisers £5.60–£7.80 ■ mains £7.80–16 ■ vegetables £6.80–£7.80
    ■ hot pots £16–£20 ■ beer £2.50

✪ Sinus-clearing Sichuan food

If you don't like your food incendiary then you probably shouldn't be venturing into this jolly little restaurant on the Chinatown fringe. As you walk through the door the air is heavy with chilli and one lungful will make softies splutter. Most of the customers here are Chinese, but there's a warm welcome for adventurers – the staff are young, savvy and alert, so ask their advice. The menu is a book and when you see three little chillies beside a dish take the hint. You'll find plenty of old-favourites: 'pock-marked lady's tofu with minced meat', which is very good tofu with a melting texture, poky sauce; or 'fire-exploded kidney flowers', which are implausibly rich. There is every part of the pig you could ever wish for from hock to tripe and intestine. Vegetable dishes are fantastic – water spinach, balsam pear (aka bitter melon), pea sprout – and they're all chilli boosted. One of the house specialities is the 'Red N Hot special fish', which comes to table as a stainless steel washing-up bowl filled with boiling oil. Part the 2-cm floating carpet of red chillies and you'll find collops of perfectly cooked white fish. This dish is very good indeed and the portions are enormous. The hotpots are popular – you get a vat of bubbling stock on a burner and then a platter of ingredients for a do-it-yourself fondue. A great place to eat if you like hot food.

Rules

35 Maiden Lane, WC2 ■ 020 7836 5314

⊖ Covent Garden

🍴 Very British

🕒 Mon to Sat 12.00–23.30; Sun 12.00–22.30

🖰 www.rules.co.uk

🖃 all major credit cards ■ 12.5% optional service added

££ starters £6.95–£14.95 ■ mains £16.95–£22.50 ■ sides £3.75–£7.95
   ■ desserts £7.25–£10.95 ■ lowest bottle price £19.95

⭐ London's oldest restaurant

Dickens, Betjeman, H. G. Wells, Thackeray, Graham Greene and
King Edward VII are just a few of the celebs who have revelled in
Rules. Rules would be a living cliché but for one saving grace – all
the fixtures, fittings and studied eccentricities that look as if they
have been custom-made in some modern factory are real. Rules is
the genuine article, a very English restaurant. The proud boast here
is that: 'We specialise in classic game cookery' – and indeed they
do, but first of all you should note that Rules is open from noon till
late, which is very handy when circumstances dictate a four o'clock
lunch. Start with a terrine made from Morecambe Bay shrimps, or
a wild mushroom and chestnut soup. Go on to game in season, or
the occasional specials: maybe Belted Galloway beef or Tamworth
suckling pig, sourced from Rules' own estate in the High Pennines.
The steak and kidney pudding with mash is a banker, as is the roast
rib of beef for two and the smoked Finnan haddock fishcake with
spinach and poached egg. Also noteworthy is the black-faced,
heather-fed mutton hot pot. Puddings, such as treacle sponge or
sticky toffee, are merciless. Why not go for the traditional blue Stilton
cheese with celery and a glass of port? Should you face visitors
in search of something old and English, Rules is a great place to
combine nostalgia with eating well.

Shanghai Blues

193–197 High Holborn, WC1 ▪ 020 7404 1668   &

⊖ Holborn

▯❙ Chinese/dim sum

🕐 daily 11.00–23.30 (dim sum until 17.00)

⌐⏦ www.shanghaiblues.co.uk

⎅ all major credit cards ▪ 12% optional service added

££ dim sum £3.50 ▪ starters £6–£29.80 ▪ mains £8–£45 ▪ sides
£8–£15.80 ▪ set lunch (to 17.00) £15 ▪ lowest bottle price £24.50

❂ Cocktails meet slick Chinese

This place is yet another example of the important role our libraries
will play after they're all converted into restaurants! Shanghai Blues
has survived the first few fragile years, despite being awkwardly
situated away from the fleshpots of Covent Garden and on a road
whose sole purpose is to volley a stream of traffic into W1. This is a
plush sort of place. At lunch there is an extensive dim sum menu with
some less obvious choices that are very good indeed – the original
Shanghai 'Xiao Long Bao' (those little dumplings filled with stock and
pork that explode in your mouth); the 'abalone rice in lily leaves' (the
abalone component by way of salty egg yolk and abalone sauce);
and the cuttlefish cake with sweet basil and lemon grass. Dim sum is
a sophisticated business here. The main menu has some dishes that
are well worth seeking out. There's the very expensive 'Three treasure'
soup that comes in a clay pot – Alaskan crab meat, abalone, and
sea cucumber; or fresh lobster steamed with egg white and topped
with flakes of gold; steamed razor clams with bean sprouts and
Chinese chives; double-cooked belly pork; and the attractively named
Shanghai Devil, which is a dish of stir-fried lamb. This restaurant is a
place to go for jazz evenings, cutting-edge cocktails and well-cooked,
stylish Chinese food. One proviso: the size of the bill will reflect these
little luxuries.

→ For branch, see index

Sitaaray

167 Drury Lane, WC2 ■ 020 7269 6422

Covent Garden/Holborn

Indian

daily 12.00–15.00 & 17.30–01.00

www.sitaaray.com

all major credit cards ■ 12.5% optional service added

££ fixed price – eat as much as you wish £18 per person ■ extras £12 ■ desserts £2.50–£3 ■ lowest bottle price £14

✪ Red plush Bollywood blowout

Rohit Khattar owns Chor Bizarre (see p. 87) and has a not-so-secret passion for Bollywood and its memorabilia. Most of his collection seems to have ended up on the walls at Sitaaray. Downstairs is another of his ventures – a monster nightclub and restaurant called Tamarai that offers cocktails and a fusion menu – and upstairs is Sitaaray (it's the Hindi word for stars). This is a charming place, the décor is Bollywood-boudoir (think lots of red) and the concept is very simple: for a fixed price you get delicious kebabs, lots of them. The food comes fresh to table in erratic waves and the menu varies but there are usually about nine different kebabs on offer. These range from salmon shahi tikka – with a dill and cumin marinade; to chicken chakundari – a real winner, the marinade containing beetroot, ginger and garlic; lamb methiwala boti – flavoured with fenugreek; a very good chicken malai tikka – made with Cheddar cheese; or maybe an oddity like mushroom galouti – a delicate, soft kebab made from puréed mushrooms reformed into a sausage. All are best eaten straight from the fire and that is how the food is served. Alongside the kebabs there is a splendidly rich dal makhani, a basket of breads, some rice and a well-made chicken curry. Seafood lovers can opt for the 'extras' and pay a supplement for some giant prawns, calamari and a very delicious portion of fried fish seasoned with carom seeds. The atmosphere is great and the 'booths' (tucked-away tables for up to 12 people) are much in demand for parties. Good food. Good fun.

Wahaca

66 Chandos Place, WC2 ■ 020 7240 1883 &

⊖ Covent Garden/Leicester Square

🍽 Mexican

🕐 Mon to Sat 12.00–23.30; Sun 12.00–22.30

🔗 www.wahaca.co.uk

🏷 all major credit cards ■ 12.5% optional service added for parties over 6

££ starters £3.25–£7.50 ■ mains £5.75–£9.20 ■ sides £1.80–£3.25
■ desserts £3–£3.40 ■ lowest bottle price £11.75

✪ Caramba! Easy-going Mexican food

What we have here is 'Tacamama' – Wagamama in a Mexican hat.
Dishes arrive when they are ready (which can make for dish envy
should your table companions get served first), there's a no booking
policy and food is keenly priced. The dining room is large, and has
a 'designer-industrial' feel to it. The guacamole is well made, with
a chunky texture and good flavour, and you can have it with 'pork
scratchings' – puffed pork rind, a good combination. Then there
are tacos, tostados, quesadillas and taquitos. The pork pibil tacos
are very sound, although you might take issue with the menu-speak
'melt in the mouth'. The mainspring of Wahaca is Thomasina Miers,
and her menu emphasises carefully sourced British ingredients. One
consequence is that you'll see a board proclaiming Market Fresh
Ingredients – and then lines like 'Habanero chillies from Devon'.
This marriage of convenience, which sacrifices Mexican authenticity
for local sourcing, is no bad thing, even if the resulting copy line
'Mexican Market Eating' jars a bit. The Wahaca salad is pleasant
enough, with Little Gem lettuce, avocado and splendid roast Poblano
chillies – well balanced. A burrito filled with chargrilled steak, black
beans and shredded cabbage is wholly successful. This is a busy,
happy place where the no booking policy seems to encourage rather
than deter. The great virtues of brisk service, low prices and sound
enough food are just what's wanted and Wahaca deserves its success.

Edgware Road and Paddington

Angelus

4 Bathurst Street, W2 ■ 020 7402 0083

⊖ Lancaster Gate

🍽 Modern French

🕐 Tues to Sat 12.00–15.00 & 18.00–23.00; Sun 12.00–15.00 & 18.00–22.00

🖰 www.angelusrestaurant.co.uk

🗗 all major credit cards ■ 12.5% optional service added

££ starters £9–£13 ■ mains £18–£27 ■ desserts £9–£12
■ lounge menu £4–£14 ■ lowest bottle price £15

✪ Modern, open-minded and French

Thierry Tomasin has a splendid track record as sommelier at Le Gavroche (see p. 89) and at Aubergine (see p. 387). In 2007 he took the big step and opened his own restaurant. It is unusual for the front of house to be the mainspring of a new restaurant but this place follows Tomasin's dream. Angelus is a converted pub and offers a comfortable dining room and exciting modern French cooking. The 'signature' starter is a foie gras crème brûlée topped with caramelised almonds, a strange dish with the creamy, livery, base topped with a nutty sweet crust. Other starters may include dishes such as steamed snails with horseradish and radish; scallops with watercress velouté and Avruga caviar; or grilled gambas, avocado and green apple Macedoine with fennel cream. Most of these dishes are original but they are all sufficiently ground in classical technique to make for good eating. Main courses range from pan-fried pollack with turmeric confit fennel and ginger seasoned tomato concasse; to orange roast duck, minced duck leg and a herb salad; chicken supreme stuffed with foie gras and mushroom, served with baby onion risotto; or parsley crusted veal fillet, bacon 'Lou Capou' and Parmesan cream. Despite its location to the north of Hyde Park, there is something pleasantly French about Angelus. The service has an agreeably formal feel to it, the wine list is enthralling, and the standard of cooking is high.

Dinings

22 Harcourt Street, W1 ■ 020 7723 0666

⊖ Edgware Road

🍽 Japanese

🕐 Mon to Fri 12.00–14.30 & 18.00–22.30; Sat 18.00–22.30

🗗 all major credit cards ■ 10% optional service added

££ cold tapas £3.85–£7.85 ■ hot tapas £3–£16
    ■ sushi/sashimi £3.90–£6.90 ■ lowest bottle price £15

✪ Small, but perfectly formed

This small and innovative Japanese restaurant was set up by
Tomonari Chiba, an ex-Nobu chef determined to plough his own
furrow. The Idea behind it is most easily pigeon-holed as 'Japanese
tapas', but Dinings manages to be all things to all men – provided
they are not very large men. The dining room, stairs, chairs and
tables are all on the small side and despite the modernist décor it's
a cramped sort of place for larger folk. As well as the main menu
there are various specials on offer, for example, 'grilled salmon
collar' – this is the chunk of the fish immediately behind the head, a
traditional Japanese delicacy but something that tends to go into the
stockpot in European kitchens. Dishes here are small and the grazing
principle means each elegant little plate arrives when it is ready. From
the 'cold tapas' try the tar tar chips, which are small u-shaped potato
chips loaded with salmon tartare or chopped sweet shrimp. Or there
may be octopus with white asparagus, yuzu and garlic; or monkfish
pate; or pork leg terrine with mustard miso. Then there is a range
of well-made sushi, plus sashimi. The 'hot tapas' might include chilli
and garlic black cod; pork belly braised with a Korean miso sauce; or
scallop with yuzu garlic sauce. Delicious dishes are well presented and
flavours and textures are distinct. Service is smiley charming.

Duke of Wellington

94a Crawford Street, W1 ▪ 020 7723 2790

⊖ Baker Street

🍽 Modern British/gastropub

🕐 Mon to Fri 12.00–15.00 & 19.00–22.00; Sat 12.30–16.00 &
19.00–22.00; Sun 12.30–16.00 & 19.00–21.00

🗃 all major credit cards ▪ 12.5% optional service added

££ starters £5.50–£8.75 ▪ mains £10–£19.75 ▪ sides £3
▪ desserts £4.50–£9.25 ▪ lowest bottle price £15

✪ Plush resto-pub

The Duke of Wellington is from the same stable as the Brown Dog
in Barnes (see p. 381). Downstairs it's a pub with real beer and bar
food, upstairs is a restauranty kind of restaurant, while on the menu
it styles itself as a 'Bar and Dining Room', which seems to take care
of every eventuality. The 24-seater upstairs dining room is a pretty,
if crowded, room. The food is restaurant food and the menu offers
seven starters and seven mains. The standard of cooking is good at
the Duke and you may be faced with a starter like spiced pig's head
'cake' with trotters on toast, fried quails' eggs and tomato sauce;
warm salad of smoked eel with beetroot purée and grilled trevisse; or
seared foie gras that comes with an amazing silky purée of butternut
squash. The main courses also impress: a feuillette of 28-day aged
'Longhorn' beef sirloin with buttered spinach and shitake mushrooms
has a few superfluous pastry elements but is a good combination,
or there may be slow-roast duck with apple sauce. Or grilled loin
of lamb with fondant potato and confit garlic, which is a dish that
works on every level – very good fondant potato, a head of garlic
cooked to melting sweetness, and tender meat. Service is friendly
and the wine list is priced fairly. Puds are good, such as Valrhona
chocolate panna cotta with blood orange caramel. Good food from a
gastro-restaurant-pub-bar.

The Mandalay

444 Edgware Road, W1 ■ 020 7258 3696

⊖ Edgware Road

🍴 Burmese

🕐 Mon to Sat 12.00–14.30 & 18.30–22.30

🖱 www.mandalayway.com

🖪 all major credit cards ■ no service added

££ starters £2.10–£5.50 ■ mains £4.40–£7.90 ■ sides £1.10–£5.50 ■ desserts £1.90–£2.90 ■ set lunch £3.90 (1 course) & £5.90 (3 courses) ■ lowest bottle price £8.90

⭐ Fancy going out for a Burmese?

Two Scandinavian-educated Burmese brothers, Gary and Dwight Ally, have become famous in this rugged stretch of the Edgware Road. Their restaurant is bizarre, with just 28 seats, an old sandwich counter filled with strange and exotic ingredients, and greetings and decoration in both Burmese and Norwegian. Gary is in the kitchen and smiley; talkative Dwight is out front. The Ally brothers have correctly concluded that their native languages are probably unmasterable by most of their customers, so the menu is written in English with a Burmese translation. But the food itself is pure unexpurgated Burmese, and all freshly cooked. The cuisine is a mélange of different local influences, with a little bit of Thai and Malaysian, and a lot of Indian. To start there are pappadums or a great bowlful of prawn crackers, which arrive freshly fried and sizzling hot (and served on domestic kitchen paper to soak up the oil). Starters range from spring rolls and samosas, to salads like raw papaya and cucumber, or chicken and cabbage. Main courses are mainly curries, or rice and noodle dishes, spiced with plenty of ginger, garlic, coriander and coconut, and using fish, chicken and vegetables as the main ingredients. The cooking is good, flavours hit the mark, portions are huge, and everything is priced very keenly indeed. Vegetable dishes are somewhat more successful than the prawn ones, but at this price it's only to be expected.

Pearl Liang

8 Sheldon Square, W2 ■ 020 7289 7000

♿

⊖ Paddington

🍴 Chinese/dim sum

🕐 daily 12.00–23.00

⌙ www.pearlliang.co.uk

🖅 all major credit cards ■ 12% optional service added

££ dim sum £2.50–£4.20 (until 17.00) ■ starters £3–£8.80
■ mains £6.80–£22 ■ sides £2–£10.60 ■ desserts £2.30–£3
■ set menus £23, £38 & £68 ■ dim sum set lunch £9.60
■ lowest bottle price £13.80

⭐ Glossy Chinese, obscure location

It is easy to find Pearl Liang in Sheldon Square, but finding Sheldon Square can be tricky (start by looking on the bridge where Paddington Station taxis queue). This is a grown-up and glossy Chinese restaurant; there's plenty of mauve, comfy chairs, and a wash handbasin in the gents painted with Chinese motifs. The management has a line of form going back to time spent at the Mandarin Kitchen (see p. 142). The dim sum are very good and reasonably priced, the stars being the Shanghai dumplings – very juicy; the king crabmeat and egg white dumpling; the crispy aromatic duck roll; the scallop dumplings – thin skinned; the barbecued pork puff – nearly as good as the ones at Royal China (see p. 80); the chueng fun; and the fried watercress meat dumpling. The main menu is the usual interminable length – highlights seem to be some of the more extravagant dishes, such as the lobster prepared in a variety of styles. Maybe it is time to give the ginger and spring onions combo a rest and try the Belaccan Malaysian hot shrimp paste? All the lobster dishes benefit from adding some noodles. There are the eco-unfriendly soups featuring abalone and shark's fin. The simpler dishes like stewed belly pork with preserved vegetables or Singapore rice noodles work well, and the service is on the ball. A good Chinese, if you're able to find it.

Ranoush

43 Edgware Road, W2 ▪ 020 7723 5929

⊖ Marble Arch

🍽 Lebanese

🕐 daily 08.00–03.00

🖱 www.maroush.com

🗄 cash only ▪ no service added

££ starters £1.25–£5 ▪ mains £3.25–£9.50 ▪ sides £1.50–£2
   ▪ desserts £3.50 (Lebanese pastries) ▪ no alcohol

✪ A cure for the midnight munchies

Ranoush is a fine, unfussy, late-opening, lively sort of pit stop that is justifiably popular with late-night folk. At the back is the juice bar, which gives you the healthy bit, and at the front is the kebab servery. In between is a counter packed with all the other items from the encyclopaedic menu. To eat here you need to know the menu and what you want, as you start by paying, then take the relevant piece of the receipt to either the kebab men at the front or the juice men at the rear – it's self-service with attitude. The starters are very sound, with lots of meze both cold and hot: houmous, tabbouleh, and warak ineb are good. The pickles are very good. The main course offerings are large plates of grilled meat – lamb shawarma; kafta meshwi (minced lamb); and riash ghanam. Best, though, to opt for the sandwiches. Ordering lamb shawarma, for example, brings a fresh round of bread wrapped around slivers of grilled lamb and lubricated with a dollop of yogurt. It arrives wrapped tight in paper and is very difficult to eat without dripping the juices down your clothes. Very good. Variants include chicken shawarma; lahm meshwi (chunks of lamb); and soujok (Lebanese spicy sausages). Have a couple, drink some juice and reflect on the night's adventures. The health-conscious will doubtless opt for the 'low-calorie platter' – six meze plus one skewer of lean meat.

→ For branches, see index or website

Rhodes W1

Great Cumberland Place, W1 ■ 020 7616 5930

⊖ Marble Arch

🍴 Modern British

🕐 Mon to Fri 06.30–10.30 (breakfast), 12.00–14.30, 19.00–22.30;
Sat 07.00–10.30 (breakfast), 12.00–14.30, 19.00–22.30

🗄 all major credit cards ■ 12.5% optional service added

££ à la carte £52 (2 courses) & £60 (3 courses) ■ lowest bottle price £24

✪ Good looking, good cooking

When Gary Rhodes opened a brasserie in the revitalised
Cumberland Hotel it settled down to steady business, despite patchy
reviews. Then in the spring of 2007 a fine dining Rhodes W1 opened
at the rear of the hotel, and with its own entrance. It's a pretty
place to eat (so much so that it has made it onto various lists as a
favourite venue for ladies who lunch). Kelly Hoppen designed the
dining room and there are chandeliers, a sea of taupe, comfy chairs,
plus much use of textiles. In the kitchen they know what they are
doing and most of the menu is made up from classic French dishes
seen through a British prism. So to start you might choose salmon
soup with steamed smoked salmon – a bowl comes to table with a
curl of smoked salmon which is 'cooked' by pouring on hot salmon
soup, very good. Or there may be pressed foie gras, duck salad and
maple syrup vinaigrette; or a splendid dish where a soft-boiled egg
is given a crisp crust and served with morels and Roquefort toast
soldiers for dipping. Mains are equally interesting – poached Cornish
lobster comes with summer vegetables; there's an extremely good
cauliflower and Lancashire cheese mousse with morels, florets and
broad beans; roast spring lamb, tomato and tarragon navarin; or fillet
of beef, braised faggot, onions, spinach and red wine sauce. Desserts
maintain the high standards: cherry trifle with iced Jersey cream or an
old fave like oeufs à la neige served with poached rhubarb and vanilla
custard. The wine list is lengthy but has some accessibly priced bottles
and service runs smoothly. All in all this is a top-end restaurant.

King's Cross

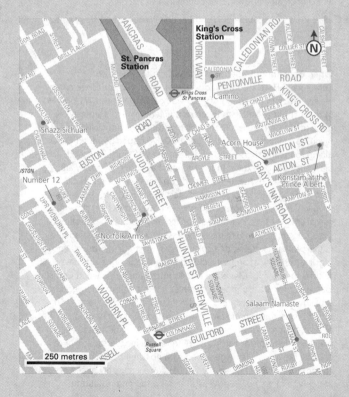

Acorn House

69 Swinton Street, WC1 ■ 020 7812 1842

⊖ King's Cross

🍴 British (They say 'modern London')

🕐 Mon to Fri 08.00–11.30 (breakfast); 12.00–15.00, 18.00–22.00; Sat 10.00–15.00 (brunch), 18.00–23.00

🖰 www.acornhouserestaurant.com

🖰 all major credit cards ■ 12.5% optional service added

££ starters £4.50–£14 mains £12–£23 ■ desserts £3.50–£6.50
   ■ tasting menu £45 (5 courses; 9 people or more)
   ■ lowest bottle price £14.50

✪ Worthy … and worth a visit

Acorn House surfed through the first couple of years on a wave of positive reviews. It seemed that most critics visited in some trepidation, worried that an eco-friendly, charitable venture that gave work and training to some needy people and was committed to sourcing sustainable produce might not be concentrating on the cooking. But this restaurant feels like a proper restaurant that just happens to have impeccable green credentials. The room is long and modern with an open kitchen at the far end, and aside from the jugs of filtered water that replace a chic mineral water there are few outward signs that you are doing good. The menu changes on a monthly basis and 'seasonal' is the watchword. Thus in January there may be a couple of soups – beetroot, cardamom and sour cream; or a very good and very rich bowlful of Jerusalem artichoke and chestnut. In March other starters range from sustainable prawns with golden salsify; or roast duck confit with apple and prune. The menu goes on to three pasta dishes and then roast English mutton, minted pear and apple – good meat. Or there may be a spinach, goat's cheese and curly kale frittata; or pan-fried salmon with taggiasca olives. Puds feature home-made caramel ice cream and a fine rhubarb sorbet. The cooking is good, the service is very chirpy and the wine list is not too aggressively priced.

Camino

3 Varnishers Yard, The Regents Quarter, N1 ■ 020 7841 7330 ♿

🚇 King's Cross

🍴 Spanish

🕐 Mon to Fri 08.00–11.30 (breakfast in the juice bar) 12.00–15.00
& 18.30–23.00; Sat 09.00–15.00 (breakfast) & 18.30–23.00;
Sun 10.00–16.00 (breakfast) & 12.00–16.00 (brunch)

🖥 www.barcamino.com

💳 all major credit cards ■ 12.5% optional service added

££ breakfast £1.25–£3.50 ■ tapas (bar) £1.25–£15
■ starters £2.25–£8.50 ■ mains £12.50–£15.50 ■ sides £3–£4.55
■ desserts £5–£5.75 ■ express lunch £12 (2 courses) & £15 (3
courses) ■ lowest bottle price £12.50

✪ The new face of King's Cross – and it's Spanish

King's Cross isn't what it was. It's not so dirty, not so dangerous,
not so dismal. For once the developers seem to have been a force
for good and polished new bars and restaurants are springing up.
Camino has already bagged a prize as best bar, bang in the middle
of the Regent Quarter (lying between Caledonian Road and York
Way). It's a sprawling Spanish establishment with a charming hidden
courtyard, a lounge, a large bar and a restaurant. The courtyard looks
like a great place for an alfresco drink or two. You can either order
tapas at the bar or adjourn to the restaurant, which is a large room
under a glass dome that makes it very light and airy. The drinks list
ranges from cava to sherry and includes some very decent Spanish
wines. The starters on the menu bear a strong resemblance to the
tapas in the bar and include good Jamón; those little pimientos
del piquillo – here they are stuffed with crab; and chorizo. There
are specials which change daily: a soup, a fish and a main. From
the main menu the lamb chops and steaks are very good, perfectly
cooked on the kitchen's huge parrilla (grill). Look to the side dishes
for an amazing treat: sarten de patata a lo pobre con huevo – fried
potatoes and green pepper topped with a fried egg and seasoned
with paprika.

Konstam at the Prince Albert

2 Acton Road, WC1 ■ 020 7833 5040

● King's Cross

🍴 Modern British

🕐 Mon to Fri 12.30–15.00 & 18.30–22.30; Sat 18.30–22.30

🔗 www.konstam.co.uk

💳 all major credit cards ■ 12.5% (for parties of 6 or more)

££ starters £5–£6.50 ■ mains £11.50–£16.50 ■ sides £2.50–£3
   ■ desserts £4.50–£6 ■ lowest bottle price £14.50

✪ Urban Chef shops local

Head chef Oliver Rowe has a decent pedigree — time spent behind the stoves at Moro (see p. 224), and then running his own charming small café called Konstam which he moved to the Prince Albert using the springboard of a telly series called the Urban Chef. Rowe's plan was to source all the ingredients for his restaurant from within the M25, or, failing that, as close as possible. Admirable but difficult, and if you think that the buying policy is eccentric just wait until you see the décor — a dark green room is festooned with a mile or two of the kind of chain that is more often seen attaching a plug to your bath. The food, however, is simple and good, with the menu changing daily. Starters might include poached egg salad with Norbury blue cheese, leeks and walnuts; charcoal-grilled Amersham pigeon breast with beetroot, marjoram and orange salad; or Rowan Tree farm goat's cheese. Mains continue the emphasis on provenance. Pan-roast Waltham Abbey chicken with braised chicory; grilled leg of Amersham lamb with barley; grilled Channel sea bass with braised spring onions; or braised leg of Stansted duck with red cabbage, lemon and fennel salad. The cooking is of a decent standard and you cannot help admiring anyone who sticks so rigidly to their principles. Puds range from London porter and currant ice cream; to the engagingly named Ealing sherry trifle.

The Norfolk Arms

28 Leigh Street, WC1 ■ 020 7388 3937

⊖ King's Cross/Russell Square

🍴 Gastropub/tapas

🕐 Mon to Sat 12.00–15.00 & 18.30–22.15; Sun 12.00–22.15

🖰 www.norfolkarms.co.uk

🖬 all major credit cards ■ 12.5% optional service added

££ tapas £1.50–£10.50 ■ starters £4.50–£8.50 ■ mains £9.50–£12.50
　 ■ desserts £4.50 ■ set menu £10 (2 courses) & £13.50 (3 courses)
　 ■ lowest bottle price £12

✪ Gastropub speaks fluent Spanish and some Italian

The Norfolk is a small corner pub that is blessed with a magnificent plasterwork ceiling, and a bar with more space behind it than in front. The tables and chairs are from gastropub central casting and the floor features sanded floorboards. So saying, the beer is well kept and the food is excellent. The two-sided menu reflects a two-sided approach to food. One side is reserved for tapas, and offers such standards as pickled guindilla peppers and caper berries; boquerones; Serrano ham; and cipollini onions in balsamic, before upping the ante to dishes like English asparagus with Manchego cheese; or rojones, which are hunks of belly pork pan fried with paprika – very good indeed. There is also a notable 'cheese selection' and 'charcuterie selection'. Turn over the menu and there are starters, mains and puds. It's hard to argue with gleaning your starters from the tapas list, but dishes like octopus, Jersey Royals and mixed leaves appeal; or a salad made from chicory, feta and pumpkin seeds with a honey dressing. There's also an understated fruits de mer – razor clams, prawns, clams, mussels, smoked salmon. Mains range from pollack fillet with clams to an artichoke risotto. The puds are ambitious and sophisticated, such as Pedro Ximénez parfait with pine nut nougatine. This is a pleasant place to eat and the service is informal but effective. What's more, there are good cooks at work here.

Number 12

12 Upper Woburn Place, WC1 ■ 020 7693 5429 ♿

⊖ Euston

🍽 Modern Italian

🕐 Mon to Fri 12.00–15.00 & 17.30–22.30; Sat 17.30–22.30;
Sun 11.00–15.00

🔗 www.numbertwelverestaurant.co.uk

💳 all major credit cards ■ 12.5% optional service added

££ starters £5.95–£9.95 mains £14.50–£18.95 ■ sides £3
■ desserts £5.95–£6.95 ■ one hour lunch £10.50 (1 course), £13.50
(2 courses) and £15.50 (3 courses) ■ lowest bottle price £15.50

✪ Unlikely home for polished Italian

Number 12 opened towards the end of 2007 and manages to
resolve the just-another-hotel-restaurant quandary, partly by the
simple expedient of having its own entrance. The dining room is
modern (in a retro kind of way) but the tables are large and the
chairs comfortable. The level of cooking is very high indeed; dishes
are complex and sophisticated with multiple elements. To start with
there is a magnificent array of different breads: a foccacia with olives;
a bread roll with smoked mozzarella; plus a handful of other options
each more tempting than the last. The chef here is Santino Busciglio
and he has successfully married British seasonal produce with Italian
flair. Starters range from potato gnocchi with spring vegetables,
butter and basil; to seared yellow fin tuna with a Sicilian sweet and
sour fennel salad; or three different ways with Claire Island Irish
salmon – a well-made terrine, an elegant salmon tartare and some
that is simply smoked (and very good). Mains are equally considered:
pan-fried Welsh sea trout from the river Towy, with crayfish, peas and
Jersey Royals; or loin of lamb with a grissini herb crust, confit garlic
and a splendid potato cake made with the shoulder, plus a shot glass
of double-strength gravy. The desserts are elaborate, such as Valrhona
chocolate as mousse, ice cream and brownie. Service is slick, the wine
list extensive – this is a restaurant that is going places.

Salaam Namaste

68 Millman Street, WC1 ■ 020 7405 3697

⊖ King's Cross/Russell Square

🍽 Indian

∏ Mon to Sat 11.30–14.30 & 17.30–23.30; Sun 11.45–14.30 & 17.30–23.00

🖰 www.salaam-namaste.co.uk

🖰 all major credit cards ■ 10% optional service added

££ starters £2.95–£4.50 ■ mains £5.50–£11.95 ■ sides 50p–£3.50
■ desserts £2.50–£4.50 ■ lunch buffet £4.95 (Mon to Fri); £5.95 (Sun)
■ lowest bottle price £11.50

✪ Aspirational local Indian

Salaam Namaste is tucked away up on the fringes of Lawyerland and it is full of local residents stopping off for their dinner and bright young people who have been working late on a brief for Rumpole. The dining room is modern and the décor is the modern equivalent of flock wallpaper – bare wood floors, light colours and mirrors. The result is a pleasant enough place to eat. The menu lists some interesting and slightly less obvious dishes including Pakistani and Bangladeshi favourites, but at some point the corporate nerve has broken and you'll find murg makhani and the strangely titled Madras vindaloo listed on the menu. Starters include a badami chicken kebab – a chicken tikka spruced up with almonds; a very good chat patti – savoury, crispy, crunchy with chick peas and chutney; spicy crab cakes; and aloo chat – spicy, sweet and sour potatoes. The 'specialities' section makes a good hunting ground for main courses, with a pistachio chicken korma, complete with edible silver foil; Bangladeshi machchi fry – a large portion of sweet freshwater fish with tomatoes, potatoes and aubergine (you will need to be bone tolerant); or Bengali gosht shatkora – lamb, a rich sauce and the citrus twang of the shatkora. The main dishes come with rice and a lot of unnecessary and prettied-up garnish. Order a laachi paratha, buttery, flaky and indulgent.

Snazz Sichuan

37 Chalton Street, NW1 ■ 020 7388 0808

⊖ King's Cross

🍽 Chinese

🕐 daily 12.00–15.00 & 17.30–22.30

🖰 www.newchinaclub.co.uk

🖶 all major credit cards ■ 10% optional service added

££ cold starters £6–£8 ■ seafood £9.80–£18.80 ■ meat mains £8.20–£12.80 ■ vegetables £5.20–£9.20 ■ sides £1–£3.50 ■ set menus £14.80 & £18.80 ■ lowest bottle price £10.50

⭐ Best-ever menu copy

Snazz Sichuan is very snazzy and the menu is littered with deadly hot, favourite dishes from Sichuan and Chong Quin. The card informs us that Snazz is a restaurant, tea house and gallery. You can see that it's a gallery, as there are some very attractive modern Chinese pictures on the wall; the tea house bit is rather tucked away; and everything is part of 'The New China Club', which is some kind of umbrella organisation. The menu is the usual large tome but for once it makes wonderful reading. Among the cold starters is what may be my all-time favourite for succinct copy – 'strange flavour rabbit'. It would surely take a very boring diner to pass up the opportunity of trying strange flavour rabbit. When it comes it is very good. The bunny has been cooked and then chopped (bones and all) into pieces the size of dice and brought to table in the dark and delicious cooking liquor – soy definitely, garlic, ginger, chilli, something pungent. A grand flavour and only a little strange. The other red-hot Sichuan dishes feature 'fire-exploded kidney flower', which is fabulous – implausibly tender, it just melts away. You could enjoy a whole salmon head or there are those cheesy preserved eggs. Listed under vegetables you will find a stellar dish: bitter melon with green and red pepper. The melons have been peeled and then undercooked so that they retain their crunch and epic bitterness. The service here is friendly and the menu a joy for the enquiring gastronaut. Snazz Sichuan is not an outrageously cheap restaurant but it is a jolly good one.

Knightsbridge, Belgravia and Kensington

Amaya

Halkin Arcade, Motcomb Street, SW1 ■ 020 7823 1166

⊖ Knightsbridge

🍽 Indian

🕐 Mon to Sat 12.30–14.30 & 18.30–23.00; Sun 12.30–14.30 &
18.30–22.30

⌂ www.realindianfood.com

🖰 all major credit cards ■ 12.5% optional service added

££ small plates £4–£11 ■ regular plates £5.40–£24 ■ salads &
vegetables £3.50–£10 ■ main dishes £12.50–£15.50 ■ set lunch
£14 ■ tasting menu £26 (lunch, or vegetarian); £30 (dinner)
■ lowest bottle price £18.50

✪ Belgravia fashionable meets modern Indian

Over the last few centuries cultured Indians have developed an
aesthetic way of progressing a meal and over the last few decades
Brits have pretty much ignored it. Amaya is a very sleek and luxurious
place, comfortable, hedonistic and with very good food. But if you
expect the familiar curry house way of doing things, think again.
At Amaya you start by grazing your way through a succession
of 'kebabs': small bites to share that come to table when they're
ready rather than in a formal succession of courses. After which the
table may share a biryani or a curry by way of a grace note. This
unfamiliarity puts a subtle strain on ordering and one good strategy
is to leave the choosing to your waiter. Otherwise, the menu is
divided up by cooking technique: dishes from the tandoor oven; from
the sigiri – a charcoal grill – or the tawa – a flat iron griddle; plus
salads and vegetables and, finally, biryanis and curries. All the food
is elegantly presented, carefully spiced and very good to eat. From
the tandoor the black pepper chicken tikka is notable, as are the tiger
prawns. From the grill the lamb chops are good and the fish options
are amazing. From the tawa the star dish is the keema kaleeji, which
is roughly chopped mince, liver and kidney griddled with rich spices.
Very delicious. And if you have room after exploring the small dishes,
the curries and biryanis are very good too. Amaya takes Indian dining
to another level.

La Bodeguita del Medio

47 Kensington Court, W8 ■ 020 7938 4147

⊖ High Street Kensington

🍽 Cuban

🕒 Mon to Sun 17.00−23.00

🖱 www.bdelmlondon.com

🖻 all major credit cards ■ 12.5% optional service added

££ tapas £4.50−£19.50 ■ mains £8.75−£19.50 ■ sides £2.50−£3.25
 ■ desserts £5.59−£6.50 ■ lowest bottle price £16.50

✪ Kensington twinned with Havana?

After a lot of effort, thought, and doubtless money, La B del M
was recreated by its acolytes in London. The Cuban original is said
to have been the birthplace of the seminal cocktail the Mojito and
a favourite of everyone from Ernest Hemingway to Errol Flynn and
Sophia Loren. The Kensington cousin is very proud of its version
of the cocktail. During the spring of 2008 this restaurant closed at
lunch time to accommodate the building work next door, but the
lunch service will doubtless re-emerge after this book has gone to
press. Service is friendly and the wine list expansive without being too
fiercely priced. The food reflects 'Cuban heritage', possibly because
authentic Cuban cooking leaves a good deal to be desired. Start
with tapas: salt and pepper squid; Bodeguita albondigas (meatballs);
a Caesar salad; swordfish ceviche; tuna carpaccio with capers; or
tiger prawns with chilli and garlic. The grills range from a La B de
M hamburger; through a range of different 21-day-aged Argentine
steaks from rib eye to fillet; a swordfish steak; or chagrilled smoked
paprika and garlic pork skewers. There is also the traditional dish
'Ropa vieja with Moros and Cristianos', a dish of rice and beans
with slow-roast beef ribs. You won't be happy here unless you crave
atmosphere, music and Mojitos (and have an admiration for the
'cigar terrace').

Byron

222 Kensington High Street, W8 ■ 020 7361 1717   &

⊖ Earls Court/High Street Kensington

🍽 Burgers

🕐 Mon to Fri 12.00–23.00; Sat 11.00–23.00; Sun 11.00–23.30

🌐 www.byronhamburgers.com

💳 all major credit cards ■ 10% service added for parties of 8 or more

££ burgers £5.50–£8.25 ■ sides £1.95–£4.25 ■ salads £7.75–£10.25
   ■ desserts £3.25–£10.50 ■ lowest bottle price £13.50

✪ A promising entry in the hamburger stakes

This, the first branch of a chain of Byrons opened indecently close
to Christmas 2007 and the watchword adopted by the proprietors is
'proper hamburgers', which by and large is something they achieve.
The dining room is large and bright and the menu is commendably
short, sticking to half a dozen burgers but offering a choice of
toppings. The rubric is pretty much the same as at the other elite
hamburger joints: 'Our hamburgers are made from Aberdeen Angus
Beef sourced exclusively from select farms in Morayshire, Scotland.
They come in a soft, plain bun with lettuce, tomato, red onion,
pickle and mayo.' The burgers weigh in at around six ounces and are
a testimonial to the virtues of doing a simple thing well. Choose a
cheeseburger (then choose the cheese: mature Cheddar, Monterey
Jack, Cashel blue, or Gruyere); or the Byron, a burger with dry-cure
bacon, Cheddar and barbecue sauce. Or there's the 'mini classic' of
three miniature hamburgers (taking a leaf from the American White
Castle hamburger company's book). Sides are traditional French
fries; hand-cut chips; onion rings; Caesar salad. Desserts range from
Knickerbocker Glory to cheesecake and chocolate brownie. The wine
list is organised rather coyly into 'good', 'better', 'great' and 'best'
but is fit for purpose. Service is efficient and this place makes a good
option when you stumble out of the cinema opposite.

The Capital

22–24 Basil Street, SW3 ■ 020 7589 5171

⊖ Knightsbridge

🍴 French

🕐 daily 12.00–14.30 & 18.45–22.30

🖥 www.capitalhotel.co.uk

🗄 all major credit cards ■ 12.5% optional service added

££ lunch £29.50 (3 courses) & £48 (5 courses) ■ dinner £55 (3 courses)
■ dégustation £70 (5 courses; add £49 for wine)
■ lowest bottle price £28

✪ Grown-up cooking in a grown-up room

It's hard to believe, but the irrepressible French star Eric Crouillère-Chavot has been head chef here since 1999, long enough to see various redesigns of the dining room. Mr Michelin gives The Capital two stars, putting it firmly in the top half-dozen restaurants in London, and for once the tyre folk have got it right. The Capital Hotel has quietly gone about its business since 1971 and the cooking has always been top-flight. The Capital is not a cheap restaurant. Chavot cooks exciting food and his menus draw on classic French cuisine, which means that dishes are full-flavoured and elegantly plated. Sometimes presentation strays into the fussy zone beloved of Michelin inspectors, but expect classically rich and satisfying dishes. Starters may include a fricassée of frogs' legs, veal sweetbread and cèpe purée; or a goats' cheese and apple salad; an assiette Landaise; a crab lasagne with langoustine cappuccino; or seared scallops with sauce ceviche and cucumber jelly. Main courses carry on in the same vein: grilled turbot with mushroom ravioli and jus Diable; roast veal cutlet with balsamic jus and mushroom fricassée; honey-roast fillet of duck with macaroni gratin and pear jelly; fillet of lamb with spicy couscous; or roast lobster with tagliolini pasta and sauce vierge. The wine list here is both extensive and expensive. Puds are elaborate, sculptural and satisfying – Chavot may be offering a praline pear crumble, or an iced-coffee parfait with a chocolate fondant.

Le Cercle

1 Wilbraham Place, SW1 ▪ 020 7901 9999 ♿

 Sloane Square

 French

⏱ Tues to Sat 12.00–15.00; 15.00–18.00 (tea); 18.00–23.00

⌖ www.clubgascon.com

🗃 all major credit cards ▪ 12.5% optional service added

££ starters £4.50–£6.50 ▪ mains £6.50–£35 ▪ desserts £3.75–£5.50
▪ cheese £4.50–£9 ▪ set lunch £15 (3 courses) & £19.50 (4 courses)
▪ pre-theatre £17.50 (3 courses, 18.00–19.00 & 22.00–23.00)
▪ 'petits gourmets': 5 courses, free for the under-12s, at lunch only
▪ lowest bottle price £20

✦ French grazing – stargazing

The first move outside Smithfield from those lively people who
set up Club Gascon (see p. 218), Le Cercle lies deep within the
bowels of a discreet and exclusive 'apartment hotel', which in turn is
tucked away up a side street. You come down a flight of steps into
a modern double-height room. The wine cellar and the cheese room
are on show and there's a long and businesslike bar. It is an all-day
operation running from lunch through afternoon tea to dinner. The
food is modern, resolutely French and is served in the Club Gascon's
trademark style of small portions and multiple courses. The lengthy
menu changes seasonally. Sections are themed – 'vegetal', 'marin',
'fermier' – and each offers six or seven options. For two people one
dish from each section is probably too little food and two dishes is
too much. The cooking is of a very high standard. Stand-outs include
organic salmon confit, frothy ginger, celeriac and celery; smoked
haddock and mustard glaze; beef onglet, confit shallots, pommes
pailles; braised wild rabbit, rich sauce and cabbage marmalade; milk-
fed Pyrenean lamb, lemon purée; and the signature dish – foie gras
'Cercle'. But this selection only scratches the surface of a multi-page
menu so feel free to graze to your heart's content. Puds are good:
look out for banana doughnut with rum-soaked raisins or chocolate
fondant with pistachio ice cream.

The Chicago Ribshack

145 Knightsbridge, SW1 ■ 020 7591 4664

⊖ Knightsbridge

🍴 North American

🕐 Mon-Sat 12.00–24.00; Sun 12.00–23.00

🖰 www.thechicagoribshack.co.uk

🗐 all major credit cards ■ 10% optional service added to tables of over 8

££ starters £3.95–£8.95 ■ salads £7.95–£8.95 ■ ribs, steaks & burgers £8.50–£35.95 ■ sides £3–£5.50 ■ desserts £4.95–£6.95 ■ lowest bottle price £12.95

⊙ Fun fun fun

The Ribshack is a one-off. Were you to open a restaurant in May 2008, would you choose to resurrect a menu and concept that had been a whizz in the 1980s? The team behind the Ribshack have done just that and are confident that they will be mining a profitable seam of nostalgia. The original Shack was the brainchild of an ebullient adman called Bob Payton and it placed a ground-breaking emphasis on 'mood', unlike anything Londoners had ever seen before. Thirty years later none of it looks so novel, but there is still plenty of residual charm. The dining room is dark brown with echoes of an American diner. The food ranges from chicken wings (sweet) to a wedge of iceberg lettuce (sweet dressing); or pork ribs (sweet); or beef ribs (sweet); or pulled pork (sweet sauce). There are also some magnificent organic steaks – very good meat indeed. Side orders include the famous 'other bits', such as chunks of baked potato coated and crisped, or the infamous onion loaf. The latter is a foot long, described by its fans as a giant onion bhaji, a dish so gross that people instinctively love it. If you want to take hungry teenagers somewhere a good deal classier than McD's, then this is the place. The cooking is steady at best and the dishes are sweet and pander to your worst vices – which may explain why it's so popular.

Nahm

The Halkin, 5 Halkin Street, SW1 ■ 020 7333 1234

⊖ Hyde Park Corner

🍴 Thai

🕐 Mon to Fri 07.00–10.30, 12.00–14.30 & 19.00–23.30; Sat & Sun 19.00–22.30 (22.00 Sun)

🖰 www.halkin.como.bz

🖶 all major credit cards ■ 12.5% optional service added

££ à la carte, dishes £7.50–£17 ■ traditional Nahm Aharna menu £55 (8 dishes over 4 courses) ■ lunch menu £20 (2 courses) & £26 (3 courses) ■ lowest bottle price £33

✪ Mind- and palate-expanding Thai

David Thompson is a gentle, soft-spoken Australian, which somehow makes it all the more surprising that he is the world's leading authority on Thai cooking and consultant to the Thai government. The dining room at Nahm is chic, stylish and quietly fashionable – much the same in feel as the hotel in which it is hidden away. The food is amazing. At Nahm every meal is founded upon a bowl of jasmine rice and then other dishes are chosen to add savour to that rice. Nam prik tua ling song is one such dish: peanuts with dried prawns and shrimp paste with steamed eggs, okra, crisp acacia and chicken livers – an amazing palette of flavours. Or there's yam pak, which is a 'salad' of different leaves and vegetables brought together by an amazing citrussy dressing. Or pla meuk pat sadtor, which is a dish of garlic stir-fried squid with sadtor beans – wonderfully aromatic and pungent. Even the 'duck salad' is a complex affair and offers a grand array of textures. There's an extensive wine list and a helpful sommelier who recommends drinking Alsace with Thai food. Nahm is a sophisticated place and not cheap, so it's important to get the most out of the experience – you should rely on the charming front of house staff to help with the ordering. Then your meal will be delicious, vibrant and totally unfamiliar – a strangely alluring and elegant combination.

One O One

Sheraton Park Tower, 101 William Street, SW1

■ 020 7290 7101

⊖ Knightsbridge

⦿ French/Fish

⏱ Mon to Fri 12.00–14.30 & 18.00–22.00; Sat & Sun 12.30–14.30 & 18.30–22.00

⌂ www.oneoonerestaurant.com

⊟ all major credit cards ■ no service added

££ ■ mains £24–£28 ■ desserts £6 ■ business lunch menu £15–£35 (2 to 6 petit plats) ■ lunch: à la carte starters £8–£10, mains £13–£15 ■ tasting menu £50 (5 courses) ■ lowest bottle price £22

⭐ Fish: the French way

Pascal Proyart is a Breton chef who is a fine fish cook. During 2007 the restaurant was completely refurbished to emerge with a new look and more importantly its own toilets (previously they were three days' march via the hotel reception). The menus have also been given the once-over and now work on a grazing principle. It's hard not to have reservations over the florid, overblown language used to describe sections of the menu. 'Low tide and wonderful discovery'; 'Delicacies from the shore and beyond'; 'High tide with its exceptional sea fishing'. But that aside, the standard of cooking is very good and it is recommended that four little dishes per person are combined to make a meal. Pascal's oyster creations (molluscs from Cancale in Brittany, natch) are well done. Have them either chilled with shallot vinegar, chilled with a yuzu sorbet or in tempura batter but impaled with a pipette of wasabi soya that is injected into the oyster by the Maitre d'. Then there's pan-fried Norwegian scallop with onsen quail eggs, truffle potato mousseline and pork belly – a good combo working well together. Or a stellar dish of pan-seared langoustine and duck foie gras with Pekin duck consommé. Or pan-roast Norwegian halibut and langoustine dumpling with a coco bean and truffle cassoulet. Puds are equally complex and include classics like coupe Liégoise with salt caramel ice cream. Service is slick.

Wódka

12 St Alban's Grove, W8 ■ 020 7937 6513

⊖ High Street Kensington

🍽 Polish

🕐 Mon to Fri 12.00–15.00 & 18.30–23.15; Sat & Sun 18.30–23.15

🖰 www.wodka.co.uk

🗗 all major credit cards ■ 12.5% optional service added

££ starters £5–£8.90 ■ mains £12.90–£16 ■ sides £3–£3.50
■ desserts £5–£6 ■ set lunch & pre-theatre (18.30–19.30) £13.50 (2 courses) & £17 (3 courses) ■ lowest bottle price £13

✪ Vodka, soup and good cheer

There's a clue to the Polish psyche in the extensive collection of moody and esoteric vodkas behind the bar. Like the spirits, Wódka is a restaurant that lies in wait for you. It's calm and bare, and the food is better than you might expect – well cooked and thoughtfully seasoned. There's a daily lunch menu that represents extremely good value, a large proportion of the dishes being refugees from the evening à la carte. Otherwise, the soup makes a good starter: grzybowa is a wild mushroom soup. Blinis are also the business: they come with smoked salmon, seared foie gras, aubergine mousse, or Oscietra caviar. Choosing a selection will get you all except the caviar. Also good is the kaszanka – grilled black pudding with pickled red cabbage and pear purée. For a main course, the fishcakes with creamed leeks are a firm favourite with the regulars. Alternatively go for summer bigos – a Polish hunters stew; or schabowy, which is breaded pork escalope. In line with the Polish love of wild game, when partridge is available it is roasted and served with a splendid mash of root vegetables; wild boar is served with roast baby beetroot and red wine shallots; or there may be braised rabbit with mustard sauce, spatzle dumplings and black cabbage. Puddings tend to be of the oversweet, under-imaginative gateau variety. Opt for the chocolate truffle cake, and your twelfth glass of vodka.

→ For branches, see index or website

Zafferano

15 Lowndes Street, SW1 ■ 020 7235 5800

⊖ Knightsbridge

🍽 Italian

🕐 Mon to Sat 12.00–14.30 & 19.00–23.00; Sun 12.00–15.00 & 19.00–23.00

🖥 www.zafferanorestaurant.com

🖪 all major credit cards ■ 12.5% optional service added

££ lunch £25.50 (2 courses), £29.50 (3 courses) & £32.50 (4 courses)
■ dinner £29.50 (2 courses), £39.50 (3 courses) & £49.50 (4 courses)
· ■ lowest bottle price £15

✪ Italy in Belgravia

When Zafferano opened, the combination of modern Italian food and decent-value fixed-price menus was a rare and dazzling new development that attracted a host of diners and a number of awards. People felt that although it wasn't cheap per se, you did get a good deal. Now Zafferano has matured and expanded – more tables, a luxurious bar and a private room. But the deal is still a simple one; you are faced with a series of multiple-course options and you merely have to decide how greedy you want to be. This is one place where you should go through the card: antipasti, pasta, main and pud. The cooking is good here, the menu is seasonal, and the ingredients carefully chosen. Fortunately, the service is slick and the wine list long, so the 'essence of Italy' mood remains unbroken. Starters may include sliced duck speck and pig's cheek with mustard fruits; warm octopus salad; or tuna carpaccio with fennel, orange and mint. Go on to the stunning pheasant ravioli with rosemary, or the fish. Then there may be something simple like pan-fried veal cutlet with mushrooms and rosti; or roast partridge with cabbage, chicken livers and capers; or truffle dishes in season – they attract a hefty supplement, but it is worth it for the baked onion filled with cheese fondue and topped with truffle. Puddings are serious – the tortino al cioccolato, chocolate fondant pudding, is worth the 12-minute wait. The tiramisù is majestic.

Zuma

5 Raphael Street, SW7 ■ 020 7584 1010
■ valet parking from 19.00   ⚹

⊖ Knightsbridge

🍽 Japanese

🕐 Mon to Thurs 12.00–14.15 & 18.00–23.00; Fri 12.00–14.45 &
18.00–23.00; Sat & Sun 12.30–15.15 & 18.00–23.00 (Sun 22.00)

🖰 www.zumarestaurant.com

🗄 all major credit cards ■ 13.5% optional service added

££ small dishes/salads/maki rolls £4.10–£13.80 ■ sushi/sashimi/tempura
£3.30–£34.80 ■ soup/rice/sides £1.80–£5.80 ■ mains £13.80–£75
■ desserts £5.80–£12.80 ■ tasting menu £96 ■ lowest bottle price £28

✪ Uber-cool celeb haven, elegant Japanese food

Chef-proprietor Rainer Becker chose the unspeakably chic Japanese
design team Super Potato to create this huge restaurant, filled with
crowds of both celebs and celeb spotters. This place is all stone,
rough-hewn granite and unfinished wood. The menu says that Zuma
is a 'contemporary Japanese Izakaya' – so now you know. In practice,
this means dishes are prepared either at the sushi bar, on the robata
grill, or in the kitchen. Everything is designed for sharing and the
dishes will pitch up in a gentle procession rather than in the more
formal order of starters, mains and puds. By way of a prelude, order
some edame – soya beans that have been steamed in the pod. Strip
the beans out with your teeth and leave the pods. Or there is tosa
dofu, which is deep-fried tofu with daikon and bonito flakes, or age
watarigani, a dish of fried soft-shell crab with wasabi mayonnaise.
The sashimi and sushi are exquisite and pricey. The skewers from
the robata grill are fresh and appealing. Try satsumaimo no goma
shoyo gake, which is sweet potato glazed with sesame; or Suzuki no
shioyaki, salt-grilled sea bass with burnt tomato; or tori no tebasaki,
chicken wings with sea salt and lime. Then there are tempura,
seafood dishes and meat dishes, every one of which is presented
stylishly. The sake list features a host of different kinds – thankfully
there's a 'sake sommelier' to help.

Marylebone and Euston

REGENT'S

The Garden Café

Diwana
Greens & Beans
EUSTON

PARK

ALBANY STREET
MUNSTER SQUARE
LONGFORD
WILLIAM ROAD
HAMPSTEAD ROAD
EUSTON RD
EUSTON RD
EUSTON RD
EUSTON RD
EUSTON SQUARE

WARREN
STREET
EUSTON
SQUARE

OUTER CIRCLE

BAKER STREET
YORK TERRACE WEST
YORK TERRACE EAST

REGENT'S
PARK

GT PORTLAND
STREET
EUSTON ST

PARK CRES

MARYLEBONE RD

Phoenix Palace

The Providores

Galvin Bistrot de Luxe
Giusto
L'Autre Pied
Royal China
Locanda Locatelli
Texture

PORTLAND PLACE

GREAT PORTLAND STREET

LANGHAM ST

MORTIMER

CAVENDISH
SQUARE

GOODGE
STREET
GOODGE ST

OXFORD STREET

OXFORD
CIRCUS

MARBLE
ARCH
OXFORD STREET
BOND
STREET

500 metres

L'Autre Pied

5–7 Blandford Street, W1 ■ 020 7486 9696

⊖ Bond Street

🍴 French

🕐 Mon to Fri 12.00–15.00 & 18.00–23.00; Sat 18.00–23.00

⌂ www.lautrepied.co.uk

🖃 all major credit cards ■ 12.5% optional service added

££ starters £7.50–£14.95 ■ mains £17.95–£21.50
  ■ desserts £5.95–£7.50 ■ tasting menu £49.50 (6 courses)
  ■ lowest bottle price £12

✪ Putting the other foot forward

L'Autre Pied is the sophisticated younger sister of Pied à Terre (see p. 10). As a general rule, spin-off, second-string restaurants tend to be gentler, simpler or less starry establishments than their older siblings. None of this applies to L'Autre Pied, however. The same Michelin ambitions that are writ large at Pied à Terre are evident on Blandford Street. The dining room is slick, chic and modern, if a little on the dark side. Starters are ambitious and everything is pretty on the plate. You might be offered a salad of smoked eel, Vichyssoise mousse and red veined sorrel; a mosaic of beetroot, soured cream and balsamic jelly; a soft-poached hen's egg with warm salad of celery and ratte potatoes, with celery emulsion; or parsley and bacon velouté with Herefordshire snail beignets. The main courses are also complex, multi-faceted dishes: roast breast of Anjou pigeon with carrot and mango purée, caramelised mango, and confit potatoes; pan-fried brill with roast chestnuts and Jerusalem artichoke purée; slow-cooked breast of veal with caramelised sweetbread, smoked potato purée and hazelnut jus; or assiette of rabbit with swede and honey purée, and lemon thyme froth. The kitchen favours emulsions, froths, jellies and purées but the seasoning is good and the flavours well matched. Puds continue the theme: pan d'épice emulsion, banana ice cream; kaffir lime panna cotta, blood orange granita. The wine list is unforgiving and races off into the high pastures pretty quickly. This place takes itself seriously and you should do likewise.

Diwana

121 Drummond Street, NW1 ■ 020 7387 5556

⊖ Euston

🍽 Indian/vegetarian

🕐 Mon to Sat 12.00–23.30; Sun 12.00–22.30

🖫 all major credit cards ■ 10% optional service added

££ starters £3.50–£4 ■ mains £5–£8.95 ■ sides 70p–£4.70
■ desserts £2.30–£3.75 ■ buffet lunch £6.50 (12.00–14.30)
■ unlicensed, BYO (no corkage)

✪ Reliable Indian veggie old-timer

Despite looking tired, with décor from another decade, Diwana is a busy place. Tables fill up and empty at a fair crack, though the atmosphere is convivial and casual rather than rushed. You can bring your own beer or wine and a full water jug is supplied on each table. This, the low prices, a chatty menu listing 'tasty snacks', and fast, friendly service combine to create a deceptively simple stage for some good Indian vegetarian cooking. There's even a lunch buffet where you can overeat to your heart's content. Starters are copious, ladled out in no-nonsense, stainless-steel bowls. The dahi bhalle chat is a cool, yogurty blend of chickpeas, crushed pooris and bulghur wheat, sprinkled with 'very special spices'. The dahi poori is a fragrant concoction of pooris, potatoes, onions, sweet and sour sauces and chilli chutney, again smothered in yogurt and laced with spices. Stars of the main menu are the dosas, particularly the flamboyant deluxe dosa, a giant fan of a pancake with coconut chutney, potatoes and dhal nestling beneath its folds. Also superb is the house speciality, thali Annapurna – a feast of dhal, rice, vegetables, pickles, side dishes, mini bhajees and your choice of pooris or chapattis, which overcomes any ordering reticence by bringing what seems like everything to table. There are extras like Bombay aloo, but the main-course portions are large enough to make them seem pretty ambitious.

Galvin Bistrot de Luxe

66 Baker Street, W1 ■ 020 7935 4007

⊖ Baker Street

🍴 French

🕐 Mon to Sat 12.00–14.30 & 18.30–23.00; Sun 12.00–15.00 & 18.30–22.30

🖥 www.galvinuk.com

🖪 all major credit cards ■ 12.5% optional service added

££ starters £5.50–£14.50 ■ mains £10.50–£17.50 ■ desserts £5–£6.50 ■ prix fixe menus: lunch £15.50 (3 courses), early dinner (18.00–19.00) £17.50 ■ lowest bottle price £13.95

⭐ Les frères Galvin cooking up a storm

Chris Galvin and his brother Jeff get on well together and after parallel careers in some of London's top kitchens they set up this, their first joint venture. The Galvin Bistrot de Luxe is a French restaurant, as French as only two Englishmen who genuinely love classic French food can make it. It's comfortable. It represents excellent value for money. The wine list doesn't pillage your plastic. The menu is short and seasonal. Dishes are honest, delicious and wholesome. A great deal of time and effort goes into sourcing fine ingredients. Starters may range from a splendid, almost juicy terrine pressé of Landaise chicken, ham hock and foie gras; to a salad of endive Roquefort and walnut; a beautifully made little Pithiviers of pigeon with a glazed chestnut – very delicious; or an omelette aux cèpes. Main courses range from a risotto of courgette and saffron; to wing of skate Grenobloise; sautéed veal kidney with wild mushrooms and grain mustard; confit pork cheeks with Puy lentils; or pavé of beef Bourguignonne pommes mousseline. Gutsy cooking. There's a braised shoulder and roast cutlet of Cornish lamb with flageolet bean purée. Puds are hardcore: St Emilion au chocolat comes in a small glass and is impressively rich; or there's pear tarte Bourdaloue; or a retro classic like oeufs à la neige. As you'd expect, there's a decent cheeseboard. For people who like food, Galvin Bistrot de Luxe really hits the spot.

The Garden Café

Inner Circle, Regent's Park, NW1 ▪ 020 7935 5729   ♿

⊖ Baker Street

⦿ Modern British

🕐 daily 10.00–dusk (09.00–20.00 May to Sep)

🖰 www.thegardencafe.co.uk

🖫 all major credit cards ▪ no service added

££ starters £4.95–£7.95 ▪ mains £7.50–£12.50 ▪ desserts £4.95
   ▪ set lunch £15.50 (2 courses) ▪ lowest bottle price £14.50

✪ A hidden gem by the rose garden

The mere words 'park café' are enough to make a gastronaut shudder, but your first visit to the Garden Café may change all that. In 1964 the new café (built under a roof made up of 31 copper hexagons) was the height of modernity and lovers of gastro trivia will enjoy the fact that this was the first 'Little Chef' in Britain. Now the building is a cherished part of our architectural heritage, but thankfully something has been done about the food which now sits easily in the setting. Service is friendly in an egalitarian sort of way – no bookings are taken – and there is plenty of room both inside and al fresco. The menu changes with the seasons, so winter starters range from honey-roast parsnip and Cox apple soup; to air-dried ham served with celeriac remoulade and rather good sourdough toast; or purple sprouting broccoli with feta cheese dressing. The menu offers comfortable, familiar dishes: braised lamb shank comes with roast shallots, mash and gravy; there may be a serious macaroni cheese; or free-range chicken with peas, bacon and pearl barley Or there may be a leek blue cheese tart; or a peppered rump steak with chips and a Béarnaise sauce. There is always a decent salad served in a large, no-nonsense bowl and, to finish up, workmanlike puds. The Garden Café is a pretty restaurant with good food, a friendly atmosphere and reasonable prices.

Giusto

43 Blandford Street, W1 ■ 020 7486 7340

⊖ Bond Street

⑩ Italian/pizzas

⏲ Mon to Sat 12.00–15.00 & 18.30–22.30; Sun 12.00–15.00

🔗 www.giustorestaurant.com

🖥 all major credit cards ■ 12.5% optional service added

££ antipasti £7–£9.25 ■ mains £15–£17.25 ■ pasta £11.50–£13.75
■ pizza £9–£12 ■ sides £4.50–£5 ■ desserts £6.95
■ lowest bottle price £8.50 (carafe)

✪ Classy (somewhat pricey) pizzas

Halfway through 2007 Giusto took over this site from La Spighetta
– presumably the new proprietors were looking for premises that
already had a large wood-fired oven. The ground floor here is so
small and unprepossessing that it comes as a real shock when you
wander downstairs into the large dining room, bar and kitchen.
You can see inside the oven and there's a cheery glow as oak billets
blaze away. The menu leaps through all the hoops. There are several
antipasti – carpaccio di manzo is sound enough; prosciutto e
pecorino is well presented – or there's the insalata Giusto, which
teams radicchio with raw broad beans, French beans and pecorino.
Then there are half a dozen 'secondi' ranging from rib eye steak to
wild sea bass. Then seven pasta dishes: gnocchi with lamb ragù; crab
ravioli. But as is so often the way, the public go straight to a different
section of the menu and the eight different pizzas are flying out of
the kitchen. This maybe due to the subliminal effect of watching
the big oven, seeing the sizzle and coveting other people's orders.
The pizzas are exceptional – crisp and with well-balanced toppings.
Try the Estiva (buffalo mozzarella, Parma ham, plum tomatoes and
rocket) or the Piccante (spinach, scamorza, n'duja and spicy salami).
The wine list has plenty of choice including some sound wines by
carafe and service is friendly.

Greens & Beans

131 Drummond Street, NW1 ■ 020 7380 0857

⊖ Euston

🍽 Vegetarian wholefood

🕐 Mon to Fri 09.00–17.00

🖱 www.greensandbeans.biz

🖶 all major credit cards ■ no service added

££ breakfast £3.25–£4.95 ■ starters £2.75–£3.95 ■ salads £5.50
■ mains £4.25–£6.95 ■ desserts £1–£3 ■ BYO £3 per bottle corkage

---

⭐ The Green machine

Greens & Beans is a small, clean, cheerful little café – one of hundreds to be found In London. What makes it a bit different is that the menu is completely vegetarian and aims to use fairly-traded, GM-free, organic local ingredients wherever possible. Greens arrival is an interesting example of the market-place theory, in that Drummond Street is already home to several Indian vegetarian restaurants, including some old-timers that are starting to look past their best. Greens reaffirms veggie credentials. You could start with an organic breakfast – Alara Fairtrade muesli, or porridge (choose from oats, millet or quinoa) then a scrambled egg sandwich. Then there are salads, including the gluten-free and vegan option 'baby greens, mixed sprouts, pumpkin and sunflower seeds with avocado and tomato'; the black bean and two peppers salad with a cumin and mint vinaigrette; or the tomato pepper and mozzarella salad, which is rather puzzlingly described as 'Munich-style'. At lunch there are several ten-inch pizzas including a Margherita – mozzarella, tomato and basil; and the house special – mozzarella, feta cheese, sun-dried tomatoes and spinach. Mains range from penne pasta with a tomato and basil sauce to that veggie ever-present 'nut roast', or crepes filled with ricotta cheese and spinach. For an all indulgent finish there are ice creams from Green & Blacks or Roskilly's of Cornwall. This is a pleasant little café serving considered and wholesome food.

Locanda Locatelli

8 Seymour Street, W1 ■ 020 7935 9088   ♿

⊖ Marble Arch

🍽 Italian

🕐 Mon to Thurs 12.00–15.00 & 18.45–23.00; Fri 12.00–15.00 &
18.45–23.30; Sat 12.00–15.30 & 18.45–23.30; Sun 12.00–15.30 &
18.45–22.00

🖥 www.locandalocatelli.com

🗗 all major credit cards ■ no service added

££ antipasti £12–£12.50 ■ pasta £8–£18 ■ mains £22–£29.50
■ sides £3.75 ■ desserts £6–£12 ■ lowest bottle price £12.50

✪ Stars in the dining room, stars in the kitchen

Giorgio and Plaxy Locatelli run a chic modern and blisteringly
fashionable Italian restaurant. Luckily, the food is very good indeed.
The room is elegant and has a real buzz that makes it something of
a celebrity magnet, all of which may be part of the reason there's
phone frenzy on the booking lines at the beginning of each month
– spontaneous here means five to eight weeks ahead. To start,
there's a splendid basket of mixed breads to keep you busy. There is
a large turnover of dishes, but the cooking is always spurred on by
the seasons and when it's truffle time there are lots of ways you can
double your bill! From the starters choose a spring salad; ox tongue
with green sauce; chargrilled cuttlefish; or pan-fried scallops with
saffron vinaigrette. Pasta dishes delight: fregola with razor clams
and tomato soup; chestnut tagliatelle with wild mushrooms; or how
about a risotto alla Amarone della Valpolicella? Every dish looks
elegant on the plate, and combines tastes and textures to their best
effect. Main courses may include roast breast of duck with spelt and
broccoli; steamed hake in garlic and parsley; roast rabbit leg with
Parma ham and polenta; or chargrilled lamb. The service is slick and
smooth and the restaurant has an established and comfortable air.
Dolci range from tiramisù to a serious chocolate soufflé. The wine list
pays homage to the Italian greats.

Phoenix Palace

5 Glentworth Street, NW1 ■ 020 7486 3515

⊖ Baker Street/Marylebone

🍴 Chinese

🕐 Mon to Sat 12.00–23.30; Sun 11.00–22.30

🖱 www.phoenixpalace.uk.com

🖃 all major credit cards ■ no service added

££ dim sum £2.20–£4 ■ starters £2.50–£32 ■ mains £7.50–£30
■ sides £2–£8.50 ■ desserts £3.80 ■ set dinner £15.80–£26.80
■ lowest bottle price £10

✪ Chinese outpost in the far North

It comes as a bit of a shock to find a rather good, large, bright, busy Chinese restaurant marooned this far north, alongside the stream of traffic intent on dodging the Congestion Charge as it crawls past Tussaud's. The chefs here know what they are doing, so this is a good place to try out something new. Starters include all the old favourites, such as chicken wrapped in lettuce leaf, but try the jellyfish with sesame seed; the soft-shell crab with chilli and garlic; the pork trotters with vinaigrette; or the chilli potsticker dumplings. The menu is a long one and it is worth a careful read as there are some interesting discoveries to be made, and a good many dishes that push the envelope. Whenever you visit an ambitious Chinese restaurant it is always worth trying one dish that you have never had before. Salt-baked chicken is a wonderful savoury roast chicken with juicy meat and crisp skin. Or there's steamed turbot with Tientsin cabbage and garlic. The fried minced pork patties with salted fish are very classy, the salt fish seasoning the pork mix successfully. You could also try baked crab and salty yolk served with steamed buns; eel with pickled mustard green; pork and stuffed beancurd cooked in a clay pot; or venison with yellow chives and celery. To find any Chinese restaurant in this out-of-the-way location is a puzzle – to find such a good one is positively incomprehensible.

The Providores

109 Marylebone High Street, W1 ■ 020 7935 6175

⊖ Baker Street/Bond Street

🍴 Fusion

🕐 Mon to Fri 12.00–15.00 & 18.00–23.30; Sat & Sun 10.00–15.00
(brunch) & 18.00–23.30

🖰 www.theprovidores.co.uk

🖶 all major credit cards ■ 12.5% optional service added

££ starters £7–£14 ■ mains £18–£24.50 ■ sides £3–£4 ■ desserts £8.80
■ cheese £9.80 ■ lowest bottle price £14.50

✪ Fusion and less confusion

When you nervously mention the word 'fusion' there is only one
chef in London with a 24-carat bankable reputation and that is Peter
Gordon, the amiable New Zealander. His showcase is this restaurant,
which he opened with a consortium of friends. The resto part
occupies an elegant room on the first floor. Chairs are comfortable,
tablecloths are white and simplicity rules. The dishes all taste
fresh, with every flavour distinct and each combination cunningly
balanced, even if the menu descriptions read like lists: 'coconut, black
cardamom and galangal laksa with lime leaf marinated squid, a fried
quail's egg, a grilled prawn, green tea noodles, crispy shallots'! Or
'crispy spiced nori soft-shell crab on avocado sesame purée pickled
tomato'. Puzzled? The laksa is a rich, creamy, sweet coconut broth
covered with a scattering of crisp bits of shallot and laced with the
contrasting textures of ribbon noodles and the tiger prawn. Or how
about Thai-style seared kangaroo loin with pomelo? Mains may
include roast turbot on roast celeriac and sherry with sautéed snails;
brown shrimp and coconut-crusted sea bass on fennel, orange,
green olive, smoked eel and dill salad; or roast New Zealand venison
loin on Jerusalem artichokes with spiced quince. Desserts are equally
elaborate: chocolate clementine 'delice' with Marscapone sorbet
espresso Manzanilla tapioca; or grenadine panna cotta with pear and
basil jelly, pomegranate and a manuka snap! Counter-intuitively, these
flights of fancy are well worth trying. Downstairs there's a walk-in,
informal, gentler-paced sort of place.

Royal China

24–26 Baker Street, W1 ◼ 020 7487 4688   ♿

⊖ Baker Street

🍽 Chinese/dim sum

🕐 Mon to Thurs 12.00–23.00; Fri & Sat 12.00–23.30; Sun 11.00–22.00; dim sum until 16.45

🖰 www.royalchinagroup.co.uk

🖥 all major credit cards ◼ 13% optional service added

££ dim sum £2.20–£3.50 ◼ mains £6.50–£24 ◼ sides £2.50–£8.50
   ◼ desserts £4.20–£6.50 ◼ set dinners £30–£38
   ◼ lowest bottle price £17

✪ Dim sum star

You'll find the Royal China Group's number one restaurant on Queensway and this, their West End outpost, used to be at no. 40 Baker Street. However, the move a few doors down to this new establishment has proved a big success. All the Royal China restos are kitted out in shiny black and gold, which makes the rather calmer look of the new dining room all the more welcome. There is a large wall mural in the black and gold idiom, but it is no longer oppressive. The dim sum are terrific. There is a long menu featuring much the same array of dishes as you find in every other Chinese establishment, but go before 16.45 and stick with the dim sum. Until Hakkasan (see p. 6) introduced the venison puff, the roast pork puff from Royal China was thought by many to be the best dim sum in town. It is still very good, light, flaky and rich. The regulars, such as steamed prawn dumplings and minced pork dumplings, are fresh and well seasoned, and the prawn cheung fun are well made and commendably thin. Also noteworthy are the prawn and chive dumplings, and the steamed curry squid. Bulk out your order with the glutinous rice in lotus leaves – a dish that is done very well here. Service is slick and quick and after you've made the choice between Chinese tea and Tsing Tao beer try as many different dumplings as you dare. Look at the specials list where you might find unusual delicacies like 'pig's skin and turnip in broth'. A treat for Baldric.

→ For branches, see index or website

Texture

34 Portman Square, W1 ■ 020 7224 0028 &

⊖ Bond Street/Marble Arch

🍴 Fusion

🕐 Tues to Sat 12.00–14.00 & 19.00–24.00

🖱 www.texture-restaurant.co.uk

🗗 all major credit cards ■ 12.5% optional service added

££ à la carte £45 (3 courses) ■ lunch £8.50 per dish (starter size)
■ tasting menu £59 (6 courses) ■ lowest bottle price £22

✪ Something different, something exciting

You have to wonder whether having an Icelandic head chef
could ever be a sufficient draw to fill an aspirational restaurant, but
fortunately Agnar Sverrisson's CV includes the magic words 'Manoir
aux Quat'Saisons'. Black wooden tables are somewhat crowded
together, the floors are uncarpeted floorboards and the high ceilings
mean that there is an echoey feel to the place, but Sverrisson's
cooking is careful and combinations of flavour and texture are
considered. At lunch time there is list of dishes served in starter-size
portions. French Jerusalem artichoke soup comes with a poached
hen's egg and black truffle – very refined soup, like perfumed
cream, a decent fresh egg and the whiff of truffle. 'Winter vegetable
textures' turns out a little too complicated and looks a bit like a
splatter painting. The 'Icelandic' cod comes with brandade, chorizo
and squid and is a wholly successful combination. The Shetland hot
smoked organic salmon is perfectly cooked. The Lancashire suckling
pig is slow cooked and served with squid and bonito sauce – once
again, good flavours. The Charolais beef cheek is slow braised with
root vegetables and red wine – Monsieur Blanc would be proud of
this one. The Cornish monkfish comes with a barley risotto, anis and
almond. The desserts include a plateful of different coconut delights,
and there is a poached pear that comes with a fine five-spice ice
cream. Sometimes spooky but generally good.

Mayfair and Bond Street

Alain Ducasse

The Dorchester, Park Lane, W1 ■ 020 7629 8866   &

⊖ Hyde Park Corner/Marble Arch

⦿ French

🕐 Tues to Fri 12.00–14.00 & 18.30–22.00; Sat 18.30–22.00

🖱 www.alainducasse-dorchester.com

🗄 all major credit cards ■ 12.5% optional service added

££ à la carte £75 (3 courses) & £95 (4 courses) ■ lunch £35 (3 courses)
■ tasting menu £115 (7 courses) ■ lowest bottle price £25

✪ Foothold for French superstar?

One of France's heaviest hitters opened in the Dorchester towards
the end of 2007. The dining room is a symphony in muted beige,
very soft, very gracious, very tranquil. Service glides about. There
is what seems to be a compulsory manifestation of dodgy French
taste – large and complicated china vegetables adorn each table.
Monsieur Ducasse has written a menu that is only a quarter turn
away from the old-fashioned, classical French cooking of yore – sauce
Vin Jaune; sauce Grand Veneur; sauce Nantua; and sauce Albufera all
feature proudly, and from a technical point of view the cooking is very
good indeed: A soft-cooked organic egg comes with crayfish, wild
mushrooms and sauce Nantua – perfectly judged egg and perfectly
made sauce, grand contrasts of taste and texture. The simmered duck
foie gras with mango and dolce forte sauce comes to table almost
quivering with an indulgent melting heart. Main courses also show
classical roots – a dish of halibut presents firm fish on spinach and
Jerusalem artichokes with a lemon and caper sauce. The roast pigeon
is a runaway winner, exceedingly tender and with a superb croute
pasted with dark meat and liver. The puds are also pretty momentous
– the rum baba comes with real rum and melts in the mouth. This
is not a cheap place (although the lunch is a bargain) and the wine
list saunters off into the stratosphere, but it is agreeably, undeniably,
French.

The Albemarle

Browns Hotel, Albemarle Street, W1 ■ 020 7493 6020   ♿

 Green Park

🍽 British

🕐 Mon to Sat 12.00–15.00 & 18.00–22.30; Sun 19.00–22.30

🖱 www.brownshotel.com

🗄 all major credit cards ■ no service added

££ starters £6.25–£16.50 ■ mains £11.50–£29.50 ■ sides £3.75–£4.25
■ desserts £6.50–£9.75 lowest bottle price £21

✪ A showcase for the best of British

Until early 2008 this restaurant was the Grill, but a formidable
wind of change has swept through this venerable hotel with much
refurbishment, a sexy new cocktail bar and a new philosophy for
the main restaurant. The newly christened Albemarle has a large,
light, bright dining room with sage green chairs (comfortable too)
and the occasional splash of gaudy modern art. The menu pays
homage to British dishes, British produce and the seasons. This is
still a plush and pricey place to eat out but the food now has an
agreeable authenticity about it. You might start with a salad of Jersey
tomatoes with lovage; baked razor clams – magnificent, with a
herby breadcrumb crust; or asparagus in scrumpy batter. There are
various fish dishes from pukka fish and chips to char-grilled cuttlefish
or steamed halibut. Then some tempting dishes for two to share – a
roast Woolley Grange Farm chicken; a whole Cornish brill; salt-baked
sea bass. Followed by a section of pies, hot pots and braises, such
as rabbit braised in cider with capers. The 'grill' section adds lamb
cutlets (served with a decent bubble and squeak made with fresh
peas), sausages and steaks. By way of homage to an earlier, clubbier,
incarnation there is still a lunch trolley: Thursday is roast Middlewhite
pork. The trolley always sells out on Wednesday which is beef
Wellington day. Good puds. Sympathetic service. Long wine list.

Automat

33 Dover Street, W1 ■ 020 7499 3033   ♿

⊖ Green Park

🍽 North American

🕐 Mon to Fri 07.00–11.00, 12.00–15.00, & 18.00–23.00; Sat
11.00–16.00 (brunch) & 18.00–23.00; Sun 11.00–16.00 (brunch).
Brasserie Mon to Fri 12.00–01.00

🖥 www.automat-london.com

🖫 all major credit cards ■ 12.5% optional service added

££ starters £7–£11 ■ mains £7–£25 ■ sides £3.50 ■ desserts £6
■ breakfast £3–£12 ■ brunch £7–£25 ■ lowest bottle price £15

✪ Mayfair plush meets Americana

Setting aside delightful images of rich little old Mayfair ladies
pitching up with their laundry for a service wash, Automat doesn't
seem like a good name for this combination of chic, slick and Yank.
Automat's dining area is divided into three parts – to the rear is a
bar and seating with a greenhousey feel, in the middle are solid and
trad booths, and to the front, smaller, less comfortable tables and
chairs crowd a sort of 'shop-window' area. The menu also splits into
appetisers, entrées, 'US beef' and sides. The starters are American
dishes that have been adapted just a little for European tastes. There's
chicken liver and foie gras mousse; and an iceberg wedge with
'house ranch dressing'; crab cakes with guacamole; or a Caesar salad.
Entrées include the Automat burger – 10oz of good meat, check;
cooked as requested, check; good bun, check; good size, check. Also
on offer are macaroni and cheese; roast Alaskan Black cod; a soft-
shell po' boy; steak tartare and a salad Niçoise with freshly grilled
tuna. In the beef section there's a New York Striploin steak and also
a rib eye. Puds range from a New York cheesecake to Mississippi mud
pie with soured cream. This place has a good reputation for brunch,
and that menu features both eggs Benedict and buttermilk pancakes.
The prices on the wine list reflect the Mayfair location, but thankfully
the service is informal and cheerful.

Benares

12 Berkeley House, Berkeley Square, W1 ■ 020 7629 8886 ♿

⊖ Green Park

🍴 Indian

🕐 Mon to Sat 12.00–14.30 & 17.30–23.00; Sun 12.00–14.30 & 18.00–22.30

🖱 www.benaresrestaurant.com

🗂 all major credit cards ■ 12.5% optional service added

££ starters £9.80–£16.95 ■ mains £17.50–£35 ■ sides £3.95–£6.95 ■ desserts £8.50 ■ set lunch £19.50 (2 courses) & £24.95 (3 courses) ■ tasting menus £65 ■ lowest bottle price £18

✪ Top-drawer Indian in plush surroundings

Atul Kochar is the man who secured one of the first Michelin stars ever awarded to an Indian restaurant in Britain, and you can be sure that at Benares he yearns to repeat the trick, while carving out a career for himself as a telly chef. This place is certainly a deluxe affair: acres of polished stone floors, pools strewn with blossoms and little candles bobbing about. The dining room is modern and stylish. Some of the pricing, and most of the wine list, 'goes Mayfair' pretty briskly, but considering the elegance of the setting, the friendliness of the service and the undoubted quality of the cooking, this is a good option as a special occasion Indian restaurant. When each dish arrives it is beautiful on the plate – lots of influences from smart French chefs, but still matching textures with good assertive tastes. Karara kekda is a crisp soft-shell crab with spicy squid and a Peruvian potato salad; or there is gosht ke shammi — delicate ground lamb kebabs with a green mango salad. The tandoor work is exemplary – lamb chops are exceedingly plump and tender, king prawns large and perky. A classic dish such as rogan josh is as good as you can get, unless you can find it served on the bone. Or there's hari machichi, which is pan-fried John Dory served with sautéed Jerusalem artichokes. The vegetable side dishes are most interesting. Achaari kadoo is a dish conjured up from yellow pumpkin and pickling spices to give a tangy, spicy finish.

Chor Bizarre

16 Albemarle Street, W1 ■ 020 7629 9802

⊖ Green Park

⦿ Indian

🕐 Mon to Sat 12.00–15.00 & 18.00–23.30; Sun 18.00–22.30

🖰 www.chorbizarrerestaurant.com

🗗 all major credit cards ■ 12.5% optional service added

££ starters £3.50–£6.50 ■ mains £6.50–£25 ■ sides £1.50–£14
■ desserts £5–£6 ■ set lunch £14.50 & £16.50
■ tasting menu (Wazwan) £25 ■ lowest bottle price £16

✪ Good Indian food, genuine Indo-kitsch dining room

This Chor Bizarre is a straight copy of the one in the Broadway
Hotel, Delhi. Its name is an elaborate pun (*Chor Bazaar* translates as
'thieves' market') and the restaurant is furnished with Indian antiques
and bric a brac. Every table, and each set of chairs, is different — you
may find yourself dining within the frame of an antique four-poster
bed. The food is very well prepared and encouragingly authentic.
Chor Bizarre does, however, carry the kind of price tag you'd expect
in Mayfair. Start with simple things such as pakoras, which are tasty
vegetable fritters, or dakshini crab cakes, which come with a coconut
chutney. Kebabs are taken seriously here, too: try gazab ka tikka,
a bestseller in Delhi, which is a kind of chicken tikka deluxe. Then,
for your main course, choose dishes such as baghare baingan, a
Hyderabadi dish combining aubergine, peanuts and tamarind; or
Konkan prawn masala, king prawns simmered in a traditional Goan
sauce with a kick of chilli; or goshtaba, the famous Kashmiri lamb
curry – very velvety. Breads are also impressive, including an excellent
naan; pudina paratha, which is a mint paratha; and stuffed kulcha.
The many imposing set meals are a good way to tour the menu
without watching your wallet implode. Try the Maharaja thali – a
complete meal on a tray. TV dinners will never be the same again.
Bravehearts will tackle the Wazwan, a multi-course banquet of rich
food from the North of India.

Galvin at Windows

28th floor, London Hilton, 22 Park Lane, W1 ■ 020 7493 8000 &

⊖ Hyde Park Corner

🍽 Modern British

🕐 Tues to Fri 07.00–10.00, Sat & Sun 07.00–10.30 (breakfast); Mon to Fri 12.00–14.30 & 18.00–23.00; Sat 18.00–23.00; Sun 12.00–14.30

🖰 www.galvinuk.com

🗗 all major credit cards ■ 12.5% optional service added

££ prix fixe lunch £29 (3 courses) & £45 (inc. wine, water, coffee) ■ dinner à la carte £58 (3 courses) ■ menu gourmand (dinner only) £75 or £110 (with wine) ■ lowest bottle price £18.50

✪ Accomplished food, amazing view

Windows, the top-floor bar and restaurant at the Hilton, used to be more about curiosity than gastronomy – the views were amazing (clear line of sight into the Queen's back garden) and the bar was always crowded with a delightful combination of sinister, shiny-suited hoods and their exotic, sexily dressed arm candy. Then the Hilton management had a brainwave and hired in the big guns, the Galvin brothers, who were wowing diners at their new venture Galvin Bistrot de Luxe (see p. 73). The large modern dining room juts out over London and has the kind of views you can only expect from the 28th floor. Better hope it's not a foggy day when you visit. The menu is typically Galvin-esque: it changes seasonally, has top ingredients, classical French flair and appetising combinations. Starters may include slow-cooked duck egg, wild mushrooms and freshwater crayfish; warm Lincolnshire smoked eel 'Bordelaise'; or cured Loch Duart salmon, Dorset crab, lemon and caviar dressing. Main courses range from roast fillet of halibut with crab and pommes écrasées to slow-roast fillet of Scotch beef, braised short rib or culotte of Anjou pigeon and foie gras. Alternatively, two people can share a baby Pyrenean lamb leg with grelot onions, peppers Basquaise and aubergine gratin. Puds are sophisticated – buttermilk panna cotta, macerated strawberries and black olives. Service is slick, the wine list can torture even a brave wallet … and the view really is awesome.

Le Gavroche

43 Upper Brook Street, W1 ■ 020 7408 0881

⊖ Marble Arch

⑩ French

🕒 Mon to Fri 12.00–14.00 & 18.30–23.00; Sat 18.30–23.00

🖰 www.le-gavroche.co.uk

🖶 all major credit cards ■ 12.5% optional service added

££ starters £19.90–£36 ■ mains £26–£46 ■ desserts £12–£28
■ cheese £13.80 ■ set lunch £48 (3 courses Mon-Fri); tasting menu
£95 (8 courses £150 with wines) ■ lowest bottle price £21

✪ Temple to gastronomy

The Roux family business is cheffing and at Le Gavroche Michel
(Jnr) plys his trade to some purpose; he's been head chef here for 17
years. This is an awesome French restaurant. Service is super slick. The
dress code is super formal (jacket and tie). The wine list is littered with
superstar bottles. And the cooking is as good as it gets. The best way
of dodging this minor fiscal problem is to opt for the set lunch, which
is one of the bargains of the age. If you enjoy 'proper' French cooking
almost anything on the menu will ring a bell, but the soufflé Suissesse
– a cheese soufflé with extra cream – is very charming; or scallops
pan fried with five-spice mixture; or an artichoke heart filled with foie
gras and truffles. Mains are equally self-indulgent: a tournedos comes
with pan-fried foie gras and truffled macaroni cheese. Or there's
roast Anjou pigeon; wild salmon; or turbot. Then it's time to hit the
trolleys – the cheese trolley is a monster, laden with cheeses in perfect
condition. Or there's one groaning with different ice creams and
sorbets. The rest of the puds are stellar. Meanwhile, the service glides
around you, not too pushy, yet you never seem to wait. The wine
list has sound bottles at the bottom end for people whose priority is
the food, and then it soars off to the top for people whose priority is
spending.

Gordon Ramsay at Claridge's

Brook Street, W1 ■ 020 7499 0099   ♿

⊖ Green Park

🍴 French

🕐 Mon to Fri 12.00–14.45 & 17.45–23.00; Sat 12.00–15.30 &
   17.45–23.00; Sun 12.00–15.00 & 18.00–22.30

🖰 www.gordonramsay.com

🗗 all major credit cards ■ 12.5% optional service added

££ à la carte £70 (3 courses) ■ set lunch £30 (3 courses)
   ■ prestige menu £80 (6 courses) ■ lowest bottle price £18

✪ Classic French food within a classic luxury hotel

Gordon Ramsay's takeover of the restaurant at Claridge's has
bedded in well; the restaurant is packed and everything hums along
smoothly. There's a good-value set lunch, which some reckon to
be an even better bargain than the set lunch at Ramsay's Chelsea
flagship (see p. 395). Unfortunately, like its sibling, Claridge's is
booked up far in advance. While Gordon Ramsay has his name
over the door, the head chef here is Mark Sargeant. The menu
changes with the seasons and among the starters you may find a
ravioli of Dorset blue lobster and salmon poached in a lemongrass
bisque; cauliflower soup, braised oxtail and parsley black Périgord
truffle; ballotine of foie gras marinated in white port; or pot-roast
wood pigeon with artichoke velouté. Main courses might include
roast Goosnargh duck with mustard glazed pear and fricassée
of celeriac and chestnuts; pan-fried stonebass, Cromer crab and
celeriac cannelloni; roast John Dory and sautéed langoustines with
violet artichoke, pink fir apple potatoes and carrot purée; fillet of
Casterbridge beef, pot au feu of root vegetables, jasmine consommé;
or loin of venison and braised haunch with parsnip fondant and
wilted baby spinach. The desserts are equally considered: Valrhona
chocolate fondant with feuillatine and malt ice cream or passion fruit
crème brûlée with white chocolate sorbet. Those with deep pockets
and an inquisitive nature should consider booking the chef's table,
which seats six in an alcove overlooking the kitchen.

The Greenhouse

27a Hay's Mews, W1 ■ 020 7499 3331 &

⊖ Green Park

⑩ French

⏲ Mon to Fri 12.00–14.30 & 18.45–23.00; Sat 18.45–23.00

⌂ www.greenhouserestaurant.co.uk

⊟ all major credit cards ■ 12.5% optional service added

££ lunch £25 (2 courses) & £29 (3 courses) ■ dinner £60 (3 courses)
■ tasting menu £75 (7 courses) ■ lowest bottle price £20

✪ High ambitions and high prices

The Greenhouse is a very Mayfair concept. The coda of this place is excellence – of ingredients, cooking, service and wines. The room is comfortable and elegant, service attentive, the wine list an absolute monster with a great many fine wines and the cooking is very accomplished. Starters may range from a Simmental beef tartare with bone marrow, black truffle and kohlrabi; to a duck foie gras terrine with pistachio vinaigrette, cocoa jelly and warm brioche; or Limousin veal sweetbread with wild garlic caramel, glazed leek and veal jus. An engaging feature of the menu is that one seasonal item is presented differently every day, so your English asparagus may come with a soft-boiled gull's egg. Among the main courses considered dishes predominate, such as Anjou pigeon with braised salsify and toasted 'sesame gomasio'; brill cooked on the bone with baby Swiss chard, maple syrup and grated nutmeg; or milk-fed veal rump with butter praline and parsnip Chantilly. There is also the 'modern classic'. This is usually a dish for two to share such as a magnificent roast 'poulard de Bresse' in two services – first the breast with morels and home-made noodles, and then the legs. Desserts are elaborate: pineapple carpaccio, crunchy cereal and coconut ice cream; fresh blood orange white chocolate cream and olive oil ice cream; or 'Carré Dubuffet' – chocolate biscuit and pralinée ice cream. The Greenhouse offers Mayfair dining at Mayfair prices.

The Grill at the Dorchester

Park Lane, W1 ■ 020 7629 8888   ♿

⊖ Marble Arch/Hyde Park Corner

🍴 French

🕐 Mon to Fri 07.00–10.30 (breakfast); 12.00–14.30; 18.00–23.00;
   Sat 08.00–11.00 (breakfast); 12.00–14.30; 18.00–23.00;
   Sun 08.00–11.00 (breakfast); 12.00–15.00; 19.00–22.00

🖱 www.thedorchester.com

🖃 all major credit cards ■ 12.5% optional service added

££ starters £10–£19.50 ■ mains £19.50–£34 ■ desserts £10.50
   ■ tasting menu £70 (7 courses) ■ set lunch Mon-Fri £25 (2 courses)
   & £27.50 (3 courses) ■ pre-theatre (16.30-19.30) £25 (2 courses) &
   £27.50 (3 courses) ■ Sunday lunch £35 (3 courses)
   ■ lowest bottle price £19

✪ Good looking, good cooking

It's hard not to admire the wild, dramatic statement made by the
Grill Room décor – a French designer has gussied up the venerable
room in an orgy of tartan; it's the kind of flamboyant 'look' that
upsets everyone equally. In the kitchen Aiden Byrne writes an
appetising menu, but cunningly he has left sections called 'Grill Room
Classics', and 'Menu of the Day' where Scottish smoked salmon,
and roast Angus beef and Yorkshire pudding delight traditionalists.
Byrne's à la carte dishes are seasonal and make use of the finest
British produce. Starters like pan-fried scallops with mushroom
duxelles and chervil sauce; braised snails with lettuce emulsion and
smoked bacon; or pan-fried smoked foie gras with baked bread soup
are magnificent. Mains may include roast veal sweetbreads with
lobster tail and broccoli purée; squab pigeon with pickled cabbage
and sweet garlic butter sauce; line-caught sea bass with shrimp
chorizo and saffron pickled vegetable; or stuffed loin of lamb with
celeriac Boulangère, artichokes and walnuts. This is cooking at its
most accomplished and inventive. Puds are real pleasers – pear and
goat's cheese salad, and a bitter chocolate mousse with beetroot!
Service is super slick, and the wine list is a monster, as can be the bill.

Hibiscus

29 Maddox Street, W1 ■ 020 7629 2999 &

⊖ Oxford Circus

🍽 French

🕐 Mon to Fri 12.00–14.30 & 18.30–22.00; Sat 18.30–22.00

🖰 www.hibiscusrestaurant.co.uk

🗗 all major credit cards ■ 12.5% optional service added

££ à la carte £60 (3 courses) ■ tasting menu £62.50 ■ 'surprise' menu £75 (5 or 6 courses) ■ lowest bottle price £16.75

❂ Fresh from the provinces

Claude and Claire Bosi moved their restaurant from Ludlow to Mayfair as recently as November 2007 and pulled off the unlikely trick of bringing one of their two Michelin stars with them. The cooking in Ludlow was exceptionally fine, even though some of the 'cutting-edge' dishes were a little too sharp for their own good. If anything the food in London is better. Starters are still complex, such as Wye valley asparagus confit in salted butter, then lightly oak-smoked, tamarillo powder, cruised soft-boiled eggs with spring Tuscan truffle. If that sounds too straightforward how about Herefordshire snails, wild garlic purée, consommé of spring onion and garlic, salad of pig's head, pickled tongue and mixed leaves? For main there's slow-grilled Pyrenean kid with caramelised spring onions and glazed white turnips. Or try the hand-reared pork that comes in two services, first crisp pork belly with a fricassée of spring vegetables, Brittany cockles and seaweed vinaigrette, followed by a warm sausage roll with mushy peas and sherry vinegar. This is a grandstand dish and the sausage roll is notable. From the dessert list, the chocolate tart is as good at Maddox Street as it was in Shropshire – ultra-short pastry and a crusted top to the molten chocolate filling; like a chocolate fondant pudding but very much better. The new Hibiscus is a friendly place with classy food, a decent wine list and service to match.

Kai

65 South Audley Street, W1 ■ 020 7493 8988

⊖ Bond Street/Marble Arch

|◉| Chinese

🕓 Mon to Fri 12.3–14.15 & 18.30–20.45; Sat 18.30–20.45;
Sun 18.30–22.15

🖱 www.kaimayfair.com

🖅 all major credit cards ■ 12.5% optional service added

££ soups and starters £11–£21 ■ mains £12–£59 ■ sides £3–£12
■ set lunch £24 ■ lowest bottle price £23

❂ Exquisite cooking, merciless Mayfair pricing

Outside, in their glossy cars, the chauffeurs sit waiting. Inside, the diners take their time over elegant and often elaborate dishes. You'll find a full complement of all those fabled Chinese dishes, with all those fabulously expensive ingredients – abalone, shark's fin, deer's pizzle. At Kai truffles and lobster are run of the mill. So, having established the ground rules (i.e. this place is not for those of feeble wallet), what's it like? The standard of both the cooking and the invention is very high, flavours are well matched, textures are inspired, and eating here is an aesthetic experience. You'll find all your favourite Chinese dishes – prawns Kung Po, spare ribs, crispy duck – but you're better off trying some of chef Alex Chow's more elaborate flights of fancy. There's a dish called Oriental lamb shank, which comes to table in a Martini glass. The bottom layer is brown soup-sludge-slow-braised-lamb and it is topped with a garlic cream – delicious. Or there are tempura prawns with a wasabi mayonnaise – crisp, crunchy, well balanced. The braised abalone (cooked for three days) has 'best-ever' status and comes with a white truffle jus. The deep-fried, soft-shell crabs with fried garlic and chilli are very good. The sirloin with black pepper and garlic flakes is a rich and sticky beef dish. The service at Kai is exemplary, careful and friendly, and the wine list matches the ambitions of the menu. Get saving.

Kiku

17 Half Moon Street, W1 ■ 020 7499 4208   ♿

⊖ Green Park

🍴 Japanese

🕐 Mon to Sat 12.00–14.30 & 18.00–22.15; Sun 17.30–21.45

🖱 www.kikurestaurant.co.uk

🗗 all major credit cards ■ 12.5% optional service added

££ sushi £1.80–£6.50 ■ mains £9.20–£35 ■ sushi combinations £18 & £33
■ desserts £4–£8 ■ lowest bottle price £14.50, sake £12

✪ Good sushi, blissfully unintimidating atmosphere

Brace yourself, because what follows is going to sound like a bit of
a porky. Kiku is a Japanese restaurant (translates as pricey) deep in
the heart of Mayfair (translates as very pricey) and one that serves
top-class sushi with a classical ambience – but without charging the
earth. Wander along smack on opening time, snatch a seat at the
counter and go for it. Knowledgeable Japanese folk always start a
meal of sushi with tamago – the sweetish, omelettey one that allows
the diner to properly assess the quality of the rice. The toro, or tuna
belly, is good; the suzuki, or sea bass, is good; the amaebi, or sweet
prawn, is – sweet; the hiramei, or turbot, is very delicate. You must
have hotate, which are slices of raw scallop, translucent and subtle
– very good indeed. From the rolled sushi section pick the umeshiso
maki, made from rice with pickled plums and fresh green shiso leaves
– really zingy. Tobiko is the roe of flying fish and is surprisingly good.
A successful strategy might be to try a few sushi and then turn to the
main menu: perhaps tempura moriawase, which is mixed tempura, or
sake teriyaki, which is grilled teriyaki salmon. If you suffer from 'long
foreign menu fatigue syndrome', there are good sushi combinations
such as tokujyo nigiri or jyongiri. Drink the very refreshing Asahi beer
and only venture into the realms of sake if you understand the stuff.

Maze

10–13 Grosvenor Square, W1 ■ 020 7107 0000   &

⊖ Bond Street

|⊙| French

⊕ Mon to Sat 12.00–15.00 & 18.00–23.00

⊕ www.gordonramsay.com

⊟ all major credit cards ■ 12.5% optional service added

££ lunch £25.50 (4 courses) & £42.50 (6 courses) ■ à la carte starters £15–£17.50 ■ mains £22–£29.50 ■ desserts £8–£10 ■ tasting menu dishes £7–£10.50 ■ lowest bottle price £30

✪ Every day is a grazing day

Part of the Gordon Ramsay empire, at Maze inspired cooking is made complicated by the mechanics of the menu. First things first: the menu here is a seasonal one, which is a wholly commendable approach. It quickly gets more complicated though. To start with, about twenty small dishes are listed and you are invited to choose between six and eight per person. But if the grazing approach doesn't ring your bell, the next spread is more conventional and offers six starters and six mains – but all dishes drawn from the first selection. The room is pleasant and modern and the service is sound enough, although all the explaining needed means it tends to drag on. 'Grazing' – and all the other derivatives of the tasting menu – is a mixed blessing. When a dish arrives that you like, you feel disappointed that there is not more of it on the plate; when a dish arrives that you don't like, you're just disappointed. If you were to visit in the spring you might be offered foie gras marinated in Pinot Noir caramel, smoked ham hock and piccalilli – good complementary textures – or roast John Dory with lemon candied aubergine and basil vinaigrette. Other highlights might be braised Royal Berkshire pork belly with Umbrian lentils and chorizo; or wood-fired squab with liver pâté and pickled apple purée. Desserts appeal – try Valrhona chocolate fondant with green cardamom caramel, sea salt and almond ice cream. Whether triumph or gimmick, Maze is saved by the quality of the cooking.

Maze Grill

10–13 Grosvenor Square, W1 ■ 020 7495 2211   ♿

⊖ Bond Street

🍴 Steaks

🕐 Mon to Sat 12.00–15.00 & 18.00–23.00

🖰 www.gordonramsay.com

🖶 all major credit cards ■ 12.5% optional service added

££ small plates £6 ■ starters £8.50–£14.50 ■ salads £9.50–£11.50
■ steaks £10–£45.00 ■ mains £13.50–£27.50 ■ sides £3.50
■ desserts £7 ■ lowest bottle price £30

⭐ Homage to the New York steakhouse

Jason Atherton is a busy man. Not content with heading up Maze
(see p. 96), in 2008 he opened this grill next door. At the door, Maze
lies to the left and the Grill to the right. It's a long and comfortable
room and a restaurant that borrows a good deal from the great New
York steak temples (when you're wrestling with the menu the waiter
parades the meat on a silver salver, and lurking in kitchen is a 'broiler'
imported from the US and capable of generating a fearsome 650°C).
To dispense with the peripherals: the small plates are well done, such
as seared octopus with confit lemon or salt and pepper squid. Starters
include a delicious tuna tartar, and there are complex salads. If you
miss the point there are fish mains – seabass and lobster – plus a
burger, a Barnsley chop, or pork chop. But steak is the mainspring
of this establishment. Pick from grain-fed Casterbridge beef aged 21
days; grass-fed Hereford aged 25 days; grass-fed Aberdeen Angus
aged 28 days; corn-fed Creekstone prime USDA aged 35 days; or
Australian Waygu '9th grade'. The meat is lovingly cooked and
presented on a board with a sharp knife. Just which option rings your
bell will depend on your taste, but for me grass-fed beef always has
the edge over grain-fed – better taste, better texture. It just remains
to choose a decent red wine and decide between French fries and
mashed potato.

Momo

25 Heddon Street, W1 ■ 020 7434 4040

⊖ Oxford Circus

🍽 North African

🕐 Mon to Sat 12.00–14.30 & 18.30–23.00; Sun 18.30–23.00

🖱 www.momoresto.com

🖬 all major credit cards ■ 13% optional service added

££ starters £6.50–£12.50 ■ mains £15.50–£21 ■ sides £3.50–£5
■ desserts £6.50 ■ set lunch £14 (2 courses) & £18 (3 courses)
■ North African Experience £90 (2 people) ■ lowest bottle price £19

✪ The men's urinal is an installation of some beauty

Blisteringly trendy, Momo is not only the eponymous owner, but also an attractive Moroccan restaurant tucked away in a backwater off Regent Street. For dinner, you usually have to book at least a week in advance and to opt for an early or late sitting. If you apply for the late shift, be prepared for a noisy, nightclub ambience. The design of the place is clever, with bold, geometric, Kasbah-style architecture, plush cushions and lots of candles. Downstairs there's an even more splendid Moorish bar, annoyingly reserved for members only. The starters include harira – a traditional vegetable soup; a selection of briouats – little pastries filled with cheese, haddock or vegetables; a pastilla of wild pigeon – a little pie made with almonds and very sweet; seared tuna with quail egg and vierge sauce; or a terrine of foie gras served with confit of quince and a cinnamon brioche with a glass of Tokay. For main course, choose from five tagines, which are North African-style stews served in a large clay pot. Try the tagine of chicken with preserved lemons, or the tagine of lamb with prunes, quinces and almonds. There are duck brochettes, a wild seas bass served with a purée of Jerusalem artichoke; or a veal cutlet with saffron baby fennel. Alternatively, opt for couscous méchoui (for two), based around roasted, spiced lamb. Desserts include pastries, deep-fried filo parcels of fruit, pancakes and meringues.

Nobu

19 Old Park Lane, W1 ■ 020 7447 4747

⊖ Hyde Park Corner

🍴 Japanese

🕑 Mon to Thurs 12.00–14.15 & 18.00–22.15; Fri & Sat 12.30–14.30 & 18.00–23.00

🖑 www.myriadrestaurantgroup.com

🗗 all major credit cards ■ 15% optional service added

££ special dishes & appetisers £5–£29.50 ■ tempura £1.25–£6 ■ kushiyaki f5.50–£10 ■ mains £15.50–£24 ■ desserts £2.50–£9 ■ bento box set lunch £25 ■ 'Omakase' chef's choice: lunch £50 & £60, dinner £70 & £90 ■ lowest bottle price £26

⭐ Good food in celeb-spotter's heaven

Nobu is home to the broom cupboard where Boris Becker qualified for his paternity suit. On the face of it, a restaurant owned by Robert de Niro, Drew Nieporent and Matsuhisa Nobuyuki sounds like the invention of a deranged Hollywood producer, but Nobu has been plying its trade for over a decade and has even spawned a couple of siblings. The restaurant is dauntingly expensive, but don't be discouraged, the food is innovative and superb. Ingredients are fresh, flavour combinations are novel, and presentation is elegant and stylish. Perhaps the best way to see for yourself is to start with the bargain lunchtime bento box, which includes sashimi salad, rock shrimp tempura, black cod and all the trimmings. Matsuhisa worked in Peru, and South American flavours and techniques segue into classical Japanese dishes. Some of the dishes (like the Anti-Cucho Peruvian-style tea-smoked lamb) defy classification but are worth trying. The sashimi is terrific: salmon is sliced and just warmed through to 'set' it, before being served with sesame seeds; the minimal cooking makes for a superb texture. The sushi rolls provide some interesting combinations like scallop and smelt egg, or fatty tuna and scallion. The black cod with miso is a grandstand dish – a piece of perfectly cooked fish with an elaborate banana-leaf canopy.

→ For branches, see index or website

Patterson's

4 Mill Street, W1 ■ 020 7499 1308

⊖ Oxford Circus

🍴 French

🕒 Mon to Fri 12.00–15.00 & 18.00–23.00; Sat 17.00–23.00

🖰 www.pattersonsrestaurant.com

🗗 all major credit cards ■ 12.5% optional service added

££ starters £5 (lunch), £13 (dinner) ■ mains £10 (lunch), £17 (dinner) ■ desserts £5 (lunch), £10 (dinner) ■ lobster lunch £25; set lunch (3 courses) £20 ■ lowest bottle price £19

✪ Ask the family for good French food

While family-run restaurants serving top-quality, classical, French food are occasionally sighted in France, they are as rare as hen's teeth in Mayfair. Patterson's is the exception. Raymond Patterson won his spurs during a fourteen-year stint in the kitchens at the Garrick Club, and somehow he has persuaded most of his family to join him in his restaurant. The menu here is littered with those satisfying, classical dishes that are so very difficult to do well. A crab cake is served with ribbon salsify, cress salad and poached quail's egg. Or there may be a parfait of foie gras, ham knuckle and chicken served with pickled pear and white bean mustard dressing. Other starters may include carpaccio and tartare of beef with avocado, frisée and Parmesan shavings. These are dishes that put the kitchen through its paces. The mains continue the theme – braised belly pork with scallops and black pudding; salt-cured duck breast with mango risotto; seared fillet of sea bass on a roulade of artichoke, potato and spinach; or tournedos of beef with veal sweetbreads wrapped in Bayonne ham with pommes Anna. The puds are good – a textbook tarte Tatin, an epic marquise of chocolate, chocolate and chilli mousse, and lemongrass chocolate ice cream. The wine list at Patterson's seems unaggressively priced, and there are a good many classic bottles. The service is charming and there is plenty of both ambition and technical ability in the kitchen. At lunch prices shrink a good deal – look out for the lobster lunches: crustacea, cheeseboard and coffee.

La Petite Maison

54 Brooks Mews, W1 ■ 020 7495 4774

⊖ Bond Street

🍴 French

🕐 Mon to Sat 12.00–14.30 & 18.00–22.30; Sun 12.00–14.30

🖱 www.lpmlondon.co.uk

🗗 all major credit cards ■ 12.5% optional service added

££ starters and salads £3.50–£16.50 ■ mains £13–£55
■ sides £3.50–£4.75 ■ desserts £5.50–£9.75 ■ lowest bottle price £21

✪ Classy informality, very good, simple food

Madame Nicole Rubi's restaurant in the heart of Nice is called La Petite Maison and it bucks the local trend by offering simple dishes. In July 2007 the chaps behind Zuma (see p. 69), who were big fans, opened a branch in London. The menu rambles along; the cooking is of a high standard; you can share dishes. Pick from a hit parade of South of France delights: pissaladière; salade d'artichauts; salade de févettes et Pecorino – the young broad beans and salty cheese is a marriage made in heaven; salade de betteraves – simple, good flavours; a salade de Nice – great dressing, large bowl, good anchovies, egg – pretty much perfect. A dish of prawns served warm with olive oil is a stunner. 'Trois saveurs de beignets', with its ultra-light batter, could just as easily be 'tempura of' courgette flower, sage with anchovies, and onions. The fishy options include turbot aux artichauts barigoule – a perfectly cooked piece of fish. Meatier dishes include côte de veau grillée (bring an appetite), and a poulet de noir au foie gras – a whole roast black-leg chicken stuffed with foie gras to share. You shouldn't miss out on the potato gratin. Puds are classy and the crème brûlée is bathtub sized and just about perfect. The wine list is interesting and, in a tribute to the original there are a dozen rosés. The atmosphere may be charming-casual, but both the service and the prices are Mayfair slick.

Ristorante Semplice

10 Blenheim Street, W1 ■ 020 7495 1509 ⟍

⊖ Bond Street

🍴 Italian

🕐 Mon to Fri 12.00–14.30 & 19.00–22.30; Sat 19.00–22.30

🖥 www.ristorantesemplice.com

🗗 all major credit cards ■ 12.5% optional service added

££ starters £9.50–£12.50 ■ mains £16–£23.50 ■ sides £2.75
   ■ desserts £6–£12.50 ■ set menus: lunch Mon to Fri £16 (2 courses)
   & £19 (3 courses) ■ lowest bottle price £13.50

⭐ Italian chic, very Bond Street

There's nothing very simple about Ristorante Semplice, which turns out to be more like Ristorante 'pretty chic and slick'. The room uses plenty of polished wood and there is flattering lighting and comfortable banquette seating. The cooking is of a high standard and the service is slick. Although the menu may list a succession of regional and rustic dishes, what comes to table is rather sophisticated. Antipasti may include carpaccio di manza Fassone all'Albese – frills of thin-cut beef (from Fassone cattle, Piedmont beef renowned for their tenderness); sliced veal tongue with chick pea sauce; or grilled octopus. The pasta and risotti are well executed – gnocchi filled with pesto; ravioli filled with potato and rosemary, braised oxtail; and a classic risotto alla Milanese with saffron and bone marrow. For mains there may be slow-cooked hake with ratatouille and fresh oyster; lemon sole with Swiss chard sauce; roast milk-fed Piedmontese veal wrapped in Parma ham; tagliata made with Fassone beef; or roast and pan-fried Italian rabbit, served with polenta, sautéed spinach and a ceps sauce. Dishes are pretty on the plate and certainly look elegant. The wine list is voluminous and there are enough middle-weight Italian bins to keep the interest of the wine buff. As well as suitably sweet Italian desserts, there is a magnificent all-Italian cheeseboard. This is a very aspirational Italian restaurant. Perhaps the use of 'Semplice' is ironic?

Scott's

20 Mount Street, W1 ■ 020 7495 7309   &

⊖ Bond Street/Green Park

🍽 Modern British/fish

🕐 Mon to Sat 12.00–15.00 & 17.30–23.00; Sun 12.00–15.30 &
17.30–22.30

🖰 www.scotts-restaurant.com

🖫 all major credit cards ■ 12.5% optional service added

££ starters £6.25–£19 ■ seafood £8–£21.50 ■ mains £15.25–£39.50
■ sides £3.75–£4.75 ■ desserts £6.75–£9 ■ lowest bottle price £17.75

✪ Full-on glamour, full-on fish

Scott's has had a chequered career. Chic in the 1970s, when Ian
Fleming would drop in and ask for his Martini shaken not stirred,
it has been revamped a couple of times since. Now the room is a
triumph and the proprietors (who also run The Ivy, Le Caprice and
J. Sheekey – see pp. 29, 127 and 30) understand the appeal of
glamour. As a centrepiece, there is an altar to seafood – crabs,
lobsters, langoustines enthroned on ice. The standards of cooking are
high and the menu has a commendable lean to British produce and
sustainable fish. Starters range from a 'best-ever' shellfish cocktail
– pink sauce, plump prawns; to grilled razor clams served with sea
vegetables; and a dish of cod's tongues and cèpes Bordelaise – a
serious and rich dish accompanied with roast bone marrow. Mains
include simple fish options like a whole Gilthead sea bream; and
Dover sole grilled or meunière, setting the foundations for more
interesting numbers like pan-fried skate with periwinkles, brown
butter and capers; hake and pork belly with braised arroncina beans;
and whole squid 'a la plancha'. Attention is also paid to carnivores,
with a Glen Fyne rib steak; rack of Shetland lamb with pan haggerty;
and game in season. Then onwards to Quenby Hall Stilton with port
jelly and fruit cake; Amedei chocolate mousse; or poire belle Hélène.
The wine list gets as extravagant as you could wish for and service is
cheerful.

Sketch, the Gallery

9 Conduit Street, W1 ■ 020 7659 4500

⊖ Oxford Circus

🍽 Modern European

🕐 Mon to Wed 19.00–23.00 & 17.30–23.00; Thurs to Sat 19.00–01.00

🖰 www.sketch.uk.com

🗗 all major credit cards ■ 12.5% optional service added

££ starters £8.50–£22 ■ pasta & noodles £8.50–£16 ■ mains £21–£32
■ sides £3.50–£5 ■ desserts £7–£13 ■ lowest bottle price £21

✪ Sophisticated playroom dining

Sketch sprawls through an elegant building on Conduit Street.
At the top there's the Lecture Room and Library, then there's the
Glade and the East Bar, plus the patissier and cake shop on the
ground floor. In the last edition of this guide we included the Glade,
which was then a lunch spot. Things change here as strange ideas
grip the proprietor Mourad Marouz (see Momo p. 98). The culinary
mainspring is Pierre Gagnaire and his food is truly cutting-edge
stuff. On the menu at the Gallery the rubric is typically distinctive. As
they put it: 'The focus of our food is always extraordinary freshness
and quality. We use the finest ingredients and cook with very little
oil, dairy or carbohydrates, ensuring that each dish is light and full
of natural flavour.' This means complex starters like roast saddle of
rabbit with rillettes with cumbawa, coco bean velouté, Venetian jelly
and caramelised pistachios; or chilled octopus casserole with pata
negra ham. Mains are also impressive, such as lobster fricassée with
bok choy and lobster bisque or grilled scallops with turnips cooked
in cider and braised turnip. As you would expect with the patisserie
skills that are on site puds are elaborate – try Pierre Gagnaire's
chocolate spring caribe chocolate cake with chocolate jelly, ice cream,
chocolate sauce and shortbread biscuit. Post midnight, after dinner,
the Gallery is for 'drinking, listening to music and watching video art
projections'.

The Square

6–10 Bruton Street, W1 ■ 020 7495 7100

⊖ Green Park

🍴 French

🕐 Mon to Fri 12.00–15.00 & 18.30–22.45; Sat 18.30–22.45

🖥 www.squarerestaurant.com

🖃 all major credit cards ■ 12.5% optional service added

££ set lunch £25 (2 courses) & £30 (3 courses) ■ dinner £65 (3 courses)
■ tasting menu £90 (7 courses) ■ lowest bottle price £18

✪ Splendid food, splendid wines, splendid service

In the gastro premier league – an arena where almost every
commentator bows to the supremacy of French chefs and French
cuisine – you cannot help a slight smirk that head chef Philip Howard,
a softly spoken Englishman, has got it all so very, very right. This is
a highly gracious restaurant. Service is suave, silent and effortless.
Presentation is elegant. The wine list seems boundless in scope and
soars to the very topmost heights. The menu changes on a broadly
seasonal basis. Starters may include roast chicken consommé with
a tasting of new season morels; roast foie gras with sweet and sour
elderflower glaze and crushed apple and lime; ravioli of baby goat
with white asparagus; or lasagne of Dorset crab with a cappuccino
of shellfish. Mains are dishes like steamed sea bass with wilted spring
leaves, new season's onions and Jersey Royals; steamed pigeon from
Bresse with hot smoked consommé and hazelnut dumplings; or herb-
crusted saddle of lamb with spring vegetables. Even the vegetarian
option appeals – cannelloni of broad beans with asparagus, morels,
new season's onions and peas. Puddings, such as warm sable
of bitter chocolate with mint ice cream; or a cocoa crème brûlée
with griottine cherries and Kirsch ice cream, are classics. Howard
is an able man and Michelin's two-star measure of his worth is an
underestimate. There's also a seven-course 'tasting' menu (only for
the entire table). This is one treat you will never regret.

Theo Randall

Intercontinental, 1 Hamilton Place, W1 ■ 020 7318 8747 &

⊖ Hyde Park Corner

🍽 Italian

🕐 Mon to Fri 12.00–15.00 & 18.00–23.00; Sat 18.30–23.00

🔗 www.theorandall.com

🖰 all major credit cards ■ 12.5% optional service added

££ antipasti £8–£12 ■ starters £9–£11 ■ mains £25–£27 ■ sides £4
   ■ desserts £6–£7 ■ set lunch £21 (2 courses) & £25 (3 courses)
   ■ cheapest bottle price £22

⭐ Honest cooking in a swish environment

Theo Randall arrived to take over this hotel restaurant burdened
with sackloads of reputation gathered during all those years when
he was the heartbeat of the River Café in Hammersmith. Randall's
eponymous 124-seater restaurant opened at the beginning of 2007.
This restaurant is a rare thing, somewhere that is bold enough to
be straightforward. The cooking is accomplished, the dishes simple,
the ingredient quality very high. Starters range from a plateful
of impeccable Parma ham with rocket and shaved Parmesan to
the freshest, perkiest, crab salad you could wish for. 'Primi' may
include a seriously good wild mushroom risotto, or something as
simple as ravioli with mixed winter greens. For mains a wood-roast
spatchcocked chicken stuffed with prosciutto, thyme lemon and
mascarpone is a runaway winner. Or there's a veal chop; or a sea bass
cooked in foil; or an Anjou pigeon given the wood-roast treatment.
Flavours are to the fore. The wine list is voluminous but with scope on
the lower slopes. Go for the three-course set lunch – bagna cauda,
minestrone verde, wood-roast lemon sole – a bargain. Then add one
of the rather good puds like the blood orange almond and polenta
cake. The food is simple and good here and anyone who doesn't see
that is missing the point.

Umu

14–16 Bruton Place, W1 ■ 020 7499 8881 &

⊖ Green Park/Bond Street

🍴 Japanese

🕐 Mon to Fri 12.00–14.30 & 18.00–23.00 (tasting menus to be ordered before 14.00 & 22.30); Sat 18.00–23.00

🖱 www.umurestaurant.com

🗗 all major credit cards ■ 12.5% optional service added

££ starters £6–£22 ■ sushi £2.50–£7 per piece ■ sashimi £11–£22
■ mains £8–£55 ■ sides £3–£12 ■ desserts £6–£10
■ set lunch from £21 ■ Kaseki tasting menus £60, £90 & £135
■ wines by the glass £6–£18 ■ lowest bottle price £27

⭐ Rarefied Japanese food, rarefied prices

The publicity blurb for this resto mentions that the chef imports all the water he uses for cooking from Japan, an obsessive attention to detail that only seems credible when you have eaten the food at Umu. This place makes no bones about targeting the A-list: the décor is slick; the service is very slick under the aegis of a talented French maitre d'; the sake list is refined and extensive; and when it comes, the bill is large enough to make a lottery winner wince. The menu offers appetisers; sashimi; classic sushi; modern sushi; main courses; soups; rices and desserts. A few generalities: the combinations of taste and of texture are magnificent; every dish looks beautiful on the plate, and the attention to detail is amazing. Simple starters like mackerel tartare or sesame tofu with fresh wasabi and nori seaweed work well. Sweet shrimp comes with sake jelly and caviar; or there's makizukuri of salmon and chives; or deep-fried oyster with lemon vinaigrette. These are all delicate and delicious. The sushi verge on 'best ever'. Modern sushi contenders are blue crab, courgette, pine nuts and red ichimi; foie gras with lily roots; and scallop, lemon confit and langoustine bisque. Main courses range from a deep-fried lobster yuba roll with yuzu salt; to grilled venison with spring onions, sesame sauce; or tempura of prawn, rabbit and ginger bud. Although pricey, the 'Kaseki' tasting menus offer a balanced choice of dishes and also suggest matched sake and wine.

Via Condotti

23 Conduit Street, W1 ▪ 020 7493 7050

⊖ Oxford Circus/Bond Street

🍴 Italian

🕐 Mon to Sat 12.00–15.00 & 18.30–23.00

🖳 www.viacondotti.co.uk

🖻 all major credit cards ▪ 12.5% optional service added

££ set lunch £19.50 (2 courses), £24.50 (3 courses) & £29.50 (4 courses)
▪ set dinner £22.50 (2 courses), £27.50 (3 courses) and £32.50
(4 courses) ▪ lowest bottle price £17

✪ Mayfair style, neighbourhood prices

The site of Via Condotti has had a chequered career, but the
restaurant opened in 2006 and looks as if it will survive. It's an
elegant dining room which manages to convey a slight feeling of
country-house-chic without ending up too chintzy for the Mayfair
fashionistas. The proposition appeals – honest, well-made Italian
dishes and a set menu formula that lets you know just what you
are letting yourself in for as you sit down. The antipasti range from
cured beef with celeriac and lemon to baked aubergine with tomato
and mozzarella or pan-fried scallops with grilled pumpkin. For
primi piatti there are some splendid pasta dishes: tortellini of pear
and Campania sausages; fresh pasta with prawns and cavolo nero;
ravioli filled with smoked mozzarella; risotti; and soups like a classic
minestrone. Secondi range from pan-fried halibut with gnocchi to
venison with Swiss chard and quince compote or the monster veal
chop – breadcrumbed and cooked 'alla Milanese'. The kitchen knows
its stuff and portion sizes are well judged. During the appropriate
season there are even more specials – scrambled eggs with white
truffle or a white truffle risotto will bump up your bill. Desserts may
include classics like rum baba or 'seadas' – those little Sardinian fried
ravioli filled with pecorino cheese. The service has the dash and élan
that you'd expect from an all-Italian front of house. This is a very
comfortable and equitably priced restaurant which positively begs for
you to opt for a leisurely three or four courses.

Wild Honey

12 St George Street, W1 ■ 020 7758 9160

⊖ Oxford Circus

🍴 Modern European

🕐 Mon to Sat 12.00–14.30 & 18.00–22.30; Sun 12.00–15.00 & 18.00–21.30

🏠 all major credit cards ■ 12.5% optional service added

££ starters £8.95–£11.95 ■ mains £15.50–£21.50 ■ desserts £6.95 ■ set lunch £16.95 (3 courses) ■ pre-theatre £18.95 (3) ■ lowest bottle price £12.50

✪ Perfectly judged cooking, accessible wines

Wild Honey is the second restaurant of those wonderful people who brought you Arbutus (p. 150) and it has the same key elements. Fine, seasonal, unfussy food and the majority of the wine list available by the 250ml carafe. Happy diners can try several different wines with the rather good food, which is the best kind of rich, hearty, honest, and downright delicious. Starters range from a slow-cooked Elwy valley lamb breast with heritage potatoes and spring onions; to warm smoked eel with sweet and sour turnips and William pear purée. The braised pig's head, potato purée, and caramelised onions is a classic of its kind and the Cornish razor clams, shallots, chilli and parsley is a wholly successful dish. Consider a 'plat du jour': a daube of beef, salsify and sauté of ceps – genuinely worth a detour, a large lump of tender slow-cooked beef, the salsify braised and melting, and a few mushrooms adding an extra texture. Not merely poetry on the plate, but poetry with a good rhyme scheme. Then there may be roast French Limousin veal, soft polenta with Parmesan; or halibut with a mushroom risotto and purple sprouting broccoli. All really good dishes. You could also enthuse about the puds: treacle tart; Savarin of Williams pears; wild honey ice cream. As to the rest of the checklist, the room is comfortable; the service is silky; and best of all, the prices are exceptionally modest for Mayfair.

Notting Hill and Kensal Green

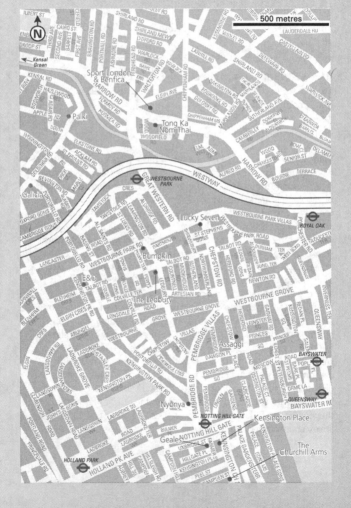

Assaggi

39 Chepstow Place, W2 ■ 020 7792 5501

⊖ Notting Hill Gate

🍽 Italian

🕐 Mon to Fri 12.30–14.30 & 19.30–23.00; Sat 13.00–14.30 & 19.30–23.00

🖅 all major credit cards except AmEx ■ no service added

££ starters £9.90–£15.90 ■ pasta £9–£12.90 ■ mains £18–£24.90 ■ sides £3.20–£4.80 ■ desserts £7.50 ■ lowest bottle price £21.95

✪ Elite Italian with prices to match

For a small, almost scruffy room above the Chepstow pub, Assaggi is enviably full and getting a table can be a problem. The prices here are unforgiving, yet Assaggi is usually packed. The reason is its uncompromising attitude to the best, and most straightforward, tenets of Italian cuisine. The menu may appear simple, but it is littered with authentic and luxury ingredients, and the cooking is very accomplished indeed. You'll find a dozen starters – with the option to have the pastas as main courses – and half a dozen main courses. Start with pasta, maybe a lasagna bianca, or a plate of sensational burrata with grilled aubergine (burrata is the ultra creamy, super-Mozzarella). Or choose grilled vegetables with olive oil and herbs. Or there may be a dish like capesante con salsa alla zafferano, a simple plate of perfectly cooked, splendidly fresh scallops. Main courses are even more pared down: calf's liver; a plainly grilled veal chop with rosemary; or fritto misto. But even a humble side salad of tomato, rucola e basilico is everything you would wish for. Puddings change daily. Look out for panna cotta – a perfect texture – and the beautifully simple dish made from spanking fresh buffalo ricotta served with 'cooked' honey. To accompany, the short wine list features splendid and unfamiliar Italian regional specialities. Be careful if offered 'specials' made with truffle or wild mushrooms – they are delicious but wallet bruising.

Bumpkin

209 Westbourne Park Road, W11 ■ 020 7243 9818

⊖ Westbourne Park

🍽 Modern British

🕐 Mon 18.00–22.30; Tues to Fri 12.15–15.00 & 18.00–22.30;
Sat 11.00–15.30 & 18.00–22.30; Sun 12.15–16.00 & 18.00–22.00

🖰 www.bumpkinuk.com

🗄 all major credit cards ■ 12.5% optional service added

££ starters £5.50–£8 ■ mains £9.50–£18 ■ sides £3–£3.50
■ desserts £5.50–£6.50 ■ Sun lunch £24 (2 courses)
■ lowest bottle price £14

✪ The town's idea of the country

There is an old saying, 'If you want to find a fool in the country better take him with you', and this aperçu springs to mind when you walk into Bumpkin, where the theme seems to be a tongue-in-cheek celebration of things rural. Anyway, the décor in the downstairs brasserie is 'Country-house-caricature', featuring some of the most garish wallpaper in Britain, with a long refectory table and battered leather-back chairs. The waiting staff wear tee shirts emblazoned Country Boy or Country Girl. And now for the good bits – the food is very sound. Dishes are plain, seasonal and rely on high-quality ingredients. The cooking is capably done. Starters range from Heritage potato soup with Welsh Rabbit toasts; to 'Sheep feet' mushrooms on toast; smoked haddock croquettes with tartare sauce; or crisp free-range egg with Secretts Farm salad and bacon. Then there is a section called 'deep pots and pies': macaroni cheese; pot-roast Devonshire Red chicken with onions and forest mushrooms. Then 'pans, roasts and grills': an accurately cooked Angus beefburger; a whole grilled sole; organic salmon with crushed potatoes, leeks and chervil butter sauce; or Herdwick lamb cutlets with baked garlic and hot pot potatoes. A side salad of various Heritage tomatoes is very good indeed. There is a fairly priced wine list and good draught beer. Get past the coyness of the concept and Bumpkin offers good fresh food.

The Churchill Arms

119 Kensington Church Street, W8 ■ 020 7792 1246

⊖ Notting Hill Gate

🍽 Thai

🕐 Mon to Sat 12.00–22.00; Sun 12.00–21.30

🖥 all major credit cards ■ no service added

££ mains £6 ■ desserts £2.75 ■ lowest bottle price £10.75

⭐ Great pub out front, great Thai out back

The Churchill has nurtured its varied clientele by the simple expedient of serving tasty and reasonably priced Thai food. The main dining area is in a back room featuring acres of green foliage, but don't despair if you find it full (it fills up very quickly) – meals are served throughout the pub. Service is friendly but the food is cooked to order, so be prepared to wait. Dishes are unpronounceable, and have thoughtfully been numbered to assist everybody. The pad gai med ma muang hin-maparn is a deliciously spicy dish of chicken, cashew nuts and chilli served with a generous helping of fluffy, boiled rice. The khao rad na ga prao is described as very hot. For once this is not an understatement; how wonderful to find a menu where hot means hot. This prawn dish with fresh chillies and Thai basil is guaranteed to bring sweat to the brow of even the most ardent chilliholic. For something milder, try the pad neau nahm man hoi, which is beef with oyster sauce and mushrooms, or the khao rad na, a rice dish topped with prawns, vegetables and gravy. Both are good. Puddings are limited in choice and ambition, but for something sweet to temper the heat try apple pie – a strange accompaniment to Thai food, but surprisingly welcome. Still a real pub with real beer; seek out a pint of well-kept Fuller's London Pride.

E&O

14 Blenheim Crescent, W11 ■ 020 7229 5454

⊖ Ladbroke Grove

🍴 Asian eclectic

🕙 Mon to Fri 12.00–15.00 & 18.00–23.00; Sat 12.00–16.00 & 18.00–23.00; Sun 12.30–16.00 & 18.00–22.30

🖥 www.rickerrestaurants.com

🏧 all major credit cards ■ 12.5% optional service added

££ starters £3.50–£7 (dim sum) ■ mains £6.50–£21.50
■ sides £3.50–£4.50 ■ desserts £5.50–£6.50 ■ lowest bottle price £15

✪ E&O stands for Eastern & Oriental

This was the first link in Will Ricker's chain of restaurants, and whereas they once seemed outrageous, now the non-traditional eating styles pioneered here are commonplace and grazing sweeps London's restos. The venue itself is modern Japanese in feel, and staff take trouble to explain if you're unfamiliar with dishes or the spirit of the place. But even more than the taste, it is the presentation that makes the food exceptional. The menu divides into soups, dim sum, salads, tempura, curries, futo maki rolls/sashimi, barbecue/roasts, specials, sides and desserts. Edamame, soy and mirin is a dish of soybeans in the pod to pop and suck out. Among the dumplings, the date and water chestnut gyosa; the prawn and chive dumplings; and the duck siu mai stand out. Chilli-salt squid is well-seasoned, crispy squid served in a Japanese newspaper cone, while baby pork spare ribs come with a sauce good enough to eat with a spoon. In the barbecue/roasts section, black cod with sweet miso is as good as this fish gets. Under curries you'll find lamb rendang with sweet potato. When you get to the puds you must choose from ices; chocolate pudding (which comes with a 20-minute wait); and a shockingly transcultural ta koh panna cotta with pineapple and mint. Wines are well chosen and reasonably priced, and there's a selection of six teas. Can't get a table? Opt for dim sum in the bar.

→ For branches, see index or website

Galicia

323 Portobello Road, W10 ■ 020 8969 3539

⊖ Ladbroke Grove

🍴 Spanish/tapas

🕐 Tues to Sat 12.00–15.00 & 19.00–23.30; Sun 12.00–15.30 &
19.30–22.30

🗗 all major credit cards ■ no service added

££ tapas £3.20–£6.95 ■ mains £7.90–£14.95 ■ sides £2.95
■ desserts £2.75–£3.25 ■ lowest bottle price £9.95

✪ Experience the Spanish side of W10

Ambling up the Portobello Road, it would be only too easy to walk
straight past Galicia – this restaurant has that strange Continental
quality of looking shut even when it's open. Make it through the
forbidding entrance, however, and Galicia opens out into a bar
(which is in all probability crowded), which in turn opens into a small,
40-seater restaurant (which is in all probability full). The tapas at the
bar are straightforward and good, so it is no surprise that quite a lot
of customers get no further than here. First secure your table, then
cut a swathe through the starters. Jamón is a large plate of sweet,
air-dried ham; gambas a la plancha are giant prawns plainly grilled;
pulpo a la Gallega is a revelation – slices of octopus grilled until
bafflingly tender and powdered with smoky pimentón. Galicia does
straightforward grilled fish and meat very well indeed. Look for the
chuleto de cordera a la plancha, which are perfect lamb chops; or
lomo de cerdo, which are very thin slices of pork fillet in a sauce with
pimentón. Or there's the suitably stolid Spanish omelette, tortilla.
You should have some chips, which are very good here. Galicia is
a pleasant place without pretension. The wine list may have the
occasional lurking bargain – older, and overlooked, Spanish vintages
at prices that have stayed reasonable. The waiters are all old-school –
quiet and efficient to the point of near-grumpiness – and the overall
feel is of a certain stilted formality. The clientele is an agreeable mix
of Notting Hillites and homesick Iberians, both of which groups stand
between you and that table reservation, so book early.

Geales

2 Farmer Street, W8 ■ 020 7727 7528

⊖ Notting Hill Gate

🍽 Fish & chips

🕐 Mon 18.00–22.30; Tues to Sun 12.00–14.30 & 18.00–23.00

🖰 www.geales.com

🖯 all major credit cards ■ 12.5% optional service added

££ starters £6–£14 ■ mains £9–£17 ■ sides £2–£4 ■ desserts £5
■ lowest bottle price £13.50

✪ From classic chippy to modernist fish resto

Geales, it says on the new signage, was established in 1939. But every vestige of nearly 70 years' endeavour has been blown away. Maybe the proprietors realised that there was not very much (other than the name) that was worth saving. It's true that the Geales of the 1970s (good fresh fish, celebrity clientele and a wall devoted to those black-and-white signed photos of the stars – you know the kind of thing, Sinatra, Roy Rogers and Trigger) had gone downhill. When it re-opened in the spring of 2007, this place had become a fish restaurant decked out in a soothing shade of grey with navy gingham undercloths, white linen and leather chairs. The menu is short and to the point: starters include yet another rebirth of the prawn cocktail – avocado, lettuce, scallion and mayonnaise; fish soup; or dressed crab. The fried fish – cod, haddock, hake and sole – are accurately cooked with a hard carapace of delicious golden batter. The chips are worthy of special note – which they should be, as they are charged for separately. Among the accoutrements there's a decent wally (aka sweet pickled gherkin) and mushy peas. There is always a fish of the day, which can be served grilled or pan fried. It strikes a nostalgic chord to see Notting Hill old-timers sitting down to a lunch of grilled John Dory with mushy peas and a glass of wine

Kensington Place

201–207 Kensington Church Street, W8 ■ 020 7727 3184　♿

🚇 Notting Hill Gate

🍽 Modern British

🕐 Mon to Thurs 12.00–15.00 & 18.30–22.30; Fri 12.00–15.00 &
18.30–23.00; Sat 12.00–15.30 & 18.30–23.00; Sun 12.00–15.30 &
18.30–22.30

🖥 www.kensingtonplace-restaurant.co.uk

💳 all major credit cards ■ 12.5% optional service added

££ lunch £16.50 (2 courses) & £19.50 (3); dinner £19.50 (2 courses) &
£24.50 (3 courses) ■ starters £7–£13 ■ mains £14.50–£29.50
■ sides £3–£5 ■ desserts £6.50 ■ lowest bottle price £16.50

⭐ Old favourite – new lease of life

**Who'd have thought that such a small thing would make so much
difference?** KP is an iconic London restaurant and it has borne the
hammer blow of losing its chef-founder Rowley Leigh (see Le Café
Anglais, p. 136) with admirable stoicism. Early in the spring of 2008
the new proprietors took the decision to add tablecloths and put
some padding on the chairs and it turned out that this was a far-
reaching change. For a decade or so half the customers at Kensington
Place have complained about how noisy it is, while the other half
have delighted in the buzzy atmosphere. Now the restaurant is a
good deal quieter and more comfortable, the atmosphere is still
there but now you can hear your companions. The food is still British,
although portion sizes seem somewhat smaller than hitherto and
the presentation may be more elegant. Starters range from English
asparagus with sauce vierge to line-caught mackerel with a sweet
shallot tart and Cornish crab lasagne to pressed rabbit terrine.
Main courses are in the same vein – a roast lemon sole comes with
clams and tomato; middle white pork belly is served with artichoke
barigoule and wild leeks; a loin of spring lamb comes with flageolets
and broad beans. Puds are very good, such as a simple strawberry tart
made with French Gariguette berries and crème patissier. The wine list
covers most eventualities and the service is slick.

The Ledbury

127 Ledbury Road, W11 ■ 020 7792 9090

⊖ Westbourne Park

🍽 French

🕐 daily 12.00–14.30 & 18.30–22.45

🖰 www.theledbury.com

🖃 all major credit cards ■ 12.5% optional service added

££ starters £9–£14 ■ mains £16.50–£24 ■ desserts £7–£10
■ set lunch £19.50 (2 courses) & £24.50 (3 courses)
■ dinner £50 (3 courses) ■ tasting menu £60 (8 courses) & £98 (with wine) ■ Sun lunch £35 (3 courses) ■ lowest bottle price £18

✪ The jewel in W11's crown

The Ledbury has settled in nicely. Restaurateur Nigel Platts-Martin and Philip Howard (his head chef at The Square – see p. 105) chose a chef from The Square brigade to head up this sibling and it has been a great success. Brett Graham's food is sophisticated, elegant to look at and well balanced. Thankfully, the front of house has not been neglected and the service is silky smooth. The menu is broadly seasonal and starters may include scallops roasted in Ras El Hanout with yoghurt and cauliflower; goats' cheese tortellini with date purée, and beurre noisette, or perhaps roast foie gras with pomegranate purée, crushed green apple and toasted grains appeals? Mains are equally confident and team contrasting tastes and textures: roast John Cornish cod with wild garlic, spinach, baby squid and blackened cassava; loin of Roe deer with sweet potato and parsley root, Douglas fir and pepper; or poached breast and confit legs of Anjou Pigeon 'Vineyard' with wild Treviso sautéed in sherry. The cooking is accomplished and flavours are upfront. The wine list is comprehensive, but the wine service manages the trick of being both informal and knowledgeable. Puds are seriously ambitious – lemon and blueberry ripple soufflé with blueberry ice cream; date and vanilla tart with cardamom and orange ice cream. The Ledbury delivers very good French food in an elegant dining room so it should be no surprise that the bill seems more West End than W11.

Lucky Seven

127 Westbourne Park Road, W2 ▪ 020 7727 6771

⊖ Westbourne Park

|◉| North American

🕐 Mon to Thurs 11.00–23.00; Fri & Sat 09.00–23.00; Sun 09.00–22.30

🔲 all major credit cards except AmEx ▪ 12.5% optional service added

££ breakfast £4.95–£7.95 ▪ mains £5–£9 ▪ sides £3.50–£5
   ▪ desserts £4–£5 ▪ blue plate specials £8–£12 ▪ lowest bottle price £15

⭐ American diner given Notting Hill gloss

Following the success of The Cow, Tom Conran shifted his attention
a few hundred yards up the road to a site that was previously a
shabby café-restaurant-drinking den and set up Lucky Seven. The
kitchen runs across the back behind a high counter and the tiny
dining area accommodates 36 people in two sets of booths. There
are engraved mirrors. A Pepsi clock. Sally didn't meet Harry here,
but doubtless she will soon. The menu is on a pegboard over the
kitchen and it opens with breakfast dishes: two eggs any style – with
sausage; with bacon; with Portobello mushrooms; and wends its
way through omelettes and eggs Benedict to buttermilk pancakes.
Then there's a section of 'soups, stews, salads, sides' before it moves
towards 'sandwiches and fries'. In the evening there's a blue plate
special dish, which ranges from club sandwich to gammon and eggs.
For chips choose between 'fat' and 'French fries'. The burgers are well
made, although on the small side for serious trenchers – but, as they
start at a reasonable price with the 'Classic hamburger', perhaps that
is best resolved by ordering two separate Classics or a special with an
extra patty of meat. In the stews section you will come across such
delights as New England clam chowder, and a Cuban black bean chilli
(both of which are sold in two sizes, by the cup or by the bowl). And
then there are salads – Cobb, Caesar and 'Garden of Eden', plus the
ominously but accurately named 'Exterminator chilli'. Sounds like fair
warning.

Nyonya

2a Kensington Park Road, W11 ▪ 020 7243 1800

⊖ Notting Hill Gate

🍽️ Malaysian/Chinese

🕐 Mon to Fri 11.30–15.00 & 18.30–22.30; Sat & Sun 11.30–22.30

🖰 www.nyonya.co.uk

🖃 all major credit cards ▪ no service added

££ starters £4.50–£8.40 ▪ mains £6.80–£8.90 ▪ desserts £3.70
▪ set lunch (Mon to Fri) £8 ▪ lowest bottle price £14

✪ Fast food meets Malay home cooking

Nyonya is ultra modern, sensibly cheap and seriously informal. It is
named after the Straits Malay 'grandmothers', who have achieved
near legendary status due to their impressive cooking skills. In Nyonya
dishes you'll find plenty of coconut cream, some chilli heat, souring
from tamarind, and that musty-savoury tang you get from fish sauce
or blachan – the seriously stinky shrimp paste. There are four long,
curved tables, so sharing is the order of the day. Service is friendly
and the food arrives briskly. Starters include the ubiquitous chicken
satay, and it is well done here. The dumplings are good, especially if
you splash out on a small saucer of 'sambal blachan' – a red sludge
made from prawns and chillies, not over-the-top hot, but which does
add a welcome belt of heat. Main courses come in decent portions.
Beef rendang arrives in a clump, and so it should – this dish should
be served almost dry with the coconut sauce reduced to a paste.
These are upfront flavours. A dish of cashew nut prawns is agreeably
mild. It's worth ordering the nyonya fried rice, which is very rich and
sticky and contains a variety of odds and ends – shrimp, chicken, peas
and egg. There is also a long list of 'hawker favourites' that includes
several 'meals-in-a-bowl' – a Penang Assam laksa, or hokkien prawn
mee soup. It is hard to object to a cold Tiger beer with this kind of
spicy food.

Palki

44 Golborne Road, W10 ■ 020 8968 8764/0393

⊖ Westbourne Park/Ladbroke Grove

|●| Indian

🕘 Mon to Thurs 12.00–14.30 & 18.00–23.30; Fri & Sat 12.00–14.30 & 18.00–24.00

🖰 www.palkionline.co.uk

🖫 all major credit cards except AmEx ■ no service added

££ starters £1.95–£5.95 ■ mains £4.95–£10.95 ■ sides £1.50–£2.95
■ lowest bottle price £8.95

✪ Honest, local curry house

For anyone judging by first impressions, Palki is a rather ordinary curry house. It has dodgy lavender-painted walls complete with strange 'works of art', there's a patterned carpet and just thirty seats. It's located on a street lined by Portuguese shops and restaurants, all of which seem busy. Palki looks like what it is – somewhere that you can get a decent curry during, or after, a good night out. What makes this little curry house worthy of a place in this guide is that the menu combines the standards (chicken tikka masala; lamb pasanda; meat Madras) with some more interesting and authentic Bengali dishes. Take special notice of the 'Chef's recommendations', where you'll find dishes from Sylhet like gosht shatkora. The shatkora is a small, sour, plum-like fruit that gives a terrific edge to this simple lamb curry – very rich, with well-balanced spicing and a tangy finish. Or there's zinuk masala, which is a dish of mussels cooked with garlic, curry leaves and coconut milk. The 'green masala' specials are also good. These are dishes made using a masala based on fresh herbs – chopped coriander and mint with tamarind and plenty of seriously hot green chillies. Good cooking with every flavour packing a punch. Service is much as you would expect in a decent local restaurant, and the pricing is very competitive. Palki does a good job for locals and visitors alike.

Sport London & Benfica

988 Harrow Road, NW10 ■ 020 8964 5142

⊖ Westbourne Park

🍴 Portuguese

🕒 daily 11.00–23.00

🖰 www.sportlondonebenfica.co.uk

🖻 all major credit cards ■ no optional service added

££ starters £1–£8.50 ■ mains £8.50–£17 ■ desserts £2.50–£3
   ■ lowest bottle price £11

✪ Football on the telly, football in the soul

A quarter of a century ago 'Sport London & Benfica' was a
successful local football team based in W11 – then they moved their
base up to 988 Harrow Road and set up a large restaurant, a no-frills
bar and club room. The food is very good, honest, straightforward,
giant portions, uncompromising. Some starters are familiar – deep-
fried squid; ham; melon with ham – and some are odd. Ordering
chourico assado brings a ribbed earthenware dish with two
substantial chorizo sausages on it. As it is placed on the table, the
waiter casually flicks his lighter and a pool of eau de vie is set alight
under the sausages. The star starter is the ameijoa à marinheira, a
plate of stunning fresh clams swimming bravely through a butter
sauce. For mains, fish gets priority, with fourteen fish dishes,
including the classic dish for two: arroz de marisco, shellfish rice.
Bacalhau na brasa is salt cod soaked in water and milk to de-salt
it and then grilled before being served with boiled potatoes. The
portions are daunting. On the meat side of things, posta à Mirandesa
is subtitled 'big beef cube'. You get about 500g of perfectly cooked
rump steak cut about 3cm thick and dressed with oil, herbs, green
onion and garlic. This may be London's best-value steak. The wines
come from Portugal and are gently priced. Puddings are very serious.
Try the Molotov – a sort of baked-egg yolk mousse with a caramel
dressing. Even if you are not Portuguese, everyone here will make you
very welcome.If you are not a football fanatic it is probably best not
to mention the fact. They would find that very puzzling.

Tong Ka Nom Thai

833 Harrow Road, NW10 ■ 020 8964 5373

⊖ Kensal Green

|O| Thai

🕐 Mon to Fri 12.00–15.00 & 18.00–22.00; Sat 18.00–22.00

🗗 cash or cheque only ■ no service added

££ starters £4.50–£4.80 ■ mains £4.70–£5.70 ■ sides £1.50–£4
    ■ desserts £2.50 ■ unlicensed, BYO (but buy soft drinks)

✪ Cheerful Thai cafe

Fresh, cheap and authentic Thai food is alive and well and hiding
out on the Harrow Road. Tong Ka Nom Thai is a small and garish
Thai restaurant with a wonderful view of the railway tracks. It is
implausibly cheap, the food is very good, and the service friendly.
For an astonishingly modest outlay you get six well-spiced tod mun
(delightfully chewy Thai fishcakes); eight popia tod (well-made mini
vegetarian spring rolls); or six goong hompha (prawns in filo). But the
star turn is gai bai toey – six morsels of chicken that are marinated,
wrapped in pandan leaf and then fried; they are seriously good. The
curries are splendid. And splendidly cheap. Gaeng kheaw wan is a
well-made green curry that comes with a choice of main ingredients.
Other options are a red curry, a yellow curry and a 'jungle curry'.
The house speciality is called 'boneless fish fillet'. This is a large hunk
of tilapia that comes in a mesmerising light and elegant sauce with
plenty of holy basil. The sauces here are good – not thickened to a
sludge with cornflour, but rich on their own account. You'll need
some rice and you should have a noodle dish – perhaps the pad phrik,
which is well balanced. At Tong Ka Nom Thai they serve delicious and
authentic Thai food. It is truly remarkable that they can do so at what
are almost Thai prices.

Piccadilly and St James's

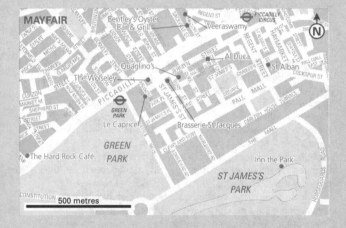

Bentley's Oyster Bar & Grill

11 Swallow Street, W1 ■ 020 7734 4756

⊖ Piccadilly Circus

🍽 British/fish

🕐 Oyster bar: Mon to Sat 12.00–24.00; Sun 12.00–22.00;
restaurant: Mon to Sat 12.00–15.00 & 18.00–22.45;
Sun 12.00–15.00 (brunch) & 18.00–22.00

🖰 www.bentleysoysterbarandgrill.co.uk

🗗 all major credit cards ■ 12.5% optional service added

££ starters £4.50–£40 ■ mains £16.50–£38 ■ sides £3.50
■ desserts £7.50 ■ set lunch £18.50 (2 courses, £22.50 with wine) or
£22.50 (3 courses, £26 with wine) ■ lowest bottle price £25

✪ Classic restaurant reborn

This stylish old restaurant seems happier under the wing of
Richard Corrigan and is buzzing again. Downstairs there is both a
charming bar and the famous oyster bar; upstairs there is the more
formal dining room. The oyster bar has the best feel to it; the craic
is good here! So are the oysters. Downstairs the menu is shorter and
all fish; upstairs half a dozen meat dishes are added. Everything is
underpinned by Corrigan's obsession with carefully sourced, top-
quality ingredients. The smoked salmon comes from Frank Hederman
in Ireland, the fillet of beef comes from West Cork, and in season
there is a choice of different oysters from different producers. From
the starters the smoked eel with crème fraîche is teamed with delicate
potato pancakes; there's a Mediterranean fish soup; and mackerel
tartare with soy and Mirin. From the fish dishes the Bentley's fish pie
is worth noting, as is the stuffed squid with chorizo and feta, and
the baked brill with Jabugo ham, pea and marjoram broth. Or you
could opt for a classic Dover sole meunière, or traditional fish and
chips. And – hurrah! – there are savouries on the menu: an Oyster
stout rarebit, or perhaps a Crozier Blue cheese that has been soaked
in Banyuls. Puds range from delightful nursery favourites to dark
chocolate mousse. The wine list is accommodating, if pitched at
Piccadilly prices. A very good place to eat.

Brasserie St Jacques

33 St James's Street, W1 ■ 020 7839 1007

⊖ Green Park

🍽 French

🕐 Mon to Sat 08.00–23.00; Sun 09.00–22.00

🖰 www.brasseriestjacques.co.uk

🖯 all major credit cards ■ 12.5% optional service added

££ starters £6–£10 ■ mains £11–£17 ■ sides £2.50–£4
■ desserts £5.50–6.50 ■ lowest bottle price £13.50

✪ Easy-going French food

Renowned French chef Pierre Koffman (see the Don, p. 204)
is building up a portfolio of consultancies and his hand is clearly
discernable behind the menu at this likeable Brasserie. Number 33
St James's has been through a good many fine dining incarnations
without being a wild success but it seems likely that this more
practical and accessible restaurant (opened in June 2008) will hit the
spot. It's probably only the designer's artifice but the room looks
French – a tall space with yellow walls and large prints. The carte is
a genuine Brasserie menu running from breakfast to late night with
a section 'Les en-cas' to bridge the gap between lunch and dinner.
There is a daily 'special' and these set the tone: on Tuesday it's
choucroute Alsacienne; Wednesday andouillette au Chablis; Friday
bourride Setoise. The starters range from a duck egg 'en meurette' –
poached in red wine and served on toast with smoked pork belly – to
(in homage to St John, p. 225) roast bone marrow with a parsley
salad. This is hearty French fare, honest and with up-front flavours.
Mains range from roast sea bass with fennel; to veal kidneys with
three mustards; or a slow-roast shoulder of lamb. Puds are classical
– oeufs a la neige, baba au rhum. There's a fine array of aperitifs and
the wine list includes a good many 50cl 'pots', which are a good way
to explore the list.

Le Caprice

Arlington House, Arlington Street, SW1 ■ 020 7629 2239

⊖ Green Park

🍽 Modern European

🕐 Mon to Sat 12.00–15.00 & 17.30–24.00; Sun 12.00–17.00 (brunch) & 18.00–23.00

🔗 www.caprice-holdings.co.uk

🗄 all major credit cards ■ no service added

££ starters £6.50–£15.75 ■ mains £14.25–£26.50 ■ sides £3.75–£7.25 ■ desserts £6.25–£9.50 ■ brunch: starters £2.75–£9 ■ mains £9.50–£15.75 ■ sides £2.50–£4.75 ■ lowest bottle price £18.50

❂ Establishment comfort zone

Every London socialite worthy of the label is a regular at this deeply chic little restaurant and everyone from royalty downwards uses it for the occasional quiet lunch or dinner. They know that this is a safe haven from paparazzi. It may not be particularly plush or comfortable, with a black-and-white-tiled floor, a big black bar and cane seats. What keeps Le Caprice full day in, day out is an amazing level of personal service, properly prepared food and a bill that holds no surprises. The much-imitated menu is enticing from the first glance. Nettle and wild garlic soup with a Keen's cheddar scone. Crispy duck comes with watercress salad, while dressed Dorset crab with celeriac remoulade is very fresh and clean. In season there are splendid specials – River Spey sea trout with steamed clams and parsley. Or perhaps a Blythburgh pork chop with flat onions and sage butter; or Glencoe venison with buttered leeks, prunes and salsify appeals? This kitchen expends time and effort on finding small producers and securing the best of everything. If you are still up for pudding, try the double-baked chocolate soufflé or a champagne jelly with rosewater ice cream. In the winter there is an array of more solid rib-stickers. The only trouble with Le Caprice is the struggle to get a table. Try booking well in advance, or go for a last-minute place at the bar.

Al Duca

4–5 Duke of York Street, SW1 ■ 020 7839 3090

⊖ Piccadilly

🍽 Italian

🕒 Mon to Fri 12.00–14.30 & 18.00–23.00; Sat 12.30–15.00 & 18.00–23.00

🖰 www.alduca-restaurant.co.uk

🗗 all major credit cards ■ 12.5% service added

££ lunch £22.50 (2 courses), £26.50 (3 courses) & £29.50 (4 courses) ■ dinner £25.50 (2 courses), £27.50 (3 courses) & £32.50 (4 courses) ■ pre- & post-theatre £15.50 (2 courses), £17.50 (3 courses) & £20.50 (4 courses) ■ lowest bottle price £18

✪ Low prices, high standards

With this kind of deal it's best not to think London but Italy. You get high-quality, sophisticated food, an agreeable setting, slick service, and all at modest prices. The entire menu changes regularly and has a seasonal bias to it. There are six or more starters at Al Duca: choose from dishes such as lemon marinated tuna with a fennel salad; bresaola with goat's cheese; or a fried duck egg served with Parmesan crisps and a potato and sun-dried tomato salad. Then there is a raft of dishes under the heading pasta, includeing linguine al vongole and maccheroni 'alla puttanesca'. This is followed by an array of main courses: roast duck breast with broccoli and a 'mulled wine' dressing; sea bass cooked sous vide; osso buco served with Sardinian cracked wheat; or calves' liver and bacon. Finally, six desserts, from the ubiquitous tiramisù; to roast pineapple with rosemary and coconut sorbet; a vanilla panna cotta with orange confit; or a rich chocolate marquise with caramel sauce. Or perhaps the selection of Italian cheeses appeals? The standard of cooking is very sound, with dishes bringing off that difficult trick of being both deceptively simple and satisfyingly rich. Overall there is much to praise here, and the slick service and stylish ambience live up to the efforts in the kitchen. Best of all, you get an opportunity to have a multi-course meal. This is the place to try four courses, Italian style.

The Hard Rock Café

150 Old Park Lane, W1 ▪ 020 7629 0382   ♿

⊖ Hyde Park Corner

🍴 North American/burgers

🕐 Mon to Thurs & Sun 11.30–24.00; Fri & Sat 11.30–01.00

🖰 www.hardrock.com

🖨 all major credit cards ▪ 12.5% optional service added to bills over £30

££ starters £3.95–£9.95 ▪ mains £8–£9 ▪ sides £1.95–£3.25
▪ desserts £4–£6 ▪ lowest bottle price £14.25

✪ Burger palace – the original and genuine

The 'Museum and memorabilia' outlet is over the road in what was once Coutts bank, which just about says it all. The Hard Rock Café was one of the first restos to understand both merchandising and the tourist market. This place is the original theme restaurant, and as such is a hard act to follow. The queue out front is legendary. There's no booking and you'll find a queue almost all day long, every day of the year. Once in, there is a great atmosphere, created by full-on rock music, dim lighting and walls dripping with rock memorabilia. The Hard Rock food is not bad, either, predominantly Tex-Mex and burgers. Scanning the menu is a serious business here. Dishes get short but complex essays attached to them, so Tupelo chicken tenders are explained as 'boneless chicken tenders, lightly breaded and coated in our Classic Rock (medium), Heavy Metal (hot) or tangy Bar B-Que sauce. Served with celery and Bleu cheese dressing'. The job of copywriter is an important one here. The burgers cover the spectrum from HRC burger to the hickory Bar-B-Que bacon cheeseburger. Veggies are catered for by the HRC veggie sandwich. Further along, among the Smokehouse Specialities, there's the pig sandwich and Bruce's famous Bar-B-Que ribs. Puddings are self-indulgent, and the hot fudge brownie elevates goo to an art form. If sweet is truly your thing there's a shooter called 'bubblegum' – Bailey's, blue Curaçao and banana liqueur.

Inn the Park

St James's Park, SW1 ■ 020 7451 9999 &

⊖ St James's Park

🍴 British

🕐 daily 08.00–21.00 or later if weather permits (breakfast until 11.00)

🖰 www.innthepark.co.uk

🗄 all major credit cards ■ 12.5% service added

££ breakfast £1–£11 ■ starters £6.50–£10.90 ■ mains £14.50–£23
■ sides £3.50 ■ desserts £6.50–£8 ■ afternoon tea £15–£25.50
(bookings taken for parties of 10 or more) ■ lowest bottle price £14.50

✪ Kicks park catering into the next century

This building is stunning – like the dwelling of an A-list hobbit.
There are lots of gentle curves, plenty of wood, and everything is
built into a grassy mound. The food is good, too – British produce,
commendably fresh, unfussy presentation and simply cooked. The
place opens for breakfast, then serves snacks, then lunch, then
afternoon tea, then dinner. The waiting staff seem friendly and service
is slick – which will all come as something of a shock to anyone
accustomed to the hot-dog-from-a-barrow that used to be the
only kind of sustenance available within the park. Breakfast offers a
choice of good things: hen's eggs or duck eggs; three different kinds
of bacon; three different black puds; and three different sausages
– perfect for anyone with an analytical turn of mind. At lunch and
dinner the 'proper' cooking is well done: for starters there's prawn
cocktail with Marie Rose sauce; ham hock terrine, broad beans, pea
shoots and spring onions; Dorset crab with green apple and toast;
and a smoked fishcake with crushed peas. For mains there's a whole
sea bass with Heritage tomatoes; smoked haddock with Colcannon
potato; roast Goosnargh chicken; or twice-cooked belly of pork with
quince jam. There are also home-made ice creams and a serious
British cheese plate. The afternoon tea of sandwiches, cakes and
scones is a serious contender, and even the snacks appeal – 'plate
of British cured and cooked meats with chutneys and pickles'. What
good, honest food and what a splendid place to eat it. And you can
now make bookings for any time of day.

Quaglino's

16 Bury Street, SW1 ■ 020 7930 6767

θ Green Park

|●| Modern British

⏱ Mon to Thurs 12.00–15.00 & 17.30–24.00; Fri & Sat 12.00–15.00 &
17.30–01.00; Sun 12.00–15.00 & 17.30–23.00

🖰 www.danddlondon.com

🗗 all major credit cards ■ 12.5% service added

££ starters £6.50–£12.50 ■ crustacea £6.50–£48 ■ mains £10.50–£26
■ sides £3.50–£5.50 ■ desserts £6–£8 ■ prix fixe lunch £14.50
(2 courses) & £17.50 (3 courses) ■ pre- & post-theatre £16.50 (2
courses) & £19 (3 courses) ■ lowest bottle price £16.50

✪ Spiritual home of the Essex crowd

In 1929 Giovanni Quaglino opened a restaurant in Bury Street
that became an instant success and the one thing it had, above
all else, was glamour. His other claim to fame was that he was the
first restaurateur to offer a hot dish as hors d'oeuvre. Years later the
ambience is still impressive – an elegant reception, the sweeping
staircase into the bar that overlooks the main restaurant, and the
second stairway down to restaurant level. If this kind of thing rings
your bell you will be happy here. The menu is simple, classy and
brasserie-style, with very little to scare off the less experienced diner.
Starters include a salad Lyonnaise – smoked bacon, poached egg
and croutons. The plateau de fruits de mer (extravagantly priced
and for a minimum of two people) is as good as you would hope,
as is the whole lobster mayonnaise. Haddock and chips is served
with home-made chips and tartare sauce and is excellent, and
there's a Quaglino's hamburger and a rib-eye steak with sauce
Béarnaise. Puddings are straightforward and agreeably predictable –
blackcurrant parfait; apple Charlotte with clotted cream. Quaglino's
staff can be brusque, but then marshalling large numbers of glamour-
seekers is a testing job. You can avoid this altogether by staying in
the bar, which offers highlights from the menu – including all the
seafood. Furthermore, Quag's is open late, which makes it perfect for
a genuine after-theatre dinner.

St Alban

4–12 Regent Street, SW1 ■ 020 7499 8558

⊖ Piccadilly Circus

🍴 Modern European

🕐 Mon to Sat 12.00–15.00 & 17.30–24.00; Sun 12.00–15.00 &
17.30–23.00

🌐 www.stalban.net

🗄 all major credit cards ■ 12.5% optional service added

££ starters £5.75–£18 ■ mains £9.25–£27 ■ sides £3.50 ■ desserts
£5–£8.50 ■ cheese £6.50–£8.50 ■ Sunday specials £12.75 & £16.75
■ lowest bottle price £15.50

✪ Seventies-looking but new-century cooking

St Alban has a perfect pedigree. It was set up by Christopher Corbin
and Jeremy King, the gentlemen whose track record stretches from
Le Caprice and The Ivy (see pp. 127 and 29) to The Wolseley (see p.
134). They still have the capacity to surprise us, and when St Alban
opened it had a completely different feel to it – the décor was a
homage to the 1970s, with curved banquettes, vibrant colours and
a carpet with abstract patterns. It works well, the carpet keeps the
noise down and the lighting makes the dining room feel bright.
The food is a take on brasserie favourites with added flair that
could probably be pigeon-holed under Modern European. Dishes
are seasonal. Starters range from broad beans with chorizo; to
squab pigeon and pearl barley salad; courgette flowers stuffed with
bacalhao; and baby squid 'a la plancha' with sweet chilli. Main
courses range from wood-baked pizzas; to slow-roast black pig
with Spanish marrow; pappardelle with ragù of rabbit and black
olives; and pan-fried wild sea trout with salsa verde. Desserts range
from wood rice pudding with marinated apricots; to espresso and
anise crème brûlée; and a dark chocolate torte with white chocolate
mousse. As you would expect from Corbin and King, the service
is very slick and the wine list touches most bases from accessible
to excessive. St Alban has already made itself indispensable to the
London scene.

Veeraswamy

Victory House, 99 Regent Street, W1 ■ 020 7734 1401

⊖ Piccadilly Circus

🍴 Indian

🕐 Mon to Fri 12.30–14.15 & 17.30–22.30; Sat 12.30–14.30 &
17.30–22.30; Sun 12.30–14.30 & 18.00–22.00

🔗 www.veeraswamy.com

💳 all major credit cards ■ 12.5% service

££ starters £6.50–£12.00 ■ mains £14–£27 ■ sides £1.50–£7.50
■ desserts £5.50 ■ set lunch & pre-/post-theatre £16.50 & £20
■ Indian Sunday lunch £20 ■ lowest bottle price £17.75

⭐ London's oldest Indian restaurant

Ever since it opened in the 1920s, Veeraswamy has been a magnet
to lovers of Indian food. It was opened by Edward Palmer (a bright
young man keen to capitalise on his success providing Indian food
for the Empire Exhibition), and under various owners managed to
cling to its reputation as a society restaurant until the 1960s. Today
it is part of the Masalaworld Group and it recently emerged from
a thorough redesign to successfully recapture some of the glitz
and glamour of the early days. The room is elegant, the chairs are
comfortable, the lighting is subtle and dramatic. The food is very
good indeed. The dishes are drawn from several regions and the
cuisine of Maharajahs jostles with street food. Start with the green
leaf bhajias – an amazing mini-haystack of herbs given a tempura-like
treatment in the lightest possible batter. Sholay chicken tikka is smoky
and very subtle. Mussels moilee teams mussels with a coconut sauce.
The duck seekh kebab is tender and well spiced. The giant 'green
prawns' are huge and juicy. From the mains choose the chicken
chatpatta – rich with tomato and spices; the Kashmiri rogan josh
– made with saffron and cockscomb flowers; the sea bream paturi
– fillets of fish in a mustard marinade steamed in banana leaf; or the
stunning Hyderabadi lamb biryani. The simple fresh pineapple curry
is also worth noting. Breads are exemplary. Puds are interesting if
you dodge the over-sweet trad Indian confections. Service is friendly;
advice is freely given and worth taking.

The Wolseley

160 Piccadilly, W1 ■ 020 7499 6996

⊖ Green Park

🍴 European

🕐 daily 07.00–11.30 (breakfast) (08.00–11.30 Sat & Sun); 15.00–18.30 (tea) (15.30–17.30 Mon–Sat; 15.30–18.30 Sun); restaurant: 12.00–15.00 & 17.30–24.00 (à la carte); 11.30–24.00 (all-day menu)

🔗 www.thewolseley.com

🗄 all major credit cards ■ 12.5% optional service added

££ breakfast £2.75–£13.25 ■ starters £5.75–£18.75
■ mains £9.75–£23.50 ■ desserts £4.50–£7.50
■ afternoon tea £8.25–£19.50 ■ lowest bottle price £16

✪ A European Grand Café docks in Piccadilly

Christopher Corbin and Jeremy King are a senior double act in London restaurants. They are the people who developed Le Caprice (see p. 127) and nursed The Ivy (see p. 29) back to health before retiring. Then they un-retired and opened The Wolseley, turning a former car showroom into a buzzing restaurant. The room is tall and theatrical, gloriously dramatic. The atmosphere is 'celebrity chic' and the feel of the place owes plenty to middle European grand cafés, as does the menu. One enterprising critic started with breakfast, and then stayed for elevenses, lunch, afternoon tea and dinner – it's probably the one sure way to secure a table for dinner! This place is so busy that it is almost impossible to get into, but worth it. Try early or late. The food is good here – unfussy, old-fashioned, and well presented. Starters include some nostalgic numbers such as chopped liver; steak tartare; and half a dozen escargots. There are salads, such as frisée aux lardons; and shellfish, including dressed Cornish crab. Onwards! Ham hock with caper sauce; whole Dover sole; a hamburger; and roast pata negra pork belly. There is even a classically presented Wiener Holstein complete with crossed anchovies and fried egg. Among the puds are butter-roast pineapple; a banana and mango Eton mess and serious ice cream coupes. The wine list is comprehensive. The service is slick and the celebrity count is very high.

Queensway and Westbourne Grove

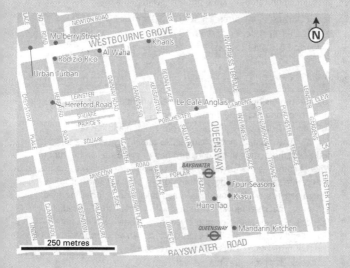

Le Café Anglais

8 Porchester Gardens, W2 ■ 020 7221 1415   ♿

⊖ Bayswater/Queensway

🍽 French

🕐 daily 12.00–15.00 & 18.30–23.00

🖰 www.lecafeanglais.co.uk

🖫 all major credit cards ■ 12.5% optional service added

££ hors d'oeuvres £3 ■ starters £5.50–£13.50 ■ mains £10–£27
■ sides £3–£11 ■ desserts £4.50–£8 ■ set lunch Mon to Sat £16.50
(2 courses) & £19 (3 courses) ■ lowest bottle price £15

⭐ A class act

Le Café Anglais opened in 2007 and is a bright, comfortable,
modern-looking Brasserie on the second floor of the Whiteleys
building on Queensway. The dining room is long and has tall
windows with elegant pastel banquettes under them on one side
and a bustling open bar, kitchen, and pair of rotisseries on the other.
When it comes to menu-writing the chef proprietor Rowley Leigh has
perfect pitch and there's no dumbing down here. Let's hear it for
'hors d'oeuvres', which comprise fifteen small dishes, including fried
anchovies; mackerel teriyaki; piperade with Parma ham; Mortadella
with celeriac remoulade; competitive rabbit rillettes with delicious
pickled endives; and that Parmesan custard with anchovy toasts – a
dish that tastes so much better than it reads. Onwards to the first
courses, such as foie gras terrine with Pedro Ximénez jelly; fonduta
with salsify and white truffles; or Parma ham with pickled damsons.
Mains are drawn from fish (half a dozen options, including a very fine
dish of steamed whiting with shrimps and a garam masala sauce)
and a section headed 'roasts' – impeccable roast chicken or rabbit
with a dandelion salad. Puds lead with fresh fruit, and then cast aside
all that cautious healthy stuff to revel in apple Charlotte, chocolate
soufflé and a succession of outrageous ice cream sundaes. The old-
world wine list gives you a decent chance of drinking at sensible
money and the service just about copes with the flood of custom.

Four Seasons

84 Queensway, W2 ■ 020 7229 4320

⊖ Queensway/Bayswater

🍽 Chinese

🕐 Mon to Sat 12.00–23.15; Sun 12.00–22.45

🗄 all major credit cards ■ 12.5% service added

££ soups/starters £2.60–£15 ■ mains £6.20–£20
■ noodles/rice £1.80–£6.80 ■ desserts £2.50–£2.80
■ set menu £15.50 & £20 ■ lowest bottle price £9

✪ Genuine Chinese food, good value

Four Seasons is an old-established restaurant that has always had a special reputation for roast duck. As with so many good Chinese restaurants, there is a stream of rumours concerning the Four Seasons; in recent years it has been murmured that the duck oven has been changed – shorthand for a less wonderfully lacquered skin. But standards never seem to suffer. That doesn't mean that service won't be brusque and that the front of house won't look at you blankly when you claim to have made a reservation. Be prepared to sit, order, eat and have a bill slapped on the table in short order. The food is good. Starters tick all the boxes from crispy seaweed to steamed scallops. The barbecued meats are splendid – the roast duck is meaty with a crisp skin; the crispy pork has a salty savoury bark that shatters in the mouth. The menu wanders on through familiar and unfamiliar dishes. Turn to the chef's specials if they are on and feast yourself on 'stuffed bitter melon with salted fish and minced pork'. This dish is a triumph – very bitter and very rich. Or there may be a sighting of that hot pot classic 'double-cooked belly pork with yam'. There are usually plenty of adventures to be had without going as far as 'duck's feet with sea cucumber and fish lips in hot pot'. A fine and workmanlike Chinese restaurant where the menu has not been dumbed down.

→ For branch, see index

Hereford Road

3 Hereford Road, W2 ■ 020 7727 1144

⊖ Queensway/Bayswater

🍴 Very British

🕐 daily 12.00–15.00 & 18.00–22.30 (22.00 Sun)

🖥 www.herefordroad.org

🖨 all major credit cards ■ no service added

££ starters £3–£7 ■ mains £8.90–£13.80 ■ desserts £4.50–£5.50
　　■ lowest bottle price £13

✪ Honest, wholesome and British

Perhaps one of the reasons why there are not more restaurants opened by disciples of Fergus Henderson and St John is that his mantra of honest, authentic, British dishes carefully made and using the finest seasonal ingredients is very hard to follow. Cooking that's so outwardly simple and so very delicious is a difficult challenge, but at Hereford Road they bring it off. To the front of the resto there are some banquettes facing the open kitchen, while to the rear there is a dining room with a large round window in the ceiling. Sit under it if you can – on a sunny day there's a delightful shaft of light. The menu is true to the spirit of British cooking. Salt duck comes with pickled chicory; lambs' kidneys on toast are perfectly cooked – faintly pink within and with buttery juices soaking into the toast; and a salad of Jerusalem artichokes shows a deft hand at work combining differing textures. The main courses may range from a peerless roast widgeon on a bed of buttery cabbage with bacon pieces – wholly successful; to tender venison, lightly cooked, and a deep dark red. The whole oxtail for two is served on the bone and about a foot and a half long, rather like a huge, meaty, Flintstone's corn on the cob. Fine cheeses get their moment of glory. Puds are good. The wine list has some modestly priced bottles and service is smooth.

Hung Tao

51 Queensway, W2 ■ 020 7727 5753

⊖ Bayswater/Queensway

🍴 Chinese

🕐 daily 11.00–23.00

🗗 cash only ■ 10% service added

££ starters £2–£2.50 ■ noodle soups £4.20–£5.70 ■ mains £4.20–£7.50
■ no alcohol

✪ Fast food, cheap food, good food

The reason to choose the Hung Tao above its neighbours is if you
fancy a one-plate (or more accurately, one-bowl) meal. One of the
first items on the menu is the 'hot and sour' soup. Appropriately, this
is hot – with fresh red chillies in profusion, sour, and delicious. There
are also a dozen different 'noodle' soups, at bargain prices. These are
the perfect all-in-one student meals – carbs and protein swimming
in a tasty broth. Then there are twenty dishes that go from duck
rice to fried fish with ginger. Plus about thirty noodle, fried noodle
and ho fun dishes, all at low low prices. The fried ho fun with beef
is a superb rich dish – well-flavoured brisket cooked until melting,
on top of a mountain of ho fun wide noodles. And the barbecued
meats displayed in the window are very tasty, too: rich, red-painted
char sui; soya chicken; duckling; and crispy pork. Towards the front
of the menu you'll find a succession of congee dishes. Congee is a
thick, whitish, runny rice porridge – one of those foods people label
'interesting' without meaning it. Plunge in at the deep end and try
the one which is styled 'preserved egg with sliced pork congee'.
As well as containing pork, there's the 'thousand-year' egg itself,
the white of which is a translucent chestnut brown and the yolk a
fetching green. Inscrutably, it tastes rather like a cheesy hard-boiled
egg.

Khan's

13–15 Westbourne Grove, W2 ▪ 020 7727 5420

⊖ Bayswater/Queensway

|◉| Indian

🕐 Mon to Thurs 12.00–14.45 & 18.00–23.45; Fri–Sun 12.00–23.45

🖰 www.khansrestaurant.com

🖶 all major credit cards ▪ 10% service added

££ starters £2.15–£3.85 ▪ thalis £9.15–£9.95 ▪ mains £4.95–£11.95
▪ sides £1.95–£3.65 ▪ desserts £2.65–£4.15 ▪ no alcohol

✪ Cavernous and echoing Indian food factory

This restaurant, in busy Westbourne Grove, is a long-standing favourite with students and budget-wary locals who know that the curries here may be the same as on a thousand menus across Britain, but that they're fresh, well cooked and generously portioned. Tables are turned in a trice, service is perfunctory and it's really noisy. Try to get a table in the vast, booming ground floor, where blue murals stretch up to the high ceilings – it feels a bit like dining in an enormous municipal swimming pool. There are some tasty breads on offer. Try the nan-e-mughziat, a coconut-flavoured affair with nuts and sultanas, or the paneer kulcha, bulging with cottage cheese and mashed potatoes. You might also kick off with half a tandoori chicken, which is moist and well cooked, or a creditable chicken tikka. For main dishes, all those curry-house favourites are listed here: meat Madras or vindalu; prawn biryani; chicken chilli masala; and king prawn curry – and they all taste good and fresh. The butter chicken is especially fine, while for lovers of tikka masala dishes, the chicken tikka masala will appeal. There's a typical array of vegetable dishes, too: bhindi, sag aloo, vegetable curry. Desserts include kulfi and various ice creams from Häagen Dazs. Then, just when you think that Khan's is an unreconstructed curry house, you spot the heart symbols on the menu – they are positioned beside the 'low fat' dishes.

Kiasu

48 Queensway, W2 ■ 020 7727 8810

⊖ Bayswater/Queensway

🍴 Malaysian/Singaporean

🕐 daily 12.00–22.30

🔗 www.kiasu.co.uk

🗄 all major credit cards ■ 10% optional service added

££ starters £2.50–£5.50 ■ mains £4.80–£8.50 ■ noodles £6.20–£7.20
■ sides £1.50–£3.50 ■ set menus £2.50–£7.50
■ lowest bottle price £11.50

⭐ The anything but dire Straits

On the menu it proclaims that 'kiasu' (from the Chinese Hokkien dialect) means 'afraid to be second best' and that the menu offers dishes from that culinary melting pot the Straits of Malacca. Which explains why you'll find Malay chicken satay and a Chinese pork satay, a Vietnamese spring roll and a Thai red duck curry. The service is smiley, charming and profoundly irritating – do not allow it to spoil what is potentially an eye-opening meal. Start with the Chinese pork satay, which is unlike most other satay – you get the crispy meat on a skewer, you get clumps of rice and cucumber shards, and you get a very good peanut sauce. The roti pratha is fun, too – two crispy, flaky, floury breads and a curry gravy to dip them into. Or you can try pai tee, which are little pastry cups filled with prawn, pork and yam. Mains are also delicious: beef rendang is suitably dry and intense; bak chor mee is a dish of noodles with minced pork and soup; the Nonya laksa is an astonishing soup noodle dish and contender for 'best-in-London'. The food is very well balanced, chilli hot or not, depending on what you ask for. Drink the agreeable Singha beer and save a little room for one of those spooky Straits desserts like chendol – shaved ice, coconut palm syrup, and pandan green blancmange noodles (honestly).

Mandarin Kitchen

14–16 Queensway, W2 ■ 020 7727 9012

🚇 Queensway/Bayswater

🍽 Chinese/fish

🕐 daily 12.00–23.30

🗂 all major credit cards ■ no service added

££ starters £1.50–£11.80 ■ soups £2.20–£8.90 ■ mains £6–£25
■ lobster 'seasonal price' (about £28.50) ■ set meals £12–£20
■ lowest bottle price £13.50

✪ Lobster HQ

The Mandarin Kitchen is something of an institution. It's a large place, busy with waiters deftly wheeling four-foot diameter tabletops around like giant hoops as they set up communal tables for parties of Chinese, who all seem to be eating – lobster. Whatever you fancy for the main course, start with as many of the steamed scallops on the shell with garlic soy sauce as you can afford. They're magnificent. Then decide between lobster, crab or fish. If you go for the lobster, you can have it as sashimi; steamed; with ginger and spring onions; or with black bean and green pepper chilli sauce (whichever way, it will be 'seasonally priced'). Be sure that you order the optional extra soft noodle to make a meal of it. The crab is tempting, too. Live crabs are shipped up from the south coast, and you can opt for a handsome portion of shells, lots of legs and four claws baked with ginger and spring onion. Fish dishes require more thought – and keep an eye on the seasonally changing per-pound prices. The menu lists sea bass, turbot, Dover sole, red snapper and pomfret. The steamed eel with black bean sauce is notably rich. The squid in chilli and black bean sauce is good. The Mandarin Kitchen serves good fresh fish, but the downside is that reservations are a waste of time – you'll be greeted by blank stares.

Mulberry Street

84 Westbourne Grove, W2 ■ 020 7313 6789

Westbourne Park/Notting Hill Gate

Pizzas

daily 12.00–24.00 (breakfast Fri, Sat 09.30–12.00)

www.mulberrystreet.co.uk

all major credit cards ■ 12.5% optional service added

££ 20" pizzas £15.99–£19.99 ■ slices £3.50–£4 ■ entrées £6.50–£12.95
■ salads & sides £3.50–£10.95 ■ desserts £4.50
■ lowest bottle price £12.95

⭐ Classy pizza, New York portions

They say everything is bigger in America, and whether that is true or not, the people behind Mulberry Street believe this adage and see it as a unique proposition for their pizza restaurant. Here they serve 20 inch 'New York' pizzas – so large that they have a tendency to topple off the natty little stands that support the platters on the tables. This is a small but busy place with a central bar and booths. A large mural strives to add some transatlantic glam and there are enough large screen televisions to conjure up a feel of NY. The menu leads with the 20" pizzas, which are not as daunting as you might expect (one makes a decent meal for two people) and you can add much needed variety by having a different topping on each half. Some of the options are as follows: the Classic – tomatoes, mozzarella and fresh basil; the New York Hot – spicy pepperoni, fresh green peppers, jalapenos and mozzarella (could be hotter); the 'Skinny Bitch' – a 'lo carb' pizza (whatever will they think of next); or 'fresh white spinach' – spinach, ricotta, mozzarella and tomato (this one works very well). If you want to add some greens there are various salads ranging from Tricolore to Caesar, and for pud there's cake or ice cream. Service is friendly and efficient. A jolly place selling large pizzas with prices to match.

Rodizio Rico

111 Westbourne Grove, W11 ■ 020 7792 4035

⊖ Notting Hill Gate

⦿ Brazilian

🕒 Mon to Fri 18.30–24.00; Sat 12.30–16.30

🖰 www.rodiziorico.com

🖸 all major credit cards ■ 10% service added

££ set meal £20.50 (£14.40 vegetarian) ■ desserts £4.40
   ■ lowest bottle price £15

✪ Meat, then meat and some more meat!

In southern Brazil this restaurant would be seen as pretty run-of-the-mill, but in W11 churrascarias are the exception rather than the rule. If you're a lover of smoky grilled meat, Rodizio Rico will come as a godsend, but it can be a rather puzzling experience for first-timers. There's no menu and no prices – but no problem. 'Rodizio' means 'rotating', and refers to the carvers who wander about the room with huge skewers of freshly grilled meat from which they lop off chunks on demand. You eat as much as you like of whatever you like, and then pay the very reasonable bill. When you're up helping yourself to some salad, look out for the tiny rolls, no bigger than a button mushroom, called pão de queijo – a rich cheese bread from the south of Brazil. Return to your seat and await the carvers – they come in random order, but they keep on coming. There's lamb, and ham, and pork, and spare ribs, and chicken, and silverside beef (called lagarto after a similarly shaped iguana). Then for offal aficionados there are grilled chicken hearts. But the star of the show is picanha – the heart of the rump, skewered and grilled in huge chunks. Taste it and the arguments over the relative merits of rump and fillet are over forever. Brazilians seem to revere the crispy bits, but if you want your meat rare you only have to ask.

→ For branches, see index or website

Urban Turban

98 Westbourne Grove, W2 ■ 020 7243 4200 ⚹

⊖ Bayswater/Notting Hill Gate

🍽 Indian

🕐 Mon–Fri 18.00–23.00; Sat & Sun 12.30–15.30 & 18.00–23.00

🖱 www.urbanturban.uk.com

🗄 all major credit cards ■ 12.5% optional service added

££ desi tapas £5.50–£6 ■ mains £5–£12 ■ bread/rice £3 ■ desserts £6
 ■ sharing platters £24 (2 people) ■ lowest bottle price £16

✪ Glorious grazing, Indian style

Vineet Bhatia already had one fine restaurant (see Rasoi Vineet
Bhatia, p. 401) but with Urban Turban he has tried something new.
The room is large and dominated by an island bar, the seating at the
round tables around the periphery is a combination of banquettes
(comfortable) and stools (less so). As for authenticity, you would
expect the street food of Mumbai to undergo a few tweaks on its
journey to London W2. The menu leads with 'desi tapas', aka the
starters. Sample a few and then move on to a curry. A good option
is one of the 'platters' which serve two people. It's not a platter but
a perspex stand and the six different dishes are presented in cones
of paper. The contents are delicious. Try machli Amritsari, which are
goujons of white fish in spiced batter – well judged; lamb seekh
kebab – a little dry, but well spiced; chicken lollipops – delicious, crisp
and tender; chilli chicken – agreeably hot; khandvi – rolled pancakes,
interesting texture; or potato chat – like moody potato salad. Good
flavours and textures. The 'mains' at Urban include a very decent
lamb biryani with crust; a spicy Punjabi chicken masala that is indeed
spicy; and a smoked aubergine and pea masala that manages to be
very light. The breads are fine, if on the small side. It is a pleasure to
eat dishes where the spicing has not been toned down and messed
about with.

Al Waha
75 Westbourne Grove, W2 ■ 020 7229 0806

⊖ Bayswater/Queensway

|O| Lebanese

🕑 daily 12.00–24.00

🖱 www.alwaharestaurant.com

🖯 all major credit cards except AmEx ■ no service added

££ meze £3.75–£7 ■ main dishes £10–£18.50 ■ sides £3.50–£3.75
■ desserts £3.50 ■ set menus £12.50–£25
■ 'Days of the Week speciality' £10 ■ lowest bottle price £12

✪ Top-notch Lebanese cooking

Anissa Helou, writer of several definitive books on Lebanese
cuisine, nominates Al Waha as London's best Lebanese restaurant.
And after eating here you'll probably agree with her. Lebanese
restaurants are all meze obsessed, and Al Waha is no exception.
What is different, however, is the way in which the chef at Al Waha
is obsessive about main courses as well. When you sit down, crisp
crudités will be brought to the table. It includes everything from some
quartered Cos lettuce to a whole green pepper. Choosing is then the
problem, as there are 21 cold starters and 23 hot ones. Houmous is
good here; tabbouleh is heavy on the parsley; and the foul moukala
is good, despite its name – broad beans with garlic, coriander and
olive oil. From the hot section, try manakeish bizaatar, which is a
mini-bread topped with thyme, like a sophisticated pizza. Or there's
batata harra, potatoes with garlic and peppers. The makanek ghanam
are tiny Lebanese lamb sausages, like very refined cocktail sausages.
For main courses, grills predominate, and they are all spanking fresh
and accurately cooked. Good choices include shish taouk, made with
chicken, and samakeh harrah, a whole sea bass. The star turn is kafta
khashkhash – a superb cylinder of minced lamb with parsley, garlic
and tomato. The various breads, hot from the oven, are exceptionally
fine. Drink the good Lebanese beer or the very good Lebanese wines.

Soho

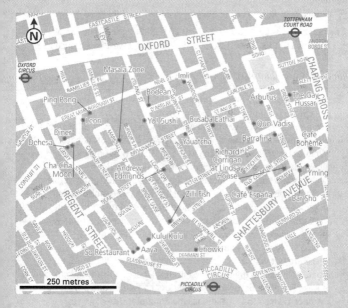

Aaya
66 Brewer Street, W1 ■ 020 7319 3888

⊖ Piccadilly Circus

🍴 Japanese

🕐 Mon to Sat 12.00–15.00 & 18.00–23.30; Sun 12.00–15.00 & 18.00–22.30

🖥 www.aaya.com

🏧 all major credit cards ■ 12.5% service added

££ appetisers £3–£9 ■ sushi £2.50–£6.50 (per piece) ■ sashimi £3.50–£6 ■ mains £6–£13.50 ■ desserts £5.50–£7.50 ■ lowest bottle price £23

✪ Superslick Japanese style palace

Nobody heard this place coming. Usually, any new restaurant is preceded by a rumble of foodie anticipation but Aaya sprang open in the spring of 2008 without anyone noticing. This was all the more surprising as the proprietor here is Gary Yau, brother of Alan (see Yauatcha, p. 169, and Cha Cha Moon, p. 156) who is a master of the whole 'tantalise pre-opening' game. Aaya occupies a large and elegant space: upstairs there is a huge cocktail bar with some tables to dine at; downstairs is a huge sushi bar with more tables to dine at. This is a very opulent setting and dishes are pretty on the plate. The cold appetisers include razor clam with Japanese mountain yam; there's a salad of warm wild mushrooms — more of a stir fry really; or tuna katsu tataki, an interesting dish with the tuna slices raw in the centre but with a crisp breadcrumb coat. Other dishes from the robata grill include grilled yuzu Chilean sea bass and corn-fed chicken teriyaki. From the braised dishes the slow-cooked Kakuni pork belly is a winner, cooked to its gelatinous melting point. The nigiri sushi are well made, as befits their top-end pricing. The service is solicitous and this is the only place to offer a choice of lemon, lime or cucumber in the tap water! This is a beautiful restaurant with beautiful food … and then you pay.

Andrew Edmunds

46 Lexington Street, W1 ■ 020 7437 5708

⊖ Oxford Circus

🍴 Modern British

🕐 Mon to Fri 12.30–15.00 & 18.00–22.45; Sat 13.00–15.00 &
18.00–22.45; Sun 13.00–15.30 & 18.00–22.30

🗗 all major credit cards ■ 12.5% service added

££ starters £2.95–£7.25 ■ mains £11.50–£16.50 ■ sides £2.75
■ desserts £3.75–£7.25 (cheese) ■ lowest bottle price £12.50

✪ Local hero from the days of old Soho

This restaurant has a loyal band of regulars, some of whom
date back to the far-off days when this place was called Andrew
Edmunds wine bar. They enjoy the imaginative bistro-style dishes,
strong flavours and bold combinations. It tends to be cosy, dark
and usually very crowded. The menu changes weekly and combines
solid favourites with bright new ideas. Despite having been around
for a very long time it doesn't feel dated – merely charming. Start
with spiced sweet potato and coconut soup; or marinated squid;
or charcuterie with red onion compote. Main courses may include
stalwart and straightforward dishes such as best end of Herdwick
lamb with olive-oil mash and sprouting broccoli; free-range chicken
breast wrapped in Speck; wild halibut, pollack fish cake on spinach;
seared scallops with a saffron and lemon risotto; or an impressive
vegetarian option like goats' cheese ravioli with wild mushrooms.
This is very like stumbling on a neighbourhood restaurant in some
affluent suburb, only you are in the very heart of Soho. Puddings
include chocolate mousse cake, the ubiquitous tiramisù, and nutmeg
ice cream. Wines are a passion with Andrew Edmunds. The constantly
changing, broker-bought list is long and special and, because of his
low mark-up policy, there are some genuine bargains to be had –
something which has not escaped the notice of the regulars! Booking
is essential as the dining room has a limited number of covers.

Arbutus

63 Frith Street, W1 ■ 020 7734 4545

⊖ Tottenham Court Road/Leicester Square

🍽 Modern European

🕐 Mon to Sat 12.00–14.30 & 17.00–22.30; Sun 12.30–15.30 &
17.30–21.30

🖰 www.arbutusrestaurant.co.uk

🖪 all major credit cards ■ 12.5% service added

££ starters £5.95–£9.95 ■ mains £14.95–£19.95 ■ sides £2.95
■ desserts £6.95 ■ set lunch (12.00–14.30) £15.50 (3 courses);
pre-theatre (17.00–19.00) £17.50 (3 courses) ■ lowest bottle price
£12.50

✪ Magnificent food, magnificently reasonable prices

As soon as Arbutus opened, it started racking up 'best restaurant
of the year' awards, and its younger sister Wild Honey (see p. 109)
has also picked up its share. For once these plaudits are thoroughly
deserved. The kitchen specialises in robust French cooking and the
menu always has two or three dishes that are made from offal or
really unfashionable cuts of meat. The pricing is sympathetic and
nearly 40 wines (including some of the smarter bottles) are available
by the 250ml carafe, so you can explore the wine list to your heart's
content without busting the bank. The food is mega, and always
seasonal. The menu changes daily. You might start with Hereford
snails, Laguiole cheese farinette; braised pig's head, potato purée,
caramelised onions; squid and mackerel 'burger', with parsley and
razor clams – strange concept, delicious dish; or guinea fowl and
foie gras boudin blanc. Mains include classics like andouillettes
de Troyes with morels à la crème; slow-cooked Elwy valley lamb,
sweetbreads and artichokes – a superb dish; pieds et paquets –
lamb's trotters and tripe, very delicious. And there is a plat du jour
which might be short rib of Rhug Estate beef with potato gnocchi,
English snails, garlic and parsley – a sort of Welsh/Italian/English
co-production. Puds are accomplished: île flottante with pink praline,
and warm waffles with crushed strawberries and vanilla ice cream.

Bar Shu

28 Frith Street, W1 ■ 020 7287 8822

⊖ Tottenham Court Road/Leicester Square

🍽 Chinese/Sichuan

🕐 daily 12.00–23.00

🖰 www.bar-shu.co.uk

🖫 all major credit cards ■ 12.5% service added

££ starters £6–£12 ■ mains £8.50–£28 ■ sides £8–£18
■ lowest bottle price £19.90

✪ Hot, hot, hot

Sometimes a restaurant opens with such a recondite cuisine that
only a fool would venture in without a guide. Bar Shu is just such
a place, and promised to bring real, full-strength, unexpurgated
Sichuan food to W1. So it was that we made up a large party,
including Fuchsia Dunlop (who has written a number of erudite
Chinese cookery books and acted as consultant to the gentlemen
setting up Bar Shu). Several lessons were rammed home: Sichuan
food can be addictively, imperiously, dangerously hot; as well as
awesome quantities of chilli there is the Sichuan pepper – a small
flower bud that makes your lips sting. To start, try the numbing-
and-hot dried beef; or slivered pig's tripe in chilli-oil sauce; or the
preserved duck eggs with green peppers – despite their dodgy
appearance, these eggs taste rich and cheesy. Mains include 'boiled
sea bass with sizzling chilli oil' – this is a bowl of hot oil with a 2-cm
layer of dried red chillies floating on top. The waitress brushes them
to the side and lifts out the fish which has been cooked in the oil –
delicious. Also good are the fire-exploded kidney flowers (it's a way of
scoring the kidney); the dish called pock-marked old woman's bean
curd; and the dry-fried green beans. This food is double-delicious
if you like things hot. Turn up, take advice from the waiters and be
prepared to experiment.

Barrafina

54 Frith Street, W1 ▪ 020 7813 8016

⊖ Tottenham Court Road

▮◎▮ Spanish/tapas

🕐 Mon to Sat 12.00–15.00 & 17.00–23.00

🖥 www.barrafina.com

🖰 all major credit cards ▪ 12.5% optional service added

££ tapas £1.90–£12.50 ▪ mains £5.50–£9.50 sides ▪ £3–£6.80
▪ desserts £4–£6.50 ▪ lowest bottle price £15

✪ Tapas bar behaving like a restaurant

This is the Hart brothers' (see Fino, p. 5) homage to tiny tapas bars
in general and Barcelona favourite Cal Pep in particular. The bar is
small – there are only 23 seats; the menu is short; and many dishes
are cooked to order. Brilliant. In Spanish tapas bars you stop by for
a drink and a couple of dishes and then drift on to repeat the dose.
In Soho things are somewhat different – parties of four turn up
and then spend a happy 90 minutes over a leisurely lunch. The Harts
would like Barrafina to be a tapas bar but the customers want to
use it as a restaurant. So turn up early, secure your seat, and tuck in.
The simple things are great: black foot ham; pimentos de Padrón;
pan tomate. The cold meats are top quality. There are mussels 'a
la plancha' – griddled on an iron sheet – or there may be blue
crabs or razor clams on the specials list. Chiperones – tiny squidlets
deep fried in batter – are crisp and hot. A dish of sweetbreads with
capers is perfectly judged. And the tortillas are worth a detour, firm
outside and runny inside – the perfect Spanish omelette. The food
is fresh and simply cooked. Puds are steady and Spanish. The short
wine list showcases several splendid sherries, then moves on to some
delightful Iberian wines. Service is polished and the atmosphere
agreeably busy.

Bodean's

10 Poland Street, W1 ■ 020 7287 7575

Θ Oxford Circus

📍 North American

🕐 Mon to Fri 12.00–15.00 & 18.00–23.00; Sat 12.00–23.00;
Sun 12.00–22.30

🖰 www.bodeansbbq.com

🖬 all major credit cards ■ 12.5% service added

££ starters £3.95–£6.95 ■ mains £4.95–£16.95 ■ sides £1.95–£4.95
■ desserts £3.25–£4.50 ■ lowest bottle price £11.75

✪ Yankophile rib palace

This is an unashamedly American eatery. Downstairs is a restaurant, complete with strident tartan carpet, wall lights made to look like antelope horns and a red-painted ceiling. Even the service is American gushy and there is an authentic 'commercial' ring to the place, something that you will either love or hate. The starters are sound but not wow – Buffalo chicken wings come either regular, hot or Diablo and they are the best of the bunch, or perhaps the clam chowder. Cut to the chase and get amongst the real smoky barbecued stuff. Baby back ribs (served by the whole or half 'slab') are considered by ribologists to be too tender and a bit of a cop-out. The pork spare ribs (again sold by the whole slab, eleven or twelve ribs; or the half, five or six ribs) are terrific. Mains come with average coleslaw and pretty good beans. Fries are good and crisp. The star dish is the beef back ribs – a Fred Flintstone dish with large flat bones, this is dry and chewy. Very good. There are other delicacies such as Boston butt, a pulled pork sandwich, but only the ribs will stick to your ribs. Puds tread the ice cream and pie route, while to drink there is a flotilla of different Bloody Marys, wine or beer. Happily, this place is very child-friendly and there is usually some sort of enticing deal on offer.

→ For branches, see index or website

Busaba Eathai

106–110 Wardour Street, W1 ■ 020 7255 8686

⊖ Piccadilly Circus/Tottenham Court Road

🍽 Thai

🕐 Mon to Thurs 12.00–22.45; Fri & Sat 12.00–23.15; Sun 12.00–21.45

🖰 all major credit cards ■ no service added

££ mains £5.80–£10 ■ sides £1.50–£7.50 ■ lowest bottle price £14.30

✪ Easy Thai, by the bowlful

This site was once a bank, but former customers stumbling into 106 Wardour Street would be more than a little surprised by this dark, designery and implacably trendy Thai canteen. This place serves decent Thai food at low prices, and with consummate lack of pretension. For all the cod philosophy, this is a jolly and energetic restaurant and you will probably have a very good time. There's no booking so there may be queuing, and the tables are large so there may be sharing. Food, grouped into categories, veers towards one-pot dishes, and vegetarians are particularly well served. If you want starters you need to peruse the side dishes. Choose from such things as po-pea jay, which are vegetable spring rolls; or fishcakes; or Thai calamari, which are not unlike everyone else's calamari. There are curries: Mussaman duck curry; stargazer monkfish green curry; green chicken curry; green vegetable curry; and aromatic butternut pumpkin curry. You'll find genuine Thai veg, such as pea aubergines, sweet basil and lime leaves, although dishes do tend to be on the sweet side. Or there's phad Thai, and thom yam chicken. Stir-fries include chargrilled duck in tamarind sauce with Chinese broccoli; ginger beef; and chargrilled cod with lemongrass and tamarind sauce. The power juice phenomenon has reached Busaba. Nam polamai is organic, and combines carrot, apple and celery with dandelion and nettle extract. Good health to you.

→ For branches, see index

Café Boheme

13–17 Old Compton Street, W1 ▪ 020 7734 0623

⊖ Leicester Square

⑩ French

⏱ Mon to Sat 08.00–03.00; Sun 08.00–24.00

⌐ www.cafeboheme.co.uk

⊟ all major credit cards ▪ 12.5% optional service added

££ starters £4–£11 ▪ mains £11–£17 ▪ sides £3.50 ▪ desserts £5
▪ lowest bottle price £15

✪ Bohemian rhapsody

Anyone pining for France and those bustling Brasseries that biff
out decent food and drink throughout the day and throughout the
night as well will be pleasantly surprised to find one in the heart
of Soho. The menu here is the brainchild of Henry Harris, who was
most recently at Racine and bears all the hallmarks of an experienced
Francophile. There's a magnificent zinc bar, a nest of rooms, informal
décor and businesslike service. The starters range from an expertly
made terrine served (as is the vogue) in a small Kilner jar; to a salad
Lyonnaise; eggs 'en cocotte'; soupe de poisson; rosette de Lyon;
snails; mussels; and oysters. There's one section of the menu devoted
to sandwiches, such as merguez baguette and frites, and another to
tartines – try Bayonne ham and celeriac remoulade on toasted pain
Poilaine. Main course dishes are a roll-call of bistro classics: lapin à
la moutarde comes with a brilliant mustard sauce, agreeably hot;
there's coq au vin; a whole gurnard served 'Grenobloise'; or lamb
gigot with flageolet beans. If you are 'going for it' there is large and
impressive chateaubriand which comes with sauce Béarnaise. Due
to our archaic licensing laws, you must eat something if you want
to drink here in the small hours. That's no hardship, however – a
Croque Monsieur and a bottle from the gently priced all-French wine
list will be most restorative.

Cha Cha Moon

15 Ganton Street, W1 ■ 020 7297 9800

Oxford Circus

Chinese/noodles

Mon to Thurs 12.00–23.00; Fri & Sat 12.00–23.30; Sun 12.00–22.00

all major credit cards ■ 10% optional service added for parties of 5 or more

££ soup noodle £3.50 ■ lao mian £3.50 ■ cold noodle £3.50 ■ wok dishes £3.50 ■ sides £3.50 ■ 250ml wine £4.90

NB prices to be revised in June

✪ Cheap, cheerful and delicious

Cha Cha Moon is the latest brainchild of Alan Yau (whose battle honours include Wagamama, p. 14; Busaba Eathai, p. 154; and Yauatcha, p. 169). So it's no surprise that this place was busy from opening day in May 2008. The resto seats 160 or so, no bookings are taken, and the layout is mainly benches and refectory tables with some stools at high counters. The elegant bamboo ceiling has its own humidifying system to stop it drying out and cracking – this level of attention to detail is a Yau trademark. The food is both remarkably cheap and remarkably simple. There are ten soup noodle dishes – roast duck comes with wolfberry, pack choi and wonton noodles; six 'lao mian' dishes – jasmin-tea smoked chicken, bean sprouts, spring onion and shrimp roe noodle; one cold noodle dish – smoked chicken, cucumber, red onion, ground fried fish and a spicy sesame dressing; eight wok finished dishes including old favourites like Singapore noodle and beef ho fun; plus sides ranging from wonton and spring rolls to greens with oyster sauce and a very good spring onion pancake. Pitch up, get a seat, order a deep bowlful of interesting stuff, slurp it up, pay the puny bill and leave. Check out the soft drinks list: Afri cola; salted lemon Sprite; Boylan black cherry soda or a particular favourite, San bitter – like a radioactive Campari and soda.

Chowki

2–3 Denman Street, W1 ■ 020 7439 1330

⊖ Piccadilly Circus

⑩ Indian

⊕ Mon to Sat 12.00–23.30; Sun 12.00–22.30

⌁ www.chowki.com

🖯 all major credit cards ■ no service added

££ starters £3.25–£4.50 ■ mains & thalis £7.95–£13.95
■ sides £2.25–£2.95 ■ desserts £2.95 ■ set lunches £4.25–£9.75
■ regional feasts £14.95 (3 courses) ■ lowest bottle price £9.75

★ Regional Indian dishes, un-Piccadilly prices

Kuldeep Singh is the head chef behind Chowki and he was also the
mainspring of Mela (see p. 32). Chowki is a large, cheap restaurant
serving authentic home-style food in stylish surroundings. The menu
changes every month in order to feature three different regions of
India. Thus April might feature the North-West Frontier, Lucknow,
and Goa, then by June it could be Kashmir or Maharashtra. Over the
course of a year Chowki showcases 36 different regional styles of
food. All the dishes are authentic and all come with accompaniments.
Chowki has 120 seats spread across three dining areas, but you'll
still probably have to wait for a table at peak times. There are three
or four starters and three or four mains from each region. When the
menu showcases the cuisine of Rajasthan, Hyderabad and Mangalore,
starters might include an epic dish of Rajasthani quail; dumplings
stuffed with banana from Hyderabad; and prawns marinated in
tamarind. Mains follow the lead and come with an appropriate
vegetable and the correct rice or bread. From Hyderabad comes a
sour mutton stew. From Mangalore there might be a dish of chicken
cooked with coconut, or a mackerel poached in spice paste. All the
dishes have the unmistakable stamp of homely cooking – rich, simple,
appetising flavours. Service is friendly and this is a comfortable,
modern place. Finding anywhere this good – and this cheap – within
earshot of Piccadilly Circus is little short of miraculous.

Dehesa

25 Ganton Street, W1 ■ 020 7494 4170

⊖ Oxford Circus

🍽 Spanish/Italian

🕙 Mon to Wed 12.00–23.00; Thurs to Fri 09.00–23.00; Sat 10.00–23.00; Sun 11.00–17.00

🖰 www.dehesa.co.uk

🗗 all major credit cards ■ no service added

££ meat tapas £5.50–£7.25 ■ fish tapas £4–£6.75 ■ veg tapas £3.25–£6.50 ■ charcuterie £2.25–£17 ■ cheese £3–£8 ■ lowest bottle price £14.50

✪ Happy as a pig in a meadow

This place is an offshoot of the Salt Yard (see p. 12). To make things clear, due to the eccentricities of our licensing laws, this is not a bar where you can get food, but it is a place to eat where you can accompany your meal with a drink. Thus in a street awash with places selling alcohol you cannot have a drink at Dehesa unless you have a 'table meal' – sometimes you wish that our lawmakers would just grow up. Dehesa is the Spanish name for the 'meadows' where the fabled pigs snuffle about putting on the silky white fat that makes them into fabled hams. At this restaurant you can compare the relative merits of black foot Iberico ham and prosciutto, or you can try a host of different Spanish and Italian cured meats and sausages. You can also try various tapas, which are done well here. There may be a roast duck breast with mustard fruits; salt cod croquetas with Romesco sauce; baby violet artichokes cooked on a plancha and served with mint; or, in season, courgette flowers with Monte Ebro cheese and honey. These are delicious and delicate options, perfect for mulling over with a glass of sherry. The array of cheeses is also formidable: gorgonzola; truffled pecorino; taleggio; payoyo, la Peral. No bookings are taken here and the hot tapas are not available all the time. Best to check.

Diner

18 Ganton Street, W1 ■ 020 7287 8962

⊖ Oxford Circus

🍴 North American/burgers

🕐 Mon to Sat 10.30–24.30; Sun 10.00–24.00

🖰 www.thedinersoho.com

🗄 all major credit cards ■12.5% optional service added

££ burgers £5–£7.50 ■ sandwiches & dogs £5.50–£7
■ blue plates £5–£8.50 ■ salads £6–£8.50 ■ sides £2.50–£3
■ desserts £3.80–£4.20 ■ lowest bottle price £13.50

✪ Transatlantic menu arrives via Shoreditch

The first link in this fledgling chain was the Diner in Curtain Road, which took over a site formerly occupied by a rather good, but often empty, Bourgeois French restaurant. Strangely, the good folk of Shoreditch clearly prefer hamburgers, as the Diner is doing well. A decent hamburger restaurant is an asset to any locale and to find one in the heart of tourist territory is a definite bonus. The Diner is comfortable and good at what it does. Burgers range from original; to bacon cheeseburger; a double decker; a 'Californian' topped with Monterey Jack cheese (comfortably the world's least inspiring cheese); a Mexican burger with chilli; and some oddities like a fish burger made from salmon or a mushroom burger. The menu section on sandwiches and dogs makes welcome reading – try classics like an open meatloaf sandwich; a bacon chilli cheese dog; or a Philly cheese steak sandwich. Or go for a 'blue plate special' – as well as onion soup or bowl of chilli you could feast on the steak burrito, which comes with a hot chipotle salsa and jalape-o sauce. Sides are worth checking out – sauerkraut; refried beans; chilli cheese fries. This diner may be a long way from the USA but it serves up pretty authentic food. Watch out for the 'hardshakes' – the one named Colonel Parker teams Bourbon, vanilla ice cream and Skippy's peanut butter.

The Gay Hussar
2 Greek Street, W1 ■ 020 7437 0973

⊖ Tottenham Court Road

🍴 Hungarian

🕐 Mon to Sat 12.15–14.30 & 17.30–22.45

🖰 www.gayhussar.co.uk

🖦 all major credit cards ■ 12.5% optional service added

££ starters £3.80–£6.85 ■ mains £9.50–£22.50 ■ sides £2.90–£3.95
■ desserts £4.25–£5.50 ■ prix fixe lunch £16.50 (2 courses) & £18.50
(3 courses) ■ lowest bottle price £14.25

✪ Unashamedly old-fashioned power lunchery

The ground-floor dining room of The Gay Hussar stretches before
you like an old-style railway carriage – there are banquettes, there are
waiters in dinner jackets, there is panelling and the walls are covered
with political caricatures. The Gay Hussar is the real thing, right down
to the faded photo of a naked Christine Keeler. Perhaps the politicos
like the food, which is solid, dependable, comfortable and tasty. It
can also be good value, especially if you stick to the set lunch. In
the evening dishes get a trifle more complicated, but the Hungarian
specialities are still to the fore. Starters include a fish terrine with
beetroot sauce and cucumber salad, and hási pástétom – a fine
goose and pork pâté. But the most famous (a house speciality that
has featured in various novels) is chilled wild cherry soup, which is
like a thin, bitterish, sourish yogurt and is rather good. Main courses
are blockbusters. Try the hortobágyi palacsinta, a pancake filled with
a finely chopped veal goulash and then sealed, deep-fried and served
with creamed spinach; or the kacsa sült – crisply roast duck with red
cabbage. There are also fish dumplings, which are served with rice
and a creamy dill sauce. Or cigány gyors tal, a 'gypsy fry-up' of pork,
bacon, onions and peppers plus a good shake of paprika. Puds are
also fierce – poppy-seed strudel comes with vanilla ice cream, while
options like chestnut purée have real substance.

Imli

167–169 Wardour Street, W1 ■ 020 7287 4243 &

⊖ Oxford Circus

⦿ Indian

⏰ daily 12.00–23.00

🌐 www.imli.co.uk

💳 all major credit cards except AmEx ■ 12.5% optional service added

££ dishes £2.95–£4.95 ■ mains £4.50–£8.95 ■ sides 50p–£1.85
■ desserts £2.95–£3.25 ■ set lunch £7.50 ■ set dinner £14.50
■ tasting menus (2 or more) £14.50–£22.50 ■ lowest bottle price
£13.95

⭐ Graze away at this slick Indian

Sharing a number of different curries has long been the modus
operandi of the curry house. At Imli, matters are formalised and a
sophisticated grazing menu holds sway. Mercifully, the prices are
wholly reasonable and allowing three or four dishes per person will
leave you happy if not belly-busted. The food is described as Indian
tapas. The menu headers are rather coy, but persevere. From 'light
and refreshing' the spiced potato cakes are very simple and good;
the over-stuffed samosas are delightful; and the 'banana dosa' –
which seems to be the potato cake dish but made with bananas – is
delicious. Under 'New Traditions' you'll find chicken wraps – breads
flecked with fenugreek and stuffed with chicken, or a seafood
platter – good crisp squid rings, a commendable fishcake and some
very large prawns. Undermining the grazing idyll, some of the
'Signature Dishes' come with a choice of paratha or rice. These are
well-balanced curries – a dish called Southern lamb curry comes in a
rich and finely textured sauce with coconut, while Goan pork is rich
and red with enough chilli heat to give the nod towards the fabled
vindalho. Puds feature some moody ices, such as raspberry and black
salt sorbet. This is a large, elegant restaurant with plenty of attentive
staff and high standards in the kitchen. Only by being a busy place
will the management be able to keep the prices so reasonable, so
plan your visit now.

Kulu Kulu

76 Brewer Street, W1 ■ 020 7734 7316

⊖ Oxford Circus/Piccadilly Circus

🍴 Japanese

🕐 Mon to Fri 12.00–14.30 & 17.00–22.00; Sat 12.00–15.45 &
17.00–22.00

🗃 Mastercard, Visa ■ no service added

££ sushi £1.20–£3.60 ■ sushi combinations £4.80–£9.60
■ mains £12.80–£30 ■ desserts £1.80 ■ lowest bottle price £12

⭐ Well-made sushi at conveyor-belt prices

Serving good sushi without being impersonal or intimidating
is a difficult trick for any conveyor-belt sushi restaurant, but Kulu
Kulu pulls it off. This place is light and airy while the atmosphere is
Japanese utilitarian. In front of you is a plastic tub of gari (the rather
delicious pickled ginger), a bottle of soy and a small box containing
disposable wooden chopsticks. The plates come round on the kaiten,
or conveyor, and are coded by design rather than colour, which could
prove deceptive. Do not worry too much, as prices are reasonable.
All the usual nigiri sushi are here, and the fish is particularly fresh
and well presented. Choose from maguri, or tuna; amaebi, or sweet
shrimp; salmon roe; hotategai, or scallops – very tender, very sweet.
Futomaki is a Californian cone-shaped roll with tuna. The top plates
tend to be ritzier fishes such as belly tuna. As well as the sushi, the
conveyor parades some little bowls of hot dishes. One worth looking
out for combines strips of fried fish skin with a savoury vegetable
purée. It counts as a basic sushi, as does the bowl of miso soup.
For the indecisive, mixed tempura is good and crisp and there's also
mixed sashimi. To drink there is everything from oolong tea to Kirin
beer by way of a special sake made in the Rocky Mountains of the
good ol' US of A.

Leon

35 Great Marlborough Street, W1 ■ 020 7437 5280

⊖ Oxford Circus

🍴 Modern British (they say Mediterranean)

🕐 Mon to Fri 08.00–22.30; Sat 09.30–22.30; Sun 10.30–18.30

🖰 www.leonrestaurants.co.uk

🖬 all major credit cards ■ no service added

££ breakfast £1.90–£5.50 ■ starters & sides £1.80–£4.30
   ■ wraps £2.95–£3.60 ■ big dishes £3.95–£5.50
   ■ desserts £2.50–£4.90 ■ lowest bottle price £15

✪ Fast food, but wholesome

Imagine a typical Carnaby Street fast-food joint: the bright lights, garish uniforms and ghastly food – then forget all that. Leon is from another planet and deserves your support. As soon as this place opened it collected a hatful of awards from judges grateful that at last someone was prepared to serve good food fast. Starting with a really decent breakfast – dry-cured English bacon, two free-range soft-boiled eggs, roast tomatoes, grilled mushrooms, hand-made wholemeal toast and home-made tomato ketchup or brown sauce – the attention to detail, and the care taken sourcing the ingredients, is impressive. The décor is a blend of the stylish and the utilitarian. The lunch and dinner menu is written seasonally and offers dishes in a variety of sizes and styles. The food is an amalgam of modern British and Mediterranean influences, so Moroccan meatballs nudge a charcuterie plate and chicken nuggets (but home-made, from real chicken – there's a shock). There are also 'Superfood Salads', like the warm mushroom and tarragon fish superfood salad, which is subtitled 'white fish from sustainable shoals, baked with sautéed mushrooms and freshly chopped tarragon, broccoli, baby spinach, toms, alfalfa, seeds, rocket and aioli'. For a tad more indulgence look no further than the puds section and the Leon hot Valrhona chocolate brownie with organic Herefordshire ice cream. You can eat well, and fairly cheaply, at Leon – while basking in the knowledge that the food is PC.

→ For branches, see index or website

Masala Zone

9 Marshall Street, W1 ■ 020 7287 9966

⊖ Oxford Circus/Piccadilly Circus

🍴 Indian

🕐 Mon to Fri 12.00–15.30 & 17.30–23.00; Sat 12.30–23.00;
Sun 12.30–15.30 & 17.00–22.30

🖰 www.realindianfood.com

🖶 all major credit cards ■ 10% service added

££ starters £3.95–£6.20 ■ thalis £7.40–£11.95 ■ mains £5.95–£8.95
■ sides 95p–£2.50 ■ desserts £2.75–£3.25 ■ lowest bottle price £10.95

✪ Good-value Indian fast food, quite at home in Soho

Masala Zone is impossible to pigeonhole. The food is Indian, but
modern Indian, with a commendable emphasis on healthy eating
– as would be the norm in India. And because it's an authentically
Indian menu, there's a long list of attractive vegetarian options. The
dining room is smart and large with a handsome mural by visiting
tribal artists, but the prices are low. The fast-food dishes tend to
be the roadside snacks of Mumbai. In all, this is an informal, stylish
and friendly place, serving food that is simple and delicious. The
menu begins with small plates of street food. There are sev puris,
dahi puris, samosas and a particularly fine aloo tikki chaat. Pick
several dishes and graze your way along – at these prices, it doesn't
matter if there's the occasional miss among the hits. At lunch there
are splendid Indian sandwiches, including a large masala chicken
burger and a Bombay layered-vegetable grilled sandwich. There are
also half a dozen curries that are well balanced and richly flavoured
– served simply, with rice. But you should move straight on to the
thalis, which are the authentic option. At Masala Zone these are steel
trays with eight little bowls containing a vegetarian snack (to whet
the appetite), a curry, lentils, a root vegetable, a green vegetable,
yogurt, bread, rice and pickles. You just choose the base curry and a
complete, balanced meal arrives at your table.

→ For branches, see index or website

Ping Pong

45 Great Marlborough Street, W1 ■ 020 7851 6969   &

⊖ Oxford Circus

🍽 Chinese/dim sum

🕐 Mon to Sat 12.00–24.00; Sun 12.00–22.30

🖱 www.pingpongdimsum.com

🖩 all major credit cards ■ 12.5% optional service added

££ dim sum £2.99–£4.50 ■ set lunch £10.99–£11.99
   ■ desserts £2.20–£3.50 ■ 'lazy Sundays' menu £17.50
   ■ lowest bottle price £13.50

✪ Plenty of seats at this modern dumpling factory

Ping Pong is a cavernous dim sum palace. There are two floors
and the chef twirling the noodles, or his colleagues steaming the
baskets, provide a floorshow for diners. There are seats at tables and
stools at sinuous counters; all is black and stylish. This place is like
a cocktail bar with a strange emphasis on food. On the one hand
the food is 'sound to good' and most of the dumplings are priced
very reasonably. On the other hand (less good) dim sum purists will
find some of the wrappers a bit thick, and some dumplings a bit
lacklustre. But Ping Pong is a jolly place, service is brisk and efficient,
and those prices go a long way to calming the inner gastronome.
Roast pork puffs are good (maybe not quite as good as the venison
puffs at Yauatcha, see p. 169), but old favourites like pork siu mai,
char sui pau, and vegetable spring roll are sound enough. Prawn
toast is reinterpreted and seems less greasy than the trad version.
Crispy prawn balls are surrounded by a sphere of deep-fried noodles.
There is Chinese beer on draught, but the most elegant refreshment
is the jasmine flower tea – you get a glass containing a ball of leaves
and when they pour on the boiling water it 'flowers' and unravels. As
they add to an ever-increasing chain of branches, the proprietors can
confirm that they have found a niche.

→ For branches, see index or website

Quo Vadis

26–29 Dean Street, W1 ■ 020 7437 9585

⊖ Leicester Square

†◎† British

🕘 Mon to Sat 12.00–14.45 & 17.00–22.45

🖱 www.quovadissoho.co.uk

🖃 all major credit cards ■ 12.5% optional service added

££ starters £6–£16.50 ■ salads/pasta/eggs £7.50–£16 ■ grills £16–£22
■ fish £16.20–£25 ■ sides £3–£4 ■ desserts £6.50–£7
■ lowest bottle price £17

✪ Celebrate the rebirth of a classic

Leoni's Quo Vadis opened in 1926 and quickly built up a reputation
for style and glamour. Fast forward 82 years and once again it is
buzzing. The Hart brothers (see Fino, p. 5, and Barrafina, p. 152)
re-opened Quo Vadis in June 2008 after a major, but sympathetic,
refit. They have done a terrific job. The 1920s design elements
have been retained and merged with modern comfort. The place is
slick once more and, best of all, the menu is British – one of those
all- embracing, all-enticing, super Brasserie menus. The Harts may
have made their name with Spanish restaurants but they grew up
in a country house hotel in Rutland and Quo Vadis has a good idea
where it's going, with carefully sourced British produce that is simply
cooked – very commendable. Unfussy starters like crab mayonnaise;
razor clams griddled with garlic and parsley; asparagus and butter;
or steak tartare are done very well indeed. There is good meat, such
as a 28-day aged Lincoln Red rib of beef for two served with chips
(the chips are good here) or 'veal sweetbread with tartar sauce'. This
dish is a joy – perfectly cooked, buttery, tender, and mercifully plain,
it might even be 'best ever'. Then there are roasts – a squab pigeon
is magnificent – and fish, such as skate with capers and lemon. Puds
like summer pudding and treacle tart are exemplary. Service is slick
and there's a sympathetic wine list.

Richard Corrigan at Lindsay House

21 Romilly Street, W1 ■ 020 7439 0450

⊖ Leicester Square

🍴 British

🕐 Mon to Fri 12.00–14.30 & 18.00–23.00; Sat 18.00–23.00

🖰 www.lindsayhouse.co.uk

🖯 all major credit cards ■ 12.5% optional service added

££ starters £9–£16 ■ mains £14–£24 ■ desserts £8
    ■ dinner £56 (3 courses) ■ tasting menu £68 (6 courses)
    ■ 'Garden' menu £68 (6 courses) ■ pre-theatre £27 (3 courses
    18.00–20.00) ■ lowest bottle price £29

✪ The best of British, and Irish, cooking

Richard Corrigan is an 'original' and the Lindsay House was the
jumping off point for an empire that includes Bentley's (see p.
125), a hotel in Dublin and an upscale presence on Park Lane that
will open after this guide has gone to press. At the Lindsay the
service is attentive and the food is very good indeed. The menus are
uncomplicated and change regularly to keep in step with what is
available at the market. If the à la carte intimidates, then the epic
six-course tasting menu is a very tempting way to relinquish control.
Starters surprise – warm poached English asparagus with poached
duck egg, morels and foie gras foam – or are traditional with a twist,
such as croquette of crubeens, salad of lady's Smock, soft egg yolk
dressing. Or how about baby squid with pressed pork shoulder? Main
courses follow the same ground rules (or lack of them): fillet of hake
poached in almond milk; or Reggie Johnson's magnificent organic
chicken from Goosnargh, which is 'butter poached' with roast
ballotine of the leg and boudin blanc. The puddings may include
poached rhubarb and Alfonso mango or a chocolate and hazelnut
tart with vanilla ice cream. The wine list is extensive and expensive,
and is particularly well matched to the cooking style, with plenty of
serious reds to complement the rich dishes. One thing distinguishes
the cuisine at the Lindsay House – Corrigan's deft touch with hearty
ingredients.

So Restaurant

3—4 Warwick Street, W1 ■ 020 7292 0767

⊖ Piccadilly Circus

🍴 Japanese

🕑 Mon to Fri 12.00–15.00 & 17.00–23.00; Sat 12.00–23.00

🖱 www.sorestaurant.com

🖯 all major credit cards ■ 12.5% service added

££ starters £6.50–£10 ■ tempura £6–£14 ■ sushi £2.50–£3.20
(per piece) ■ sashimi £2.50–£3.20 ■ mains £11–£20
■ desserts £6.50–£7.50 ■ lowest bottle price £23

✪ Comfortable contemporary Japanese dining

So Restaurant walks a fine line between being modern (the menu
changes with the seasons, the décor is bright) and more formal.
There is a 'low' table for diners whose knees are up to it and the
shelves around the room are crammed with Japanese paraphernalia.
The menu promises 'hints of European cuisine' and 'dishes cooked
over volcanic rocks from Mount Fuji'. Despite these somewhat
complex multiple signals the food here is good and the service
exemplary, being both charming and efficient. Tebasaki are chicken
wings but in this instance a French black leg chicken's wings — very
good; there's Scottish salmon 'mi-cuit'; a duck and walnut salad;
or very decent squid tempura, with tender squid and featherlight
batter. This is a good menu to explore and nobody seems to mind if
you order an eclectic array of dishes. Main course options range from
pan-fried foie gras served on a bed of rice; to grilled lobster; grilled
venison with hot pepper sauce; or black cod in Saiyko miso. The nigiri
sushi is well made and gently priced. Another welcome initiative is the
flight of four different sakes complete with informative tasting notes
— a good move and good value as well. This is a friendly restaurant
and the atmosphere is much enhanced by the helpful staff. Ignore the
lime green paint and concentrate on the good, well-presented food.

Yauatcha

15 Broadwick Street, W1 ■ 020 7494 8888

⊖ Piccadilly Circus

|○| Dim sum/teahouse

⏱ (teahouse) Mon to Sun 11.00–23.45; Sun 11.00–22.30; (dim sum)
Mon to Sat 12.00–23.30; Sun 12.00–22.30

🖰 all major credit cards ■ 12.5% optional service added

££ teas £3–£29.50 ■ dim sum £3–£38 ■ desserts £6–£13.50
■ set tea (12.30–18.00) £19, £26 with a glass of champagne
■ lowest bottle price £24

✪ Long on dim sum, long on style

On the one hand, the critics rave about Yauatcha and on the
other the snipers snipe about a booking policy that only secures your
table for 90 minutes. This place offers an elegant designery take on
dim sum from Alan Yau, the man who set up Hakkasan (see p. 6),
and the food is amazingly, blisteringly good. The little dishes here
sweep effortlessly to a 'top notch' rating, and if you cannot stuff
yourself greedily in 90 minutes you should be ashamed. It is hard to
oppose tea by way of accompaniment – there's a lady who is a kind
of tea sommelier and there are half a dozen regional and specialised
Chinese teas, some of which are stratospherically expensive. There
are dumplings – all are good, some are amazing, most come three to
a portion. Chinese chive dumpling is a delicate green pastry basket
with a savoury middle; prawn and enoki mushroom dumpling has a
thin, translucent casing; box dumpling is round and solid, with pastry
outer and savoury middle; five-spice roll is like an über sausage roll,
meaty with crisp exterior; pork and spring-onion cake is ring-shaped,
with light pastry crust and rich filling; venison puffs are the best puff
pastry with a meaty filling. Don't worry, choose what you like and you
will not be disappointed. At ground level there is a tearoom, which
offers an appealing combo of fine Chinese teas and super slick French
pâtisserie.

Yming

35–36 Greek Street, W1 ■ 020 7734 2721

⊖ Leicester Square

🍴 Chinese

🕐 Mon to Sat 12.00–23.45

🖥 www.yminglondon.com

🖪 all major credit cards ■ 10% optional service added

££ starters £3–£11 ■ mains £8.50–£26 ■ rice & noodles £1.90–£6.50
■ set menu (until 18.00) £10 ■ lowest bottle price £11

✪ Chinatown's bridgehead in Soho

Yming is a calm sort of place. The mint green walls and unhurried service give you confidence, which is fair enough, as this is an old-established restaurant. It's a classy place – you could take your bank manager to lunch here and he wouldn't feel slighted. The menu tends to concentrate on the more familiar dishes, but there are one or two excursions into less familiar territory. Several years ago Yming adopted the interesting strategy of annotating the menu to say just which critic liked which dish. It's more low-key now but the double-braised pork in a pot is famous as the particular favourite of Matthew Fort, Jay Rayner and Jonathan Meades (though Jonathan stopped writing resto pieces some time ago, which means this information may be a little dated). It's a good dish, rich and porky. Squid with chilli and salt is done well; there are three kinds of spare ribs; sesame prawn toast; and various lettuce wraps. The mains include some interesting dishes: Empress beef is slow-cooked flank with star anise while Zhacai delight is shredded pork with chilli and preserved vegetables. Or there's Dongan chicken – a sweet and sour dish that originated in Hunan – as well as standards like lemon chicken. There's an underlying formality about Yming that makes it a very soothing place to eat, and if you fancy eating Chinese while avoiding the hurly burly of Chinatown it's a good option.

Yo! Sushi

52 Poland Street, W1 ■ 020 7287 0443

Piccadilly Circus/Oxford Circus

Japanese

daily 12.00–23.00

www.yosushi.co.uk

all major credit cards ■ no service added

££ sushi/sashimi/maki £1.70–£5 ■ box sets £4–£8 ■ desserts £5
■ lowest bottle price £12.50

⭐ Let the sushi come to you

This was the first Yo! Sushi to open, with what was then a largely
new concept – kaiten or conveyor-belt sushi. It's a place of dark
wood and comfortable booths, and over the years the food has been
refined and continues to be more consistent than the hype would
have you suspect. Plates are colour-coded according to their price,
and when satiated you simply call for a plate count, and your bill is
prepared. You sit at the counter with a little waiters' station in front
of you. There's gari (pickled ginger), soy and wasabi, plus some little
dishes and a forest of wooden chopsticks. By way of refreshment,
Kirin beer, a small warm sake and unlimited amounts of Japanese tea
vie for your attention. The list of cooked dishes that can be ordered
has been expanded, so you'll need to integrate your choices with
plates from the belt. If in doubt, ask. The sushi range from roasted
pepper and avocado; through salmon, crabstick and avocado; tuna,
grey mullet and salmon skin; and so on up to yellowtail and fatty
tuna – which carry a warning that they are on offer 'as available'.
There are about twenty different maki rolls (with vegetarians well
catered for), at all prices. The ten different sashimi and five different
gunkan all command the higher orange and pink prices. Yo! Sushi is a
practical, easy and inexpensive place to eat.

→ For branches, see index or website

Zilli Fish

36–40 Brewer Street, W1 ■ 020 7734 8649

⊖ Piccadilly Circus

🍽 Italian/fish

🕒 Mon to Sat 12.00–23.30

🖰 www.zillialdo.com

🖫 all major credit cards ■ 12.5% optional service added

££ starters £7–£13.50 ■ mains £8.50–£30 ■ sides £3.25–£4
■ desserts £6.50 ■ pre- & post-theatre £20 (2 courses) & £25 (3 courses) ■ lowest bottle price £16.50

✪ Telly chef cooks fish for glitterati

Bright, brittle and brash, Zilli Fish is a part of Aldo Zilli's empire, which extends to books, telly stardom and anything else that buoys up the profile. You can see into the surprisingly calm kitchen through a large window as you walk along Brewer Street. Inside, the restaurant serves a modern Italianate fish menu to London's media workers and the rest of the young Soho crowd. Tables are close and everything is conducted at a racy pace. Not ideal for a secret conversation or for plighting your troth, unless you want the whole place to cheer you on. The starters here are an attractive bunch: pan-fried squid with sweet chilli sauce; mussels arrabbiata with bruschetta; tuna carpaccio with rocket and Parmesan. Then there are the pasta dishes, such as penne arrabiatta and spaghetti vongole (clams with Italian cherry tomatoes and basil). The menu goes on to feature a section entitled 'Fresh from Billingsgate Market'. These are dishes such as whole roast lemon sole; spaghettini with fresh lobster; traditional beer-battered cod with fat chips and tartare sauce; or pan-fried sea bass fillet, served with julienne vegetables and grated bottarga. For unrepentant carnivores there is a fillet steak wrapped in pancetta. Puddings include a ricotta and amarena cherry tart with cherry coulis; a home-made tiramisù with Pavesini; and pecorino and Gorgonzola with honey. But for something genuinely excessive, what about 'fried banana spring rolls with white chocolate ice cream'?

→ For branches, see index or website

Victoria and Westminster

Atami

37 Monck Street, SW1 ■ 020 7222 2218

⊖ St James's Park

🍽 Japanese

🕐 Mon to Fri 11.00–15.00 & 17.30–23.00; Sat 17.30–23.00

🔗 www.atamirestaurant.com

🖥 all major credit cards ■ 12.5% optional service added

££ starters £6–£21 ■ sushi/sashimi £2–£4.75 (per piece)
■ mains £13.50–£21.50 ■ sides £3.75 ■ lunch £18 (2 courses)
■ tasting menu £45 (10 courses, dinner only, minimum 2 people)
■ lowest bottle price £23

✪ Japanese chic

Atami is an elegant, modern, surprisingly large Japanese restaurant.
It has a cocktail bar, a platoon of smiley and helpful staff and is
trying hard to banish any lingering tendency for upscale Japanese
restaurants to be seen as intimidating by all but Japanese diners.
The tables are large and plain, the chairs are modern and the floor
is polished concrete. The food is sophisticated, sometimes surprising
and presented with great elegance. There is a sushi counter where
the chefs painstakingly assemble all the old favourites plus some
novelties. Try the foie gras sushi roll – bound with papery nori
and with a foie gras centre, the liver lubricating the rice in a most
delicious manner. Or perhaps the 'new style sashimi' – razor clam
with a ginger spring onion vinaigrette. From the starters the marble
beef with hot oil, tempura chive and ponzu stands out; the crispy
baby squids are crisp but could do with more chilli; or there's Atami
tar tare – avocado, tuna, salmon, sweet shrimp and caviar. From
the special dishes the Chilean sea bass is magnificent – very rich
flesh, tasting almost buttery and complimented by a black truffle
and ponzu sauce. There are also dishes like quail with five-spice and
plum sauce or king crab with yuzu sauce. This is not a cheap place to
dine, but the kitchen is aiming high and dishes are very well thought
through. Treat yourself.

Boisdale

15 Eccleston Street, SW1 ■ 020 7730 6922

⊖ Victoria

🍽 Scottish

🕐 Mon to Fri 12.00–01.00; Sat 19.00–01.00

🖰 www.boisdale.co.uk

🖶 all major credit cards ■ 12.5% service added

££ starters £7.50–£17.50 ■ mains £15–£28.50 ■ sides £3.50–£3.95
   ■ desserts £6.50 ■ Flying Scotsman lunch £14 ■ '1780' menu £18.70
   ■ lowest bottle price £15.95

✪ Braveheart – the restaurant

Ranald Macdonald, who is next in line to be the Chief of Clanranald, owns Boisdale, and if that information gives you a premonition of what the restaurant is like you are probably thinking along the right lines. This is a very Scottish place, strong on hospitality, and with a befuddlingly large range of rare malt whiskies. Fresh produce – correction, fresh *Scottish* produce – rules wherever possible, and it is no wonder that the clubby atmosphere makes this a haven of choice for local businessmen. There are various Boisdale menus: one is a two-course menu with a choice of five starters and five mains. Or there's the 'Flying Scotsman', a limited choice lunch, presumably for people in a rush. Starters range from marinated Orkney herring and mini roast Macsween haggis to dill-marinated Scottish salmon. Main courses veer from crofter's pie to smoked haddock fishcakes to – you've guessed it – roast Macsween haggis. The à la carte includes a good many luxury ingredients. As well as Lochcarnan smoked salmon from South Uist, and Rannoch Moor smoked venison with black truffle dressing, there's a rabbit, pigeon and foie gras terrine with pear chutney. Commendably, the mains feature fresh fish of the day, and fresh offal of the day. There are various Aberdeen Angus beef steaks: fillet with Béarnaise sauce and chips or rib eye with black truffle, pommes Dauphinoise, spinach and wild mushrooms.

→ For branch, see index or website

Cinnamon Club

Old Westminster Library, Great Smith Street, SW1

■ 020 7222 2555

⊖ St James's Park

🍴 Indian

🕓 Mon to Fri 09.30–10.00, 12.00–14.30 & 18.00 to 22.45;
Sat 12.00–14.30 & 18.00–22.45

🖰 www.cinnamonclub.com

🖵 all major credit cards ■ 12.5% optional service added

££ breakfast £10–£16 ■ starters £8–£12 ■ mains £11–£29
■ sides £2.50–£6 ■ desserts £6–£8 ■ prix fixe weekday lunch & pre-/
post-theatre £19 & £22 ■ lowest bottle price £16

✪ Sleek and accomplished modern Indian restaurant

Libraries and restaurants can have a good deal in common.
Lofty ceilings, large doors, old wood floors and plenty of panelling
are just the features you need for a cracking formal eaterie. So it
shouldn't surprise that what was once Westminster Library is now
the Cinnamon Club. The whole operation is elegant, substantial
and very pukka. Service is polished and attentive, the linen is snowy-
white, the cutlery is heavy, the toilets opulent, and there are huge
flower arrangements. The cooking is very good, and each dish offers
a finely judged combination of flavours, every one distinct. There's
an informed wine list. You can even pitch up for a power breakfast
if you're seeking to influence the nearby parliamentary movers
and shakers. And yes, unlikely as it may sound, this is an Indian
restaurant. From the 'Appetisers' section of the menu there's tandoori
halibut in Rajasthani spices; sandalwood-flavoured chicken breast; or
Bengali-style grilled half lobster. Such dishes set the tone. Mains are
also well conceived: spice-crusted tandoori monkfish with tomato
and lemon sauce; or Goan-style wild boar chop with vindaloo sauce
– not something you'd find on the High Street. Go for the basket of
breads as a side dish – a selection of unusual parathas, naans and
rotis. Desserts are elegant: try the warm apple lassi with champagne
granita, or the spiced banana tarte Tatin with a deep-purple berry
sorbet.

The Goring

15 Beeston Place, Grosvenor Gardens, SW1 ▪ 020 7396 9000 ♿

⊖ Victoria

🍴 Very British

🕐 Mon to Fri 07.00–10.00 (breakfast), 12.30–14.30 & 18.00–22.00;
Sat 07.00–10.30 & 19.30–22.30; Sun 07.30–10.30 12.30–14.30 &
18.00–22.00

🖰 www.goringhotel.co.uk

🖵 all major credit cards ▪ 12.5% optional service added

££ lunch £35 (3 courses) ▪ dinner £47.50 (3 courses) ▪ sides £3.75
▪ lowest bottle price £25

⭐ Rule Britannia

The Goring Hotel is a delight. This place has been family run for
generations and is an eccentric antidote to a world increasingly
cluttered with faceless chain hotels. The dining room looks a little
like a hotel dining room although a redesign by Linley perked it up
and added Swarovski crystal chandeliers. The food is unashamedly
British and it is no surprise to hear that young Mr Goring is off in
the Goring Bentley scouring the countryside for new delicacies for
the menu: gull's eggs; elvers; well-aged mutton; British truffles;
and rare British cheeses for the trolley. Such stubborn dedication
deserves recognition. The menu is seasonal and may include starters
like eggs Drumkilbo – a lobster dish that was said to be a favourite
of the late Queen Elizabeth the Queen Mother – or roast marrow
bones with breadcrumbs, parsley and toasted onion bread; a terrine
of duck confit; a glazed Scottish lobster omelette; or something as
simple and seasonal as potato and nettle soup. Main courses also
rely heavily on astute sourcing – wild sea trout, roasted then served
with fennel and clams; braised lambs' hearts with haggis; confit of
Lincolnshire pork belly with hogweed, apple purée and sage sauce; or
perhaps fillet of beef Wellington from the trolley appeals? Puddings
are old-fashioned, nursery-led, self-indulgent, masterpieces. Service
is comfortable and the wine list is extensive enough for the most
classical oenophile.

Hunan

51 Pimlico Road, SW1 ■ 020 7730 5712

⊖ Sloane Square/Victoria

🍴 Chinese

🕑 Mon to Sat 12.30–14.00 & 18.30–23.00

🗗 all major credit cards ■ 12.5% service added

££ à la carte (lunch only): starters £8 ■ mains £8.50–£9.50 ■ sides £7
■ desserts £4 ■ tasting menus £28.80 (lunch) & £38.80 (dinner)
■ lowest bottle price £14

✪ Interesting Chinese food, provided you do as you're told

Hunan is now the domain of Mr Peng, Junior. As you venture into his restaurant you put yourself into his hands, to do with you what he will. You order the boiled dumplings – and the griddle-fried, lettuce-wrapped dumplings turn up, 'because you will like them more'. Peng Junior is following principles established by his father, who developed the tasting menu arrangements. The Hunan 'feast' is a multi-course extravaganza, varied according to the maestro's whims, and it might include pigeon soup. Or goose. Or a dish of cold, marinated octopus. This fine food and attentive service is matched by Hunan's elegant surroundings, but be warned – the prices are Pimlico rather than Chinatown. If you want to defy two generations of Pengs and act knowledgeable, there is an à la carte at lunchtime. Stand-outs include hot and spicy beef; sizzling prawns; braised scallops in Hunan sauce; and spicy braised eggplant. However, for all but the strongest wills, resistance is useless and you'll probably end up with what is described on the menu as 'Hunan's special leave-it-to-us-feast – minimum two persons.' As is says, 'We recommend those not familiar with Hunan cuisine and those who are looking for a wide selection of our favourite and unusual dishes to leave it to us to prepare a special banquet. Many of the dishes are not on the menu'. Even Alexis Gauthier, Roussillon's Michelin-starred head chef (see p. 182), leaves it to the Pengs.

Pomegranates

94 Grosvenor Road, SW1 ▪ 020 7828 6560

☻ Pimlico

🍴 Eclectic/multi-national

🕐 Mon to Sat 12.30–14.00 & 19.00–23.00

🗄 all major credit cards ▪ 12.5% service added

££ starters £6.75–£12.75 ▪ mains £13.75–£24.75 ▪ desserts £6.75
▪ lunch £15.95 (crudités & 2 courses) & £18.95 (3 courses)
▪ dinner £19.95 (crudités & 2 courses) & £22.95 (3 courses)
▪ lowest bottle price £19

✪ Clubby, comfortable and downright eccentric

This basement restaurant is dark, comfortable and resolutely old-fashioned. 'Pistol' pattern cutlery, bentwood chairs and a certain formality about the service. Start with one of Patrick Gwyn-Jones's very serious Bloody Marys. The menu is eclectic and reads pretty much the same as it did in 1974. Starters include Jamaican fish tea (an elegant fish soup); the much-vaunted home-made gravadlax, which is very sound; the escargot and wild mushroom pie; or melon with port. Taramosalata comes with hot pitta bread; there's chicken satay; or fresh terrine of foie gras. Main courses also lead you from cuisine to cuisine with minimum of fuss: crab cakes with sorrel and pea purée; Hong Sui Yeung (crisp breast of lamb) with Sichuan sauce; Welsh salt duck; or West Indian curried goat. There is also a section devoted to Aberdeen Angus beef: a sirloin steak comes with maitre d'Hotel butter and there's a carpet bagger steak – just as it should be, top-quality steak lifted by the iodine tang of oysters. The steak tartare also comes as 'tartare Baltique' – perfectly seasoned steak with the addition of a little finely chopped roll mop herring. This is a real winner and may qualify as 'best ever' steak tartare. Eating here is like eating in an old-established private club that has been frozen in time. You get a personal welcome, interesting dishes and a wine list that is considered and features some quality bottles.

La Poule au Pot

221 Ebury Street, SW1 ▪ 020 7730 7763

⊖ Sloane Square

|⊙| French

🕐 Mon to Fri 12.30–14.30 & 18.45–23.00; Sat 12.30–16.00 & 18.45–23.00; Sun 12.30–16.00 & 18.45–22.00

🖻 all major credit cards ▪ 12.5% service added

££ starters £6.75–£17 ▪ mains £15–£24.50 ▪ sides £3.50–£4.75 ▪ desserts £4.50–£6 ▪ prix fixe lunch £17.75 (2 courses) & £19.75 (3 courses) ▪ lowest bottle price £18

⭐ La belle France – as found in Chelsea

La Poule au Pot is a bastion of France in England, and has been for more than three decades. What's more, several of the staff have worked here for most of that time, and the restaurant itself has hardly changed at all, with its huge dried-flower baskets and comfortable rustic atmosphere. You are in trouble here if you don't understand at least some French, as the waiters have a Gallic insouciance and delight in incomprehension. A small dish of crudités in herb vinaigrette is set down as a bonne bouche. Different fresh breads come in huge chunks. The menu is deceptive, as there are usually several additional, fresh, daily specials. As a starter, the nine escargots deliver classic French authenticity with plenty of garlic and herbs. The soupe de poisson is not the commonly served thick soup, but a refined clear broth with chunks of sole and scallop, plus prawns and mussels. There's a classic French onion soup. A main course of bifteck frites brings a perfectly cooked, French-cut steak with red-hot chips. The gigot aux flageolets is pink and tender, with beans that are well flavoured and not overcooked. There's calves' liver, and carré d'agneau à l'ail – rack of lamb with garlic. And, of course, there's poule au pot. The pudding menu features standards such as crème brûlée – huge, served in a rustic dish, and classically good. The wine list is unadventurous.

The Quilon

41 Buckingham Gate, SW1 ■ 020 7821 1899

☻ Victoria

🍴 Indian

🕐 Mon to Fri 12.00–14.30 & 18.00–23.00; Sat 18.00–23.00; Sun 12.30–14.30 & 18.00–22.30

🔗 www.thequilonrestaurant.com

🗗 all major credit cards ■ 12.5% service added

££ starters £5.50–£8.25 ■ mains £8.50–£23 ■ sides £2–£8.50
■ desserts £5–£5.25 ■ prix fixe lunch £12.95 & £15.95
■ lowest bottle price £19.50

⭐ Classy South Indian cooking

The Quilon is a sophisticated restaurant. As it is part of the Taj hotels group, this should come as no surprise, yet words like sophisticated and élite are still the exception rather than the rule when the subject is Indian restos. Given that this restaurant is tacked onto the end of a hotel, that the dining room is large, and that the plush décor is rather anodyne, it has a very good feel to it. The staff are helpful and there is an appreciative buzz. The stellar bargain is the set lunch, which is priced very keenly indeed. Starters include some interesting South Indian delicacies: a Cochin mixed seafood broth; karvari fried fish – very crisp and very dry outside, firm within; pepper shrimps – agreeably spicy; and crab cakes – rich with curry leaves and ginger. As befits any Keralan restaurant, when you come to choose main courses fish is a good option. There is 'baked black cod', a truly splendid dish with the black cod (not an Indian species by several thousand miles) marinated in a tamarind mixture that accentuates its butteriness. The pistachio lamb curry is good and rich. The chicken masala is admirably intense and dry. Veg dishes are very strong – a raw jackfruit thoran is perfectly balanced with coconut and curry leaves. The breads are good as well, particularly the flaky, buttery Malabar paratha. The cooking here is very accomplished and dishes have finesse without losing the rich spicing of Southern India. Quilon should also be commended for its beer list – some very intriguing matching suggestions.

Roussillon

16 St Barnabas Street, SW1 ■ 020 7730 5550

⊖ Sloane Square/Victoria

|●| French

⏱ Mon to Fri 12.00–14.30 & 18.30–22.45; Sat 18.30–22.45

🖰 www.roussillon.co.uk

🖻 all major credit cards ■ 12.5% service added

££ menu de déjeuner £55 ■ menu légumes £48 (7 courses, lunch) & £60 (dinner) ■ menu dégustation £58 (8 courses, lunch) & £70 (dinner), plus £45 (with wine) ■ lowest bottle price £24

✪ Top-notch French cooking, in the modern style

It is somehow surprising that Roussillon has been around for over a decade with the same talented French chef at the helm, Alexis Gauthier, a man obsessed with the quality and freshness of ingredients. To see the advantages of being seasonal, and market-driven, try the excellent set lunch. The main menu offers three courses and if you feel the urge to splash out there are multi-course, showing-off menus. Service is formal and slick. The menu changes with the seasons. You might open with sesame-crusted langoustines with sweet and sour pepper; or a spring vegetable risotto with veal jus, crisp bacon and black truffle; or thin warm smoked eel tartlet. The mains also pay particular attention to combinations. Try squab pigeon roast in a pot with young asparagus and crayfish, or there may be a spring Welsh lamb in three ways – leg, shoulder, cutlet. Puddings include the spectacular croustillant Louis XV, which may be the ultimate chocolate pudding, and a warm plum and almond tart. Vegetarians are particularly well served here and the 'menu légumes' brings out the best of seasonal ingredients. Choose from broad beans with shallots and chervil; wild garlic and mashed potato; salsify and curry; cheeses and quince; and almond meringue with rhubarb compote and yoghurt mousse. Astute combinations also come into play in the tasting menu – scallops and apple; asparagus and morels; venison and pumpkin; sea bass and artichokes. This is accomplished and cerebral cooking.

Tate Britain Restaurant

Millbank, SW1 ■ 020 7887 8825   ♿

⊖ Pimlico

🍽 Modern British

🕐 Mon to Fri 11.30–15.00 (lunch); Sat & Sun 10.00–11.30 (breakfast),
11.30–15.30 (brunch) & 15.30–17.00 (tea)

🖱 www.tate.org.uk

🗗 all major credit cards ■ 12.5% optional service added

££ breakfast £4.75–£6.50 ■ starters £5.95–£7.50 ■ mains £15
■ sides £2.95 ■ desserts £5.95–£7.50 ■ afternoon tea £3.75–£6.95
■ lowest bottle price £15

⭐ Still a place of pilgrimage for wine lovers

In these days of 'sandwich at the desk' office culture, you have
to think before recommending a restaurant that doesn't open for
dinner. For the foodie, the Tate Britain Restaurant is worth a visit; for
the winey, a visit is essential. This restaurant's love affair with wine
began in the 1970s, when the food was dodgy and it seemed as if
the only customers were wine merchants smug at the impossibly low
prices. Today there may be fewer florid gents enjoying a three-bottle
lunch, but the atmosphere is soothing and the wine list not only
fascinates, but offers outstanding value as well. The menu changes
on a regular basis and offers admirably seasonal dishes. Starters may
include a new season vegetable broth; devilled kidneys; or steamed
Cornish cockles with wild garlic. Mains touch most of the bases:
spring chicken with baby vegetables and morels; 'fish of the day'
from the Newlyn day boats; rump of lamb with black kale and mint
jus; and lemon sole with buttered samphire and brown shrimps.
There are tempting puddings (like a stalwart sticky toffee pud) to
team with dessert wines. The wine list is wonderful, and changes
constantly. Don't be intimidated by the vast book – take your time
and listen to knowledgeable wine waiters. Bottles are served at the
right temperature and decanted without fuss when necessary. Two
tips – don't overlook the half bottles, and ask advice.

The Thomas Cubitt

44 Elizabeth Street, SW1 ■ 020 7730 6060

⊖ Victoria

🍴 Modern British

🕒 Mon to Fri 12.00–15.00 & 18.00–24.00; Sat 18.00–24.00

🖰 www.thethomascubitt.co.uk

🗗 all major credit cards n 12.5% optional service added

££ starters £7.–£10.50 ■ mains £15.50–£22.50 ■ sides £4
■ desserts £7.50 ■ set lunch £19.50 (2 courses) & £24.50 (3 courses)
■ lowest bottle price £14

⊗ Belgravia posh

This pub may be very handy for Victoria coach station but its
soul is closer to Eaton Square. On the menu, cards and so forth the
heading is 'The Thomas Cubitt Belgravia', a statement of intent.
Downstairs is the pub bit and the gastropub bit – on a warm evening
the pavements are crowded with happy drinkers fenced in behind
a rope. The bar is heaving – a brawling, braying bearpit of a place.
But as you walk up the stairs to the first-floor restaurant the din
fades into the background and you find yourself in a high-ceilinged
room with dove-grey walls, comfy chairs and fine linen tablecloths.
This is a grown-up restaurant with grown-up prices. The food is
praiseworthily seasonal and admirably British. Starters range from
bacon-wrapped smoked eel with celeriac purée; to gammon ham and
foie gras terrine, with pear relish; baked Loch Crinan diver scallops,
with prawns and a lemon dressing; or a salad of goats' cheese with
figs. Mains range from roast Lincolnshire rabbit with a champagne
sauce – an interesting juxtaposition; to beef Wellington; or herb-
crusted Welsh lamb with butter beans. Among the desserts you
can enjoy warm sticky toffee pudding with vanilla bean ice cream
or strawberry and mint salad with crushed meringue and white
chocolate soup. There's also a good British cheeseboard. Service is
smooth and slick and the wine list has enough at the lower end to
suit non-Belgravians.

Waterloo and South Bank

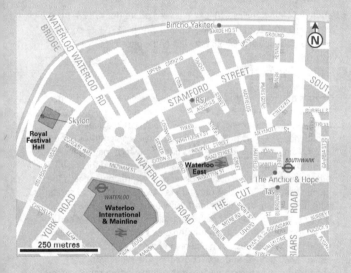

The Anchor & Hope
36 The Cut, SE1 ■ 020 7928 9898

⊖ Southwark/Waterloo

|●| British/gastropub

🕒 Mon 18.00–22.30; Tues to Sat 12.00–14.30 & 18.00–22.30;
Sun lunch 14.30 (one sitting, bookable)

🖪 all major credit cards except AmEx ■ no service added

££ starters £4–£7 ■ mains £10–£22 ■ shared dishes (for 4) £28–£100
■ sides £2.60–£3.20 ■ price fixe lunch & dinner £15.95 (2 courses) &
£18.95 (3) ■ desserts £4–£6 ■ lowest bottle price £15.25

✪ Champion gastropub

There's one marker that infallibly signals really excellent food.
You might spot it in the way the menu is written, in the presentation
of the dishes, or in the way things taste, but that key quality is
confidence. The Anchor & Hope has confidence aplenty. It's a rough-
looking dining area and there is no booking (which may mean
queuing, unless you are ready and waiting when the doors open),
but the pricing is fair and the cooking is very confident indeed. The
menu changes twice a day, but starters may include smoked sprats
with horseradish; or crab on toast (how understated is that?); leeks
gribiche; a warm snail and pig's head salad; or Spanish ham and
green tomatoes on toast. Among the mains are the economically
named tripe and chips; roast pigeon and semolina gnocchi; scallops
escarole and morels; and slow-cooked Middle White pork with
choucroute. Then there are a few dishes that are for sharing, such
as a 7-hour cooked shoulder of lamb. Or how about ordering up a
Lancashire hotpot to feed six? The cooking is inspired and owes a
good deal to the time one of the chef-proprietors spent at St John
(see p. 225). The wine list is un-graspingly priced and service, which
can get ruffled, is in tune with the surroundings. Puds are pukka –
chocolate pot; pear and almond tart; or a lemon and almond cake
with blood oranges.

Bincho Yakitori

2nd Floor, Oxo Tower, Bargehouse Street, SE1

■ 020 7803 0858   &

⊖ Waterloo/Southwark

🍽 Japanese

🕓 Mon to Fri 12.00–15.00 & 18.00–23.30; Sat & Sun 12.00–15.30 &
17.00–23.30 (22.30 Sun)

🖰 www.bincho.co.uk

🗗 all major credit cards ■ 12.5% optional service added

££ yakitori/kushiyaki £1.40–£2.60 ■ mains £3.90–£15.50
■ desserts £1.50–£5.50 ■ lunch £10 ■ lowest bottle price £14.50

✪ Slick Japanese resto skewers the market

The second floor of the Oxo Tower has a great view that's lured a
succession of restaurateurs to their doom. Bincho, however, seems
to have cracked it and this long and stylish Japanese grill house does
good business. There's something very agreeable about the relays
of little skewers – and it's in tune with the trend towards grazing
menus. To eat well here you should go with the flow; order three
different skewers to try, then order a fistful of your favourites. Yakitori
usually refers to chicken and Kushiyaki refers to other meats. There
are also salads and some rice dishes – indeed, the yasai yaki meshi
(fried rice with Japanese vegetables) is very good indeed. Choice
of skewers will depend upon your personal preferences but here
are some tips: the tebaski (chicken wing) is good and meaty; the
leba (chicken liver) is good; the kawa (chicken skin) is on the greasy
side and not as good and crisp as at Jin Kichi (see p. 285); the sori
(chicken oysters) is tremendous; the unagi (eel) is double tremendous;
the buta (pork belly) is sweet, rich and melting; the hitsuji (lamb) is
rather greasy; and the honetsuki gyu (beef rib on the bone) is good
and chewy with an intense flavour. Bincho is cleverly pitched, both
the concept and the food are accessible. This is a good option for a
few skewers, a cold beer and a view of the river.

→ For branch, see index or website

RSJ

13a Coin Street, SE1 ■ 020 7928 4554

⊖ Waterloo

🍴 Modern European

🕐 Mon to Fri 12.00–14.00 & 17.30–23.00; Sun 17.30–23.00

🖱 www.rsj.uk.com

🗄 all major credit cards ■ 12.5% service added

££ starters £6–£8.95 ■ mains £10–£18.95 ■ sides £2.75
   ■ desserts £5.75 ■ prix fixe lunch & dinner £15.95 (2 courses) &
   £18.95 (3 courses) ■ lowest bottle price £15.25

✪ The definitive Loire wine list

Rolled Steel Joist may seem a curious name for a restaurant but it
is appropriate – they can point out the RSJ that is holding up the first
floor if you wish! What's more interesting about RSJ is that it's owned
by a man with a passion for the wines of the Loire. Nigel Wilkinson
has compiled his list mainly from wines produced in this region, and
it features dozens of lesser-known Loire reds and whites – wines that
clearly deserve a wider following. The menu is based on classical
dishes, but with a light touch and some innovative combinations
as well. The starters might include warm white asparagus, Hereford
fried egg and parmesan; linguine, scallops, and chorizo; or cold roast
Suffolk pork with capers, gherkins, tuna and anchovy sauce. Moving
on to the main courses, typical choices might include pan-fried Red
bream, grapefruit, mango and caramelised endive; Denham Castle
lamb, roast leeks and anchovy gratin; grilled 10oz Pulford Farm
sirloin steak, Stilton cheese and red onion. The menu also features
an above-average number of vegetarian options, such as fresh sage
gnocchi with a blue cheese sauce, new season peas and broad beans.
The puddings can be serious stuff: steamed spiced pineapple pudding
with coconut custard or banana mousse with chocolate brownie.
Wine lovers captivated by the Loire should check out the RSJ Wine
Company, or visit the website if they fancy some online shopping.

Skylon

Southbank Centre, Belvedere Road, SE1 ■ 020 7654 7800

⊖ Waterloo

🍴 Modern British

🕐 daily 12.00–23.45 (the grill); Mon to Sat 12.00–14.30 &
17.30–22.45; Sun 12.00–16.00 (restaurant)

⌀ www.skylonrestaurant.co.uk

🗗 all major credit cards ■ 12.5% optional service added

££ (the grill) starters £6.50–£13.50 ■ mains £11–£21 ■ sides £3–£3.50
■ desserts £5 ■ (restaurant) £37.50 (2 courses) & £42.50 (3 courses)
■ lowest bottle price £18

✪ A great view, through the window and on the plate

The Royal Festival Hall emerged from a major refurb early in 2007,
and the People's Palace became Skylon. Money and design skills have
been lavished on the project but the restaurant retains its greatest
asset – a stunning view across the Thames. The head chef is Helena
Puolakka, who made her name at Harvey Nichols 5th Floor restaurant
and bases her menus on the twin planks of seasonality and careful
sourcing of ingredients. The room is elegant, the service is very crisp
and the food is honest and well cooked. Skylon splits into grill and
restaurant. Both have an amazing view of the river and, when it's
not obscured by murky drizzle, a splendid sunset. In the restaurant
starters may include scallops with boudin noir, leek fondant, vanilla
velouté; or cream of pumpkin, Parmesan flan and anchovy Melba;
or a Pithivier of quail with confit leg, sauce diable. Mains range from
pan-fried halibut, choucroute, morteau sausage and smoked belly; to
braised pork cheeks, roast lobster, caramelised salsify, green mango
and pumpkin salad; or Anjou pigeon roast in confit pepper, risotto of
Sharpam Park spelt, broccoli cream. Dishes sophisticated enough for
all-comers. Puddings are also impressive: a luxurious milk chocolate
mousse is teamed with dark chocolate fondant and white chocolate
ice cream. For cooking of this standard prices are very competitive;
there's an extensive wine list; and that amazing view.

Tas

33 The Cut, SE1 ■ 020 7928 1444

⊖ Waterloo

🍴 Turkish

🕐 Mon to Sat 12.00–23.00; Sun 12.00–22.30

🖰 www.tasrestaurant.com

🖬 all major credit cards ■ 12.5% service added

££ starters £3.35–£4.25 ■ mains £4.95–£14.45 ■ sides £2.05–£3.25
   ■ desserts £3.35–£3.95 ■ set menus £8.95–£18.50
   ■ lowest bottle price £13.20

✪ Lively, cheap and Turkish

Tas is heaving with office parties and stag or hen nights because
it is a bright and bustling Turkish restaurant where eating is cheap.
The various menus and set menus offer a baffling choice and there
is often live music. Consider the set menus as a simple way through
the maze. The Sahan menu includes starter and main; the Renk menu
is a mixed mezze. There's even a set menu called the Aslan, which
is presumably aimed at lion-sized appetites. The main menu has
everything – there are four soups, a dozen cold starters, a dozen
hot starters, eight salads, a dozen vegetarian dishes, plus casseroles,
fish and grilled meats aplenty. Take a breath and then treat Tas like a
simple Turkish eatery. Start with some mezze. There's tarama salata;
calamari; houmous; cacik – a simple cucumber and yogurt dip; and
hellim – a rather good grilled cheese. Then go on to try some grilled
meats: tavuk shish is chicken kebab; kofte is a minced lamb kebab. Or
there are casseroles. Hunkar begendi is aubergine topped with lamb;
and incik is lamb cooked on the bone. One element of the menu
that makes Tas stand out from other Turks is the long list of fish and
shellfish dishes. As well as kalamari there is balik bugiulama, which
is steamed cod, and pirasali mercan, pan-fried dorade. Baklava is all
very well, but it is probably outsold by chocolate cake.

→ For branches, see index or website

The City and east

Brick Lane and Spitalfields

Bengal Village

75 Brick Lane, E1 ■ 020 7366 4868   ♿

⊖ Aldgate East/Liverpool Street

🍴 Indian

🕐 daily 12.00–24.00

🗂 all major credit cards ■ no service added

££ starters 60p–£3.95 ■ mains £4.50–£12.95 ■ sides £1.90–£3.95
■ desserts £3–£3.50 ■ lunch menu £5.95 ■ lowest bottle price £6.95

✪ Bangladeshi cooking – the genuine article

Ignore the rabidly commercial curry houses and seek out
something more satisfying. Where once all was BYO restaurants
serving rough-and-ready curries at bargain-basement prices to
impoverished punters seeking chilli, there's now a growing crop of
slick new establishments on Brick Lane serving authentic Bangladeshi
cooking. At the Bengal Village there's a blond wood floor and
modernist chairs, but it's about more than just design. The menu
touches all the bases: trad curryholics can still plough their way
through more than a hundred old-style curries, but now they can also
try some more interesting Bangladeshi dishes. Bucking what seems to
be becoming the trend, starters are not the best dishes at the Bengal
Village. Bowal mas biran is boal fish that has been deep fried and is
served with a rich sauce. There are four shatkora curries, the shatkora
being a small green fruit that has a delightful bitter-citrus tang and
goes very well with rich meats – lamb shatkora, for example. Then
there are ureebisi dishes, traditionally made with the seeds of a large
runner-bean-like plant – try chicken ureebisi. There are also some
interesting vegetarian options: chalkumra – subtitled 'ash-ground',
made with a pumpkin-like gourd. The marrow kofta is a curry with
large and satisfactorily dense vegetable dumplings floating, or
rather sinking, in it. If charm is to be the decider, you must try bhug
mas bhuna, described as 'a large fish spotty like a leopard found in
Bangladesh'.

Canteen

2 Crispin Place, EC1 ■ 0845 686 1122

⊖ Liverpool Street

⦿ British

🕐 Mon to Fri 08.00–23.00; Sat & Sun 09.00–23.00

🖱 www.canteen.co.uk

🖪 all major credit cards ■ 12.5% optional service added

££ breakfast £2–£8 ■ starters £4.50–£8 ■ mains £7–£13.50 ■ sides £3
■ desserts £5 ■ lowest bottle price £12.50

✪ The modern face of traditional cooking

The new face of Spitalfields Market is a rather welcome one,
with office blocks jostling with boutiquey food shops and various
restaurants. Canteen's manifesto bangs on about 'honest food,
nationally sourced, skilfully prepared and reasonably priced' and in
the main this is a resto that lives up to its billing. The dining room
is modern and you get to choose between booths and long tables.
The menu changes with the seasons and starts with various breakfast
favourites – bacon sandwich; Marmite toast; bacon, fried eggs with
bubble and squeak; and eggs Benedict – all of which are served
throughout the day. Then there are starters like hot buttered Arbroath
Smokey; onion and sage tart; devilled kidneys on toast; and the
rather good potted duck, which comes with piccalilli. Mains range
from macaroni cheese; to fish and chips; gammon with potatoes
and parsley sauce; rump steak with mushrooms; or the 'pie of the
day' – which might be as simple, and as good, as chicken, ham and
mushroom. This is a very successful dish and something of a bargain.
Canteen is a 'helpful' unfussy sort of place – there is a section of the
menu listing dishes that are for 'fast service', but everything else is
cooked to order. Puds are trad – rice pudding with jam; treacle tart.
There's a cheeseboard sourced from Neals Yard plus a 'cake counter'
to provide a sugar rush for those mid-afternoon moments.

→ For branch, see index or website

Hawksmoor

157 Commercial Street, E1 ▪ 020 7247 7392

⊖ Liverpool Street

▮●▮ Steak

🕐 Mon to Thurs 12.00–24.00; Fri 12.00–01.00; Sat 18.00–01.00

🖰 www.thehawksmoor.com

🖰 all major credit cards ▪ 12.5% optional service added

££ starters £6.50–£9 ▪ mains £10–£21.50 ▪ sides £3–£6
   ▪ desserts £5–£6 ▪ lowest bottle price £22

✪ Amazing cocktails, amazing steaks

This is the place to ponder the meaning of life and work your
way through as many subtle variations of the Sazerac cocktail as
you are able. Hawksmoor is either a bar that thinks it is a restaurant
or a restaurant with a bar fixation. Roughly equal weight is given
to strong drinks and magnificent steaks. The room is long and dark
and can get noisy when busy. The menu is short and single-minded:
someone here has taken to heart the idea of seeking out really good
ingredients and the menu bears witness. The pork comes from
happy Tamworths, the lamb from flocks of Swaledale and Black
Face sheep, and the steaks are from Longhorn cattle and have been
hung for at least 28 days. Foodists will by now have pin-pointed
Hawksmoor's butcher as The Ginger Pig, a seriously good outfit from
North Yorkshire. Starters range from Tamworth ribs; to grilled shrimp;
grilled scallops with salsa verde; and a Caesar salad with or without
chicken. But you'll just be putting things off, the steaks are immense
and with 48 hours' notice you can order something even larger, or a
Chateaubriand – now there's a thought. The main list offers hanger
steak (skirt in Britain and onglet in France); a bone-in 600g sirloin;
a ribeye (choose between 400 and 600g); or half a kilo of rump.
Making up the numbers are a rump of lamb; a roast loin of pork
and a whole sea bream. The steaks are very good indeed, accurately
cooked, with decent meat. The triple-cooked chips are also good. A
few greens is all you need add. Finish things off with an ice cream list.

Kolapata

222 Whitechapel Road, E1 ■ 020 7377 1200

⊖ Whitechapel

🍽 Indian

🕐 daily 12.00–23.00 (Fri 13.30–23.00)

🖰 www.kolapata.co.uk

🖵 cash only ■ no service added

££ starters £1.95–£2.50 ■ mains £4.50–£6.95 ■ sides 50p–£1.95
■ desserts £2–£4.50 ■ no alcohol

✪ Bangladeshi food at its most interesting

There's a magnificent leprechaun-bright greenness to the dining area at Kolapata: green lights, green-shirted waiters, green napkins, plus some shockingly modern furniture. But you're here for the food. At last I see the point of haleem. Haleem is a dish of pounded lentils and meat that combines the texture of breakfast porridge with rich meaty flavours. Most examples are unbearably sticky and slimy with an unappealing gloopiness. At Kolapata haleem is delicious – more like a smooth dal with small chunks of lamb (on the bone) lurking in its depths. The flavour is rich and with a fried luchi bread it makes a very good starter. There are plenty of fish dishes – koi, hilsa, rupchanda and ayer all get a mention – but the menu has its chaotic moments and plenty of crossing out. The specials board is a reliable source of information. Try the murog pulao, which differs from a biryani in that a whole chicken joint is buried in a mountain of rice and accompanied by a bowl of nutty, sweet-savoury sauce complete with hard-boiled egg. Very delicious. Or there may be beef bhuna, a rich, heavily spiced, slow-cooked curry. The breads are good and a traditional vegetable dish called labra is a good accompaniment (if rather over-cooked by Western standards). Kolapata serves good and interesting food at bargain prices and the waiting staff are notably helpful and friendly. Good fun.

The Lahore Kebab House

2–10 Umberston Street, E1 ■ 020 7481 9737

Whitechapel/Aldgate East

Indian

daily 12.00–01.30

all major credit cards ■ no service added

££ starters 75p–£9.50 ■ mains £5.50–£9.50 ■ sides £3.50–£7.50 ■ desserts £2.50–£4.50 ■ unlicensed, BYO (no corkage)

✪ A chillied success story

This is a nondescript, indeed dowdy-looking, kebab house serving decent and reasonably priced food. What was once a cherished secret among a handful of curry lovers is now big business. Thankfully, the food is still good and spicy, and the service brusque enough to disabuse you of any thoughts that the smart tables and posh shop front are signs of impending mediocrity. What they do here, they do pretty well. Rotis tend to arrive unordered – the waiter watches how you eat and brings fresh bread as and when he sees fit. For starters, the kebabs are stand-outs. Seekh kebab, mutton tikka and chicken tikka are all very fresh, very hot and very good, served with a yogurt and mint dipping sauce. The meat or chicken biryanis are also splendid, well spiced and with the rice taking on all the rich flavours. The karahi gosht and karahi chicken are uncomplicated dishes of tender meat in a rich gravy. And on Friday there is a special dish – lamb chop curry. Also noteworthy is the masala fish. The dal tarka is made from whole yellow split peas, while sag aloo brings potatoes in a rich and oily spinach purée. For dessert try the delightful home-made kheer, which is a special kind of trad rice pudding with cardamom. BYO by all means – but remember, when it comes to chilli burn, lassi is way more cooling than lager will ever be.

St John Bread & Wine

94–96 Commercial Street, E1 ■ 020 7251 0848

⊖ Liverpool Street

🍴 British

🕐 Mon to Fri 09.00–22.30; Sat 10.00–22.30; Sun 10.00–16.30

🕘 www.stjohnbreadandwine.com

🖪 all major credit cards ■ 12.5% service for parties of 6 or more

££ breakfast £2.50–£6.80 ■ starters £2–£13.20 ■ mains £11.20–£13.20
■ desserts £3.60–£7.60 ■ lowest bottle price £16

✪ Best British Restaurant – award winner

This place is younger brother to St John in nearby Clerkenwell
(see p. 225) and is home to what may be London's most civilised
elevenses – 'seed cake and a glass of Madeira'. It's a stylish but
utilitarian room with small, tightly packed tables and chairs, and the
whole place is dominated by an open-plan bakery and kitchen. The
food is honest here. Simple. Delicious. Very good value. The menu has
its own timeline: 09.00 could mean a Middle White bacon sandwich
or porridge and prunes. The seed cake combo features at 11.00. By
lunchtime at noon you'll find cauliflower soup; jellied pig's head;
smoked mackerel and horseradish; and herring and oatmeal; or you
could splash out on lemon sole. The menu changes with the seasons
and what is available at market, so perhaps there'll be braised
cuttlefish or red mullet served with chicory and anchovy. Maybe
pigeon with mushy peas appeals? Or veal heart, pickled walnut
and watercress. Or rabbit kidneys with mustard. All these dishes
are supported by fabulous bread, and a fairly forgiving selection of
wines. You shouldn't expect anything elaborate or fancy pants, but
you can be sure of big flavours and intriguing combinations of taste
and texture. Puds are good – rhubarb cobbler and custard; treacle
tart and vanilla ice cream; or blood orange jelly. Should you be feeling
Proustian, take half a dozen madeleines home with you and see what
you remember.

Tayyabs

83–89 Fieldgate Street, E1 ▪ 020 7247 6400   ♿

⊖ Whitechapel/Aldgate East

🍽 Indian

🕐 daily 12.00–24.00

🖰 www.tayyabs.co.uk

🗇 all major credit cards ▪ no service added

££ starters 50p–£10 ▪ mains £5.50–£12 ▪ sides £4.50–£4.80
     ▪ desserts £2 ▪ unlicensed, BYO (no corkage)

✪ Join the queue, relish the prices

Tayyabs has come a long way since those first days in 1974. After
the initial café came the sweet shop, and then Tayyabs took over
what was once the corner pub. Now it's a slick 180-seater, with
art on the walls, smart lighting and chairs in leather and chrome.
Miraculously, the food remains straightforward Pakistani fare: good,
freshly cooked and served without pretension. And more miraculous
still, the prices have stayed lower than you would believe possible.
Booking is essential if you don't want to queue and service is speedy
and slick: this is not a place to um and er over the menu. The simpler
dishes are terrific, particularly the five pieces of chicken tikka, served
on an iron sizzle dish alongside a small plate of salady things and a
medium-fierce, sharp, chilli dipping sauce. They do the same thing
with mutton, or there's a plate of four large and splendid lamb
chops. Sheekh kebabs and shami kebabs are bought by the skewer.
There are round fluffy naan breads, but I would go for the wholemeal
roti, which is deliciously nutty and crisp. The karahi dishes are simple
and tasty: 'karahi chicken' is chicken in a rich sauce; karahi aloo gosht
is lamb with potatoes in another rich sauce, heavily flavoured with
bay leaves. Or there's karahi mixed vegetables. A list of interesting
daily specials includes dishes such as the trad mutton curry nihari,
which is served every Monday.

Wild Cherry

241 Globe Road, E2 ■ 020 8980 6678

⊖ Bethnal Green

|●| Vegetarian

🕙 Tues 10.30–16.00; Wed 10.30–19.00; Thurs to Sat 10.30–16.00

🖥 Mastercard, Visa ■ no service added

££ Sat £3.90–£5.95 (all-day breakfast) ■ starters £1.50–£2.70
■ mains £5.75–£5.95 ■ desserts £2.75–£3.95
■ unlicensed, BYO (£1 corkage)

✪ Vegetarian, and proud of it

Wild Cherry is an offshoot of the London Buddhist Centre and it's a genuine vegetarian restaurant that, as the mission statement by the door proclaims, 'exists firstly to provide fresh home-cooked vegetarian meals for the local community'. This is a bright, clean, self-service venue. A blackboard lists the daily menu and you choose from selections like Stilton and cauliflower soup; cream cheese, spinach and polenta with roast vegetables; vegetarian lasagne; or hot quiche of the day (such as courgette) with two salads. On to a choice of three different salads every day – maybe beetroot, carrot and ruby chard with orange hazelnut dressing. There's always a quiche and two further hot dishes. In season, baked potatoes come with comforting fillings like houmous, grated Cheddar or tzatziki. Salads (which vary in size from a single scoop to regular or large) include choices like aramé rice; ruby chard, cherry tomato and fresh chive; mixed leaf; Moroccan chickpea with rocket; and coleslaw with vegan mayonnaise. Puddings are homely and all the better for it, and may include trifle; hot fruit crumble; and banoffee pie. Choose from fourteen different teas, ten of them herbal, plus Free Trade coffee (by the mug, or by the cafetière), and a choice of soya or cow's milk. There are usually wheat-free, gluten-free and sugar-free options available. All the portions here are huge; everything tastes wholesome and the value is amazing.

The City

1 Lombard Street – the Brasserie

1 Lombard Street, EC3 ■ 020 7929 6611

⊖ Bank

🍽 Modern European

🕐 Mon to Fri 07.30–11.00 (breakfast) & 11.30–22.00

🖥 www.1lombardstreet.com

🗄 all major credit cards ■ 12.5% optional service added

££ breakfast £9.50–£16.50 ■ starters £6.50–£9.75
   ■ mains £14.50–£28.50 ■ sides £3.75–£4.95 ■ desserts £6.50–£7.50
   ■ lowest bottle price £22

✪ City stuff for City people

The Brasserie occupies an imposing room and the circular bar
sits under a suitably impressive glass dome. The brasserie menu is a
model of its kind, long but straightforward, with a range of dishes
that is up to any meal occasion. It delivers on pretty much every front,
serving satisfying dishes made with good fresh ingredients, both
stylish and unfussy at the same time. The bar, meanwhile, is like any
chic City watering hole – loud, brisk and crowded, with simultaneous
conversations in every European language. There is a smaller,
40-seater room at the rear, set aside for fine dining at fancy prices.
The brasserie menu changes every couple of months to satisfy the
band of regulars, and there are daily specials in addition. The starters
can be ambitious, such as seasonal game terrine, or simple, like
Scotch broth, while further down the menu there will be some even
more comfortable options, such as soft-boiled free-range egg served
with smoked haddock and spinach gratin. There's enough listed
under shellfish and crustacea to fuel even the wildest celebrations,
including griddled scallops with black pudding, leeks and brown
butter; and casserole of mussels and clams. The Classics section has
coq au vin à la Bourguignon or roast suckling pig. The Meat section
lists steak, sausages and liver. Puds triumph – there's an indulgent
warm chocolate fondant – and there's something on the wine list to
suit most tastes.

Café Spice Namaste

16 Prescot Street, E1 ■ 020 7488 9242   ♿

⊖ Aldgate/Tower Hill

🍽 Indian

🕐 Mon to Fri 12.00–15.00 & 18.15–22.30; Sat 18.15–22.30

🖰 www.cafespice.co.uk

🖶 all major credit cards ■ 12.5% optional service added

££ starters £4.75–£6.95 ■ mains £12.25–£18.55 ■ sides £4.75–£6.50
■ desserts £3.75–£6.25 ■ lowest bottle price £15.50

✪ Gifted chef lifts Indian cooking

Lunchtimes and even weekday evenings the pace in this brightly
painted dining room is fast and furious, but paradoxically, come
Saturday nights, things get calmer and you can settle back and
really enjoy Cyrus Todiwala's exceptional cooking. The menu, which
changes throughout the year, sees Parsee delicacies rubbing shoulders
with dishes from Goa, North India, Hyderabad and Kashmir, all of
them precisely spiced and well presented. The tandoori specialities,
in particular, are awesome, fully flavoured by cunning marinades.
Start with a voyage around the tandoor. The murg kay tikkay tastes as
every chicken tikka should, with yogurt, ginger, cumin and chillies all
playing their part. Or there's venison tikka aflatoon, which originates
in Gwalior and is flavoured with star anise and cinnamon. Also
notable is the papeta nay eeda na pattice – a potato cake perked up
with egg, coconut, green peas and Parsee-style hot tomato gravy.
For a main course, fish lovers should consider the patra ni machchi,
pomfret stuffed with green coconut chutney. If you're going for meat
you should try the dhansaak, which is a truly authentic version of
the much-misrepresented Parsee speciality. It is served with a small
kebab and brown-onion rice. Breads are also excellent, and some of
the accompaniments and vegetable dishes belie their lowly status at
the back of the book-sized menu. Try baingan bharta – an aubergine
classic. It's also worth checking out the weekly changing 'specials
menu'.

→ For branch, see index

The Don

20 St Swithins Lane, EC4 ■ 020 7626 2606

⊖ Bank

🍴 Modern European

🕐 (restaurant) Mon to Fri 12.00–14.30 & 18.00–22.30; (bistro) Mon to Fri 12.00–15.00 & 18.00–22.00

🖱 www.thedonrestaurant.com

🖪 all major credit cards ■ 12.5% optional service added

££ starters £5.90–£9.75 ■ mains £8.95–£23.95 ■ desserts £5.95–£7.50
■ lowest bottle price £16.95

⭐ Rich food in a rich setting

George Sandeman first took over the cellars at 20 St Swithin's Lane in 1798. And very fine cellars they are too, complete with an ornate black iron 'Capital Patent Crane' for lowering barrels into the depths. Now it is home to The Don restaurant and bistro, which takes its name from the trademark portrait of Sandeman port's 'Don'. The lofty room on the ground floor makes a striking restaurant, while the vaulted brick cellars make a grand backdrop for the bistro. The ground-floor restaurant is the more sophisticated – and rumour has it that during 2007 the great Pierre Koffman took up an advisory role in the kitchens. The food is accomplished and under Koffman's influence leans towards classical French cooking: starters range from soupe de poisson Marseillaise; wild pigeon chicory and lambs lettuce salad; or a foie gras crème brûlée with sorrel; to Scottish scallops en coquille, with fines herbes. Mains may include pork belly and pig's trotter with white cabbage; hare 'à la Royale!' with celeriac purée; monkfish 'à la Gasconne' with haricot beans and chorizo; or a loin of young New Zealand venison with Savoy cabbage and a bitter chocolate sauce. These are dishes with strong flavours and good combinations of texture. Puds are comforting – dark chocolate tart with mandarin sorbet; nougat glacé; roast pineapple with star anise. To boost numbers at Friday dinner there are occasional, but very attractive, wine offers.

Kasturi

57 Aldgate High Street, EC3 ■ 020 7480 7402 &

⊖ Aldgate

🍴 Indian

🕐 Mon to Sat 11.00–23.00; Sun 12.00–15.00 & 18.00–23.00

🖱 www.kasturi-restaurant.co.uk

🖥 all major credit cards ■ no service added

££ starters £3.95–£9.50 ■ mains £7.95–£14.95 ■ sides £1.95–£4.95
■ set lunch/dinner £15.95 & £18.95 ■ lowest bottle price £13.95

✪ Sleek modern Indian, sleek modern food

There was a time when a 'curry in the City' meant a pretty
roughly doughty sort of meal; when the whole concept was very
much associated with pubs, chucking out time and the last train
home. Times have changed and so have City curry houses. The once
infallible rule (that the starters taste better than the mains) is slowly
giving way. Here the starters are fine but not exceptional – the
kebabs are good: chicken tikka is very sound as are the drake lamb
chops, although they are on the thin side. Team some nibbles with
the excellent lacchi paratha. Move on to the mains, which are most
impressive – it is always a very good sign when each and every curry
looks and tastes completely different from the others. Stand-outs are
the all mas, a superb dry lamb curry, hot and with a belt of sourness.
Or there's dahi macula, which is tilapia with turmeric. The Hyderabadi
lamb biryani is exemplary, rich and with tender meat. The dahi machli
is very good too – fillets of tilapia in a very mild creamy sauce. The
veg section hides some good things such as a dish of baby aubergines
cooked with peanuts and poppy seeds – for all the world like a smart
satay – and a dish of baby new potatoes cooked with pomegranate.
Kasturi is a pleasant, businesslike restaurant which serves above-
average Indian food.

The Mercer

34 Threadneedle Street, EC2 ■ 020 7628 0001   &

⊖ Bank/Liverpool Street

🍴 British

🕐 Mon to Fri 07.30–10.00, 12.00–15.00 & 18.00–21.30

🖱 www.themercer.co.uk

🖪 all major credit cards ■ 12.5% optional service added

££ starters £6–£15 ■ mains £12.50–£26.50 ■ sides £3–£4.50
■ desserts £5–£6.50 ■ quick lunch £18 (2 courses) & £24 (3 courses)
■ lowest bottle price £16.50

✪ Modern British meets traditional British

From the look of it the Mercer is yet another reclamation of an elegant and lofty banking hall; presumably nowadays all banks live in a computer chip offshore and have no need of imposing premises. The room is dominated by a long and seemingly excessively well-stocked bar, where rare spirits jostle with one of those chrome machines that enables restaurants to serve a single glass of fine wine and stop the rest of the bottle from going off. The menu here treads a fine line between Modern British (starters like roast wood pigeon salad with pancetta and pink grapefruit) and more traditional stalwarts (potted Yorkshire ham hock with piccalilli). There are daily specials which range from corned beef hash on Monday to rabbit casserole on Thursday and fish pie on Friday. Mains continue the theme, including the Mercer pie — a decent, deep-dish affair with light pastry — and a satisfying rump steak, with mushroom and London porter interior. Sound gravy. A roast haunch of venison comes with truffled artichoke, Granny Smith apples and cashew nuts (that one's in the Modern British camp); or perhaps seared scallops with peas, pancetta and lobster sauce appeals? Puds are trad with fresh fruit salad, ice creams and sorbets leading the way. The wine list is extensive and not over-grasping and you have the valuable option of 250ml or 500ml carafes. Service is particularly good — the perfect combination of friendly and efficient.

Mugen

26 King William Street, EC4 ■ 020 7929 7879

⊖ Monument

🍴 Japanese

🕐 Mon to Fri 12.00–15.00 & 18.00–22.00

🗗 all major credit cards ■ no service added

££ sushi £3.00–£6.20 ■ sashimi £5.80–£10.80 ■ mains £4.20–£10.80
■ set lunches £9.20–£14.20 ■ lowest bottle price £12.50

⭐ Businesslike Japanese for salary men

This restaurant is a makeover of an earlier Japanese restaurant that stood on this site. Why the old one closed is not clear, but in its new incarnation as Mugen it seems impressively busy. The Japanese (at least in the City) take their lunch pretty early and on the dot of noon this restaurant fills up. To the left as you go in there's a glossy kaiten (sushi conveyor belt) while to the right there's an array of tables. The décor is modern and the atmosphere is as businesslike as the customers. The set meals are well done. At lunch time you might tuck into an assortment of fresh nigiri sushi and rolls flanked by miso soup, a mixed salad and a portion of fruit. It will arrive lightening quick and the service is friendly but slick – they really do believe the adage that time is money. Other options are a pork katsu curry; salmon teriyaki; all manner of tempura; and a serious bowl of noodles – the Mugen special ramen, a big bowl laden with noodles, several different vegetables and a soft-boiled egg. From the à la carte you could pick out grilled yellowtail with teriyaki sauce; or grilled chicken with ponzu sauce and white radish. For drinkers the sake is reasonably priced and there are Japanese beers. Anyone with a lively disposition will be pleased to see a line-up of potent cocktails. Beware.

Northbank

Millennium Bridge, One St Paul's Walk, EC4 ■ 020 7329 9299

⊖ St Paul's

🍽 Modern British

🕐 Mon to Sat 12.00–23.00; Sun 12.00–17.00

🖰 www.northbankrestaurant.com

🖬 all major credit cards ■ 12.5% optional service added

££ starters £6–£9.50 ■ mains £12.50–£23 ■ sides £3.50
■ desserts £5.50 ■ set menu (12.00–15.00 & 18.00–19.00) £13.50 (2 courses) & £17.50 (3 courses) ■ lowest bottle price £15

✪ Comfortable riverside restaurant

Northbank is tucked away at the foot of the North East end of the Millennium Bridge and from the terrace, or indeed the dining room, you can watch the Thames sweep by and a steady succession of joggers plodding past. These intimations of mortality add purpose to the excellent range of beers and cocktails available here, there is time enough for fitness in due course. The menu is sensibly crafted and changes with the seasons, there is little to shock and much to comfort. Starters range from English asparagus with smoked salmon, poached egg and Hollandaise; to goats' cheese salad with pomegranates and pine nuts; roast veal bone marrow and caramelised snails on toast; and Falmouth crab and clotted cream tart. Half a dozen mains include rump of lamb with sautéed kidneys and herb mash; grilled sirloin steak with confit tomatoes; steamed fillet of sea bream with Cornish clams and samphire; and roast pork belly with mash and black pudding. Puddings veer from vanilla panna cotta and champagne-poached strawberries to a chocolate brownie with candied kumquats; or white wine and summer fruit jelly. And there is also a commendable West Country cheeseboard. After some accessibly priced bottles the wine list offers some smarter drinking. The terrace tables are a very good place to enjoy a spot of lunch on a sunny day. Service is good enough to cope with the briefest of City lunch breaks, or the longest!

Paternoster Chop House

Warwick Court, Paternoster Square, EC4 ■ 020 7029 9400 ♿

⊖ St Paul's

🍽 Very British

🕐 Mon to Fri 12.00–15.00 & 17.30–22.00; Sun 12.00–16.00

⌐ www.danddlondon.com

🗄 all major credit cards ■ 12.5% optional service charge added

££ starters £6.50–£7.50 ■ mains £12.50–£23.50 ■ sides £3.50–£6
■ desserts £5.50–£7.50 ■ Sun lunch £16.50 (2 courses) & £20 (3
courses) ■ lowest bottle price £16.50

⭐ British food – carefully chosen, carefully cooked

By City standards Paternoster Square may be a relatively new
creation, but the food and hospitality on display at the restaurant
is top notch. This place makes no bones about its targeting of City
folk: there's real ale on offer, simple fish dishes, roast meats, plenty
of shellfish and seafood, while the prices are pretty much what you
would expect. So saying, everything is done well. Ingredients are
carefully sourced from the length and breadth of Britain, the menu
changes seasonally and the cooking style is sympathetic. Start with
Scotch broth with pearl barley; Dublin bay prawns with salad cream;
or potted Devon white crab. Comfort food fans may be tempted
by the pure-bred Hereford beef cottage pie. They are proud of the
meat cookery here and pure-bred Angus beef is hung for five weeks
before ending up as twelve-hour roasted brisket, or a flank steak. In
season, there's plenty of game. Or you could opt for the Norfolk Horn
mutton with mint sauce; or Brymoor veal and white wine stew. As
befits anywhere showcasing British food, fine cheese plays a leading
role – the Cheddar comes from James Montgomery; the Stilton from
Cropwell Bishop; while the Welsh rarebit is made with Lancashire
cheese and comes topped with a poached egg. The wine list runs
from reasonable to rarefied and the service is slick, but best of all, this
place flies the flag for British cuisine.

The Place Below

St Mary-le-Bow Church, Cheapside, EC2 ▪ 020 7329 0789

⊖ Bank/St Paul's

🍴 Vegetarian

🕐 Mon to Fri 07.30–15.30 (lunch 11.30–14.30)

🖰 www.theplacebelow.co.uk

🗗 all major credit cards ▪ no service charge

££ breakfast £1.20–£2.30 ▪ soup £3.10 ▪ mains £5.65–£7.75 (£2 off 11.30–12.00 & 13.30–14.30) ▪ sandwiches £4.50 ▪ desserts £1.50–£2.80 ▪ unlicensed, BYO (no corkage)

✪ Wholesome veggie food that tastes good as well

The Place Below is a vegetarian restaurant, and yes, it is in the crypt of the St Mary-le-Bow Church. But persevere: it has a splendidly low worthiness rating. Wander into the wonderfully elegant Wren church and look for the staircase down to the crypt. You'll see that the resto is split into two halves: the first has an open kitchen at one end and acts as coffee shop and servery – good pastries and breakfast buns; the other is the restaurant proper, which is open at lunch (with prices a pound or two cheaper if you turn up early or late). Choose from the reassuringly short, daily-changing menu, push a tray along the canteen-style rails, and the chefs will fill a plate for you. The dining room is lofty, with the large, central, communal dining table being the only one with a tablecloth. There are a couple of soups, a hot dish, a quiche option, a salad of the day, good trad puds and that's about it. The soups are hearty, such as split green pea and mint, or butternut, lemongrass and basil. The salad of the day can be triumphant: crisp green beans, a rich savoury dollop of wild rice, shredded carrot with sesame seeds and plenty of fresh leaves. Or how about a hot dish like Emmental and white wine hotpot with root vegetable mash? The field mushroom, fennel and Gruyère 'quiche of the day' is also well made. There are always puddingy puddings like a marzipan and cranberry cake or passion fruit syllabub with lavender shortbread. Good cooking, great value.

Rajasthan III

38—41 Houndsditch, EC3 ■ 020 7626 0033

⊖ Aldgate

🍽 Indian

🕐 Mon to Fri 11.30–15.00 & 18.00–23.00

🔗 www.rajasthanIII.co.uk

🗄 all major credit cards ■ 12.5% optional service added

££ starters £3.20–£5.80 ■ mains £7.90–£14.50 ■ sides £2–£3.80
    ■ set meal £24 (2 courses) ■ lowest bottle price £12.50

✪ Currying flavour

The Rajasthan III is situated on Houndsditch. Walk past the window
at lunch and you cannot fail to notice that it's rammed. Waiters in red
mess jackets struggle to keep up with the cries for 'more Cobra' that
ring out from every table. This place has such a buzz to it that many
a West End restaurant would love to know their secret. In essence
the Rajasthani (and there are three branches) does a simple thing
very well. The curries are well balanced, the portions are large and
the prices are only slightly cheeky – this is the City after all. What's
more, the menu offers some interesting, less commonly seen dishes.
From the starters look at items like murgh liver – small nuggets of
liver spiced and deep fried; or there's nazakat – a sweet chicken
tikka variant; or stuffed chillies – a cheese-filled, deep-fried chillies.
For main course try one of three different duck dishes – the haash
mirchi comes with a rich gravy and plenty of fierce little green chillies.
Or there's tawa gosht Lahori – it may not look like it's seen a tawa
but it's a good rich curry nevertheless. For the unadventurous there
are all the old familiars from chicken tikka masala to lamb vindaloo.
Side dishes and breads are good, service is quick and chipper. A very
agreeable curry house serving better food than you would expect.

Rosemary Lane

61 Royal Mint Street, E1 ■ 020 7481 2602

⊖ Tower Hill/DLR Tower Gateway

🍽 French/Californian

🕒 Mon to Fri 12.00–14.30 & 18.00–22.00; Sat 18.00–22.00

🖰 www.rosemarylane.btinternet.co.uk

🖯 all major credit cards ■ 12% optional service added

££ starters £8–£11 ■ mains £13–£18 ■ desserts £6 ■ prix fixe lunch £15 (2 courses) & £18 (3 courses) ■ Sat tasting menu £30 for 9 courses ■ lowest bottle price £12

✪ Californian charisma, fresh seasonal food

The prime mover at Rosemary Lane is a Californian chef called Christina Anghelescu and her menus show an agreeable reliance on seasonal produce while displaying the same dogged determination to use only the best quality ingredients that we associate with Alice Waters and the other West Coast stars. This even extends to running a 'pot luck' tasting menu on Saturdays that is based around whatever was good at Borough Market that morning. The main menu changes every six weeks or so. The dining room looks like a lick-of-paint-makeover of a dodgy saloon bar – which is just what it is. Service is slick, in a Gallic sort of way. The food is good. Dishes are pleasantly light, and presentation just about manages to stay elegant without tipping over the edge into elaborate or over-complicated. In the winter, starters may include a Duke of York and baby leek potato Vichyssoise; or pate de foie gras with celeriac and green apple remoulade; or prosciutto with winter mushrooms and white truffle essence. Mains are considered combinations – duck breast with Peruvian purple potatoes and pomegranate; Maine diver scallops with a ragout of yellow cherry tomatoes, fresh spinach and shallots; or slow-roast Gloucestershire pork belly with braised sweet potato and a creamy mustard sauce. Puds are good – Venezuelan chocolate fondant with caramel core; or Bartlet pear and ginger cobbler. As befits the City location, there's a grown-up wine list with some good stickies.

Terranostra

27 Old Bailey, EC4 ■ 020 3201 0077   &

⊖ St Paul's

🍽 Italian/Sardinian

🕐 Mon to Fri 12.00–15.00 & 18.00–22.00; Sat 18.00–22.00

🖰 www.terranostrafood.co.uk

🖬 all major credit cards ■ 12.5% optional service added

££ antipasti £6.90–£8.60 ■ pasta £7.90–£10.90 ■ mains £11.90–£15.90
■ sides £2.90–£4.50 ■ desserts £4.50–£5.50 ■ lowest bottle price £15

⊛ Briefs encounter Sardinian local

Look around the crowded dining room of this small and
unpretentious Italian restaurant and you can play the guessing game.
Here we are with a fine view of the heavily secured back door of the
Old Bailey and your challenge is to say which of your fellow diners
are well heeled barristers and which are well heeled defendants.
Terranostra is a valuable find as it offers sound Italian food lifted
by a few Sardinian specialities, plus a gentle, 'neighbourhood'
atmosphere, whereas every other restaurant hereabouts has stellar
ambitions and prices to match. The simple antipasti are good, such
as carpaccio di manzo; calamari ripeno – grilled baby squid stuffed
with their tentacles, herbs and tomatoes; or buffalo mozzarella.
The pasta dishes beg to be elevated to main course choices. Choose
from linguine with crab; malloreddus a la campidanese – a Sardinian
special with a tomato sauce made with sausage; spaghetti with
bottarga; or culurgiones – pasta stuffed with potatoes and cheese
and served with a tomato and mint sauce. From the mains the simple
veal escalope is very good indeed – hammered out, implausibly thin
and flash cooked; or there's spada alla griglia – grilled swordfish.
Service is friendly and you get the feeling that this is a family-run
restaurant. For dessert round up the usual suspects then plump for
the warm chocolate and almond cake. To drink, look out for the
Sardinian beer Ichnusa with four Moors on the label, or rifle the
gently priced wine list.

Thai Square City

136–138 The Minories, EC3 ■ 020 7680 1111

⊖ Aldgate/Tower Hill

🍽 Thai

🕐 Mon to Fri 12.00–20.00

🖰 www.thaisq.com

🖪 all major credit cards ■ 12.5% optional service added

££ starters £4.50–£7.75 ■ mains £6.25–£18.95 ■ sides £2.25–£5.75
■ desserts £3.50–£3.95 ■ Lunch Express (in Bar) £7.95–£13
■ set menus £19.95 (2 courses) & £39.99 (3 courses)
■ lowest bottle price £11.95

✪ Loud City Thai for loud City types

You enter a vast room decorated with temple bells, Buddhas, pots, carved panels, teak, wooden flowers and gold-mosaic rooftop dragons, where friendly staff greet customers with a genuine smile. Downstairs there's a 100-seater cocktail bar with a 16.00–19.00 happy hour. On Thursday and Friday the basement turns into a club with a drink and dancing licence until 0200. The lengthy menu lists both familiar dishes from the Thai repertoire as well as some more novel ideas. Toong thong is a dish of minced prawn and chicken in purse-like little sacks, and very moreish. Tod man poo, or Thai crab cakes, will satisfy connoisseurs seeking this favourite, and tom yam kung will delight lovers of the classic lemongrass soup. Moo ping, or barbecued pork served with a sweet and incredibly hot sauce, is tender and good. The menu suggests that it's especially good with sticky rice, and it is. Six Thai curries offer a choice of red or green and different main ingredients. There are the classic noodle dishes like pad Thai. Other treats include Chu-chee lobster, which is deep-fried lobster with special curry paste, coconut milk and lime leaves. Puddings include banana with coconut syrup and sesame seeds; Thai egg custard; and ice creams and sorbets. The wine list starts gently, threads its way through some decent choices at the accessible verging on expensive mark, and then rockets to show-off bottles like a Château Cheval Blanc St Emilion.

→ For branches, see index or website

Clerkenwell and Smithfield

The Ambassador

55 Exmouth Market, EC1 ■ 020 7837 0009 &

⊖ Angel/Farringdon

🍴 Modern European

🕐 Mon to Fri 09.00–11.45 (breakfast), 12.00–14.30 & 18.00–22.15
(18.00–19.00 pre-theatre); Sat 11.00–16.00 (brunch) & 18.30–22.15;
Sun 11.00–16.00

🖰 www.theambassadorcafe.co.uk

🖶 all major credit cards ■ no service added

££ starters £4.50–£6.50 ■ mains £6.50–£15.50 ■ sides £3.50
■ desserts £4.50–£6.50 ■ set lunch & pre-theatre £12.50 (2 courses)
& £16 (3 courses) ■ lowest bottle price £14

✪ Edgy décor, grounded food

Exmouth Market has established itself as a thriving gastro locale,
and the Ambassador has secured its own niche. The décor is a bit
bleak (in a stylised Americana sort of way) but the menu makes up
for everything. This kitchen turns out food that is seasonal, simple,
carefully sourced and good to eat. It's British in concept but not
afraid to swipe the best French classical techniques. Starters may
include chilled watercress soup, soft boiled egg; pickled sardines
crème fraiche and radishes; a spinach and mascarpone risotto; a
marinated seafood salad, pickled shallots and monk's beard; or a
ballotine of rabbit with Bayonne ham. Mains range from hand-cut
pappardelle with globe artichokes; to roast pollack with a parsnip
purée and Alexander root; black-leg chicken and mushroom pie;
or glazed pork faggot with celeriac and onion gravy. There is a very
decent cheeseboard. Puds run the gamut from warm chocolate
fondant with Muscovado ice cream; sticky date pudding with
butterscotch sauce; to vanilla mousse with poached Yorkshire
rhubarb; and a blood orange jelly with ice cream. The set lunch
is worth noting – how about rare beef and beetroot salad with
balsamic; steamed skate, buttered leeks and chives; followed by the
run of the cheeseboard? A pretty tempting prospect. The wine list
is pleasantly accessible and there's a 'wine recommendation' on the
menu that is usually something interesting at a sensible price.

Bleeding Heart

Bleeding Heart Yard, off Greville St, EC1 ▪ 020 7242 2056

⊖ Farringdon/Chancery Lane

🍽 Modern British

🕘 Mon to Fri 12.00–14.30 & 18.00–22.30

🖰 www.bleedingheart.co.uk

🗗 all major credit cards ▪ 12.5% optional service added

££ starters £5.95–£10.95 ▪ mains £12.95–£23.95
▪ desserts £6.45–£7.95 ▪ lowest bottle price £16.95

✪ Traditional dining rooms, trad food, trad pricing

Part of the Bleeding Heart empire – restaurant, bistro, tavern, crypt, plus The Don restaurant (see p. 204) – the restaurant here was described by the New Yorker, as 'bleeding hard to find' and for once they have got it about right. Once you do manage to locate it, your first glance around the panelled basement rooms will tell you instantly what kind of a place this is. The clientele is from the City, the menu is written with Square Mile superiority, and the wine list is priced for bonus-laden wallets. Just right for the pukka, suit-wearing, claret-loving kind of City folk. Even during a glorious summer these plush underground dining rooms will still be packed, and booking is vital should the forecast veer towards the windy and rain-swept. The menu changes seasonally and dishes form a bridge between classical French cooking and its Modern British descendants. Starters may include truffled parsley soup with a poached egg; a terrine of rabbit and foie gras; or a warm salad of smoked eel. The mains range from a papillote of sea bass with crab; to roast rump of lamb Niçoise; an escalope of salmon with a fennel risotto; or a tournedos of Scottish beef with five peppercorn crust. There's always Stilton cheese on offer and sound, trad puds. The wine list is formidable. The *Wine Spectator* says that this place has 'one of the most outstanding restaurant wine lists in the world'.

Club Gascon
57 West Smithfield, EC1 ■ 020 7796 0600

⊖ Farringdon

🍴 Very French

🕐 Mon to Fri 12.00–14.00 & 19.00–22.30; Sat 19.00–22.30

🖱 www.clubgascon.com

🖪 all major credit cards ■ 12.5% optional service added

££ starters £8.50–£18.00 ■ mains £17–£21 ■ desserts £7–£12
■ menu marché (5 courses) £42 & £65 (inc. matched wines)
■ express lunch menu £28 (3 courses) ■ lowest bottle price £25

⭐ Notably authentic food from south-western France

Club Gascon has become a well-established and revered institution.
If you want a booking, they advise calling two or three weeks ahead,
though you may strike lucky with a cancellation. Pascal Aussignac
is chef here, and his cooking is an authentic taste of south-western
France. In the evening there is an à la carte but at lunch all is set
menus. As the restaurant has a complicated way of doing things
– lots of little dishes under various rather coy headings – this is
no bad thing. Here are some promising dishes: venison carpaccio
with black truffle; wild mushroom casserole with veal sweetbreads;
goose foie gras with sherry, plum and prunes; glazed black cod with
verjuice; cappuccino of black pudding and lobster; foie gras popcorn;
embers-grilled artichoke, barigoule and diabolo sauce; Pyrenean
milk-fed lamb with wood cedar sauce; or red sake-marinated scallop
and berry piquillos coulis. There is always some superior cheese and
suitable indulgent chocolate pudding. But whenever you think you
have a grasp of things Monsieur Aussignac's imagination darts off
in another direction. There is one constant among all this change –
standards are very high in the kitchen and dishes are well balanced
and well seasoned, which makes for good eating in a strangely old-
fashioned way, despite those cutting-edge credentials. Service is Gallic
brisk but like the diners the waiters must make sense of a constant
flow of little dishes. The wines – mainly show-casing the South West
– are splendid.

→ For branches, see index or website

Comptoir Gascon

61–63 Charterhouse Street, EC1 ▪ 020 7608 0851

⊖ Farringdon

🍴 Very French

🕐 Tues to Wed 12.00–14.00 & 19.00–22.00; Thurs to Sat 12.00–14.00 & 19.00–23.00

🔗 www.clubgascon.com

🖮 all major credit cards ▪ 12.5% optional service added

££ starters £4–£7.50 ▪ mains £11–£13.50 ▪ sides £4.50–£6
▪ desserts £3.50–£4.50 ▪ lowest bottle price £16

✪ Shop and bistro, both Gascon through and through

Emulating the Parisian practice of setting up a more modest operation close to the full-on original – a 'bistro en face' – the Gascons have the Comptoir. On one side of Smithfield Market there's the Club and on the other there's the Comptoir. At the Comptoir you can drop in to buy fine bread, pâtisserie, cheeses and the wines of the South West. You can also sit down to a bowl of cassoulet. The food is good, well cooked, simply presented and comes in satisfyingly large portions. Prices are reasonable and you can even drink very well without breaking the bank, as at head office the fine wines of the South West are to the fore. Starters may include the cheekily named 'piggy treats' – a serious pork-fest; potted duck rillettes; fresh oysters with grilled chipolatas; mackerel and fondant potato on toast; and a great deal of stunning rustic bread. Mains range from a perfect steak tartare; to grilled squid with pearl barley and rouille; grilled tuna, crackling pork belly and celery; smoked sturgeon 'civet' celeriac mash; onglet with sauce Bordelaise; mini cheese ravioli with pistou; and roast shoulder of lamb and aligot. The cassoulet Toulousain is stellar, but everything is good. For pud run amok at the cake counter or try the fabled crème Catalan; or the regional cheese plate. This bistro provides a friendly and inexpensive way to eat some very good dishes indeed.

→ For branches, see index or website

The Eagle

159 Farringdon Road, EC1 ▪ 020 7837 1353

⊖ Farringdon

🍽 Mediterranean/gastropub

🕐 Mon to Fri 12.30–15.00 & 18.30–22.30; Sat 12.30–15.30 & 18.30–22.30; Sun 12.30–15.30

🗗 Mastercard, Visa, Switch ▪ no service added

££ tapas £4–£7 ▪ mains £8–£15.50 ▪ desserts £1.20
▪ lowest bottle price £11.75

✪ Gastropub, the original and genuine

Way back in 1991, the Eagle was taken over by food-minded entrepreneurs who transformed it from grubby boozer into a restaurant-pub turning out top-quality dishes. They were pioneers: there should be a blue plaque over the door stating that this site was the starting place of the great gastropub revolution. The Eagle has remained a crowded, rather shabby sort of place. The kitchen is truly open; the chefs work behind the bar, and the menu is chalked up over their heads. It changes daily, even hourly, as things run out or deliveries come in. The food is broadly Mediterranean in outlook with a Portuguese bias, and you still have to fight your way to the bar to order and pay. The menu changes like quicksilver, but you may find the likes of the famous cal do verde – the Portuguese chorizo and potato soup that takes its name from the addition of spring greens – or a grilled swordfish with peppers, mint, new potatoes and Balsamico; a delicious and simple dish like roast spring chicken with preserved lemons, potatoes, mustard leaves and aioli; or a rib-eye 'tailgate' with green beans and mixed leaves, radishes and horseradish. To finish, choose between a fine cheese – perhaps Wigmore served with rhubarb jam and toast – or the siren charms of those splendid, small, Portuguese, cinnamon custard tarts – pasties de natal. Enjoy the lack of frills and the service that comes with a helping of attitude.

Fox & Anchor

115 Charterhouse Street, EC1 ▪ 020 7250 1300

⊖ Barbican/Farringdon

🍴 British/gastropub

🕐 Mon to Fri 12.00–22.00

🔗 www.foxandanchor.com

🖹 all major credit cards ▪ 10% optional service added

££ starters £4.50–£7.95 ▪ mains £10.50–£12.95 ▪ sides £3
▪ desserts £5 ▪ lowest bottle price £12.95

⊗ Restoring the glory of the British pub

The Fox & Anchor opened towards the end of 2007 after a
rigorous refurb that aimed to preserve the décor intact. It has a
handful of bedrooms, and what is particularly interesting about the
Fox is that the aim was always to open a pub – not a gastropub.
Such an ambition makes you think about just what the differences
are between the two classes of establishment. Pubs always have
good beer and the kind of atmosphere that underpins the serious
business of drinking with food that is wholesome, not over-priced
and practical rather than fancy. But atop the Fox & Anchor menus
the strap line reads HOPS&CHOPS, CUVEES&DUVETS which is hardly
pub-speak. The food at the Fox is very good, honest, and seasonal:
potted pigs head and piccalilli; prawns by the half pint; mussels
cooked in Aspall's cider; Welsh rarebit. Listed under mains is a large
ham hock with Colcannon mash and parsley sauce, which is very
good indeed. Or there's steak and oyster pie – fine crust, fine gravy,
extra oysters – or traditional fish pie. Great care is taken with sourcing
British ingredients from small producers. The goose-fat chips are
majestic. There is a long bar, the beer is well kept and the staff are
friendly. This place manages to be more pub than gastropub, despite
a serious wine list and good food. Wouldn't it be fabulous if we
could replace all those tired old gastropubs with genuine, hospitable,
'public houses'?

Hix Oyster & Chop House

35–37 Greenhill Rents, EC1 ■ 020 7017 1930

⊖ Farringdon

|●| Very British

⏲ Mon to Fri 12.00–15.00 & 17.00–22.30; Sat 17.00–22.30; Sun 12.00–15.00

🖥 www.restaurantsetcltd.co.uk

🗗 All major credit cards ■ 12.5% optional service added

££ starters £7.25–£17.50 ■ mains £12.50–£19.25
   ■ sides £3.25–£3.75 ■ desserts £6.75
   ■ lowest bottle price £14

✪ Honest British food done very well indeed

Hix burst onto the scene in the early summer of 2008. It is a remarkable place, not just because it is the Mark Hix's first solo venture (although he is a veteran of the London scene, having headed up Le Caprice, p. 127, the Ivy, p. 29, Scotts, p. 103 and J. Sheekey, p. 30) but rather due to his unerring ability to put his finger on the mood of the times. This restaurant felt comfortable, confident and old-established from the very first week. The menu is a roll call of all that is best in traditional, seasonal, British food. Start with a magnificent salad of French beans and ox-cheek – contrasting textures, rich flavour and a simple dressing; another salad brings together pennywort, beetroot and Little Wallop goats' cheese; there may be a stellar rabbit brawn; fresh asparagus simply cooked; or outrageously good De Beauvoir smoked salmon 'Hix cure', which comes from a smoker in Mark Hix's back garden! Mains range from a grilled gilthead bream to mutton chop curry, or a hanger steak served with baked bone marrow. Special praise must be reserved for the beef flank and oyster pie with its ambrosial gravy. There is also the option of two diners sharing a whole Wooley Park Farm free-range chicken with wild garlic sauce. The important details are right here, from the battered assortment of mismatched silver serving dishes, to the unaggressively priced wine list and friendly service.

Medcalf

40 Exmouth Market, EC1 ■ 020 7833 3533

⊖ Farringdon/Angel

⦿ Modern British

🕐 Mon to Thurs 12.30–15.00 & 18.00–22.00; Fri 12.00–15.00 & 18.00–22.00; Sat 12.00–16.00 & 18.00–22.30; Sun 12.00–16.00

⌂ www.medcalfbar.co.uk

🖯 all major credit cards ■ 12.5% optional service added

££ starters £4.50–£8 ■ mains £10.50–£14.50 ■ sides £3.25 ■ desserts £5–£6.50 ■ lowest bottle price £13.75

⭐ A resto that thinks it's a gastropub

The frontage may look like Albert Sydney Medcalf's 1912 butcher shop, but the long bar looks very like a pub bar, the tables look like pub tables and the menu is a pubby sort of menu. All of which doesn't matter a damn because, whichever pigeonhole you choose to file it in, Medcalf makes a very decent job of being an informal eatery. The menu is seasonally driven and changes every session, so starters may range from Welsh rarebit to sweet potato soup; sautéed duck livers pancetta and confit chestnuts; or squid with chilli and ginger – a good, well-balanced dish with assertive flavours and accurately cooked squid. The main courses listed are honest and have a pleasing simplicity. There may be pan-fried pollack with curly kale; or a collar of bacon with broth and new potatoes. Or how about a serious and suitably trad fish pie, fluffy mash on top and creamy gunk within? There may be braised beef with Guinness and neeps; pan-fried calves' liver with a red wine risotto; and a roasted fig and goat's cheese tart. The pud list is headed by 'selection of British cheeses with oatcakes and chutney', but for the sweeter tooth there is chocolate and almond cake; rice pudding with blackberry compôte; or plum syllabub. The wine list is priced sensibly, there is real beer on offer and service is confident and attentive without getting too pushy.

Moro

34–36 Exmouth Market, EC1 ◼ 020 7833 8336 &

⊖ Farringdon/Angel

🍴 Spanish/tapas

🕐 Mon to Sat 12.30–14.30 & 19.00–22.30

🖰 www.moro.co.uk

🖭 all major credit cards ◼ 12.5% service added for parties of 6 or more

££ starters £6–£7.50 ◼ mains £14.50–£19.50 ◼ desserts £5.50–£7.50
◼ lowest bottle price £12.50

✪ Good food – both Moorish and more-ish

Moro has a secure place on the list of London's 'must visit'
eateries. In feel it's not so very far away from the best pub-
restaurants, although the proprietors have given themselves the
luxury of a slightly larger kitchen. This has also become a place of
pilgrimage for disciples of the wood-fired oven, and the food here
hails mainly from Spain, Portugal and North Africa. You'll probably
have to book. The à la carte changes every fortnight. There's usually a
soup, and it's usually among the best starters. How does cauliflower
and yoghurt soup sound? Or morcilla with hispi cabbage? Main
courses are simple and often traditional combinations of taste and
textures. Look out for wood-roasted sea bass with poached sweet
and sour leeks; wood-roasted Old Spot pork with sprouting broccoli
and romesco sauce; charcoal-grilled mackerel with cabbage and
caraway salad, walnuts and flatbread; or perhaps chicken cooked in
Pedro Ximenez, or slow-roast kid with new season's garlic, Fino and
mashed potato. Do not miss the splendid Spanish cheese selection
served with membrillo and a glass of Oloroso. And there's no excuse
for avoiding the Malaga raisin ice cream, or the serious chocolate
and apricot tart. This is a place that effortlessly combines top-quality
ingredients with very good cooking and comfortable service, and
there is a grand list of moody sherries into the bargain.

St John

26 St John Street, EC1 ■ 020 7251 0848

⊖ Farringdon

🍽 British

🕐 Mon to Fri 12.00–15.00 & 18.00–23.00; Sat 18.00–23.00

🖰 www.stjohnrestaurant.com

🗗 all major credit cards ■ no service added

££ starters £4–£12.80 ■ mains £12.80–£22.50 ■ sides £3.20–£7.20
■ desserts £3.40–£7.40 ■ lowest bottle price £14.50

✪ A national treasure, the best British cooking

American chef, food writer, wild man and all-round good egg
Antony Bourdain names the St John bone marrow and parsley salad
as his 'desert island dish'. Good call. One of the most frequent
requests, especially from foreign visitors, is 'Where can we get some
really English cooking?' Little wonder that the promise of 'olde
English fare' is the bait in so many tourist traps. The cooking at St
John, however, is genuine. It is sometimes old-fashioned and makes
inspired use of strange and unfashionable cuts of meat. Technically,
the cooking is of a very high standard, while the restaurant itself is
completely without frills or design pretensions. You'll either love it
or hate it. The menu changes every session, but the tone does not,
and there's always a dish or two to support the slogan 'nose to tail
eating'. Charcuterie, as you'd imagine, is good: a simple terrine will
be dense but not dry – well judged. Or, for the committed, what
about a starter of crispy pig's skin and dandelion? Or celery soup?
Main courses may include calf's liver and swede, or oxtail and mash.
Maybe there will be a dish described simply as 'fennel and Berkswell
cheese'; perversely, in this den of offal, the veg dishes are a delight.
Puddings are traditional and well executed: custard tart and rhubarb,
or a slice of strong Lancashire cheese with an Eccles cake. Joy of joys,
sometimes there is even a seriously good Welsh rarebit. The place
has won shedloads of awards, and booking is a must. St John serves
good food at its most genuine.

→ For branch, see index or website

Smiths, the Dining Room

67–77 Charterhouse Street, EC1 ■ 020 7251 7950

⊖ Farringdon

🍴 Modern British

🕐 (café) Mon to Fri 07.00–17.00; Sat & Sun 12.30–17.00; (restaurants)
Mon to Fri 12.00–14.45 & 18.00–22.45; Sat 12.00–16.00;
Sat 18.00–22.45; Sun (top floor) 12.30–15.45 & 19.00–22.45
(dining room closed)

🖱 www.smithsofsmithfield.co.uk

💳 all major credit cards ■ 12.5 % optional service added

££ larder/starters/soups £5.50, £6.50 & £4 ■ mains/grills £12.50
■ daily lunch Market Special £11 ■ sides £3
■ Sweet Tooth £4.50 ■ lowest bottle price £12.75

⭐ The Café is allegedly Jamie Oliver's favourite
breakfasting place

Smith's is a large and vibrant temple to eating and drinking
spread over many floors. On the ground floor there's a bar and
café serving drink and practical, sensible food. On the second floor
is the 130-seater 'Dining Room'. The culinary mainspring here is
an enlightened buying policy – quality, quality, quality. The Dining
Room is a large space around a central hole that looks down onto
the smart bar area. Eating here is rather like sitting at the centre of a
deactivated factory. The menu is divided into Larder, Starters, Soups,
Mains, Grills, Daily Lunch Market Specials, Sides, and Sweet Tooth.
The starters are simple and good: grilled mushrooms and Taleggio on
toasted sourdough; Portuguese-style salt cod fritters; foie gras and
chicken liver parfait. Main courses may include crisp belly of pork with
mashed potato and green sauce; chicken and morel pie with buttered
green beans; a serious 10oz beef burger with mature cheddar; or
roast cod with roast salsify and Hollandaise. The lunch specials are
from the comfort-eating school, and feature such delights as cottage
pie. Puds are good. Try the chocolate and pear pithivier. The 'Top
Floor' is an élite affair specialising in well-matured steaks from rare-
breed steers – expensive, but very good indeed. Inevitably, it has
become something of a favourite with bonus boys.

Vanilla Black

17–18 Took's Court, EC4 ■ 020 7242 2622

⊖ Chancery Lane

🍴 Vegetarian/Modern British

🕐 Mon to Fri 12.00–14.30 & 18.00–22.00

🖰 www.vanillablack.co.uk

🖯 all major credit cards ■ 12.5 % optional service added

££ £24 (2 courses) & £30 (3 courses) ■ set lunch £18 (2 courses) & £23 (3 courses) ■ lowest bottle price £14.50

✪ Veggie star

In its previous location – York! – this restaurant made it onto the list as one of the top veggie restos in Britain. But even so it takes a good deal of courage to up sticks and transplant the venture to London, and it's debatable whether Took's Court in the arid heart of Lawyerland is the most promising place to end up. Several things about this restaurant which opened in May 2008 will appeal to any foodie (not just vegetarians). The chef makes good use of decent cheese in his cooking and has a confident approach to cooking with spices. This is not the coarse, 'wholemeal' kind of cooking that fits the veggie stereotype and dishes are stylish and well-presented. Starters range from green beans with toasted sesame, croutons and lemon; to aged feta and toasted orange cake with peach chutney and green olives; or 'deconstructed Puy lentil dhal with potato puree and curry oil' – very good indeed, with upfront curry flavours and agreeably contrasting textures. Mains are also delightful: hickory-smoked duck egg and Duckett's Caerphilly pudding with pommes purée croquette and pineapple pickle – good flavours. Or steamed cabbage and Longman's cheddar with braised beans. Or a baked Blue Vinney and Bramley apple galette. Puds include good chilled melon soup or chocolate parfait. The wine list is sensibly priced and service friendly. Whether you're veggie or not this is a good place to eat.

Vivat Bacchus

47 Farringdon Street, EC4 ■ 020 7353 2648

⊖ Farringdon

¶❢ South African

🕐 Mon to Fri 12.00–14.30 & 18.30–21.30

⌐⌐ www.vivatbacchus.co.uk

🗗 all major credit cards ■ 12.5 % optional service added

££ starters £5.50–£12.50 ■ mains £13.75–£18.50 ■ sides £3.50–£7
■ desserts £5–£8.50 ■ lunch £15.50 (2 courses) & £17.50 (3 courses)
■ lowest bottle price £15.50

⭐ Fine cheeses and fine wines

Vivat Bacchus is an unusual restaurant. For one it places a heavy emphasis on both cheese and wine and for a second the chef is from South Africa. In practice this means that at the start of the meal you will be asked to get up and choose your wine from the temperature-controlled glass-walled wine rooms, and at the end of the meal, when thoughts turn to cheese, you can visit another temperature- and humidity-controlled enclosure to pick cheeses. The wine list is extensive – Vivat may have London's best range of South African wines. In the meantime the menu features starters like smoked chicken and piquillo pepper soup; escarole, pear and Roquefort salad, and mojama de Atun (mojama is air-dried tuna – a sort of piscine jamon). You could also try the waygu and foie gras burger, this century's version of Richard Corrigan's 1990's classic. The mains betray more South African influences: wild mushroom, Parmesan and maize meal galette; roast whole bream served with beetroot orange and aged balsamic; rabbit saffron and green olive stew with home-made tagliatelle; or seared medallion of springbok. Puds range from a classic Dom Pedro (ice cream and Amarula) to sticky toffee pudding – both an excuse to try some Klein Constantia vin de Constance. Service is slick, as it has to be with everyone wandering from wine room to wine room. Good fun.

The White Swan

108 Fetter Lane, EC1 ▪ 020 7242 9696

⊖ Chancery Lane

🍽 Modern British/gastropub

🕐 Mon to Fri 12.00–15.00 & 18.00–22.00

🖱 www.thewhiteswanlondon.com

🗗 all major credit cards ▪ 12.5% optional service added

££ starters £6.50–£9 ▪ mains £14–£17 ▪ sides £3.50–£4
▪ desserts £5.50–£9.50 (for cheese) ▪ prix fixe lunch £23 & £28
▪ lowest bottle price £16

✪ A good restaurant posing as gastropub

'It's certainly a pub, but not as we know it.' The White Swan may
be sister to The Well, but it is one of a completely different breed of
gastropub. These places are not content to knock out homely food
in homely surroundings; their aspirations are tuned to a world of fine
dining where there is little room for junkshop tables and mismatched
cutlery. Downstairs the pub ethic dominates, with real ale and decent
bar food; upstairs there's the dining room. The seating is luxurious
beige leather, the ceiling is mirrored, there's a cheese trolley. The
food is very good. The presentation is simple but elegant. Flavours
are well matched, and for cooking of this quality prices seem very
fair. Start with chilled cucumber soup with smoked salmon strips
and horseradish crème fraîche; sautéed veal sweetbreads with
carrot purée, girolles and Sauternes sauce. Or something seasonal,
like asparagus with hot melted butter. On to the mains: wild sea
trout with curried mussel nage, saffron potatoes, mango coriander
and cucumber salsa; roast Barbary duck breast with sweet potato
and carrot à l'orange; new season rump of lamb with Puy lentils,
watercress and mint purée. Very satisfying. Puds are good; the 'blood
orange marmalade sponge pudding with custard' has a real tang.
Having a go at the extensive cheeseboard ups the ante, but it is worth
it to see so many fine British cheeses. Service is slick and the wine list
has some decent bottles at the cheap end. This is a really good place
to eat.

The Zetter

86–88 Clerkenwell Road, EC1 ■ 020 7324 4455 &

⊖ Farringdon

🍴 Modern Italian

🕐 Mon to Wed 07.00–10.30, 12.00–14.30 & 18.00–22.30; Thurs & Fri 07.00–10.30, 12.00–14.30 & 18.00–23.00; Sat 07.30–11.00, 11.00–15.00 (brunch) & 18.00–23.00; Sun 07.30–11.00, 11.00–15.00 (brunch) & 18.00–22.30

🖰 www.thezetter.com

🖶 all major credit cards ■ 12.5% optional service added

££ breakfast £4.50–£16.50 ■ brunch £5.50–£12.50
■ starters £5.50–£8.50 ■ mains £12–£16.50 ■ sides £3.50
■ desserts £5.50–£7.50 ■ menus: lunch & dinner £21.50 (2 courses + glass of champagne) ■ lowest bottle price £16.50

⭐ Boutique hotel, boutique restaurant

Formerly HQ to Zetter's Football Pools, this place has become the spiritual home of the style police. Here you'll find 59 bedrooms and 7 rooftop suites. The plus side of this arrangement is that the Zetter is open pretty much all day. The dining room curves around a large bar, the tables and chairs are utilitarian and the high ceiling can make for a noisy, echoey experience. The food is Italian, but seen through Modern British eyes; it changes monthly and strives to keep in step with the seasons. Winter will see hearty soups – pumpkin and chestnut with salame N'Duia, very rich with a welcome belt of chilli; garlic roast prawns with chorizo sweet potato and glazed pork belly; or dandelion and smoked chicken salad with crisp bacon. Pasta dishes are well done – chicken and pancetta cannelloni with walnut-smoked paprika and parmesan; or 'roast leg of lamb' risotto. Mains range from pan-fried plaice with piquillo pepper, fregola, smoked bacon and mussels; to braised osso buco with saffron risotto 'A la Milanese' and gremolata'; grilled skate with steamed fennel, fiat beans and toasted almonds; or guinea fowl with pancetta and thyme. Puds are considered – pear and Strega sorbet, or perhaps a chestnut ice cream with bitter chocolate sauce. The wine list touches a few helpful bases.

Docklands

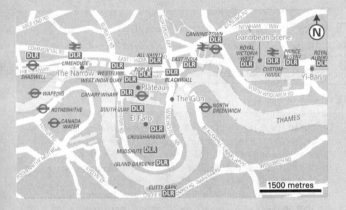

Caribbean Scene

Excel Marina, 17 Western Gateway, Royal Victoria Dock, E16

■ 020 7511 2023 &

DLR Custom House

West Indian

Mon 18.00–23.00; Tues to Thurs 12.00–23.00; Fri & Sat 12.00–24.00; Sun 12.00–23.00

www.caribbeanscene.co.uk

all major credit cards ■ 10% optional service added

££ starters £4.50–£7.50 ■ mains £11.50–£20 sides £4.50
■ desserts £4.50–£7 ■ set menu £30 (3 courses)
■ lowest bottle price £13.50

✪ Glossy Windies outpost

Caribbean Scene is a short walk from the Excel Exhibition centre and is a better option than the restaurants that are closer. While most Caribbean restaurants tend to be in the 'no-frills' category — home-cooking, laid-back service, good takeaway trade — Caribbean Scene does not lack ambition (as the various proudly displayed awards will confirm). Décor-wise, both the restaurant and the presentation of dishes on the plate are equally over the top. Diners are expected to believe that they are eating in a small West Indies beach café — something rather at odds with the view of the murky dock waters through the windows. For starters try the plantain and ginger drops. These are fritters with a good crisp coat. Or there are saltfish fritters; or saltfish and ackee moneybags. The main courses include some interesting options: 'oxtail cassoulet' is a rich stew bulked up with butter beans; there's curried goat (served as a parcel, why?); or escovitch fish, which turns out to be a sea bass marinated and served with wilted onions. Stuffed jerk chicken is breast meat rolled around a plantain and spinach mixture. The staples are well done — rice and peas; coleslaw with attitude and macaroni pie. For pudding try the coconut cake with rum ice cream. There's a large bar serving Windies beers and rum punch, and some tables outside. All that is needed is some West Indian weather.

El Faro

3 Turnberry Quay, Pepper Street, E14 ■ 020 7987 5511

⊖ DLR Crossharbour/London Arena

⦿ Spanish

⏱ Mon to Sat 12.00–15.30 & 17.00–23.00; Sun 13.00–17.00

⟟ www.el-faro.co.uk

⊟ all major credit cards ■ 10% optional service added

££ tapas £3.45–£14.50 ■ mains £13.45–£18 sides £3.25–£3.95
   ■ desserts £5.50–£7.50 ■ lowest bottle price £14

✪ Slick Spaniard on the dockside

El Faro is the second Spanish restaurant to seek fame and fortune
at this location and gradually, as the neighbourhood evolves,
prospects improve. The restaurant juts out like a prow pointing
towards the murky waters of the dock, which are enlivened by sailing
dinghies and dragon boats. There are some outdoor tables and this
is a good place to while away some time with a glass of Fino and a
succession of tapas. There's an epic Spanish cheese plate – Idiazabal,
Manchego and Tetilla y Cabrales; all the usual Jamón and charcuterie;
well-made ham croquettas; pulpo a la Galegga – octopus with sweet
paprika; pimientos del Padrón; a really superb home-made pâté de
foie gras with fig purée; or cubes of confit suckling pig with honey
and rosemary that are implausibly, meltingly delicious. Main courses
range from redoubtable steaks; grilled red tuna loin with onions,
Sichuan pepper and duck liver; to oven-roast suckling pig (check
availability); and monkfish with clams, prawns and asparagus. Or you
could break the bank and opt for grilled native lobster or some of
the complex seafood extravaganzas. The standard of cooking is high
and these dishes are sophisticated. Side orders include patatas bravas
and olive-oil chips. For pudding how about warm chocolate brownie
with vanilla ice cream; olive oil chocolate cake; or a traditional crème
Catalan? Service is friendly and the wine list offers a good range of
sherries and Spanish wines.

The Gun

27 Coldharbour, E14 ■ 020 7515 5222

⊖ DLR South Quay/Canary Wharf

🍽 Modern British/gastropub

🕐 Mon to Fri 12.00–15.00 & 18.30–22.00; Sat & Sun 11.30–16.00 &
18.00–22.30 (brunch 11.30–13.00)

⊘ www.thegundocklands.com

🖻 all major credit cards ■ 12.5% optional service added

££ starters £6–£7.50 ■ mains £15–£17.50 ■ sides £4 ■ desserts £5.50
■ bar menu £4.50–£12.50 ■ lowest bottle price £13

✪ A slick restaurant – disguised as an award-winning
gastropub

It is said that Horatio Nelson liked The Gun. But that may be on
account of the charms of Emma Hamilton, whom he is supposed to
have met regularly in an upstairs room. This sprawling riverside pub
has a warren of rooms and a splendid terrace. First things first, the
pub side of The Gun works very well; there's real beer and a roast
suckling pig sandwich with apple sauce. The restaurant side of things
also delights; well-cooked food, river terrace, suave service, private
dining room, rampaging wine list. But if your idea of a gastropub is
somewhere scruffy with good food at rock-bottom prices, The Gun
doesn't qualify. However, it is full to bursting with happy customers
who can pay their way. The menu changes regularly, dishes are
seasonal, and ingredients are carefully chosen – venison from the
Denham estate, Longhorn rib eye. The cooking is very sound: starters
may include celeriac, truffle and wild mushroom soup; ham hock and
foie gras terrine; a butternut squash and sage tart; or pan-fried king
prawns with a smoked cherry tomato relish. Mains include a series
of daily specials from the blackboard, like a roast grouse, or a whole
sea bass, which are well cooked and well presented. Or you might
find roast Barbary duck breast with kumquats; or a canon of Welsh
lamb for two to share. Puds range from Valrhona chocolate tart with
espresso ice cream to a banana tart Tatin.

The Narrow

44 Narrow Street, E14 ■ 020 7592 7950

⊖ DLR Limehouse

🍽 British/gastropub

🕐 Mon to Fri 11.30–15.00 & 18.00–22.30; Sat 12.00–22.00;
Sun 12.00–21.30

🖱 www.gordonramsay.com

🖰 all major credit cards ■ 12.5% optional service added

££ starters £4–£7 ■ toasts £5 ■ mains £9–£14.50 sides £2.75–£3
■ desserts £4–£4.50 ■ cheese £7 ■ lowest bottle price £13.50

⭐ Gordon does gastropub

The Narrow was Gordon Ramsay's first venture into the gastropub market. It may be counter-intuitive, but less formal restaurants with lower prices can deliver more revenue than wildly expensive, Michelin-starred, fine-dining establishments. Lots of bums on lots of seats, reasonable prices and lower staffing levels mean more income. The Narrow was a genuine Limehouse boozer and to Ramsay's credit, some of that feel remains. The dining room is to the side of the bar and (when the weather co-operates) spills out onto a terrace overlooking the river. The food is commendably British – as is the vogue. Starters range from corned beef and tatties to grilled Dorset mackerel with crushed celeriac or English asparagus with mayonnaise. Then there's a section called 'on toast' – brilliant stuff, an idea first pioneered by The Rivington (see p. 255). Here the devilled lambs' kidneys on toast are particularly fine. Main courses offer a splendid trad fish and chips; a smoked ham and chicken pie and mash; Essex saddleback pork chop with spinach; and Cumberland bangers with champ. Inventive puddings such as rhubarb and ginger crumble or chocolate and cherry trifle vie with old-timers like treacle tart and custard. The cooking here is reliable, service is friendly, the wine list has plenty to offer at reasonable prices and the place is packed. But it's best not to set your heart on chatting to Mr Ramsay when you visit.

Plateau

4th Floor, Canada Place, Canary Wharf, E14 ■ 020 7715 7100

⊖ Canary Wharf

🍽 Modern British

🕒 restaurant: Mon to Fri 12.00–15.00 & 18.00–22.30; Sat 18.00–22.30;
bar & grill: Mon to Sat 12.00–15.00 & 18.00–22.30; Sun 12.00–16.00

⌐ www.danddlondon.com

🖶 all major credit cards ■ 12.5% optional service added

££ starters £8.50–£15.00 ■ mains £22.50–£26 ■ sides £4
■ desserts £7–£9 ■ prix fixe dinner Fri & Sat £35 (3 courses) & £40 (4
courses) ■ lowest bottle price £21

✪ High-level room, high level of ambition

Plateau juts out from the fourth floor of a giant glass office block
and looks out over a square that is surrounded by even larger towers.
Visit at night, the view is amazing – spooky in a slightly sci-fi sort of
way, verging on Bladerunner. The menu at Plateau offers starters like
lobster and celeriac cannelloni; duck salad roll with a sesame crepe;
or foie gras and ham hock terrine. Main courses also tick a few boxes:
spice-crusted sea bass; fillet of beef with salsify and beetroot; or
confit pork belly with langoustine. There are some more extravagant
dishes like rotisserie black-leg chicken, foie gras with black truffle
mash potato; or John Dory with orange and almond powder and bok
choi. The service is sound and unruffled. The wine list is refreshingly
egalitarian – in such a lofty and aspirational establishment it is hard
not to feel nervous but there is plenty of good drinking at earthbound
prices before the wine list wings off into the stratosphere. Puds
are sound: chocolate-filled pancake with chestnut jelly and rum ice
cream, or tarte Tatin. At lunch Plateau is odds on to do good business
in a directors' dining room sort of way, but in the evening it is worth
a visit purely to gaze out of the window. It is also worth noting that
the adjacent Plateau bar and grill shares the view and offers a slightly
less formal menu.

Yi-Ban

London Regatta Centre, Royal Albert Dock, E16

■ 020 7473 6699

⊖ DLR Royal Albert Dock

🍽 Chinese/dim sum

🕐 Mon to Sat 12.00–23.30; Sun 11.00–22.30

🔗 www.yi-ban.co.uk

🖫 all major credit cards ■ 12.5% optional service added

££ dim sum £2–£3.50 ■ mains £6–£25 ■ sides £5–£8
■ desserts £2–£3.50 ■ set menus £18–£35 ■ lowest bottle price £13

✪ Sophisticated Chinese, good dim sum

If your mission was to find a rather good Chinese restaurant, it's unlikely that your first thought would be to go to a barren corner of Docklands and then make your way upstairs to a rowing club bar. Persevere – at one end of the room you'll find Yi-Ban, complete with lots of tables and friendly staff. If you turn up at lunch you'll find the room full of happy Chinese customers, which is somehow very reassuring. The room is comfortable in a modernist sort of way, so settle yourself at a large round table. The dim sum are good and cheap: snow pea dumplings are prawny, green herby numbers; mini glutinous rice rolls are mini and suitably glutinous; the crystal prawn dumplings are good, as are the prawn fun guo. The fried options are dry and crisp: sweet and sour wan tun; deep-fried seafood dumplings; Vietnamese sugar-cane prawns. Strangely there are no steamed cheung fun on the menu here, but you can indulge any whims for exotica by ordering chicken claws Thai-style. The lengthy main menu is 'standard Chinese sophisticated': steamed scallops; baked lobster (beware, it attracts the dreaded 'seasonal price'); honey spare ribs; lemon chicken. Or perhaps 'walnut prawns' – crisp prawns, walnuts and salad cream – tickles the fancy? This is a very pleasant restaurant with a terrific view, smiling, helpful staff, and bargain dim sum for lunch – not bad for a converted rowing club bar.

→ For branch, see index or website

Hoxton, Shoreditch and Hackney

N

CANONBURY
ST PAUL'S
ROAD
BALLS POND
Istanbul Iskembecisi
ARDULA ST
19 Numara Bos Cirrik 1
Mangal 2
KINGSLAND HIGH ST
DALSTON KINGSLAND
DALSTON LANE
GRAHAM
DALSTON LANE
DALSTON LA
HACKNEY DOWNS
ROAD

The Scolt Head
Huong Viet
FORBAT ROAD
Prince Arthur
LONDON FIELDS
Empress of India →

The Waterhouse
GREAT ROAD
KINGSLAND ROAD
Buen Ayre

Bacchus
HACKNEY ROAD
CAMBRIDGE HEATH

Fifteen Trattoria
CITY ROAD
Fish Central
LEVER STREET
BATH STREET
The Bavarian Beerhouse
Pinchito Tapas
OLD STREET
OLD STREET
FEATHERSTONE
CITY ROAD
GREAT EASTERN STREET
STREET
Viet Grill
Gay Tre
The Rivington
Green & Red
SHOREDITCH
BETHNAL
Gourmet San
GREEN
Maida

500 metres

19 Numara Bos Cirrik '1'

34 Stoke Newington Road, N16 ■ 020 7249 0400

Hackney Central BR

Turkish

Sun to Thurs 12.00–24.00; Fri & Sat 12.00–01.00

all major credit cards ■ no service added

££ starters £2–£8.50 ■ mains £8–£21.50 ■ sides & salads £3.50–£7.50 ■ desserts £3 ■ lowest bottle price £12

⭐ Best ever Turkish grill house

There are those moments when only the salty indulgence of perfectly grilled meat will do, and you know it is time to visit a Turkish grill house. Which leaves the denizens of N16 with a large choice, and they even have to choose between 19 Numara Bos Cirrik '1' and 19 Numara Bos Cirrik '2'. That's pretty easy though, as the original (No 1) is slightly less formal and with real charm. You sit at tables that are ranged in rows (like the desks in a schoolroom) with the teacher's place taken by the grill. Portion size is taken seriously here. You may order a starter on your first visit but you probably won't on your second. It's not that they aren't splendid – good cacik (cucumber and yoghurt); good patlican soslu (aubergines); good muska bora (cheese pastries). But your main course includes a plateful of decent salad that turns up before the meat, plus a plateful of astonishingly good grilled onions and some stunning bread, and if you are still ploughing your way through a starter it can be unsettling. From the mains the shish kebab is worth noting, as are the bildircin – grilled quail; the uykuluk – sweetbreads; and the pirzola – lamb chops. But best of all is the kaburga – impeccably crisp lamb spare ribs. Service is brisk and friendly, and the cold Efes beer is the perfect accompaniment. This is a great place to eat.

→ For branch, see index

Bacchus

177 Hoxton Street, N1 ■ 020 7613 0477

 Old Street

🍴 Fusion

🕐 Mon to Sat 18.00–22.00

🖥 all major credit cards ■ 12.5% optional service added

££ tasting menus £45 (5 courses) & £60 (7 courses)
■ lowest bottle price £18

⭐ Fervent disciple of molecular gastronomy

Do you remember when Nouvelle Cuisine segued from being 'the next big thing', to a single sprout paired with a solo strawberry on a sauce splattered plate, and a label that became synonymous with small portions? The same kind of dank future could lie in wait for 'molecular gastronomy'. Bacchus chef-proprietor Nuno Mendes is keen to emphasise that 'we dabble with modern and old cooking techniques to create a very casual "fine dining" atmosphere – the food is a very personal reflection of my travels and work with many talented, passionate and beautiful people.' This place looks like a gastropub, service is friendly and the food is very complicated. Mendes is a good cook and is particularly adept at combining textures – he seems to have a bit of thing for crumbs. On the 7-course tasting menu several dishes have a gritty, crunchy, flavour element. There's a rosemary gomasio with the tuna toast – sesame crunch; there are coral crumbs with the yuzu crab; and there's black olive migas with the confit potatoes and cepes. You'll also find powders, papers, foams and jellies. The flavours are good and (unusually for a lengthy tasting menu) the dishes seem to get better and better as you work your way down the list. By the time you get to 'crispy suckling pig, fresh and dried figs with their caramel, Iberico ham, marscapone cubes, almond basil powders' things are really singing. Molecular but fun.

The Bavarian Beerhouse

190 City Road, EC1 ▪ 020 7608 0925

⊖ Old Street

|O| German

◷ Mon to Thurs 12.00–22.00; Fri 12.00–02.00; Sat 13.00–22.00

⌁ www.bavarian-beerhouse.co.uk

⊟ all major credit cards ▪ 10% optional service added

££ starters & snacks £1.95 to £4.90 ▪ mains £6.50 to £13.50
  ▪ desserts £3.50 ▪ lowest bottle price £12.50 (wine)

✪ Beer and frolics

The Bavarian Beerhouse is a jolly, if unprepossessing, place.
Little effort is made to hide the fact that this mighty engine is
driven by our love of beer. The beer is excellent Paulaner Munich
lager and Paulaner Dunkel dark beer plus Erdinger Hefe Weissbier
– which means that you shouldn't have to resort to the special
offer: a 1.5-litre jug of Jagermeister and Coca Cola! The food is
uncompromising and is quickly in conflict with that famous dining
rule: 'Never eat anything bigger than your head'. There are some
starters, including Nurnberger bratwurst – elegant little sausages
served with sauerkraut and a pretzel. Or there are Vienna sausages;
or a serious goulash soup. The mains run from meatloaf through
Bavarian cheese noodles to a range of schnitzels – there's Weiner;
Jager (with mushrooms); Holstein (with egg and bacon – a sad lack
of anchovies); or ziguener (a hot pepper and onion sauce). Only those
foolishly confident of their appetite should climb the mountain that is
the Munchener schweinshaxe. This is the stump end of a leg of pork
and outrageously large, one of those dishes where you cannot help
but be bored with the food long before you finish it. Puds are equally
immense and the chopped pancake with raisins and ice cream would
nourish a family of four. So there you have it: jolly atmosphere, great
beer, cheerful service, giant portions.

Buen Ayre

50 Broadway Market, E8 ■ 020 7275 9900

⊖ Bethnal Green

🍴 Latin American

🕐 Mon to Fri 18.00–22.30; Sat & Sun 12.00–22.30

🖱 www.buenayre.co.uk

🗄 all major credit cards except AmEx ■ 12.5% optional service added

££ starters £4–£4.50 ■ mains £7.50–£22 ■ sides £4–£4.50
   ■ desserts £3–£5.50 ■ lowest bottle price £11.80

⭐ Significant meat mountain, sizzling at your table

This resto seeks to recreate an Argentine 'Parrilla' – a kind of
grill house. There is a nod to vegetarians, but as a guideline, think
meat. Start with empanadas – there are three kinds on offer: beef,
chicken, and spinach with cheese. These small pastries are made with
a good, light, crisp shortcrust pastry. The main courses are split into
two sections: first there are the 'platos principales' and then there
are the 'parrilladas'. The platos are simple – an 8oz or a 14oz prime
Argentine sirloin steak; or rib-eye steak; or fillet steak; or rump steak.
There are also good home-made sausages, and 'vacio', which is an
Argentine speciality – veal flank steak. The 'Parrillada' (or brazier)
is a small, table-top griddle plate over a charcoal fire. Ordering any
parrillada means you get a meat mountain. The 'Buen Ayre' brings
two large sausages, well seasoned and meaty; black pudding, very
decent, floral and not too fatty; sweetbreads, marginally overcooked;
kidneys, ditto; short ribs, excellent crispy bits; and flank steak, very
close-grained and fatty. The side order of chips is a worthwhile
addition – very crisp, very fluffy. Service is sound and the wine list
un-grasping. Pud-wise, the famous and ultra sweet dulce de leche
turns up in flans and cheesecakes. Best to opt for the moody coffees
– 'bombon' is a shot glass with a thick layer of condensed milk that
has an espresso floating on top of it.

Cây Tre

301 Old Street, EC1 ■ 020 7729 8662

⊖ Old Street

🍴 Vietnamese

🕐 Mon to Thurs 12.00–15.00 & 17.30–23.00; Fri & Sat 12.00–15.00 &
17.30–23.30; Sun 12.00–22.30

🖥 www.vietnamesekitchen.co.uk

🖶 all major credit cards ■ 12.5% optional service added

££ starters £2–£22.50 ■ mains £6–£9.50 ■ sides £2–£6
■ desserts £3.50–£4.50 ■ special menus £16 (meat) & £19 (seafood)
■ lowest bottle price £10.95

✪ Jolly, bustling Vietnamese – strong on fish

You'll find Cây Tre on Old Street, a short distance from 'little
Vietnam' on the Kingsland Road. It stands out because the food is
so good, the prices are so reasonable and the resto has retained an
engaging family-run feel. The menu is fascinating and includes many
authentic and complicated Vietnamese dishes. Start with the bò cuôn
bánh tráng (for two). A griddle is set up on your table for you to grill
thinly cut steak. While you're waiting, soak rice papers until soft, then
add sauce and parcel up the beef with pickles. Also prepared at table
is cha cá La Vong, a dish that hails from a notable restaurant on Cha
Cá Street in Hanoi. Sliced marinated monkfish is cooked in a frying
pan at table on fresh fennel with a shrimp sauce. Another superb
starter is the bò lá lôt, parcels of minced savoury beef wrapped in
aromatic sapu leaves. From the mains, bò lúc lâc, shaking beef, is
made with tender rib-eye steak. There is a wide selection of noodle
soups including the classic pho, and you can get that most delicious
of Vietnamese vegetable dishes, rau muông xào to'i, stir-fried water
spinach with garlic dressing. There are two ways to make the most
of Cây Tre's charming service and very good food: either opt for one
of the 'meals-in-a-bowl' and dine quickly, or order up an array of
starters and feast.

→ For branch, see index or website

The Empress of India

130 Lauriston Park Road, E9 ■ 020 8533 5123

⊖ Mile End

🍴 Modern British/gastropub

🕐 Mon to Fri (breakfast) 08.30–11.30, (lunch) 12.00–15.00, (tea)
15.00–18.00, (dinner) 18.00–22.00; Sat (breakfast) 9.00–11.30,
(lunch) 12.00–15.00, (tea) 15.00–18.00, (dinner) 18.30–23.00; Sun
(breakfast) 9.00–11.00, (lunch) 12.00–16.00, (dinner) 18.30–21.30

🖰 www.theempressofindia.com

🖫 all major credit cards except AmEx ■ 12.5% optional service added

££ starters £4.50 to £9 ■ mains £9.50 to £16.50 ■ sides £3.50
■ desserts £5.50 ■ lowest bottle price £13.50

✪ Glossy gastropub

Behind the bar at the Empress is a fine and gloriously exotic
period mirror that was retrieved from an Indian cinema; apparently
the mirror came first and the bar was built around it. The people
behind this gastropub (which opened towards the end of 2006)
have a proven track record – see also The White Swan, p. 229 –
and it shows! They have got the ambience right, the food right and
the pricing right. There are some decent beers on draught and a
sympathetic wine list. Service is slick. Starters may include a pint of
prawns served with mayonnaise; a dressed Dorset crab; or a rabbit
and prune terrine – well made and well seasoned. Main courses
change with the market and reflect the seasons: there may be
herb-crusted hake, mousselline potato, peas and tarragon; or meat
balls made from Gloucester Old Spot pork with prune and apples.
Sometimes there's game pie: a large china pie dish comes with a
decent pastry crust, although there is a suspicion that the game
element may be bolstered with a tad too much beef. The 'thrice-
cooked' chips are very sound. Puds range from lemon tart to spotted
dick and a pear Tatin with Calvados ice cream. When gastropubs
started they were roughty-toughty sort of places with patchy service
and only occasionally inspired cooking. The Empress is a much more
polished operation with high standards and deserves to do very well.

Fifteen Trattoria

15 Westland Place, N1 ■ 0871 330 1515

⊖ Old Street

🍴 Italian

🕐 Mon to Sat 07.30–11.00 (breakfast), 12.00–14.30 & 18.00–23.00;
Sun 09.00–11.00, 12.00–14.30 & 18.00–23.00

🖥 www.fifteen.net

🖬 all major credit cards ■ 12.5% optional service added

££ antipasti £8 ■ mains £9–£18 ■ desserts £6 ■ lowest bottle price £16

✪ Your way to support the Fifteen Foundation Charity

When Jamie Oliver's restaurant Fifteen first burst onto our television screens it quickly became apparent that the stated objective, 'To give opportunities to unemployed youngsters and help them change their lives by becoming the next generation of star chefs', would not be an easy task. Some years further on and dogged determination seems to be paying off. The more pukka establishment downstairs is very busy and somewhat pricey, while the Trattoria on the ground floor offers customers sound Italian food, chirpy service and glimpses of the telly stars, and then makes them pay enough to support the endeavour. For a cold-hearted, careful-with-money diner, the prices here will be high enough to elevate the wince factor, certainly higher than you would pay for this level of cooking elsewhere. But come on – this is for charity, so evaluate the rosy glow instead. Thankfully, the menu copy has been toned down a bit and puffery has given way to provenance: the beef comes from Buccleugh; the olives from Amalfi; and the olive oil from Cerro del Masso. In a similar vein, 'the lightest potato gnocchi' are very good and come with Isle of Wight mushroom. Tagliatelle with horse mushrooms, mascarpone, thyme and Parmigiano is sound enough. 'Secondi' offers whole baked rainbow trout; slow-roast shoulder of lamb with smashed celeriac; and confit of duck with lentils di Casteluccio, Italian spinach and mostarda di Cremona. The cooking is sound and the service is slick, so be charitable when you catch sight of the bill.

Fish Central

151 King's Square, Central Street, EC1 ■ 020 7253 4970

⊖ Barbican

🍴 Fish & chips

🕐 Mon to Thurs 11.30–14.30 & 17.00–22.30; Fri & Sat 11.30–14.30 & 17.00–23.00

🖰 www.fishcentral.co.uk

🖽 all major credit cards ■ no service added

££ starters £3.45–£7.90 ■ mains £5.45–£19.90 ■ sides £1.50–£2.45 ■ desserts £3.50 ■ lowest bottle price £9.45

⭐ Top-notch fish and chip restaurant

Apart from the theatres and concert hall, one of the main attractions of the Barbican is its proximity to Fish Central, which holds its own with the finest fish and chip shops in town. People tend to be very snobbish about fish and chip shops, but Fish Central is just the place to dispel such delusions. Though at first sight it appears just like any other superior chippy – a takeaway service one side and an eat-in restaurant next door – a glance at its menu lets you know that this is something out of the ordinary. All the finny favourites are here, from cod and haddock to rock salmon and plaice, but there's a wholesome choice of alternatives, including grilled Dover sole and roast cod with sautéed potatoes. These dishes are cooked to order, and a menu note prepares you for a 25-minute wait. You can eat decently even if you are not in the mood for fish. Try the Cumberland sausages, with onions and gravy. If you think your appetite is up to starters, try the prawn cocktail – the normal naked pink prawns in pink sauce, but genuinely fresh. Chips come as a side order, so those who prefer can order a jacket potato or creamed potatoes. There are mushy peas, which are, well, mushy, and pickled onions and gherkins. In keeping with its role as fish restaurant rather than fish shop, there is even a wine list. Champagne anyone?

Gourmet San

261 Bethnal Green Road, E2 ■ 020 7729 8388

Bethnal Green

Chinese

Mon to Sun 16.30–24.00

all major credit cards ■ no service added

££ starters £3–£6 ■ mains £6–£16 ■ sides £1–£2 ■ desserts £3 ■ lowest bottle price £7.50

Well worth waiting in the queue

Visiting Gourmet San is an epic adventure – especially if you are one of the 15% of customers who is not Chinese and must ask for the menu in English. On a quiet, mid-week night there may be 25 people crammed into a disorderly queue, while waitresses wriggle through it from table to table bearing huge bowls of food and piles of barbecue skewers. So if you're shy don't bother. The food is magnificent, fresh, with amazing tastes and textures, and lots of unusual items. The house speciality is 'xingjiang-style lamb on skewer'. These are very good, dry, marinated lamb kebabs – take the deal that offers 12 skewers for £10. The BBQ squid is also good, with a great texture. The rabbit leg is also good. Then how about 'lamb and fish soup', which is a well-flavoured citrussy broth with chunks of sea bass and slices of lamb – an unlikely combo but one that works terrifically well. There's lots of offal: £6 gets you 8 or 9 braised pigs' feet – gluey and unctuous. Or there's a stellar dish of cumin fried fish – perfectly cooked sea bass. Another of the more charming dishes is also one of the simplest: stir-fried green beans with chillies. It's very crunchy, and has an impressive depth of flavour. The best strategy is to keep your eyes open while queuing and order whatever appeals. The food here is cheap, exotic, well balanced and eye-opening.

Green & Red

51 Bethnal Green Road, E1 ■ 020 7749 9670

⊖ Liverpool Street

🍴 Mexican

🕐 Mon to Thurs & Sun 18.00–23.00; Fri & Sat 18.00–01.00

🖥 www.greenred.co.uk

💳 all major credit cards ■ 12.5% optional service added

££ starters £2.50–£3.75 ■ mains £10.50–£14.50 ■ sides £1–£3.50
■ desserts £3–£5.50 ■ lowest bottle price £14

✪ Food from Jalisco, mood via tequila

Named for its location (at the junction of Bethnal Green Road
and Redchurch Street), this buzzing bar restaurant has done more
to redeem the reputation of Mexican cooking than anywhere else.
The cocktails are superb and for once it is well worth setting a few
parameters – sweet, fruity, strong, sharp – and then leaving it to
the mixologist. It is also worth noting the range of Mexican beers,
all of which go very well with the food. The presentation is informal
and the cooking is home style, but each of the starters has a different
character and differing varieties of chilli are used to good effect.
Albohondigas is a dish of beef meatballs with chipotle chilli and
tomato salsa; calamar frito is deep-fried squid served with a tomatillo
salsa and lime; while ensalada de jicama y cacahuates is a splendid
salad – jicama with cucumber and roast peanuts dressed with lime,
arbol chilli and sheep's milk cheese. From the mains, the carnitas
stands out – slow-roast pork belly and ribs seasoned with pasilla
chilli and orange salt, and with an avocado salsa. The pollo rostizado
is a pleasantly exotic take on a roast chicken – heavy with achiote
spices. All the dishes come with corn tortillas and re-fried beans, but
the side dishes are stars in their own right. You should try the chile
arbol – roast arbol chillies with lime; the guacamole; and the salsa
Mexicana. For pud there is the sandia con chile y limon – a strangely
successful combination of watermelon with piquin chillies and lime
– or the amazing combo of churros (crisp and squiggly doughnuts)
with spiced hot chocolate.

Huong Viet

An Viet House, 12–14 Englefield Road, N1 ■ 020 7249 0877 ⚕

⊖ BR Dalston Kingsland

🍴 Vietnamese

🕐 Mon to Fri 12.00 to 15.30 & 17.30 to 23.00; Sat 12.00 to 16.00 & 17.30 to 23.00

🖢 www.huongviet.co.uk

🗗 Mastercard, Visa ■ 10% optional service rising to 12% for parties of 8 or more

££ starters £3.30–£6.50 ■ mains £4–£6.50 ■ desserts £1–£3 ■ set [lunch] £6 for 2 courses ■ lowest bottle price £7.45

✪ Vietnam HQ

This former council bathhouse is home to Huong Viet – the canteen of the Vietnamese Cultural Centre. The resto has a well-established reputation for really good, really cheap food, and regulars have stuck with it through a couple of general refurbishments. Surprisingly, there is even a thriving lunch trade. The food is fresh, unpretentious, delicious and cheap, while the service is friendly and informal. Start with the spring rolls – small, crisp and delicious. Or the fresh rolls, which resemble small, carefully rolled-up table napkins. The outside is soft, white and delicate-tasting, while the inside teams cooked vermicelli with prawns and fresh herbs – a great combination of textures. Ordering the prawn and green leaf soup brings a bowl of delicate broth with greens and shards of tofu. Pho is perhaps the most famous Vietnamese 'soup' dish, but it is really a meal in a bowl. The pho here is formidable, especially the Hanoi noodle soup, filled with beef, chicken or tofu. Hot, rich and full of bits and pieces, it comes with a plate of herbs, crispy bean sprouts and aromatics that you must add yourself at the last moment so none of the aroma is lost. The other dishes are excellent, too. Look out for mixed seafood with pickled veg and dill, which works exceptionally well. You should also try the noodle dishes – choose from the wok-fried rice noodle dishes, or the crispy-fried egg noodles.

Istanbul Iskembecisi

9 Stoke Newington Road, N16 ■ 020 7254 7291

⊖ BR Dalston Kingsland

🍽 Turkish

🕐 daily 12.00–05.00

🔁 all major credit cards ■ no service added

££ starters £3–£3.75 ■ mains £7.50–£12.95 ■ sides £2.50–£3
■ desserts £3 ■ lowest bottle price £10

✪ Stay up late, the Turkish way

Despite being named after its signature dish – iskembe is a limpid
tripe soup – the Istambul is a Turkish grill house. Admittedly it is a
grill house with chandeliers, smart tables and upscale service, but
it is still a grill house. And because it stays open until well into the
early morning, it is much beloved by clubbers and chefs – they are
just about ready to go out and eat when everyone else has had
enough and set off home. The atmosphere of raffish elegance at the
Istambul has real charm and even the iskembe, or tripe soup, has its
following. Large parties of Turks from the snooker hall just behind the
restaurant insist on it, and you'll see the odd regular downing two
bowlfuls of the stuff. For most people, however, it's bland at best,
and even the large array of additives (salt, pepper, chilli – this is a
dish that you must season to your personal taste at the table) cannot
make it palatable. A much better bet is to start with the mixed meze,
which brings a good houmous and tarama, a superb dolma, and the
rest drawn from the usual suspects. Then on to the grills, which are
presented with more panache than usual. Pirzola brings three lamb
chops; shish kebab is good and fresh; karisik isgara is a formidable
mixed grill. For a more interesting option there's arvnavaut cigeri-
sicak – liver Albanian style.

→ For branches, see index

Mai'da

148–150 Bethnal Green Road, E2 ■ 020 7739 2645

⊖ Bethnal Green/Shoreditch

🍽 Indian

🕐 daily 11.00–23.00

🖑 www.maida-restaurant.co.uk

🖨 all major credit cards ■ no service added

££ starters £2.95–£4.95 ■ mains £3.95–£14.95 ■ sides £3.25–£5.50
    ■ desserts £2.50–£4.75 ■ no alcohol

✪ Thrills, grills and milkshakes

Mai'da means 'dining table' or 'banquet', and that is what you
get at this glitzy, modern Indian restaurant. No alcohol is served but
there are formidable milkshakes. This place is the very agreeable face
of enlightened fast food – no frozen meat; sustainable fishes; no
artificial food colours; ingredients from local suppliers and of English
origin. The menu is a magnum opus. There are good kebabs, such as
murgh seekh kebab; chicken tikka; burhansi kebab (with beetroot);
and kachay aam ka murgh tikka (chicken tenderised with fresh
mango). These are freshly cooked, served hot and very good indeed.
Travelling onwards through the small print you'll find old faithfuls
like lamb pasanda and chilli chicken. Then you get to a section of
'Chinese'-style dishes, including some that are firm favourites in
Mumbai, such as prawns Kung Po or Manchurian vegetables. But
the best dishes here are the kebabs. Team them with superb breads
and a veg dish. Some locals reckon that the food here is better than
at the nearby local hero Tayyabs (see p. 199). That's not the case,
but it is a close-run thing. End your meal with a tooth-killer; they
make milkshakes here that have various chocolate bars as the central
ingredient. So you can sample a milkshake made from Kinder egg;
Toblerone; Oreo cookies; Mars Bar; Kit Kat; Bounty... it's enough to
make a Glaswegian Mars Bar fryer look to his laurels.

Mangal 2
4 Stoke Newington Road, N16 ■ 020 7254 7888

⊖ BR Dalston Kingsland

🍽 Turkish

🕐 Mon to Fri 17.00–01.00; Sat 14.00–01.00; Sun 12.00–01.00

🗄 cash or cheque only ■ no service added

££ starters £2.75–£3.95 ■ mains £7.95–£8.95 ■ desserts £3.25
■ menus (for 2) £29.50pp ■ lowest bottle price £10.75

✪ Cheap, cheerful and magnificent grilled meats

Mangal 1 had a slot in the last edition of this guide, and Mangal
2 was featured in the edition before that. It seems only fair to include
both restaurants turn and turn about, as they both have the same
high standards. So, it's back to Mangal 2 for this edition! Despite its
slightly posher High Street location the ambience at 2 is agreeably
laid-back. Prices are low and portions enormous. Baskets of fresh
bread are endlessly replenished and there's a vast range of tempting
mezeler (starters). The 25 options include simple houmous and
dolma; imam bayildi, aubergines rich with onion, tomato and green
pepper; thin lahmacun, meaty Turkish pizza; and karisik meze, a large
plate of mixed dishes that's rather heavy on the yogurt. The main
dishes are sumptuous, big on lamb and chicken, with limited fish and
vegetarian alternatives. The patlican kebab is outstanding – melt-in-
the-mouth grilled minced lamb with sliced aubergines, served with a
green salad, of which the star turn is an olive-stuffed tomato shaped
like a basket. The kebabs are also superb, particularly the house
special, ezmeli kebab, which comes doused in Mangal's special sauce.
On rare occasions the grilled quails listed on the menu are actually
available, and are a 'must-have' item. They are very good indeed.
After that you might just be tempted by a slab of toothachingly-sweet
baklava. Alternatively, round off the evening with a punch-packing
raki.

→ For branch, see index

Pinchito Tapas

32 Featherstone Street, EC1 ■ 020 7490 0121

⊖ Old Street

🍽 Spanish

🕐 Mon to Fri 08.00–24.00; Sat 17.00–24.00

🔗 www.pinchito.co.uk

🗗 all major credit cards ■ 12.5% optional service added (tables only)

££ pinchos £1 ■ tapas £2–£6 ■ platters (cheese/charcuterie) £5–£12 ■ desserts £2.50–£4.50 ■ lowest bottle price £14

✪ Plenty to drink, plenty of ballast

It's not often that we are faced with a new concept that has been imported from such a faraway and exotic location – Brighton. That jewel of the Sussex coast is home to the Pinxto People, who have been running amok in their massive, eponymous bar-nightclub-restaurant for several jolly years. Pinchito has industrial décor – bare walls, garage doors – and makes most factories look like a TV home-design epic. The first statement of intent is the large number of bar stools and the generous amount of space to sit at the bar. There's Cruzcampo beer on draught, a splendid range of sherries and a long Iberian wine list. The pinchos change daily: they are small (two mouthfuls), made with a chunk of bread and whatever the chef's whim dictates – perhaps tuna, salad leaves and mayonnaise. They work out pretty cheap. Move on to tapas proper and look for traditional dishes: pa amb tomaquet – tomato bread; pimentos de Padrón – small grilled peppers; deep-fried squid; an oniony Spanish omelette; escalibada – a kind of grown-up, sweetly rich ratatouille. There is always a 'tapas of the day', and service flies the dishes over the bar with the minimum of fuss and the maximum flourish. Wednesday is 'paella day' and bargains are to be had. This is a friendly drinking den where good food makes a long session enjoyable: it works really well. For breakfast you can have those rich doughnutty churros with a cup of hot chocolate.

Prince Arthur

95 Forest Road, E8 ■ 020 7249 9966

Bethnal Green

Modern British/gastropub

Mon to Fri 18.00–22.00; Sat 10.30–13.00 (brunch); 12.00–16.30 & 18.00–22.00; Sun 10.30–12.00 (brunch); 12.00–16.30 & 18.00–22.00

www.theprincearthurlondonfields.com

all major credit cards except Amex ■ 10% optional service added

££ starters £4.50–£10.50 ■ mains £9.95–£11.95 ■ sides £3 ■ desserts £4.50 ■ lowest bottle price £12.50

✪ A local sort of local

The Prince Arthur is one of the recent additions to the Martin Brothers' portfolio (see the White Swan, p. 229) and like their other gastropubs, it has been cleverly tailored to suit its catchment area. The Arthur retains a decent measure of pubbyness, the interior has the warm, dark-brown feel that you get in comfortable pubs, and the bar offers a couple of real ales. The menu is short – seven starters and five mains all sensibly priced. Start with the terrine – a little chilly from the fridge but well made and well seasoned. Or a home-made pork pie; a pint o'prawns with mayonnaise; or a pickled beetroot salad with goats' cheese curd, walnuts and sticky dates – an interesting combination of flavours. Main courses are blissfully straightforward; pork belly comes with sound crackling, roast parsnips, Brussel tops and a tart apple sauce. The combo of scampi, fat chips and sauce tartare is tried and tested and none the worse for that. The chicken pie with roast ceps and Blue Wensleydale is worth noting. Service is smiley and dishes fly out of the kitchen – another benefit of the short menu approach. Puds range from lemon tart to 'deep-fried jam sandwich with plum chutney and Carnation milk ice cream' and spotted dick. It is very difficult to judge just how casual the cooking in a local pub should be, but this one should run and run.

The Rivington

28–30 Rivington Street, EC2 ■ 020 7729 7053

⊖ Old Street

🍴 British

🕐 Mon to Fri 08.00–11.00 (breakfast), 12.00–15.00 & 18.30–23.00;
Sat 12.00–23.00; Sun 12.00–22.00

🖰 www.rivingtongrill.co.uk

🗗 all major credit cards ■ 12.5% service added

££ breakfast £1.50–£9.50 ■ starters £5.50–£14.00
■ mains £9.75–£26.50 ■ desserts £5.50–£7.75 ■ Sunday set menu
£22.50 (3 courses until 16.00) ■ lowest bottle price £15

✪ Seasonal British food at its best

The Rivington flies the flag for superior neighbourhood restaurants.
This place has an elegant, high-ceilinged, white-painted dining room,
a comfortable bar with high stools for solo diners, and plenty of
sofas. The menu manages to be both stylish and seasonal. This food
is not Italian, it is not French, it is not fancy and it is not formal. The
dishes don't even answer to Modern British. If there is such a cuisine
as Ordinary British, then this is it. On the face of it, everything looks
simple, but these combinations work well together. There may be
Scotch duck eggs with caper mayonnaise; a beetroot and goat's
cheese salad with walnuts; devilled kidneys on toast – lamb's kidneys
cooked perfectly and with a well-made, sharp sauce. Or deep-fried
skate cheeks with tartare sauce. Main courses also satisfy. There's
hamburger and chips; honey-baked ham with mustard sauce; home-
made fish fingers and chips with mushy peas; roast suckling pig with
pumpkin and quince sauce; or whole grilled gilthead sea bream.
Puddings range from blood orange trifle to steamed chocolate
pudding and trad numbers like banana custard. The wine list starts
steadily but then skitters on through a handful of pricey bottles to
Vosne-Romanée and the like. Stick with the middleweights for the
best value. Ask about the 'feasts' served on platters for a large table –
whole suckling pig, or a huge roast fish. Good food on a grand scale.

→ For branch, see index or website

The Scolt Head

107a Culford Road, N1 ■ 020 7254 3965

⊖ Dalston Kingsland BR

🍽 Modern British/gastropub

🕐 daily 12.00–16.00; 18.30–22.00

🗗 all major credit cards except AmEx ■ no service added

££ starters £4.50–£5 ■ mains £8–£13.50 ■ sides £3 ■ desserts £5
　　■ lowest bottle price £12.50

✪ Pubby sort of pub, gastro sort of food

Taking over a fairly down-at-heel pub called the Sussex and
re-naming it after a bird sanctuary on the Norfolk coast seems a
surprisingly De Beauvoir town sort of thing to do. Quirky, media-savvy
and a complete break with the past. The Scolt Head is a clean, large,
no-frills pub with decent beers and lagers, a small beer garden to the
front and a dining room off to one side. The restaurant part opened
without too much hype in the spring of 2007 and it is rumoured
that Trish Hilferty, whose pedigree includes The Eagle (see p. 220)
and latterly The Fox in Shoreditch, had a hand in setting the tone for
the kitchen. Her fingerprints are certainly all over the menu, which
is gloriously short – four starters, four mains and four puds. Short
menus are just fine provided you like the sound of every dish so much
that choosing is a problem. Short menus mean seasonal and market
driven. Short menus imply that the kitchen is concentrating and will
get things right. For starters you may face a choice between wild
mushroom and nettle soup; asparagus, fried egg and Parmesan –
perfectly cooked asparagus, but needed a runnier egg yolk; potato,
onion and sorrel frittata – well seasoned; and ox tongue, potatoes
and salsa verde. Mains bring a steady, trad boeuf Bourguignon with
mash; a grilled rump steak with sauté potatoes; and pan-fried skate
wing with chips, rocket and tartare sauce. Then on to a flourless
chocolate cake or a lemon posset. The presentation is low key but
then so are the prices. The cooking is good and the service friendly
and informal. The wine list offers reasonable wine at reasonable
prices. The Scolt Head is a neighbourhood asset.

Viet Grill

58 Kingsland Road, E2 ■ 020 7739 6686

⊖ Old Street

🍴 Vietnamese

🕐 Mon to Thurs 12.00–15.00 & 17.30–23.00; Fri & Sat 12.00–15.00 &
17.30–23.30; Sun 12.00–22.30

🖰 all major credit cards except AmEx ■ 12.5% optional service added

££ starters £3.50–£22.50 ■ mains £6–£9.50 ■ sides £2–£7
■ desserts £3.50–£4.50 ■ tasting menu £19 ■ lowest bottle price £15

✪ Authentic, sometimes too authentic, Vietnamese food

Those rather good cooks at Cây Tre (see p. 243) are behind this
establishment on the Kingsland Road. Like its sibling, this is a
functional dining room rather than a slick designery sort of place.
The food is pretty uncompromising stuff – a good place to eat a
duck embryo straight from the shell. But there are still plenty of less
eccentric and more accessible dishes. Starters include a lotus stem
salad with pork, shrimp and basil; soft-shell crab with tamarind;
and a dish called 'feudal roast beef', which is the house special of a
famous restaurant in Hanoi and has a back story featuring torture –
something to do with stripping off pieces of human flesh to the beat
of a drum. The fresh, soft summer rolls are very good. And the soupy
meal-in-a-bowl that is pho is well done here. Mains range from a dish
of mullet cooked in a clay pot; or mackerel baked in banana leaf; to a
grilled turmeric lamb chop; and a curried duck dish from the north of
Vietnam. Service is friendly and explanations are forthcoming. There
is a tasting menu that offers a wave of different dishes, and a good
option is to use it as a starting point and then add a few favourites.
Much is made of 'wine-matching' on the menu but it is hard to resist
the allure of a cold beer.

→ For branch, see index

The Waterhouse

10 Orsman Road, N1 ■ 020 7033 0123

⊖ Old Street

🍽 Modern British

🕐 Mon to Fri 08.00–11.30 (breakfast), 11.30–17.00 (lunch),
17.00–22.00 (dinner); Sat 08.00–17.00 (brunch) & 18.00–22.30
(dinner); Sun 10.00–17.00 (brunch)

🖱 www.waterhouserestaurant.co.uk

🖃 all major credit cards ■12.5% optional service added

££ starters £4–£10 ■ mains £12–£16 ■ sides £2–£7 ■ desserts £3.50–£5
■ lowest bottle price £16.50

✪ 'Changing the world one drop at a time'

The Waterhouse is sister restaurant to Acorn House (see p. 51) and
has similar eco-charitable-extra-worthy credentials. It is located in
the heart of a modernist block of flats and looks out over the canal.
Surrounded by small factories makes parking a difficult proposition
and the restaurant is a long way from the tube. So get a bus and
support this worthwhile venture. It's always a moot point how much
we are prepared to forgive a restaurant simply because it is run
on a charitable basis. At the Waterhouse you'll get a sound meal
in contemporary surroundings and pay just a little over the odds.
Starters range from a mix and match of anti pasti: Violette artichokes;
various charcutiere items; salmon rillettes; pecorino. The menu is
seasonal and may offer starters like a smoked mackerel, fennel and
radish salad; burrata on bruschetta with taggiasca olives – admirably
fresh; or a ravioli of ricotta and spring herbs. Mains may include
grilled leg of lamb with sprouting broccoli and salsa verde; spaghetti
with sustainable prawns, fennel, tomato and chilli; and duck confit
on a bed of parsnip mash with a caramelised pear – suitably sweet,
sticky and indulgent. The puds include spooky ice creams (violet,
anybody?) and a well-made panna cotta. This is not a preachy place,
but sip a glass of filtered water as you look down the cheap end of
the wine list and feel the glow.

North

Camden Town, Primrose Hill and Chalk Farm

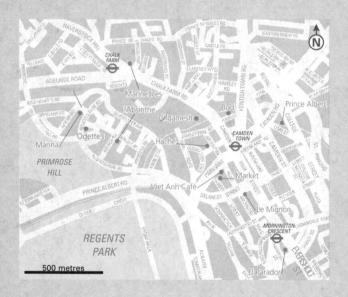

L'Absinthe

40 Chalcot Road, NW1 ■ 020 7483 4848

⊖ Chalk Farm

🍴 Very French

🕐 Tues to Fri 12.00–14.30 & 18.00–22.30; Sat 12.00–16.00 &
18.00–22.30; Sun 12.00–16.00 & 18.00–21.30

🖭 all major credit cards ■ 12.5% optional service added

££ starters £4.25–£6.95 ■ mains £8.75–£14.50 ■ sides £2.50–£2.75
■ desserts £4.25–£5.50 ■ menu du jour £8.50 (2 courses Tues–Fri)
■ lowest bottle price £11.95

✪ Good eating, better drinking

Jean-Christophe Slowik is a man with a mission. After time spent
working for Marco Pierre White as front of house, he has set up his
own place in Primrose Hill. This site has had a chequered history;
it has struggled as an Italian restaurant, an Indian restaurant and
everything in between. L'Absinthe is a neighbourhood French
restaurant serving classic bistro food – traditional dishes done well
and simply presented. Slowik's masterstroke is the wine list: wines
are priced at retail cost plus a fixed mark-up. Day to day bottles
attract £6 corkage, good bottles carry £8, magnificent bottles are
plus £10, while the grand cru have no corkage at all! The result is a
resto where you can drink a bottle of Vosne Romanee, Domain Daniel
Rion 2001 for £38.10, while a bottle of the 1996 Chateau Cantenac
Brown, Margaux costs £55. Prices and vintages may change, but
there are amazing bargains to be had. In the meantime the food
is very enjoyable. Start with a salade Lyonnaise – frisée, lardons,
egg, vinegary dressing; or French onion soup; or Bayonne ham with
celeriac remoulade. Go on to a pork chop 'Charcutière' with mashed
potatoes; a papilotte of sea bream; or a decent steak frites. Puds
range from tarte Tatin to a crème brûlée made with absinthe. Service
is beguilingly French – brisk and with passion. What a nice place to
drink better wine than you deserve.

Bod

30 Hawley Crescent, NW1 ■ 020 7482 5937

⊖ Camden Town

🍽 Spanish/tapas

🕐 daily 12.00–23.00

🖰 www.bodegadetapas.co.uk

🖃 all major credit cards ■ 12.5% optional service added

££ soups £3 ■ tapas £4–£12 ■ desserts £3.50–£5
   ■ lowest bottle price £12.50

✪ Tapas bustle – a good bod

The towering glass frontage at Bod invites passers-by to gaze
longingly into the welcoming bar. It's just off the main and merciless
Camden thoroughfare and is handy for the University halls of
residence. Spiritually, bod is Spanish, (Bodega de Tapas) and there's
as much emphasis on drinking as there is on eating; Cruzcampo beer
on draught, lots of keenly priced wine and several sherries. The food
is very good indeed. Start with the 'sticks' – simple skewers, three
or four to a portion, and with such delights as crispy glazed belly
pork in Moorish spices and blossom honey – good, sweet, rich and
crisp; chicken hearts with apples and Oloroso sherry – tender, good
combination of textures; or home-made morcilla with cracked pepper
crust – very good black pud. On to other tapas: the pan-fried paella
cake with crab is good; and once you've got over the artifice of the
Asturian bean casserole with salt pork and morcilla coming in a large
teacup, it too is a well-made dish. The broad beans with air-dried
ham and a coddled egg is also good. As well as the usual charcuterie
and cheese options there may be the most delightful menu mistake
of the year: 'Pan-fried pink fur apple potatoes'. The whole of the
extensive and inexpensive Spanish wine list is available by the glass.
Service is attentive – this is a friendly place to alternate drinks and
tapas as you gently refuel.

Gilgamesh

Camden Stables Market, Chalk Farm Road, NW1

■ 020 7482 5757

⊖ Camden Town/Chalk Farm

🍽 Asian eclectic

🕐 Mon to Thurs 18.00–24.00; Fri & Sat & 12.00–00.30; Sun
12.00–24.00

🖰 www.gilgameshbar.com

🗗 all major credit cards ■ 12.5% optional service added

££ starters £3.60–£16.80 ■ mains £6–£25.80 ■ sides £2.40–£6.50
■ desserts £6–£16.50 ■ set menus £45 & £55 pp; £35 vegetarian
option ■ lowest bottle price £19

✪ Over the top and down the other side

When Gilgamesh opened, one reviewer wrote a witty piece about
how waiting for a table was a good opportunity to meet a selection
of Essex's finest getaway drivers. This is one of those restaurants that
sets great store by glitz and it certainly seems to strike a chord with a
clientele that isn't too bovvered about the food, preferring cocktails,
champagne and celebrity. As you come up the giant escalator the
huge room opens out before you: there is a great deal of Oriental
carved wood; there is a roof that rolls back whenever the weather
co-operates; there are tables for hundreds of diners; and there is a
huge bar. It is a theme park crossed with a bar and second cousin to a
playpen. Given the feel of the place, the food is surprisingly good. The
sushi is very sound if on the pricey side – some specials like the spicy
spider roll and the salmon inside out roll work very well. Then there
are salads – scallop, crispy pork and pea shoot, or Thai rare beef with
red nahm jim. There are dim sum. You could opt for tempura. Or
Gilgamesh dishes, which may merge several disciplines – a red roast
duck and lychees curry; or hoba miso Chilean seabass. The whole
place is geared up for superficial eating – toying with a succession of
grazing dishes while keeping an eye out for a soap star. If that's your
desire, Gilgamesh will deliver … at a price.

Haché

24 Inverness Street, NW1 ■ 020 7485 9100

⊖ Camden Town

🍴 Burgers

🕐 Mon to Sat 12.00–22.30; Sun 12.00–22.00

🖰 www.hacheburgers.com

🖪 all major credit cards ■ 12.5% optional service added

££ burgers £5.95–£8.95 ■ sides £1.95–£2.50 ■ desserts £2.95–£4.50
  ■ lowest bottle price £10.95

⭐ Steak haché – French for posh burger

They may be made from Angus beef, or chicken, or vegetables, or
even tuna, but they are still burgers. Haché is a very modern kind of
burger place, and within the limits of a burger restaurant, it does a
very good job. The dining room looks good, with small chandeliers
and comfortable seating, and ingredients are signwritten along the
walls (think back a decade to the design of the original Belgo). This
whole place asserts that it is not a burger place, but steak haché
looks like a burger, tastes like a burger and costs about the same
as a premium burger. The burgers are good; the quality of meat is
good; and they are cooked as requested. The ciabatta buns are good.
The fries are good. The chunky chips are good. The onion rings are
suitably greasy and disgusting. When you tire of permutations of
an Angus beef hamburger (with chorizo, or Stilton, or Portobello
mushrooms, or sweet cure bacon), you could opt for the 'chicken
Spanish' – chicken, sweet roast red pepper and goat's cheese; the
'veggie blue cheese' – fresh vegetables and chickpeas topped with
Stilton; or even the tuna Haché burger. There are also seasonal
specials, such as 'Mexicain' (sic), with Cajun spices and salsa. The
desserts are eminently missable – ice cream and cake masquerading
as brownie; and there is a sensibly short wine list. Service is sound.
The true 'Haché experience' is to tuck into a well-made burger that
doesn't cost the earth. Experience it soon.

→ For branch, see index or website

Manna

4 Erskine Road, NW1 ▪ 020 7722 8028

⊖ Chalk Farm

🍴 Vegetarian

🕐 Mon 18.30–23.00; Tues-Sat 12.30–15.00 & 18.30–23.00; Sun
12.30–15.00 & 18.30–22.30

🖱 www.manna-veg.com

🖪 Mastercard, Visa ▪ 12.5% optional service added

££ starters £5.50–£7.25 ▪ mains £9.50–£13.25 ▪ salads £4.75–£6.95
▪ desserts £3.95–£7.50 ▪ lowest bottle price £11.50

⭐ Veggie heaven

Manna has certainly been around long enough to earn its stripes.
Currently bright and less old-fashioned following a periodic refurb,
it is no less popular. The cooking is very sound, portion sizes verge
on the formidable and if there is such a thing as a peculiarly 'veggie'
charm, this place has plenty of it. And there's even a menu code: (v)
= vegan dishes; (vo) = vegan option; (org) = organic dish; (n) =
contains nuts; and (g) = gluten free. The menu changes regularly, but
may include starters such as roast aubergine pockets filled with goats'
cheese, honey and thyme; organic piroghi made with Puy lentils and
winter herbs; Thai tempeh falafel balls flavoured with lemongrass
and galangal; or an organic beetroot gratin made with Duddeswell
sheeps' cheese. Then there are the rather good salads – organic
grilled halloumi on quinoa, wild rice and pistachio; or maybe Asian
pear in plum wine on lambs lettuce appeals? Mains are an equally
eclectic bunch: a stout and oyster mushroom pie – puff pastry and
mustard mash; a tagine made with baby vegetables and apricots; a
Creole sweet potato galette baked with Monterey Jack cheese and
topped with black bean; or 'organic baked Madras glazed tofu' (with
seasonal vegetables and a curry-spiced yoghurt sauce). Puds are
serious: organic warm chocolate fondant; tropical fruit cinnamon
Pavlova. The Manna organic fruit crumble is a challenge to all but the
stoutest appetite.

Marine Ices

8 Haverstock Hill, NW3 ■ 020 7482 9003

⊖ Chalk Farm

🍴 Italian/ice cream

🕐 Tues to Fri 12.00–15.00 & 18.00–23.00; Sat 12.00–23.00; Sun 12.00–22.00

🖰 www.marineices.co.uk

🖬 all major credit cards except AmEx ■ no service added

££ starters £3.45–£6.95 ■ pasta and pizza £5.95–£9.25 ■ mains £8.50–£13.75 ■ sides £2 ■ ice cream £1.50 (1 scoop) to £5.80 ■ lowest bottle price £10.50

✪ Old-time Italian, old-time ice cream

Marine Ices is a family restaurant from a bygone era. In 1947 Aldo Mansi rebuilt the family shop along nautical lines, kitting it out in wood with portholes (hence the name). In the half-century since, while the family ice-cream business has grown and grown, the restaurant and gelateria has just pottered along. That means old-fashioned service and home-style, old-fashioned Italian food. It also means that Marine Ices is a great hit with children, for in addition to the good Italian food there is a marathon list of stunning sundaes, coupes, ice creams and sorbets. The menu is long: antipasti, salads, pastas and sauces, vitello, fegato, carne, pollo, pesce, specialities and pizzas. Of the starters, you could try selezioni di bruschetta. Pasta dishes are home-made: mix and match various sauces with various pasta. You've got starters, mains, 'oven' dishes such as cannelloni and lasagne, and then the menu lists nearly every old-style Italian dish you have ever heard of. Onwards to a host of pizzas – immense, freshly made and very tasty. When you've had your meal, demand the gelateria menu. There are sundaes, from peach Melba to Knickerbocker Glory, and there are bombe, coppe, cassate and, best of all, affogati – three scoops of ice cream topped with hot chocolate or, even nicer, espresso coffee. Or run amok among fourteen ice creams and eight sorbets. A takeaway tub of the Mansis' ice cream has been the making of many a dinner party.

Market

43 Parkway, NW1 ▪ 020 7267 9700

⊖ Camden Town

🍴 Very British

🕐 Mon to Sat 12.00–14.30 & 18.00–22.30; Sun (roast) 13.00–16.00

🗗 all major credit cards ▪ 12.5% optional service added

££ starters £4.50–£8.50 ▪ mains £9–£12.50 ▪ sides £2.50–£3
   ▪ desserts £4.50–£6.50 ▪ lunch menu £10 (2 courses, Mon to Fri)
   ▪ lowest bottle price £13

⊕ Honest, wholesome and jolly good

Market is a small, friendly restaurant that is unashamedly
influenced by the 'Gospel according to St John', as we shall now
have to start calling it. Seasonal ingredients, a menu in constant
flux, depending on what is best at the market, honest, hearty,
well-flavoured dishes. See also St John (p. 225), Magdalen (p
346), Anchor & Hope (p. 186) and Hereford Road (p. 138)   it's
amazing how vibrant this sub sector has become. There are some
familiar dishes on the menu at Market, but there are also some
interesting new developments, albeit from within the canon.
Starters may include devilled kidneys; home-smoked mackerel pate,
pickled cucumber; pig cheeks morcilla and peas; or a goats' cheese
watercress and beetroot salad. They come to table unadorned and
unfussily plated – full marks. Flavours are upfront. Mains follow
on seamlessly. There may be a chicken and ham pie; Gloucester Old
Spot pork belly with lentils; or mutton cutlets, potato cake and caper
sauce – the tiny bones would imply that they come from a small
breed sheep, perhaps Herdwick or Soay, and the rich red meat is full
of flavour. Or try organic salmon with mash and baby leeks. .Puds
range from a plum frangipane tart to jam sponge pudding. Service is
charming and friendly; the people here care about the food and the
customers. The wine list is priced accessibly. The set lunch is a steal.

Le Mignon

98 Arlington Road, NW1 ■ 020 7387 0600

☻ Camden Town

🍴 Lebanese

🕐 daily 12.00–15.00 & 18.00–24.00

🗗 all major credit cards ■ 12% optional service added

££ cold mezze £2.75–£6.50 ■ mains £9.50–£18.50 ■ sides £2.50–£3.50
   ■ desserts £3.50 ■ lunchbox £9.50 ■ lowest bottle price £11.75

✪ A little corner of Lebanon

It's easy to forget that before it became so war-torn Beirut had
much in common with Paris. By all accounts it was a beautiful and
civilised city where you could get a good cup of coffee, wonderful
pastries and decent baguettes. Perhaps that is why Le Mignon has a
French name, despite being a thoroughly Lebanese restaurant. Inside,
the handful of tables and small bar have had a décor bypass and
would be at home in a dodgy after-hours drinking club, but you can
be sure of a warm welcome The menu is a long one – which seems
to be the way with Lebanese restaurants; you are forced to decide
between two options, either trying mezze after mezze until you burst
or picking a couple by way of starters and then following with a main
course from the list. Highlights of the mezze are: the tabbouleh;
the moutabal (a.k.a. baba ganoush); the labneh – a set yogurt; the
sujuk – heavyweight spiced beef sausages; or the moujadra, which is
a mix of lentils and rice topped with a haystack of fried onions – very
good indeed. Hot bread arrives unbidden whenever you run out. The
main courses range from Dover sole to grilled sea bass stuffed with
coriander; quails; chicken; and every conceivable way of grilling lamb
from mince through to fillet. Service is friendly and the restaurant has
a homely feel – in the nicest possible way.

Odette's

130 Regents Park Road, NW1 ▪ 020 7586 8569

⊖ Chalk Farm

🍴 Modern European

🕐 Tues–Sat 12.30–14.30 & 18.30–22.30; Sun 12.30–15.30

🖰 www.odettesprimrosehill.com

🖰 all major credit cards ▪ 12.5% optional service added

££ starters £12.50 ▪ mains £25 ▪ sides £3.50 ▪ desserts £6.00–£8.00
▪ lunch & dinner £35 (2 courses) £40 (3 courses) ▪ set lunch
£17.95 (2 courses) & £21.95 (3 courses); Sunday lunch £27 & £32
▪ lowest bottle price £20

⊗ Neighbourhood stalwart reinvigorated

After decades of jogging along as a small, old-fashioned, rather
twee establishment where the food varied wildly (depending on
which of the sometimes short-lived chefs was in charge when you
called by), Odette's has settled into a new era. The dining room is
still a tad country-house-cosy but it looks a good deal better, the
chairs are comfortable and the multitude of mirrors has gone. If
the changes to the décor are radical, the changes to the kitchens
are also significant. Head chef Bryn Williams is a talented fellow
and he's written a menu that is driven by the seasons. Dishes are
priced separately but most people opt for the all-in price. Classic
combos like roast scallop, butternut purée, chestnut and apple
work well – spanking fresh scallops working with the nutty purée.
Seared swordfish comes with tuna tartare and marinated beetroot.
Ballotine of pig's head is teamed with black pudding. Main course
dishes include the occasional surprise – pan-fried turbot comes with
cockles and oxtail (this is the dish that won the day on BBC2's Great
British Menu); or you could try roast loin of venison, braised red
cabbage and parsnip purée. A perfectly cooked poached then roast
pigeon is served with roast salsify. Puds include a glazed lemon tart;
and a warm Valrhona chocolate fondant. Service is smooth. The only
slight drawback is the wine list, which sometimes marks up a tad too
enthusiastically.

El Parador

245 Eversholt Street, NW1 ■ 020 7387 2789

⊖ Mornington Crescent

🍽 Spanish/tapas

🕐 Mon to Thurs 12.00–15.00 & 18.00–23.00; Fri 12.00–15.00 & 18.00–23.30; Sat 18.00–23.30; Sun 18.30–21.30

⌂ www.elparadorlondon.com

🖬 all major credit cards ■ 10% optional service added for parties of 5 or more

££ tapas £4–£7 ■ desserts £4–£5.80 ■ lowest bottle price £13.90 ■ Mon to Fri lunch '3 tapas for the price of 2'

✪ Tasty tapas, tasty prices

El Parador seems to be somewhat stranded in the quiet little enclave around Mornington Crescent, pinched between King's Cross and Camden. It serves very tasty tapas at very reasonable prices and has a friendly, laid-back atmosphere, even on busy Friday and Saturday nights. As ever with tapas, the fun part of eating here is choosing several dishes from the wide selection on offer, and then sharing and swapping with your companions. Allow at least two or three tapas a head – more for a really filling meal – and go for at least one of the fish or seafood dishes, which are treats. Highlights include chipirones salteados, which are baby squid pan fried with sea salt and olive oil; bacalao rebozado – salt cod goujons deep fried in a beer batter; or gambas al romero, which are nice fat tiger prawns pan fried with rosemary and garlic butter. Carnivores shouldn't miss out on the jamón serrano – delicious Spanish cured ham; or the morcilla del Parador, sausages that are a cousin of black pudding. The vegetarian tapas are particularly good here. Try tortilla Espa–ola, a classic Spanish omelette. Desserts keep up the pace: marquesa de chocolate is a luscious, creamy, home-made chocolate mousse, while flan de naranja is a really good orange crème caramel. The alfresco tables hidden in the garden behind the resto are sought after and should be booked in advance. It's worth checking out El Parador's strong selection of Spanish wines as there are some good-value options.

Prince Albert

163 Royal College Street, NW1 ■ 020 7485 0270

⊖ Camden Town

🍴 Modern British/gastropub

🕐 Mon to Sat 12.00–15.00 & 18.30–22.00; Sun 12.30–17.00

🌐 www.princealbertcamden.com

🗗 all major credit cards ■ 12.5% optional service added

££ starters £4.00–£8.50 ■ mains £10–£18 ■ sides £3–£4
■ desserts £4.50–£7.00 ■ bar menu £4–£13 ■ global tapas £3.50–£5
■ lowest bottle price £12.50

❂ Multi-tasking gastropub

The Albert is a venerable Charringtons corner pub that has been dragged into the 21st century. It is still recognisable as a pub, with a handsome bar and a scatter of downstairs tables, but there is now a first-floor dining room. It is easy to get confused but there is a restaurant menu served on the first floor; a bar specials blackboard downstairs and, for good measure, a 'Global Tapas' menu into the bargain. Meanwhile, the pubby side of things also barrels along – three real ales and an interesting wine list. In the resto, as a starter you may be offered sautéed chorizo, Granny Smith apple and black pudding; or pan-fried scallops, parsnip, black truffle and sauce d'epices. Follow this with mains such as grilled turbot, braised oxtail, thyme shallots, mushrooms, and herb mash; or rump of lamb, flageolet purée, balsamic shallots, fondant potato and confit garlic. The global tapas are equally eclectic offerings: game pie; Shanghai shellfish risotto (a set-back for Sino-Italian relations?) or grilled goats' cheese, quince sorbet and horseradish wafer. Perhaps the most attractive menu is the blackboard in the bar: toad-in-the-hole made with venison sausages; grilled Brixham sardines; or ox-liver, pancetta and black pudding hot pot – a dark and mysterious casserole topped with mash which is rich and good. For pud, how about caramelised apple and shortbread pie? There is something to be said for keeping things simple…

Viet-Anh Café

41 Parkway, NW1 ■ 020 7284 4082

⊖ Camden Town

🍽 Vietnamese

🕐 daily 12.00–16.00 & 17.30–23.00

🗗 all major credit cards except AmEx ■ 10% optional service added

---

££ starters £1–£7 ■ mains £4.50–£10 ■ lowest bottle price £10

✪ Cheap, cheerful and Vietnamese

Authentic, it says on the card, and authentic it tastes on the plate. Viet-Anh is a bright, cheerful café with oilcloth-covered tables, run by a young Vietnamese couple. In complete contrast to the occasionally intimidating feel of some of the more obscure Chinese restaurants, this is a friendly and welcoming place. If there is anything puzzling or unfamiliar, you have only to ask. Vietnamese vegetarian spring rolls and Vietnamese chicken pancake are classic starters. The former are crisp, well seasoned, and flavoured with fresh coriander; the latter are a delight – two large, paper-thin, eggy pancakes stuffed with vegetables and chicken and served with large lettuce leaves. You take a leaf, add a slice of the pancake, roll it up, then dip it in the pungent lemony sauce and eat. Hot and cold, crisp and soft, savoury and lemony – all in one. Ordering prawn sugar-cane stick brings large prawns skewered on a piece of sugar cane. Eat the prawn, then chew the cane. Pho chicken soup is made with slices of chicken and vegetables plus flat rice-stick noodles in broth. Slurp the noodles and lift the bowl to drink the soup. Lemongrass chicken on boiled rice is a more fiery dish – seriously hot. There are over a hundred items on the menu, and most are satisfying one-plate meals. Wines are priced sensibly, or you could try the Shui Sen tea – more fragrant than jasmine tea and just as beguiling.

Crouch End and Wood Green

La Bota

31 Broadway Parade, Tottenham Lane, N8 ■ 020 8340 3082

⊖ Turnpike Lane/BR Hornsey

🍴 Spanish/tapas

🕐 Mon to Thurs 12.00–14.30 & 18.00–23.00; Fri 12.00–14.30 &
18.00–23.30; Sat 12.00–15.00 & 18.00–23.30; Sun 12.00–23.00

🖑 www.labota.co.uk

🖬 all major credit cards except AmEx ■ no service added

££ tapas £2.25–£4.50 ■ mains £7.50–£12.75 ■ desserts £2.25 –£3.25
■ lowest bottle price £10.50

✪ N8 Tapas zone

This bustling tapas bar and restaurant enjoys a healthy evening
trade, and with good reason. It's a Galician establishment (from
north-western Spain), and that's always a plus sign, particularly for
seafood. Your first decision is a crucial one: do you go all out for
tapas – there is a long, long list? Or do you choose one of the main
courses – Spanish omelette, paellas, steaks, chicken, fish and so
forth? Perhaps the best option is to play to La Bota's strengths and
order a few tapas, then a few more, until you have subdued your
appetite and there's no longer a decision to make. In the meantime,
enjoy the air conditioning – and the house wine at a very reasonable
price. Start with simple things. Boquerones en vinagre brings a plate
of broad, white anchovies with a pleasant vinegar tang. Jamón
serrano is thinly sliced, ruby-red and strongly flavoured – perfect with
the basket of warm French bread that is on every table. Then move on
to hot tapas: mejillones pescador is a good-sized plate of mussels in a
tomato and garlic sauce; chistorra a la sidra is a mild sausage cooked
in cider; ri–ones al Jerez is a portion of kidneys in a sherry sauce,
rich and good. Alas de pollo barbacoa is an Iberian take on chicken
wings. Then there's arroz al campo – rice cooked with saffron and
vegetables; chicken riojana; and patatas bravas – potatoes in a mildly
spicy tomato sauce. Just keep them coming…

Matsu

50 Topsfield Parade, N8 ■ 020 8340 7773

⊖ Turnpike Lane/BR Hornsey

🍴 Japanese

🕐 Tues to Sat 18.00–23.00; Sun 18.00–22.00

🛱 all major credit cards ■ no service added

££ nigiri sushi £1.50–£2 (per piece) ■ sashimi £1.80–£2 (2 slices)
■ mains £7–£12 ■ sides £1.50–£5.50 ■ desserts £5–£6.50
■ lowest bottle price £11.80 ■ sake (from) £3

⭐ Small, elegant and perfectly formed

Shigeki Matsushima grins a lot, but then he also bows a lot and cuts up a lot of fish. This little restaurant makes maximum use of a single shop front on Topsfield Parade. There are plain tables and plain chairs for the 36 customers, abstract pictures on the walls and a tiny bar. The music is a puzzle. Sometimes it is jazzy – 'Take Five' rattles out – and sometimes it is awful piano tinklings. In a quaint way, it goes well with the ambience, which is friendly but reserved. Start (although some may find the mixed nigiri set large enough to be the main event) with some sushi. The sushi here passes all the main tests – rice at room temperature, fish neatly cut, and none of the dread chill factor as you bite into each piece. Not stellar but very good. Then there are various hand roll options (including the rather horrid one of making your own). On to the main dishes, which tend to come with a bowl of rice and miso soup. There's chicken teriyaki; or pork katsu – a chunky pork escalope which comes with a cabbage salad. The tempura is very good here, light but crisp batter, with huge prawns and crunchy vegetables. The green tea ice cream for pudding is certainly green but also astringent and bitter. Service is very smiley and everyone seems concerned that you enjoy yourself.

Mosaica

Building C, The Chocolate Factory, Clarendon Road, N22

■ 020 8889 2400 ♿

☍ Wood Green

🍴 Modern British

🕐 Tues to Fri 12.00–14.30 & 18.30–22.00; Sat 18.30–22.00; Sun 12.00–15.00

⌐ www.mosaicarestaurants.com

🗗 all major credit cards ■ 10% optional service added

££ starters £5.95–£10.50 ■ mains £12.50–£16 ■ sides £2–£4
■ desserts £5–£6.50 ■ lowest bottle price £13.50

✪ Good food in a moody location

Up in the high pastures of Wood Green there is a straggle of large, run-down buildings called The Chocolate Factory that have been colonised by artists, potters, designers and anyone arty needing a cheap, no-frills space. You'll find Mosaica hidden at the heart of Building C, and it is an amazing place – spacious, stylish and comfortable. There is a long bar made up of cinder blocks, topped with a twenty-foot sheet of glass. There's a huge open kitchen. And for once they've got the atmosphere dead right – stylish but informal, neighbourhood but sharp. The food is a complete surprise. It's terrific. The dishes achieve their objective of being both familiar and interesting. The menu at Mosaica is short and changes daily – all is seasonal and all is fresh. Starters might include charred Peruvian asparagus with Balsamic and 'parmy'; grilled squid with chilli jam; black leg ham with mozzarella; wild rabbit ragu with pappardelle; or sardines with gremolata. Mains range from halibut with cavolo nero to artichoke, garlic and confit leek ravioli. Or try rare rib eye with garlic mash and morels; calves' liver with creamed Savoy, pancetta and shallots; or slow-roast pork belly with red cabbage. Notable puds: try the panna cotta with espresso top; or the framboise cheesecake with crème Chantilly. The wine list is short and the service more enthusiastic than polished, but the food is great and the prices are forgiving.

O's Thai Café

10 Topsfield Parade, N8 ■ 020 8348 6898

⊖ Turnpike Lane/BR Hornsey

🍽 Thai

🕐 Mon 18.30–23.00; Tues to Sat 12.00–15.00 & 18.30–23.00;
Sun 12.00–15.00 & 18.30–22.30

🖰 www.oscafesandbars.co.uk

🖰 Mastercard, Visa ■ 10% optional service added for parties of 5 or more

££ starters £1.95–£8.95 ■ mains £5.95–£12.95 ■ sides £4.25
■ desserts £1.95–£2.50 ■ set lunch & dinner £6.50 & £13.95
■ lowest bottle price £10.95

⭐ Friendly neighbourhood Thai

O's Thai Café is young, happy and fresh, rather like O himself. With
his economics, advertising and fashion-design background, and a
staff who seem to be having fun, O brings a youthful zip to Thai
cuisine. His café is fast and noisy, and the music is played at high
volume. But that's not to say the food is anything less than excellent,
and it's very good value, too. Order from the comprehensive and
well-explained menu, or from the blackboard of specials, which
runs down an entire wall. Of the many starters, satays are tasty,
prawn toasts and spring rolls are as crisp as they should be, while
paper-wrapped thin dumplings really do melt in the mouth. Tom ka
chicken soup is hot and sharp, with lime leaf and lemongrass. Main
courses include Thai red and green curries – the gaeng kiew wan, a
spicy, soupy green curry of chicken and coconut cream, is pungently
moreish – as well as an interesting selection of specials such as
yamneau, a.k.a. weeping tiger – sliced, spiced, grilled steak served
on salad with a pungent Thai dressing. If you like noodles, there
is a selection of pad dishes – stir-fries with a host of combinations
of vegetables, soy sauce, peanuts, spices, chicken, beef, pork, king
prawn or bean curd. Puddings may include khow tom mud, banana
with sticky rice wrapped in banana leaf, or Thai ice cream. There's a
wide and varied wine list, with Budweiser, Budvar, Gambrinus and
Leffe beers on draught.

→ For branch, see index or website

Sosta

14 Middle Lane, N8 ■ 020 8340 1303

⊖ Turnpike Lane/BR Hornsey

🍴 Italian

🕐 Mon to Fri 18.30–22.45; Sat 12.00–15.00 & 18.30–22.45;
Sun 12.00–22.15

🔗 www.sosta.co.uk

🖫 all major credit cards ■ 10% optional service added

££ starters £3.95–£6.95 ■ mains £8.95–£14.95 ■ sides £2.95–£4.75
■ desserts £3.25–£4.25 ■ menus: Mon 'regional' £11.95; Tues–Fri
nights & Sat lunch 'degustazione' £12.95; Sun lunch £9.95 & £11.95
■ lowest bottle price £10.95

✪ Old-school Italian, old-school values

During the 1970s Silvano Sacchi was at the helm of two of
London's more fashionable eateries: the Barracuda (a smart Italian
fish restaurant in Baker Street) and San Martino (an Italian tratt in St
Martin's Lane). Having sold out to a plc, Sacchi retired to Italy with
his money and memories. Then a few years ago he dived back into
the maelstrom of the London restaurant scene and opened Sosta.
The antipasti include insalata tricolore – a mozzarella, avocado
and tomato salad; carpaccio di spada – fresh swordfish; or tomato
bruschetta. Onwards to 'primi', where you'll find pasta e fagioli alla
Veneta, a thick pasta and borlotti bean soup; and pasta dishes such
as gnocchi al pomodoro e basilico; spaghetti al frutti di mare; and
tagliolini alla rusticana. Pasta dishes incur a small supplement when
taken as a main course. 'Secondi' offers six fish and seven meat
dishes. Try bocconcini de coda di rospo – medallions of monkfish;
piccata di vitello al tartufo nero – escalopes of veal with black truffle,
or tagliata di Angus – fillet steak. Puds are sound: semi freddo; panna
cotta; tiramisù. The wine list has some trad Italian bottles that appeal
greatly. At Sosta the service is slick and the tables are close together.
The huge pepper mill of the 1970s may have been replaced by a natty
modernist Parmesan grater, but everyone is attentive in what now
seems like an old-fashioned way.

Hampstead, Golders Green and Belsize Park

Bloom's

130 Golders Green Road, NW11 ▪ 020 8455 1338

⊖ Golders Green

🍽 Jewish

🕐 Mon to Thurs & Sun 12.00–22.30; Fri 10.00–13.30 (15.00 in summer)

🔗 www.blooms-restaurant.co.uk

🖯 all major credit cards ▪ no service added

££ starters £3.95–£5.95 ▪ mains £9.95–£19.95 ▪ sides £1.20–£2.50
▪ desserts £3.90–£4.25 ▪ lowest bottle price £14.95

✪ Trad, but new, Jewish diner

Bloom's goes way back to 1920 when Rebecca and Morris Bloom first produced their great discovery – the original veal Vienna. Since then 'Bloom's of the East End' has carried the proud tag as 'the most famous kosher restaurant in the world'. Setting aside the indignant claims of several outraged New York delis for the moment, given its history it's a shame that the East End Bloom's was forced to shut, and that they had to retrench to their Golders Green stronghold in 1965. Then it was business as before – until 2006, when it was finally time for a makeover. Meanwhile, the food stayed the same. No modern interpretations here. Start with some new green cucumbers – fresh, crisp, tangy, delicious – and maybe a portion of chopped liver and egg and onions, which comes with world-class rye bread. Or go for soup, which comes in bowls so full they slop over the edge. There's beetroot borscht and potato, which is very sweet and very red; lockshen, the renowned noodle soup; or kreplach, full of dumplings. Go on to main courses. The salt beef is as good as you might expect (although it has been noted that it is a great deal leaner than it was in days of yore). Try it in a sandwich on rye bread and, if you feel brave enough, order extra side dishes like the dreaded, heart-stopping fried potato latke.

→ For branch, see index or website

Czechoslovak House Restaurant

74 West End Lane, NW6 ■ 020 7372 1193

⊖ West Hampstead

🍴 Czech

🕐 Tues to Fri 17.00–22.00; Sat & Sun 12.00–22.00

🖰 www.czechoslovak-restaurant.co.uk

🖶 cash only ■ 10% service added

££ starters £1.50 to £7 ■ mains £4 to £12 ■ sides £1.50 to £2
   ■ desserts £2.50 to £3 ■ lowest bottle price £12

⭐ Just the place to meet the Third Man

Over sixty years ago the Czechoslovak National House moved
from Holborn to West End Lane (the club committee of the day took
exception to the WC1 licensing magistrates refusing to allow the sale
of beer!), and it's true to say that nothing much has changed since.
The restaurant décor is relatively unchanged since the 1970s and
the kitchen had a shake-up a couple of years ago, but thankfully the
charm of the place remains intact. First equip yourself with a beer
— Gambrinus, Pilsner Urquell or the smooth dark one called Bernard
(licensing eccentricities mean you have to fetch your drinks from the
bar). Among the starters are intriguing options, such as brawn and
bread (very solid, very meaty) or bramborák se slaninou, which is a
potato pancake topped with slices of fat bacon. From the mains there
is goose breast served with sauerkraut; goulash; roast duck; and a
whole smoked pork knuckle — very good, very smoky, very large.
Dumplings are ever present — bread dumplings that are actually
quite light, and potato dumplings that are not. For pudding you can
have an apricot dumpling. A whole apricot is encased in dumpling
and then the resulting hand-grenade is served in a bath of melted
butter with a topping of cream. Service is gentle and conscientious,
prices are very friendly. Be especially wary of a Czech liqueur called
Becherovka.

Elephant Walk

98 West End Lane, NW6 ■ 020 7328 3308

West Hampstead

Sri Lankan

Mon to Fri 17.00–23.00; Sat 12.00–15.00 & 17.00–23.00;
Sun 12.00–23.00

www.elephantwalk.biz

all major credit cards except AmEx ■ 10% service added

££ starters £2.90–£3.25 ■ mains £4.95–£7.90 ■ sides £2.25–£3.50
■ desserts £2.50–£2.75 ■ lowest bottle price £9.85

✪ Happy hoppers!

Elephant Walk is one of those small and friendly restaurants
that almost gives the impression that it is an amateur or charitable
venture. Service is attentive and smiling, the menu lists dishes from
Sri Lanka and Southern India, vegetarians are well catered for. If
you like your Sri Lankan food with an authentic chilli burn you will
probably have to insist that the kitchen complies, otherwise things
may end up somewhat tamed — not from carelessness but rather
because of a concern that you do not know what you are getting
into. To start with, try the rolls, which are made with lamb, chicken
or vegetables and are like a spring roll — a pancake filled, rolled and
then deep fried. Move on to string hoppers. These are rather like a
new generation of chow mein — rice noodles are steamed and then
tossed in a wok with chicken or lamb and served with a curry sauce
on the side. Other good dishes are the devilled lamb and devilled
chicken — an admirably dry dish flavoured with ginger and garlic and
a healthy issue of chilli. If you want this authentically hot it's best to
ask for it that way. Fish dishes are also worth trying, such as squid
stars in thallo Mirisatta cooked with lemon juice and coconut. Note
the lemon rice and the gothamba rotis; as in so many Sri Lankan and
South Indian establishments, care is lavished on the accompaniments.

Goldfish

82 Hampstead High Street, NW3 ■ 020 7794 6666

Hampstead

Chinese/dim sum

Sun to Thurs 12.00–15.00 & 18.00–22.30; Fri & Sat 12.00–15.00 &
18.00–23.00; dim sum at lunch

---

all major credit cards ■ 10% optional service added

££ appetisers £4.50–£9 ■ salads £7–£8.50 ■ soups £3.80–£5
■ mains £6–£18 ■ sides £1.80–£8 ■ desserts £6.50–£7
■ lowest bottle price £12.50

❂ Plush restaurant, plush food

Goldfish is something of an enigma. It's a Chinese restaurant and
very decent dim sum are on offer at lunch time, but thereafter the
waters muddy somewhat. The food here, (which is much loved by
the NW3ers) is very different from what's on offer elsewhere in the
locality. Perhaps this is due to the odd attitude towards restaurants
that prevails in Hampstead, where ambitious restaurants have a
record of opening, suffering and closing. Goldfish, however, has
survived the difficult first years and seems prosperous. No MSG is
used and the predominant flavour notes are sweet, but there are
some other diverting combinations of flavour too. Try the wasabi
prawns – large prawns fried in a light batter and then covered in a
green sauce made from avocado and spiked with wasabi. Strange but
not so strange as the Mocha ribs – spare ribs in a sticky sauce made
with Valrhona chocolate and coffee, a great dish if you like things
sweet. Goldfish has a reputation for serving very good fish dishes.
Take your pick from steamed sea bass with minced ginger and spring
onions; steamed cod; or Jade seared salmon and Dover sole with chilli
and black bean sauce. All very elegant on the plate. And for the less
adventurous there are all the old favourites such as aromatic duck
with pancakes; soft-shell crabs; or sweet and sour pork. Service is
attentive, but be warned – the bill can creep up to a very Hampstead
sort of figure.

The Horseshoe

28 Heath Street, NW3 ■ 020 7431 7206

⊖ Hampstead

🍽 Modern British/gastropub

🕐 Mon to Sat 10.00–23.00; Sun 10.00–22.30

🏠 all major credit cards ■ 10% optional service added

££ starters £5–£9.50 ■ mains £9.50–£14.50 ■ sides £3.50
■ desserts £6–£7 ■ lowest bottle price £12.50

★ Fluent gastropub spoken here

As you walk into the Horseshoe you can bask in the pleasant
glow of all things familiar. This is a light, bright, clean sort of place.
Informal and casual, it is pretty much what most of us hope a
gastropub should be. The old pub functions of drinking, socialising
and drinking have been retained but towards the back of the bar
enough dining tables have been shoe-horned in to keep the kitchen
busy. The menu changes regularly but sets some store by provenance
and the seasons — the bacon comes from Blythburgh in Suffolk,
and the T-bone steak is from a Red Poll steer. Starters range from
simple dishes like a potato, spiced sausage and black cabbage soup;
to the esoteric such as lamb kidneys and sweetbreads with wild
mushrooms and salsify — complex combinations of flavour and
texture — by way of a black pudding and venison terrine served with
pickled cauliflower. The main courses can be bold, such as mackerel,
chorizo, white beans and roast garlic; or traditional, such as sardines
lemon and parsley. A duck breast comes with Jerusalem artichokes
and mushrooms; and there may be a simple classic like a haunch of
venison served with potato purée. Puddings pull of the trick of being
both modern and comfortably old-fashioned, so you have chocolate
truffle tart and clotted cream; or apple cobbler and custard. The beers
are well kept, and the wine list is sensibly priced.

Jin Kichi

73 Heath Street, NW3 ▪ 020 7794 6158

⊖ Hampstead

†⊙† Japanese

🕐 Tues to Fri 18.00–23.00; Sat 12.30–14.00 & 18.00–23.00; Sun 12.30–14.00 & 18.00–22.00

🖱 www.jinkichi.com

🗗 all major credit cards ▪ no service added

££ skewers £1.40–£2.30 ▪ mains £4.80–£14.80 ▪ sides £3.20–£5
▪ desserts £3.20–£4 ▪ set lunch £7.70–£14.90
▪ lowest bottle price: wine £18; sake £6.60

❂ Charming Japanese grill house

Unlike so many Japanese restaurants, where the atmosphere can range from austere to intimidating, Jin Kichi is a very comfortable place. It's cramped, rather shabby and has been very busy for over a decade (tables are booked up even on the quiet nights of the week). The bar dominates the ground floor and is home to a small and fierce charcoal grill, where an unhurried chef cooks short skewers of this and that. By all means start with sushi. Ordering the nigiri set brings seven pieces of fresh fish for an eminently reasonable price. But then go for the 'grilled skewers'. Helpfully enough, there are two set meals offering various combinations, and each delivers seven skewers. These make for a very splendid kind of eating, since each skewer comes hot off the grill. Be adventurous – grilled skewer of fresh asparagus and pork rolls with salt is a big seller. Grilled skewer of chicken wings with salt is simple and very good, but the duck with spring onion is even better. Chicken gizzard with salt is chewy and delicious, while the grilled skewer of chicken skin with salt is crisp and very moreish. But the top skewer must be the ox tongue with salt. Drink ice-cold Kirin beer served in a frosted glass. The remainder of the menu leads off to fried dishes, tempura, different noodle dishes, soups and so forth, but the undoubted star of the show is the little grill.

Kimchee

887 Finchley Road, NW11 ■ 020 8455 1035

⊖ Golders Green

🍴 Korean

🕐 Tues to Sun 12.00–15.00 & 18.00–23.00

🏱 all major credit cards ■ 10% optional service added

££ starters £1.90–£7.90 ■ mains £6.50–£7.90 ■ sides £1.90–£3.90
■ lunch menus £5.90–£6.90 ■ lowest bottle price £9.95

✪ A neighbourhood star – but Korean

Kimchee is a charming place with a well-mannered clientele
split fifty-fifty between homesick Koreans and adventurous Golders
Greenites. Korean food majors in strong flavours, and in dishes that
are finished at the table (each table has a barbecue built into the
middle of it and your waitress will cook at least part of your meal in
front of you). Start with some pickles: kimchee, fermented cabbage
with loads of salt and fierce chilli-hot red bean paste, is the most
famous. The sliced radish with vinegar is milder and the pickled
cucumbers are very good indeed. There is also yuk whe, the Korean
equivalent of steak tartare – shredded raw beef bound together with
egg yolk and slivers of pear. Implausibly good. Koon mandoo, large
pan-fried dumplings, have very good crispy bits. For your main course
try one of the table-grilled dishes. There's bulgogi, marinated beef
cooked on the metal plate in front of you; or sliced pork; or seafood.
The 'pot dishes' are also interesting: a stone pot is heated up until it
is sizzling, a layer of rice is then added and on top of that are placed
some meat, vegetables and an egg yolk. When it arrives at table your
waitress mixes it all together and you get dol bibim bab – instant
fried rice cooked by the hot pot. To drink, either stick to Korean beer
or try 'soju', a clear spirit served on ice from a mini-bottle.

The Wells

30 Well Walk, NW3 ■ 020 7794 3785

⊖ Hampstead

🍴 Modern British/gastropub

🕘 Mon to Fri 12.00–15.00 & 19.00–22.00; Sat 12.00–16.00 &
19.00–22.00; Sun 12.00–16.00 & 19.00–21.30

🖰 www.thewellshampstead.co.uk

🗗 all major credit cards ■ 12.5% optional service added

££ starters £5.50–£9.50 ■ mains £9.95–£22.50 ■ sides £3–£4
■ desserts £5–£8.50 ■ lowest bottle price £14

✪ A very Hampstead gastropub

As the gastropub revolution rolled over London, it deposited The
Wells smack in the middle of old Hampstead. After a flamboyant
start, The Wells has retrenched and gently re-positioned the menu
to introduce some more gastropubby and less restauranty dishes,
while easing up a little on the formality. Dinner here still carries a
pretty evening-out-in-a-restaurant price tag, but the kitchens cook
accessible food. There are a couple of dining rooms, which are lofty
and elegant, and there's plenty of bar space for the dedicated toper.
The menu changes to take account of the seasons, but starters might
include carrot, celery and onion soup; a squid and rocket salad with
chorizo dressing; beetroot Roquefort, pecan and balsamic endive
salad; sautéed chicken livers, marinated mushrooms; or pan-fried
scallops teamed with curried parsley root purée. The short list of main
courses is supplemented with grills and specials – so you could have
fillet of sea bass with courgette fettucine; a veal chop with saffron
risotto and gremolata; a Scotch Angus burger; a fillet of halibut with
Jerusalem artichoke purée; salt marsh lamb rump with Dauphinoise
potato; or simple stalwarts like Cumberland sausages with mash and
onion gravy. Puds range from fruit crumble with custard to blueberry
cheesecake with cream; or rice pudding with a caramel sauce and
pistachios. The wine list is user-friendly, service is slick and (as befits
a gastropub) the cuisine just about stays on the comfort side of
restaurant dishes.

XO

29 Belsize Lane, NW3 ■ 020 7433 0888

⊖ Belsize Park

🍽 Pan Asian

🕐 Mon to Fri 12.00–14.30 & 18.00–22.30; Sat 12.00–15.30 & 18.00–22.30; Sun 12.00–15.30 & 18.00–21.30

🔗 www.rickerrestaurants.com

🖥 all major credit cards ■ 12.5% optional service added

££ starters £3.50–£6.50 ■ mains £9–£21 ■ sides £2.50–£5.50 ■ desserts £5–£6.50 ■ lowest bottle price £13

✪ Crisp style palace

It's pretty awesome what a good hose down with plenty of cash can do for a site. Within living memory number 29 Belsize Lane was a scruffy pub called the Belsize Tavern, then it made the change to a gastropub and then another transformation saw it become the latest feather in Will Ricker's cap (see E&O on p. 114 for another of his ventures). This is an affluent neighbourhood and perhaps the very thing the area needs is a slick and stylish exotically Asian restaurant and bar. It is certainly busy enough. Starters include a range of dim sum, including chicken and bean curd dumplings; or there are baby pork spare ribs with black beans – very tender, if on the sweet side. From the tried-and-tested contingent, there is chilli salt squid served in a twist of Chinese newspaper. Or you could try the tempura soft shell crab; or there is sashimi. The most expensive dish – and given the portion size it works out seriously pricey – is the black cod with sweet miso. This is the dish that started at Nobu (see p. 99), migrated to Zuma (see p. 69) and is now a must-have for any classy, style-led Asian resto. Here it is sound enough but, like a great deal of the cooking, seems to lurch towards the sweet end of the taste spectrum. At XO drinks are exotic, service polished, and the décor chic.

→ For branches, see index or website

Harrow and Wembley

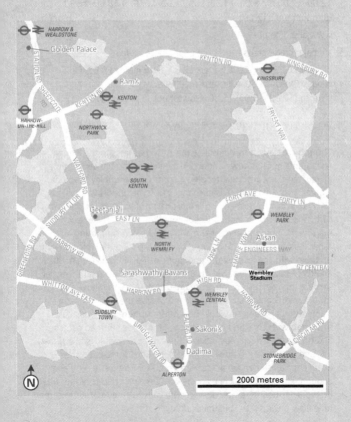

Alisan

Wembley Retail Park, Engineer's Way, Middx

■ 020 8903 3888

⊖ Wembley Park

🍽 Chinese/dim sum

🕓 Mon, Wed & Thurs 12.00–17.00 & 18.00–23.00; Fri & Sat
12.00–17.00 & 18.00–23.30; Sun 12.00–17.00 & 18.00–22.30
(dim sum until 17.00)

🖱 www.alisan.co.uk

🗗 all major credit cards ■ 10% optional service added

££ dim sum £2.30–£4.20 ■ starters £2.80–£8 ■ mains £5.80–£28
■ sides £1.80–£7.50 ■ desserts £1.80–£8.50
■ lunch (12.00–15.00) £5.50 ■ lowest bottle price £11.50

✪ We're on our way to Wembley

Though cast adrift in Wembley, this resto has links to the Aroma
restaurants in Chinatown and a dim sum chef who has served time
at Yauatcha. For anyone attending a concert at Wembley Arena or
a game at the stadium, Alisan changes from being 'off the beaten
track' to a 'handy godsend' in pretty short order. From the dim
sum list some of the more unusual dumplings catch the eye: white
marrow prawn dumpling; prawn and enoki mushroom dumpling;
asparagus cheung fun; and baked barbecue pork puff, which is right
up there with the leaders: the pork puffs at Royal China (see p. 80)
and the venison puffs at Hakkasan (see p. 6). You'll find all the usual
suspects on the main menu – steamed scallops with ginger and
spring onion come up rather small and maybe the stir-fried razor
clams with garlic shoots would be a better option; or there's baked
fresh crab with chilli and black pepper. Ignore the stir-fried ostrich
and go for the simple roast duck. The Singapore noodle is full of tasty
bits and pieces. The lengthy menu also includes some curiosities –
anyone for a fish congee made with sea bass? The service is friendly
enough, although it will need to be very crisp on concert nights when
everyone in the 200-seater dining room calls for their bill at the same
time after having the 'Stadium event day set menu'.

Dadima

228 Ealing Road, Wembley, Middx ■ 020 8902 1072   ♿

⊖ Alperton

🍽 Indian/vegetarian

🕐 Mon to Fri 12.00–15.00 & 17.00–22.00; Sat & Sun 12.00–22.00

🗄 all major credit cards ■ no service added

££ starters £2–£4 ■ mains £3–£4.50 ■ sides 50p–£3 ■ desserts £2
    ■ lunch thali (until 21.00) £3.49 ■ lowest bottle price £2.20 (180ml)

✪ Good veggie food, easy-going atmosphere

There's something very charming about these small Gujarati cafés
that quietly go about their business feeding lots of people: their
food is wholesome, prices are spectacularly low, and the atmosphere
invariably cheery. Inside, Dadima has undergone a refurbishment so
it's lighter and brighter. The starters and snacks are very good. Pani
puri are small, crunchy, and savoury, with flavours well balanced:
simply load a teaspoon of the sharp sauce into each small flying
saucer and devour them whole. For something a bit spookier try the
khichi. This is a strange dish, with a strange texture – it is basically
a very solid rice flour sludge; you dress each mouthful with a little
oil and then some finely ground hot red pepper. Kachori are much
more accessible, small balls, crisp outside and with a core of spicy
lentil mix – very satisfying with a dollop of the sweet, sharp tamarind
sauce. Onwards towards main courses, which are also very good:
palak paneer is a smooth spinach purée with a few chunks of chewy
cheese scattered through it; or try the dal makhni, a rich stew with
black lentils and kidney beans – floating on the top is the makhni
part, a large enriching lump of butter. With your meal pile into the
breads, which are very well done here. The wine is also worthy of a
mention as it comes in those handy little airline bottles which means
it's never stale.

Geetanjali

16 Court Parade, Watford Road, Middx ■ 020 8904 5353 ♿

⊖ North Wembley/Wembley Central

🍽 Indian

🕐 daily 12.00–15.00 & 18.00–24.00

🏠 all major credit cards ■ 10% optional service added

££ starters £2.50–£4.50 ■ mains £7.90–£10.50 ■ sides £4–£5
■ desserts £2.90–£3.50 ■ lowest bottle price £11.50

⭐ Best ever tandoori chops

On the face of it, the menu at Geetangli is pretty straightforward, with plenty of familiar dishes listed – chicken tikka masala, rogan josh and so on and so forth. But Geetanjali has a secret weapon, a dish that brings customers from far and wide. This place serves the best tandoori lamb chops in North London. The chop lover's haven has a large, roomy dining room. The service is attentive, if a little resigned when you pitch up and single-mindedly order a raft of beers and several portions of tandoori chops – or, as the menu would have it, lamb chopp. The chops are good of course. Very good. Thick-cut, exceedingly tender and very nicely spiced. The tandoor chef knows his stuff. Accompany them with a luccha paratha, warm and flaky and presented in the shape of a flower with a knob of butter melting into its heart. The alternative is the intriguingly named bullet nan, which promises to be hot and spicy, and delivers in good measure. Even if you're not a complete chopaholic you can do well here. Go for starters such as the good chicken tikka, made with chicken breast. Rashmi kebab is also good, made from minced chicken and spices. Main courses include methi chicken, which is chicken with fenugreek, and lamb badam pasanda. And should this emphasis on meat leave you craving some of the green stuff, there's sag aloo or karahi corn masala.

Golden Palace

146–150 Station Road, Harrow, Middx ■ 020 8863 2333   ♿

⊖ Harrow & Wealdstone

🍽 Chinese/dim sum

🕐 Mon to Sat 12.00–23.30, Sun 11.00–22.30 (dim sum until 17.00 every day)

🗃 all major credit cards ■ 10% optional service added

££ dim sum £2.20–£3.50 ■ starters £3.50–£5 ■ mains £5.20–£10 ■ sides £2.80–£5 ■ desserts £1.50–£3.50 ■ lowest bottle price £11.50

✪ Excellent dim sum

The Golden Palace would be a seriously busy restaurant even if it were in the heart of Chinatown, but to find a buzzing and sophisticated dim sum specialist in suburban Harrow is a shock. Inside all is chic and slick, and large tables of young Chinese ladies-who-lunch sit happily alongside families with babies in highchairs. Everyone is eating dim sum. The dim sum here are very good indeed and the best strategy is to order several — some familiar and some exotic – and then repeat those you like best. All the dumplings are keenly priced. Bear in mind that most of the dumplings come in threes. Stand-outs are the crystal prawn dumplings – thin, steamed dumplings full of fresh, almost crunchy prawn; and the prawn and chive dumplings, which are similar but with the green of fresh chives showing through the translucent pastry. Deep-fried shredded squid is quite simply the best, tenderest, crispest 'calamari' you have ever eaten. And try the truly amazing mini lotus-wrapped glutinous rice with meat: they come two in a portion, you open the lotus leaves and there's a stunning sticky rice ball with a centre of slow-cooked pork, which is rich, delicious and intense. The sheer variety of the dishes on offer is impressive, but it is even more unusual to find them all done so well, and at such a reasonable price. Service is brisk but friendly, and the tea is – well, tea.

Ram's

203 Kenton Road, Harrow, Middx ■ 020 8907 2030

⊖ Kenton

🍽 Indian/vegetarian

🕐 daily 12.00–15.00 & 18.00–22.00

🗗 all major credit cards ■ 10% optional service added

££ starters £3–£4.50 ■ mains £4–£5 ■ desserts £2.10–£3.90
■ lunch thali £5 ■ lowest bottle price £9.90

✪ Stunning Indian veggie food

Anyone in downtown Mumbai will tell you that India's best
vegetarian food comes from the Gujarati city of Surat. Luckily, London
has its very own Surti restaurant – Ram's. The staff rush around,
eager and friendly; their pride in both the menu and their home town
is obvious and endearing. Gujarati snacks make great starters. Petis
are small balls of peas and onions coated in potato and deep fried.
Kachori are the same kind of thing, but with mung daal inside a
pastry coat. Patras are made by rolling vegetable leaves with a 'glue'
of chickpea flour batter; the roll is then sliced across, and each slice
becomes a delicate and savoury pinwheel. Stuffed banana bhaji is
a sweet and savoury combo. The kand is a Surti special – slices of
purple potato in a savoury batter. Sev khamni is a sludge of well-
spiced chickpeas with coconut, served topped with a layer of crisp
sev. Flavours are clear and distinct, and some dishes have a welcome
chilli heat. Mains do not disappoint. The famous undhiu – a weekend
special – is a complex dish of vegetables 'stuffed' with a Surti spice
paste. It combines aubergines with three kinds of potatoes (purple,
sweet and white), as well as bananas and peas. The peas pilau is
simple and good. The methi parathas are dry and tasty. The puris are
fresh, hot and as self-indulgent as only fried bread can be.

Sakoni's

127–129 Ealing Road, Alperton, Middx ■ 020 8903 1058

⊖ Alperton

🍴 Indian/vegetarian

🕐 Mon to Thurs & Sun 11.00–23.00; Fri & Sat 11.00–23.30

🗗 Mastercard, Visa ■ 10% optional service added

££ starters £2.75–£4.60 ■ mains £4.95–£5.50 ■ desserts £2–£3
■ set menus: Sat & Sun breakfast buffet/lunch & dinner buffet £7.99
& £10.99 ■ unlicensed

✪ Top-notch Indian veggie food factory

From a décor point of view, the dining area here is somewhat clinical unless you like a huge square yardage of white tiling. But the veggie food is terrific and Sakoni's is crowded with Asian families, all of whom seem to be having a seriously good time. Many of them dive straight into the 'Chinese' dishes. These tend to be old favourites such as chow mein and haka noodles, cooked with Indian spicing. Unless curiosity overwhelms you, it probably makes sense to stick to the splendid South Indian dishes. Sakoni's is renowned for its dosas. These are pancakes so crisp that they are almost chewy, and delightfully nutty. They come with two small bowls of sauce and a filling of rich, fried potato spiced with curry leaves. Choose from lain dosa, masala dosa and chutney dosa, which has spices and chilli swirled into the dosa batter. Try the farari cutlets, not cutlets at all, in fact, but very nice, well-flavoured dollops of sweet potato mash, deep fried so that they have a crisp exterior. Also worth trying are the bhel puri, the pani puri and the sev puri – amazingly crisp little taste bombs. Pop them in whole and the flavour explodes in your mouth. Some say that the juices at Sakoni's are the best in London, and while that may be hyperbole, they certainly are very good indeed. Try madaf, made from fresh coconut.

Sarashwathy Bavans

549 High Road, Wembley, Middx ■ 020 8902 1515

⊖ Wembley BR

🍴 Indian/vegetarian

🕐 daily 12.00–23.00

🖱 www.sarashwathy.com

🗗 all major credit cards ■ no service added

££ starters 40p–£5.75 ■ dosas £2.95–£9.95 ■ mains £2.50–£4.95
■ sides £1.50–£4.50 ■ desserts £1.35–£4.75
■ thalis £6.95–£19.95 (family) ■ lowest bottle price £8.95

✪ Dosa central

If there were a prize for sheer exuberant length of menu then
Sarashwathy Bavans would be in with a shout: 3 soups, 22 starters,
25 dosas, 12 iddly and uthappams, 27 mains, 4 Chinese-style
dishes, 10 breads, 3 Sri Lankan specials, thalis, drinks, sundries. The
restaurant is bright and light with a décor that combines lots of LEDs
in the ceiling (to imitate stars?) with some classical columns and a
tiled floor. From the starters some of the simple things are the most
impressive. Ordering sambar vadai brings two of the little doughnuts,
but these are exceedingly light, almost fluffy. It's odd, but they really
do melt in the mouth. Or the samosas, which have a crisp pastry and
a well-spiced filling. Or the bhel poori – a superb balance of tastes
and textures. One of the Chinese dishes also features on the starters
list – 'gobi Manchurian', which is florets of cauliflower, battered,
deep fried and then served in a hot sauce. It's strictly so-so. On to
the dosas, which are magnificent, large and crisp. Other dishes from
the menu here have real personality – the dhal butter fry is opulent
and very rich, a far cry from the austere veggie food that you can
encounter. Best dish of all is the paneer biryani, every grain of rice
fragrant and fluffy, no hint of greasiness and rich with aromatics. A
friendly place serving good food at bargain prices.

Holloway and Highgate

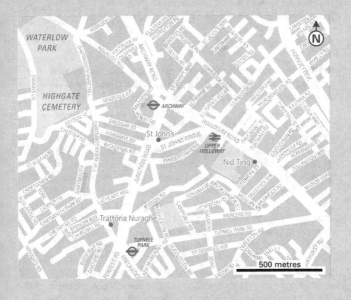

Nid Ting

533 Holloway Road, N19 ■ 020 7263 0506

⊖ Archway

🍴 Thai

🕔 Mon to Sat 18.00–23.30; Sun 18.00–22.15

🖰 all major credit cards ■ no service added

££ starters £3.95–£4.95 ■ mains £5.25–£8.95 ■ desserts £2.50
■ set dinner £15 ■ lowest bottle price £10.95

✪ Neighbourhood value, neighbourhood Thai

Nid Ting is a local restaurant that feeds people well, serving good, unfussy Thai food. The dishes here have not been tamed to suit effete Western palates, and you'll get plenty of chilli heat and pungent fish sauce. You'll also get good value and brisk service – both of which obviously appeal, as the place is usually packed. This is a genuine neighbourhood restaurant at ease with its surroundings and popular with the locals. The starters are neat platefuls of mainly fried food: chicken satay is sound, although the sauce is a bland one; a much better bet is the 'pork on toasted' – a smear of rich, meaty paste on a disc of fried bread. The prawns tempura are large and crisp, and the peek ka yas sai is very successful – stuffed chicken wings, battered and deep fried. The menu then darts off into numerous sections: there are hot and sour soups, clear soups, salads, curries, stir-fries, seafood, rice, noodle dishes, and a long, long list of vegetarian dishes – all before you get to the chef's specials. From those specials try the lamb Mussaman curry, which is rich and good, made with green chillies and coconut milk. From the noodles try pad see ew, a rich dish made with thick ribbon noodles and your choice of chicken, beef or pork. As a side order, try the som tum, which is a pleasingly astringent green papaya salad.

St John's

91 Junction Road, N10 ■ 020 7272 1587

⊖ Archway

|◉| Modern British/gastropub

🕐 Mon to Thurs 18.30–23.00; Fri 12.00–15.30 & 18.30–23.00;
Sat 12.00–16.00 & 18.30–23.00; Sun 12.00–16.00 & 18.30–21.30

🗗 all major credit cards ■ 12.5% optional service added for parties of 5
or more

££ starters £5.50–£7 ■ mains £9.75–£16 ■ desserts £5–£6
■ lowest bottle price £12

✪ Great gastropub

This was one of the first genuine gastropubs and here the
emphasis is firmly on the gastro, with a passion for all things rich,
earthy and flavoursome. Not only that, but the dining room, which
lies beyond the pub itself, looks fabulous — all louche, junk store
glamour with its high, gold-painted ceiling, low chandeliers and
plush banquettes. There's an open kitchen at one end of the room
while at the other a giant blackboard displays the long menu. As
an opening move, the friendly staff bring fresh bread and bottles
of virgin olive oil and balsamic vinegar. The menu changes day by
day, but there will probably be a soup – perhaps asparagus with a
poached egg. Other starters might be mussels, chorizo, red onions,
garlic and parsley; or jellied pig's head with celeriac purée. The food
is robust and mercifully unpretentious. Main courses range from the
traditional – chargrilled ribeye, chips and watercress with a béarnaise
sauce – to the more adventurous, such as hake steak, fennel, squash,
shallot broth and rouille; venison steak with black pudding, beetroot,
pear and hazelnut dressing; or lamb cutlets with couscous salad,
harissa and yoghurt dressing. You may need to take a breather before
venturing into pud territory. Choose from churros con chocolate;
vanilla cheesecake with butterscotch sauce; berry Pavlova; or a
chocolate and caramel tart with double cream. The intelligent wine
list includes a dozen by the glass, with a notable Cava.

Trattoria Nuraghe

12 Dartmouth Park Hill, NW5 ■ 020 7263 4560

🚇 Tufnell Park

🍴 Sardinian

🕐 Mon to Sat 18.00–23.00; Sun 12.00–22.30

💳 all major credit cards ■ 12.5% optional service added

££ starters £3.95–£8 ■ pasta £7.95–£11.50 ■ pizza £5.50–£9
■ mains £10.70–£13.80 ■ desserts £3.50–£4.50
■ lowest bottle price £11.50

✪ Ignore the décor, enjoy the food

It is hard to do justice to the décor at this small, family-run,
neighbourhood trat. The walls have swirls of red, there are swirls of
other colours, the chairs were designed by Torquemada and will have
you wriggling before the main course arrives. Thankfully, the food
is unpretentious and authentically Sardinian. Anyway, good food at
sound prices is a welcome find. The starters range from the steady –
tomato and mozzarella salad – to the very steady – charcuterie or
fritture misto (deep-fried squid, whitebait and prawns). The pastas
are inspired. There are Sardinian specialities like cullurgiones – large
home-made ravioli with a ricotta, pecorino and orange filling.
Alternatively, go for 'ravioli Nuraghe', filled with chestnuts, potatoes,
saffron and pecorino cheese. Or fregola con gamberoni – jumbo
prawns. There are main courses – lamb steak or a fish stew called
cassola – and there is a back page given over to decent pizzas. These
are freshly baked, crisp and topped with fresh ingredients. Look out
for the 'bottarga', topped with tomato, mozzarella, and grated Grey
Mullet roe. The pizzas are much in demand to take away. Desserts
include sebadas – the famous Sardinian pastries filled with cheese
and honey; and a Marscapone mousse with chocolate and Amaretto.
There's a decent bottle of Cannonau on the wine list – deep, dark
and fruity. Team it with some home-style pasta … and rely on dark
glasses to mitigate the décor.

Islington and Highbury

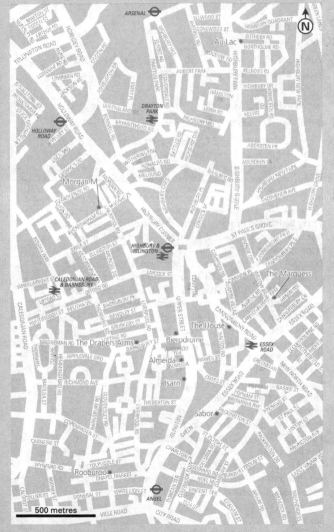

Almeida

30 Almeida Street, N1 ■ 020 7354 4777

⊖ Highbury & Islington

🍽 French

🕐 Mon to Sat 12.00–14.30 & 17.30–22.45; Sun 12.00–21.00; the Terrace: May to October 09.00–12.00 & 12.00–14.30; tapas in the bar 12.00–23.00

🖱 www.danddlondon.com

🖃 all major credit cards ■ 12.5% optional service added

££ lunch £20 (2 courses) & £24.50 (3 courses) ■ dinner £25 & £29.50 ■ regional lunch, also pre- & post-theatre £14.50 (2 courses) & £17.50 (3 courses) ■ lowest bottle price £14.50

⊗ Haven for Francophiles

It may be located in smugly-trendy Islington opposite the home base of the Almeida Theatre, and it may be yet another outpost of the sprawling D & D empire, but spiritually Almeida is stuck in some faintly remembered rural France. The menu manages to be a distillation of all that is good about an old-fashioned, gently familiar kind of French cooking and eating. On top of which, the large dining room is comfortable and the service is slick without being oppressive. There is a comprehensive wine list, with a good selection available by the glass. This is a place to overdose on nostalgia. Butternut squash velouté may come with sage and chestnuts; there may be a ballotine of duck foie gras, port jelly and sourdough; or Cornish crab, avocado and tomato confit, with lemon olive oil. But best of all, there's the trolley of charcuterie. This chariot is wheeled round to your table and you can pig out on well-made terrines, pâtés and rillettes to your heart's content. Mains carry the theme forward triumphantly: sea bass en papilotte; honey-glazed duck; seared scallops with black pudding. There are pukka pommes frites. For pud there's an apple tarte fine, or petit pot au chocolat. With such a single-minded menu, Almeida could have ended up as something of a French resto theme park, but the kitchen is passionate about the classic dishes, and the mood ends up affectionate rather than reverential.

Au Lac

82 Highbury Park, N1 ■ 020 7704 9187

⊖ Arsenal

🍴 Vietnamese

🕐 Mon to Wed 17.30–23.00; Thurs to Fri 12.00–14.30 & 17.30–23.00;
Sat & Sun 17.30–23.00

🗗 Mastercard, Visa ■ 10% optional service added

££ starters £2.20–£7 ■ mains £4.50–£8 ■ desserts £2.50
■ set dinner £11–£16.50 ■ lowest bottle price £8.50

✪ Informal neighbourhood Vietnamese

London's Vietnamese restaurants divide into two kinds. On the
one hand there are the Spartan canteens – no frills, no nonsense and
no concessions to non-Vietnamese speakers. And on the other there
is a sprinkling of glossy, West End establishments. Au Lac has a foot
in both camps. Hidden away in Highbury, it has a dining room that
is comfortable in an informal, shabby sort of way. Start with the soft
rice-flour pancakes wrapped around crunchy veg and chicken. Then
there's goi tom – you get large steamed prawns, a small pot of hot
and spicy sauce, and several large iceberg lettuce leaves. Take a leaf,
add sauce and prawn, wrap, eat, enjoy. The deep-fried monkfish
with garlic and chilli is very good and there are good soups, too. The
noodle soups – pho, bun bo, and tom hue – come in large portions.
They are cheap and tasty, good for eating when alone. For a more
sociable, sharing meal, try the chicken with lemongrass and chilli.
The noodles are also very good – pho xao do bien is a grand dish of
stir-fried rice noodles with fresh herbs and seafood, providing a good
combination of flavours and textures. Another very impressive dish is
the 'minced pork with aubergine in hot pot'. Ordering this brings a
small casserole whose contents appear almost black. Very dark, very
rich, very tasty. If offered special 'Vietnamese sake' beware – this clear
hooch is very ferocious indeed.

→ For branch, see index

Bierodrome

173–174 Upper Street, N1 ▪ 020 7226 5835 ♿

⊖ Highbury & Islington

🍴 Belgian

🕐 Sun to Thurs 12.00–15.00 & 18.00–23.00; Sat & Sun 12.00–23.00

🖰 www.belgo-restaurants.co.uk

🖬 all major credit cards ▪ 12.5% optional service added

££ starters £5.25–£6.95 ▪ mains £7.50–£17.95 ▪ sides £1.95–£2.25
▪ desserts £4.25 ▪ menus: lunch £5.50 (Mon to Fri 12.00–15.00) &
evening meal deal (18.00–19.30) £9.95 ▪ lowest bottle price £12.50

✪ HQ Belgian beers

Bierodrome is part of the Belgo organisation (see p. 17) and shares
its emphasis on modernist design. This place is a temple to beer,
and with that beer you can eat if you wish. The beer and wine list
makes stunning reading, with more than seventy beers to pore over
and ultimately pour out. As you work your way through a series of
delicious glassfuls, what you will need is some food. Unsurprisingly,
the beeriness spreads through the menu, which introduces a change
of pace from the other branches of this organisation – yes, there is
life after mussels! Here you can start with grilled squid and chorizo
salad; or a grilled goats' cheese; or tiger prawns with garlic and
ginger, before moving on to Haddock Hoegaarden – deep fried in a
beer batter; roast duck breast; burgers (including a lamb burger); surf
and turf – half a Canadian lobster with a rib eye steak; roast duck;
croquettes and frites. Wild boar sausages are served with stoemp, a
superior kind of mashed potato indigenous to Belgium. Then there
are the famous Belgo mussel pots that can be enjoyed marinière,
Provençale or even Thai – the latter cooked with creamed coconut
and coriander. Or there's a range of gourmet burgers. Steaks include
a 10oz aged rib eye with frites and a Béarnaise sauce. There is an
'express' lunch bargain that lumps together mussels, frites and a
drink. As you'd expect from a 'beer-driven' establishment, this place
can get lively.

→ For branches, see index or website

The Drapers Arms

44 Barnsbury Street, N1 ■ 020 7619 0348

⊖ Highbury & Islington

🍴 Modern British/gastropub

🕐 Mon to Sat 12.00–15.00 & 19.00–22.30; Sun 12.00–15.00 (breakfast 12.00–13.30) & 18.30–21.30

🔗 www.thedrapersarms.co.uk

🗄 all major credit cards ■ 12.5% optional service added

££ Sun breakfast £8.50–£10 ■ starters £6–£8 ■ mains £13–£16.50 ■ sides £3–£4 ■ desserts £5.50–£6.50 ■ lowest bottle price £13.50

✪ Friendly gastropub

The Drapers started life as an old-fashioned, double-fronted Georgian pub and quite a lot of the period features have been retained, despite its new role as a gastropub. There's a bar downstairs and a dining room upstairs, and out the back is a large walled yard that has been paved over and kitted out with tables and chairs to seat another 45 diners, and huge awnings in case of rain. The menu changes twice daily and reflects the seasons, but starters may include fish soup with rouille and Gruyère; chorizo and baby squid with a frisée salad; an artichoke and thyme tart with a soft poached egg; chicken liver and foie gras parfait with cranberry and gin compote; or a rare beef salad with marinated beetroot. Mains might include a wild mushroom risotto cake with artichoke purée; Drapers Arms fish stew; a roast double pork chop with mash, lentils and black pudding; sweet potato gnocchi with roast squash; fish and chips with pea purée and crème fraîche tartare; or an aged rib eye steak with chips and Béarnaise. The chips are stellar, and side dishes include welcome combos such as French beans with lemon butter. Puds are sound, and sensibly the kitchen sticks to favourites like dark Valrhona chocolate tart with black cherries and crème fraîche; and raspberry and white chocolate crème brûlée. Good sandwiches and bar snacks mean that this is a good place for more 'pubby' than 'gastro' manoeuvres.

The House

63–69 Canonbury Road, N1 ■ 020 7704 7410 &

⊖ Highbury & Islington/BR Essex Road

🍽 Modern British/gastropub

🕐 Mon 18.00–22.30; Tues to Fri 12.00–14.30 & 17.30–22.30; Sat 11.00–12.00 (brunch) 12.00–15.30 (lunch) & 18.00–22.30 (dinner); Sun 11.00–12.00 (brunch), 12.00–16.00 (lunch) & 18.30–21.30 (dinner)

🖱 www.inthehouse.biz

🖪 all major credit cards except AmEx ■ 12.5% optional service added

££ starters £5.50–£9.50 ■ mains £12–£22.50 ■ sides £2.50–£4.50 ■ desserts £5.50–£8.50 ■ menu du jour Tues to Fri £10 (1 course), £15 (2 courses) and £17.50 (3 courses) ■ lowest bottle price £13.50

⭐ A restaurant masquerading as gastropub

As befits a location in one of Islington's smarter enclaves, The House seems more gastro than pub. But what is most unusual about this N1 establishment is that for once aspirations on the menu seem matched by real talent in the kitchen. The House made the transition from dodgy local to chic eating seem easy – and has been busy ever since. Service is friendly and unstuffy. The kitchen is an open one and before you even get to your food the signs are good – the chefs work quickly, quietly and neatly. On the top of the grill there is an imposing piece of meat warming through: the chargrilled Angus rib of beef, with shallot crust, gratin Dauphinoise, green beans and jus gras. Whoever gets to share this particular rib will be thankful that it wasn't straight from fridge to grill. From the starters, fresh Dorset crab spring rolls with ginger and spring onion; foie gras and chicken liver parfait; and the red onion Tatin all stand out. Mains also hit the spot: roast haunch of venison, spiced red cabbage and celeriac mash; a tarragon, crayfish and Pernod risotto; the house shepherd's pie. When talking shepherd's pie, a price tag as large as you will find here takes some living up to, but this shepherd just about delivers. Large chunks of lamb, good gravy, unctuous mash, crisp top. Puds are good – warm gingerbread with clotted cream; Valrhona hot chocolate pudding. Brunch is big.

Isarn

119 Upper Street, N1 ■ 020 7424 5153   ♿

⊖ Angel

🍴 Thai

🕐 Mon to Fri 12.00–15.00 & 18.00–23.00; Sat 12.00–23.00;
Sun 12.00–22.30

🖰 www.isarn.co.uk

🖯 all major credit cards ■ 12.5% optional service added

££ starters £3.50–£6 ■ mains £6.50–£14.50 ■ sides £1.50–£4
■ desserts £5.50 ■ set lunch box £5.90 ■ lowest bottle price £19

✪ Chic Thai fits Islington collar

Tina Juengsoongneun must have a real problem signing within
that little box on the back of credit cards. How she must yearn for her
maiden name – Yau. The name Yau is enough to make any foodie pay
attention because Alan Yau is the man behind a range of splendid
restaurants, most notably Hakkasan (see p. 6), and Tina is Alan's
sister. With her Thai husband Krish Juengsoongneun, Tina has set
up a very good, very modern Thai restaurant. The room is long and
fashionably austere, service is attentive (if sometimes a little clumsy)
and the food is fresh tasting with good strong flavours and plenty
of contrasting textures. Starters include the ubiquitous Thai fish
cake – chewy and agreeably musty; and chicken satay – good peanut
sauce. The curries range from monkfish green curry with kuchai and
basil to a beef massaman curry, which is suitably rich. Then there is
an array of seafood dishes such as salt and pepper squid, and various
poultry and meat dishes, including some good stir-fries; chicken and
green aubergine comes with yellow bean and sweet basil. The trad
noodle dishes like pad thai turn out well – pad thai with prawns,
Chinese chives and tofu is particularly successful. Puds are trad and
interesting. In the spirit of adventure you should opt for 'Tago with
taro and lotus seed'. There's a wine list that touches the right bases
for N1. Isarn is a new restaurant that is already perfectly at ease with
its surroundings.

The Marquess

32 Canonbury Street, N1 ■ 020 7354 2975

⊖ Angel/Highbury & Islington

🍽 Modern British/gastropub

🕐 Mon to Thurs 17.00–23.00; Fri 17.00–24.00, Sat 12.00–24.00; Sun 12.00–23.00

🔗 www.themarquesstavern.co.uk

🖥 all major credit cards ■ 12.5% optional service for parties of 6 or more

££ starters £5–£9 ■ mains £9.50–£17.50 ■ sides £3 ■ desserts £5–£6.50 ■ lowest bottle price £14

✪ Careful sourcing drives Canonbury gastro-haven

The Marquess is certainly trying to do things right. The bar is still a bar-like sort of bar, and the lofty dining room is elegant. The strategy here is to concentrate on sourcing the very finest ingredients and the supplier gets a credit on the menu. So you get fish from Islington uber-fishmonger Steve Hatt, and rare breed pork, Herdwick lamb and mutton from Farmer Sharp in the Lake District. There are interesting beers, the wine list is a tad more original than most and service is sound. This is an eminently likeable concept. All dishes are seasonal and come and go from the menu as availability dictates. You might start with razor clams and samphire; devilled kidneys on toast; potted salmon with pickled cucumber; cured beef fillet; or pumpkin soup. Mains may include organic roast chicken with bread sauce and watercress; or a shearer's stew – lamb and ale – served with greens. The nomenclature may be a bit Dorothy Hartley but the dishes are tempting enough. A whole Gilthead bream is served with burnt butter and pink fir apple potatoes; or there's a Gloucester Old Spot chop with creamed leeks and beer sauce. Four diners can share a shoulder of Herdwick lamb braised with lavender while a 28-day hung forerib of Yorkshire beef can be cooked for a table of 2, 3–4, or 5–6 people. Puddings are steady – baked apple and custard; rice pudding; chocolate pudding. And there is a magnificent all-British cheese board.

Morgan M

489 Liverpool Road, N1 ■ 020 7609 3560

Highbury & Islington

French

Tues 19.00–22.00; Wed to Fri 12.00–14.30 & 19.00–22.00;
Sat 19.00–22.00; Sun 12.00–14.30

www.morganm.com

all major credit cards except AmEx ■ 12.5% optional service added

££ lunch £19.50 (2 courses) & £23.50 (3 courses); ■ dinner £36 (3
courses) £45 (6 courses); 6-course dégustation menu £39 or £36 (veg)
■ garden menu: 6 courses for £39 ■ lowest bottle price £15

⭐ Very French and very classy

Morgan Meunier is a short, passionate and very accomplished
French chef. Morgan M is very much his baby, and he controls the
look of the place, the menu and the service with the intense grip
of a true perfectionist. The restaurant is dark green outside, with a
cool interior and well-spaced tables. Foodies now make this resto
a place of pilgrimage, and in the main they are right to do so.
The style of the place is very French, very haute cuisine; dishes are
complex and elegant on the plate, but the seasoning is spot on and
it all works well. Pricing is straightforward: at dinner you opt for the
three courses, or get stuck into the six-course dégustation. Starters
may include a ravioli of snails in Chablis with poached garlic; or a
carpaccio of Scottish lobster tail – very delicate, very fresh flavours.
Onwards to a roast fillet of monkfish with crayfish ravioli with
celeriac; grilled Anjou squab pigeon; or a splendid combination lamb
dish – roast rack and confit shoulder with a Jerusalem artichoke
soubise. Puds are featured – there's a dark chocolate moelleux (you
get to specify dark or plain chocolate) which comes with milk sorbet
and a chocolate Armagnac milky drink! Or there's a perfectly judged
strawberry soufflé. The wine list scampers up to some very fine wines
indeed, but there are enough bottles on the lower slopes to slake the
thirst of mere mortals.

Rooburoo

21 Chapel Market, N1 ■ 020 7278 8100

⊖ Angel

🍴 Indian

🕐 Mon 18.00–23.00; Tues to Sun 11.00–23.00

🖱 www.rooburoo.com

🖥 all major credit cards ■ 12.5% optional service added

££ starters £2.25–£4.95 ■ mains £5.25–£9.95 ■ sides £1.50–£2.50
■ desserts £3.75 ■ set lunch £11 (3 courses)
■ lowest bottle price £11.95

✪ Chirpy modern Indian

Rooburoo is a very clean-cut restaurant with a spacious modern dining room lined with reproductions of Rudolph Swoboda's paintings featuring Victorian India. The menu is an interesting one, partly because it is short – which gives you confidence in the dishes – and partly because there are some unusual items. Starters range from samosas and momos (the little steamed dumplings) to machli pattice, which are upmarket fishcakes. Then there's a section of rolls and wraps: chilli chicken roomali, a thin handkerchief bread filled with shredded chicken and green peppers; or kakra aloo anarkali, a crab and potato combo in a chapati. The 'rooburoast' section covers dishes from the tandoor and it's great to see three variants on chicken tikka: traditional; malai (with sour cream and fenugreek); and 'ooty tooty', a green herb tikka presumably named after Ootakahmund, the famous hill station known as 'snooty ooty'. The curries are also good – a lamb pepper fry comes dry, but with a bowl of dopiaza sauce on the side – spices are well balanced and the standard of cooking is high. There is a star turn lurking among the side orders: 'fried bitter gourd crisps'. They aren't crisp but they are very delicious. Service is friendly and not over-formal, in keeping with the laid back look of the place. It's great to see a modern Indian restaurant serving traditional dishes in such a friendly and accessible fashion.

Sabor

108 Essex Road, N1 ■ 020 7226 5551

⊖ Angel

⑩ Latin American

🕐 Mon to Fri 17.00–23.00; Sat & Sun 11.00–23.00 (brunch
12.00–17.00)

🖰 www.sabor.co.uk

🖰 all major credit cards except AmEx ■ 12.5% optional service added

££ starters £4.95–£7.75 ■ mains £10.50–£19.50 ■ sides £2.50
■ desserts £4.50 £5.50 ■ dinner Mon to Thurs £15 (2 courses) &
£17.50 (3 courses) ■ lowest bottle price £12.50

✪ Nuevo Latino, for nuevo Islington

Essex Road has always cowered in the shadow of larger, brasher
Upper Street. But Sabor tries to redress the balance. Sabor is a
light, bright, modernist restaurant with food that is 'inspired by
the flavours of countries across Latin America, including Colombia,
Brazil, Peru and Argentina'. Flavours here are pin-sharp, and dishes
both light and elegant. Among the starters you'll find empanadas
– miniature half-moon-shaped pasties which are so often solid and
unforgiving, but at Sabor they are light and crisp. There are two
ceviches listed – cod or sea bass. The results are stunning: the fish has
been 'cooked' thoroughly by the high acidity, and the flavours of the
citrus, passion fruit and lots of fresh coriander sing out. Really good.
Main courses are well presented and well crafted: rabo encendido is
a slow braised oxtail in a fiery Rioja sauce and served with roast garlic
and yucca mash. There's aji de gallina, which is a Peruvian chicken
dish. Or how about moqueca, a coconut-driven fish stew? The rib eye
and fillet steaks are Argentine while the t-bone is Aberdeen Angus.
They all come with chimichurri. The steaks are accurately cooked
and the chimichurri is a revelation – a thick and chunky sauce made
from parsley and garlic bound together with oil. Light and green
and delicious. Puds include a markedly self-indulgent dulce de leche
cheesecake and a mango and Caipirinha sorbet. The wine list majors
in South America.

Kilburn, Queens Park and Willesden

Ida

167 Fifth Avenue, W10 ■ 020 8969 9853

⊖ Queen's Park

⥥ Italian

🕐 Mon to Sat 18.00–23.00

⌁ www.idarestaurant.co.uk

⊟ all major credit cards except AmEx ■ 12.5% optional service added

££ antipasti £5.50–£7 ■ primi £8–£13.50 ■ mains £12.50–£14.50
■ sides £3.50–£45 ■ desserts £4.50–£6 ■ lowest bottle price £11.75

✪ Chiantishire in Kensal Green

Before it became Ida in 2007, number 167 was a greengrocer for
many years, then briefly an ill-favoured Middle Eastern café. When at
last it became a good value, honest, authentic neighbourhood Italian
restaurant the sighs of relief from the locals must have reached gale
force. Ida is in the heartland of a large block of small but immensely
desirable houses. This is not a cheap locale, so the reasonable prices
at this restaurant are all the more remarkable. The menu sprawls over
several pages. There is usually a 'region of the month' that provides
some 'primi' specials, then there are pasta specials, then antipasti,
then more primi, then secondi, contorni, and dolce. The antipasti
are done well – decent cold meats or perhaps baby octopus in a
tomatoey-garlicky sauce. Great play is made of the handmade pasta
– eggs, OO flour and a rolling pin – and a dish of maltagliata with a
slow-cooked rabbit ragù is excellent. Freshly made pasta at the right
thickness and with the rough surface needed for the sauce to stick
– hard to fault. The mains are honest – steak; sea bass; monkfish
stew. A side dish of green beans, rocket and tomatoes with olive oil,
vinegar, garlic and ground anchovies is particularly fine. Service is
as good as the rather crowded room will allow, and the wine list is
equably priced. A jolly place with good food.

Paradise – by way of Kensal Green

19 Kilburn Lane, W10 ■ 020 8969 0098

⊖ Kensal Green

🍽 Modern British/gastropub

🕐 Mon to Fri 18.30–22.30; Sat 12.00–16.00 (brunch) & 18.30–22.30;
Sun 12.00–20.00

🖱 www.theparadise.co.uk

💳 all major credit cards ■ 12.5% optional service added

££ starters £5.75–£9.50 ■ mains £12.50–£17.50 ■ sides £2.95–£3.95
■ desserts £5.75–£8.50 ■ lowest bottle price £12.95

⭐ Stylish room home to very stylish food

A great deal of care and effort has been lavished on this classic
1890's pub. It re-opened during the autumn of 2007 to universally
approving reviews. The front bar is comfortable and easy going, there
is a music room upstairs and the dining room is genuinely shabby-
elegant – splendid glass chandeliers, swagged curtains, random
tables and chairs. The head chef is Tim Payne, who served time with
Marco Pierre White and really knows his stuff. The level of cooking
here puts it into the upper branches of the gastropub tree. Dishes
benefit from cheffy touches – a starter like Jerusalem artichoke soup
is lifted by adding some trompette mushrooms. The charcuterie
work is very accomplished – a parfait of foie gras and chicken livers
is just about parfait and potted ham hock and parsley with mustard
dressing is unreservedly delicious. From the mains, roast rump of
Swaledale lamb comes with clams and Dauphinoise potatoes; confit
pork belly comes with roast langoustines and creamed potatoes. Or
how about wild halibut with chanterelles and confit garlic? A side
order of cauliflower cheese nearly steals the show – good cheese
makes all the difference. Puds are top notch – a splendid crème
brulée; and a dark chocolate mousse with salted caramel swirl vie for
you're attention. Add a wine list that gives your wallet a chance and
helpful service and you have very good dining indeed.

Penk's

79 Salusbury Road, NW6 ■ 020 7604 4484

⊖ Queens Park

🍴 French

🕐 Mon to Thurs 12.00–15.00 & 18.00–23.00; Fri 12.00–15.00
&19.00–23.00; Sat 10.30–15.00 & 18.00 to 23.00; Sun 10.30–22.30

🔗 www.penks.com

🔒 all major credit cards except AmEx ■ no service added

££ brunch Sat & Sun £5–£14 ■ starters £5–£9 ■ mains
£8–£17 ■ sides £2.50 ■ desserts £6–£9 ■ lowest bottle price £14

✪ Bistro is as bistro does

Penk's is very much a family resto and over the years it has turned
into a model of what a neighbourhood restaurant should be. Penk's
is all about bold strokes — but only when under-pinned by the
familiar. The décor is all primary colours, a bright exterior leading to
a long, thin room. At Easter 2008 Penk's took over the shop next
door to nearly double the capacity and that expansion is proof that
Penk's is hitting all the right buttons. There is a private room to the
rear that is great for parties of up to 20. The dinner menu sets the
tone with starters such as salmon and lemon sole terrine with herb
butter sauce; griddled scallops with a pea purée; or grilled fillet of
lamb with hummus and chilli oil. Attractive combinations of classic
French bistro cooking with some modern influences. Mains may
include a 'blanquette' of pork in cider and cream; crispy roast duck
'à l'Orange'; fish cakes with sorrel and cream sauce; grilled sausage
'Languedoc style' with sage and capers; and poached halibut 'bonne
femme' with a mushroom velouté. Plus a backstop — grilled rib
eye steak with chips and Béarnaise sauce. For puds choose from
chocolate and pecan nut brownie, fudge sauce, vanilla ice cream;
rhubarb crème brûlée; or crêpes Suzette. There are continuing reports
that Penk's does one of the best brunches in NW6, including smoked
haddock kedgeree and eggs Benedict.

The Salusbury

50–52 Salusbury Road, NW6 ■ 020 7328 3286

⊖ Queens Park

🍴 Italian/gastropub

🕐 Mon to Thurs 12.00–15.00 & 19.00–23.00; Fri 12.00–15.00 &
19.00–22.30; Sat 10.30–15.00 & 19.00–23.30; Sun 10.30–22.30

🖻 All major credit cards except AmEx ■ 12.5% optional service added

££ starters £4.50–£8 ■ mains £10.50–£17 ■ sides £2.75–£4
■ desserts £4.50 ■ lunch special £6 ■ lowest bottle price £11.50

✪ The gastropub goes to Italy

**The Salusbury has become one of London's most popular
gastropubs.** Broadly speaking, it occupies a U-shaped space. You
go in one door, move through the bar and continue round the bar
to come out in the dining room – a quieter room filled with the kind
of tables your mum had in her living room, stripped and scrubbed,
and with a display of eclectic art lining the walls. If sound, Italian-
accented cooking coupled with excellent value is what rings your
bell, you'll like The Salusbury a lot. The varied menu follows a mainly
modern Italian theme rather than the more predictable Modern
British bias of so many gastropubs. Starters (and a wave of dishes
that could either be starters or mains) may include sautéed prawns
with chilli and rocket; grilled tomino with red onion jam and chestnut
bread; fillet of beef carpaccio with Parmesan and rocket; pappardelle
with duck ragu; or pumpkin risotto. There's a practical emphasis on
pasta and risotto. Main courses may include monkfish wrapped in
speck with roast peppers and saffron mash; osso buco alla Milanese;
or guinea fowl with mushroom sauce. Moving on to pud territory,
Amaretto, ricotta and almond pudding vies with sgroppina – a soft
lemon sorbet doused in grappa – and pure chocolate tart. The wine
list is not large, but it is well chosen. Service is friendly and un-pushy.
And there is the Salusbury Food Store at no. 56 – good deli, and
pizzas to go.

Shish

2–6 Station Parade, NW2 ■ 020 8208 9290 ♿

⊖ Willesden Green

🍽 Middle Eastern

🕐 Mon to Fri 11.00–23.30; Sat 10.30–24.00 (brunch 10.30–16.00);
Sun 10.30–22.30 (brunch 10.30–16.00)

🏠 www.shish.com

🗠 all major credit cards ■ 12.5% optional service added

££ brunch £4.50 £5.95 ■ mezze £2.25–£5.25 ■ shish £5.25–£8.75
■ desserts £2.50–£3.95 ■ kid's menu £4.25 ■ lowest bottle price £11.95

✪ The new face of the kebab

A large, curved-glass pavement frontage displays a sinuous bar
counter that snakes around the dining room, leaving grills, fridges
and chefs' stations in the centre. Shish is pretty slick. Diners take a
stool at the counter; it is for all the world like being at a modernist
sushi bar. This place owes a debt to Israeli roadside eateries, with its
falafel and shish kebabs, but the 'concept' is much more inclusive.
The inspiration for Shish is the food of the Silk Road. Attention
has been paid to sourcing the best ingredients and Suffolk lamb,
free-range chickens and Charolais beef all get credits on the menu.
Starters are divided into lots of cold mezze and a shorter list of hot
mezze. The Afghan pumpkin is honey roasted. The red and green
falafel are well made – the red variety is engagingly spicy. The hot
bread is as delicious as only freshly baked hot bread can be. Kebabs
are served in two different ways: either plated with rice, couscous or
French fries, or in a wrap. The shish kebabs are really rather good.
Mediterranean lamb comes up very tender; apricot and ginger teams
chicken with good tangy apricot flavour; the Sichuan chilli beef is
made with rib eye; or there is king prawn shish. The portions all seem
decent-sized and there are further fish and vegetarian options. Die-
hard kebabbers can even insist on a satisfactorily fierce squelch of
chilli sauce.

→ For branch, see index

Sushi Say

33b Walm Lane, NW3 ■ 020 8459 2971

⊖ Willesden Green

🍽 Japanese

🕐 Tues to Fri 12.00–14.30 & 18.30–22.30; Sat 13.00–15.30 & 18.00–23.00; Sun 13.00–15.30 & 18.00–22.00

🖪 all major credit cards ■ no service added

££ starters £3.90–£6.50 ■ assorted sushi £12.10–£20.10
■ assorted sashimi £15–£25 ■ mains £6–£12 ■ desserts £2–£4.80
■ set lunch £9.40–£14.80 ■ set dinner £21–£35
■ lowest bottle price £12; 200ml carafe of sake £8

⭐ Expert sushi for novice diners

Yuko Shimizu and her husband Katsuharu run this small but excellent Japanese restaurant and sushi bar. It has a very personal feel and is a welcoming and intimate space. *Shimizu* means pure water, and the cooking is pure delight. The menu offers a full classical Japanese selection, making it a difficult choice between limiting yourself to sushi or going for the cooked dishes. Perhaps adopting the European style, and having sushi or sashimi as a starter and then main courses with rice will bring you the best of both worlds. Sitting at the sushi bar allows you to watch Katsuharu at work. With a sumo-like stature and the widest grin this side of Cheshire, his fingers magic nigiri sushi onto your plate. In the lower price brackets you'll find omelette, mackerel, squid and octopus. At the top end there's sea urchin, fatty tuna and yellowtail. In between there is a wide-enough range to delight even the experts. Nigiri toku brings you eleven pieces of nigiri and seaweed-rolled sushi, and it's a bargain – heavy on the fish and light on the rice. Cooked dishes do not disappoint. Ordering ebi tempura brings you crispy battered king prawns, the batter so light it's almost effervescent. It's worth trying the home-made puddings, such as goma (sesame) ice cream. For experts, there's half-frozen sake – Akita Onigoroshi – not so much a slush puppy, more of a slush mastiff.

Maida Vale,
Swiss Cottage and
Finchley Road

Natural Burger Company

12 Blenheim Terrace, NW8 ■ 020 7372 9065

⊖ Maida Vale

🍴 Burgers

🕑 Mon to Sat 12.00–23.00; Sun 12.00–22.30

🗗 all major credit cards ■ 12.5% optional service added

££ starters £3.75–£4.95 ■ burgers £5.75–£7.95 ■ grills £8.75–£12.95 ■
sides £1.45–£3.95 ■ desserts £3.95–£4.10
■ lowest bottle price £12.95

✪ Doing a simple thing well

There are enough fancy restaurants in the world that charge
plenty, and there are enough chain restaurants that claim to have
mastered a specific dish (like the hamburger) and promise cheap food
that rarely lives up to that billing when all the extras are factored in.
At the Natural Burger Company they offer a decent hamburger, one
that has been accurately cooked, and comes in a very good, fresh,
ciabatta bun – which looks a bit odd as it is square, but tastes just
fine. The starters are a bit of fig-leaf: there's some deep-fried squid
served with mayonnaise on a bed of green leaves; there are buffalo
wings with a blue cheese dip on the side; and grilled Portobello
mushrooms. But good sense will probably hustle you straight to the
burgers. All the beef is billed as Aberdeen Angus and you can have
a plain burger; one with cheese; one with avocado and bacon; one
with a Jalape–o sauce; the Italian job with mozzarella and basil – and
a handful more. The burgers are good. And so are the chips, which
are large, dry, and crisp – a basic standard that so many places fail
to achieve. There are some grilled dishes on offer – rib steak; lamb
steak; tuna; and chicken – as well as salad favourites like Caesar and
Niçoise, and a curtailed list of puds. Have a hamburger and a glass
of red.

Raoul's

13 Clifton Road, W9 ■ 020 7289 7313

⊖ Warwick Avenue

🍽 European/deli

🕐 Mon to Fri 08.30–22.15

🖰 www.raoulsgourmet.com

🗗 all major credit cards ■ 10% optional service added

££ breakfast £4.75–£7.75 ■ starters £4.95–£8.50 ■ mains £9.30–£16
■ sides £2.95–£4.95 ■ desserts £4.10–£4.95
■ lowest bottle price £12.95

⭐ A comfortable neighbourhood institution

Raoul's certainly looks like a café (although a stylish, film-setty, modern café) and it is certainly open for long hours each day. But Raoul's is more of a restaurant that thinks it's a café than the other way around. The waiters are unhurried without seeming world-weary. The room is modern without being aggressively designery. And the menu offers all things to all customers and is backed up by a blackboard listing daily specials. No wonder it is full of people waiting out the day. The breakfast dishes are good. For a café this place is more eggs Benedict than fried bread, but the full English comprises scrambled or fried eggs, bacon, sausage, grilled tomatoes and toast; the American and modernist influences don't become apparent until further down the page – bagels with smoked salmon and cream cheese, or tortillas. Sandwiches are modernist on the one hand – focaccia with melted mozzarella, grilled peppers, rocket and sun-dried tomatoes – and trad on the other, with croque monsieur. Good quality, very fresh ingredients, and well presented food. If you dock here during a main-meal time turn to the blackboard; there may be starters such as grilled spare ribs and spinach salad; then mains such as crab and chilli linguine; grilled sea bass with risotto cake; Raoul's organic hamburger; or a well-aged Argentine rib eye steak with garlic butter and French fries. There's a short wine list with economical house wines, and service is cheerful. A very comfortable place.

→ For branch, see index or website

Red Pepper

8 Formosa Street, W9 ■ 020 7266 2708

⊖ Warwick Avenue

🍴 Pizza/Italian

🕐 Mon to Fri 18.30–23.00; Sat 12.00–23.00; Sun 12.30–22.30

🗄 Mastercard, Visa ■ 12.5% optional service added

££ starters £6–£9.50 ■ mains £8.50–£15 ■ sides £3.50–£4
■ desserts £5–£6.50 ■ lowest bottle price £13

✪ Terrific pizzas, tiny resto

The Red Pepper may not be the largest restaurant in Maida Vale, and it certainly isn't the most elegant. The service hovers on the edge of brusque, and for what is a neighbourhood pizza joint the prices would be high enough to raise an eyebrow anywhere less sleek than W9. But it is packed. Over the years, every review of Red Pepper has opened with a complaint that the tiny tables are crammed in too tightly, jostling together so that the waiters have to combine an aptitude for slalom skiing with the skills of a limbo dancer. No matter. There are half a dozen starters, a few pasta dishes, some specials, and the list of pizzas. The starters are light and fresh; a dish of baby octopus with potato and black olive salad; carpaccio of beef; a soup made with borlotti beans and mussels; or that classic melanzane alla parmigiana. But you should turn your attention to the pizzas. They are large, flat and thin, but not too thin. Cooked to a crisp and with top-quality toppings. As well as the usual suspects – Margherita, Napoli, stagioni – the 'porro' pizza, with mozzarella, leeks, ham and Parmesan is worthy of special mention. Or the 'diavolo', with tomato, mozzarella and spicy salami. The 'primavera' is also very good, topped with San Daniele ham, Parmesan and a handful of rocket leaves. The all-Italian wine list has some interesting bottles at gentle prices – check out the Sardinian reds.

Singapore Garden

83a Fairfax Road, NW6 ■ 020 7328 5314

⊖ Swiss Cottage

🍴 Singaporean

🕐 Mon to Thurs 12.00–15.00 & 18.00–23.00; Fri & Sat 12.00–15.00 & 18.00–23.00; Sun 12.00–15.00

🖰 www.singaporegarden.co.uk

🖶 all major credit cards ■ 12.5% optional service added

££ starters £4–£11 ■ mains £7–£29 ■ sides £2–£9
   ■ desserts £4.50–£6.50 ■ lowest bottle price £15

✪ Large, sprawling, jolly, family restaurant

Singapore Garden performs a cunning dual function. A good deal of the cavernous but well-appointed dining room is filled with well-heeled family groups from Swiss Cottage and St John's Wood, treating the restaurant as their local Chinese and consuming crispy duck in pancakes. The other customers, drawn from London's Singaporean and Malaysian communities, are tucking into the Teochew braised pig's trotters. So there are both cocktails and Tiger beer on offer, but this is a busy restaurant, so don't even think of turning up without a reservation. The food is interesting and good. Start with a chiew yim prawns – dry-fried with garlic, pepper and chillies. Or go for old favourites like the spare ribs, the satay or the money bag chicken. If you're feeling adventurous, follow with a real Singapore special – the Teochew braised pig's trotter, which brings half a pig's worth of trotters slow-cooked in a luxurious, black, heart-stoppingly rich gravy. Or maybe try the claypot prawns and scallops, which delivers good, large, crunchy prawns and a fair portion of scallops, stewed with lemongrass and fresh ginger on glass noodles. Very good indeed. From the Malaysian list you might pick the rendang – slow cooked and coconutty; the squid blachan, rich with the strange savoury taste of prawn paste; or a simple dish such as archar, which is a plate of crunchy pickled vegetables sprinkled with ground peanuts. Good food, happy place.

Stoke Newington

Rasa

55 Stoke Newington Church Street, N16 ■ 020 7249 0344

⊖ BR Stoke Newington

🍴 Indian/vegetarian

🕐 Mon to Thurs18.00–22.45; Fri 18.00–23.00 Sat & Sun 12.00–15.00 &
18.00–23.30

🖱 www.rasarestaurants.com

💳 all major credit cards ■ 12.5% optional service added

££ starters £2.75–3 ■ mains £3.70–£5.95 ■ sides £2.25–£4
■ desserts £2–£3 ■ Kerala Feast £16 ■ lowest bottle price £9.95

⭐ South Indian veggie – the original and genuine

Rasa has built up a formidable reputation for outstanding South
Indian vegetarian cooking, but as well as great food, you'll find that
the staff are friendly and helpful, and the atmosphere is uplifting.
Inside, everything is pink (napkins, tablecloths, walls), and a colourful
statue of Krishna playing the flute greets you at the entrance. Rasa's
proprietor and most of the kitchen staff come from Cochin in Kerala.
As you'd expect, booking is essential. This is one occasion when
the set meal – or 'Kerala Feast'– may be the easiest option. But
however you approach a Rasa meal, everything is a taste sensation.
Even the pappadoms are a surprise: try the selection served with six
home-made chutneys. If you're going your own way, there are lots
of starters to choose from. Mysore bonda is delicious, shaped like
a meatball but made of potato spiced with ginger, coriander and
mustard seeds; or there is kathrikka, slices of aubergine served with
fresh tomato chutney. The main dishes are good, too. Cheera parippu
curry is made with fresh spinach, toor dal and a touch of garlic while
moru kachiathu combines mangoes and green bananas with chilli
and ginger. Or go for a dosa (paper-thin crisp pancakes). Masala dosa
is packed with potatoes and comes with lentil sauce and coconut
chutney. Puddings sound hefty, but arrive in mercifully small portions;
the pal payasam is a rice pudding with cashew nuts and raisins. A fine
end to a meal.

→ For branches, see index or website

Rasa Travancore

56 Stoke Newington Church Street, N16 ■ 020 7249 1340

⊖ BR Stoke Newington

🍽 Indian

🕐 Mon to Thurs 18.00–22.45; Fri & Sat 18.00–23.30; Sun 12.00–15.00 & 18.00–22.45

🌐 www.rasarestaurants.com

🗄 all major credit cards ■ 12.5% optional service added

££ starters £2.75–£4.95 ■ mains £3.90–£7.95 ■ sides £2–£3.45
   ■ desserts £2–£2.75 ■ Travancore feast £20
   ■ lowest bottle price £9.95

✪ Exploring Syrian Christian cuisine

Rasa Travancore is painted glow-in-the-dark Rasa pink, just like the original Rasa, which faces it across the roadway. Rasa Travancore moves the spotlight onto a particular facet of Keralan cuisine: Syrian Christian cooking, and a very welcome move it is, too. All the South Indian flavour notes are there – coconut, curry leaves, ginger, chillies, mustard seeds, tamarind – but as well as veggie specialities, Syrian Christian dishes feature fish, seafood, mutton, chicken and duck. The menu is a long one and great pains have been taken to explain every dish. Apparently the king prawns in konjufry have been marinated in 'refreshing spices'. Or there's Kerala fish fry, a large steak of firm-fleshed kingfish dusted with spice and pan fried. Very delicious. The lamb puffs are made from light pastry with a filling of lamb and vegetables. The main course dishes are fascinating and richly flavoured. Kozhy olathu curry – billed as a famous 'Christmas speciality' – is a rich, dryish, oniony chicken curry. Erachi olathiyathu is a dry lamb curry with lots of pepper. Kappayyum meenum vevichathu is a triumph – a soupy fish curry, delicately flavoured and served with floury chunks of boiled tapioca root dusted with coconut. Excellent accompaniments are the tamarind rice, which has an amazing depth of flavour, and the flaky, buttery Malabar paratha. This place has all the charm of the original veggie haven over the road, with the added pluses of some rare and interesting meat and fish dishes.

→ For branches, see index or website

Testi

38 Stoke Newington High Street, N16 ■ 020 7249 7151

BR Stoke Newington

Turkish

daily 12.00–01.00

www.testirestaurant.com

all major credit cards except AmEx ■ no service added

££ starters/mezze £3–£6.50 ■ mains £5.50–£11.95 ■ sides £3–£3.90
■ desserts £3 ■ lowest bottle price £10.50

✪ Honest Turkish grill house

Testi is a large and bustling Turkish restaurant and, somewhat
disappointingly, the testi from which it takes its name are not testicles
(as the rumour would have it) but the Turkish word for water jug.
At the centre of the dining room is the obligatory open grill and the
design theme is frills with a red ceiling splattered with fine white
squiggles. The staff manage to be both efficient and friendly, prices
are low and the grill chef is significantly gifted. Starters are very
sound: hummus is nutty and smooth; ali nazik is a dish of aubergine
in creamy yogurt; and kisir is stunning – bulghur wheat plus very
finely chopped tomatoes and peppers. The hot bread is wonderful.
For main course you should order what are billed on the menu as
'Thesticals' – koc yumurtasi – and to avoid confusion, subtitled 'lamb
testicles marinated and chargrilled'. They are delicious. A soft texture,
crisp outside, yielding within, and smoky from the grill. And while
you're at it, the grilled kidneys are good, the liver is good, and the
grilled quail is good. The 'kaburga', lamb spare ribs, is outstandingly
good – chewy, crispy and salty all at the same time. But if you cannot
bring yourself to grab dinner by the thesticals, the menu lists all the
old favourites: shish kebab, chicken wings, lamb chops. The grills here
are served with some very fine accompaniments, including a dish of
charred sweet onions that comes in sumac and lemon juice.

Yum Yum

183–187 Stoke Newington High Street, N16 ■ 020 7254 6751

⊖ BR Stoke Newington

🍴 Thai

🕐 Mon to Fri 12.00–15.00 & 18.00–23.00; Sat & Sun 12.00–23.30

🖱 www.yumyum.co.uk

🗗 all major credit cards ■ 10% optional service added

££ starters £4–£8 ■ soups £4.95–£5.15 ■ curries £6–£10.50
　■ sides/rice/noodles £2.65–£7.90 ■ desserts £4
　■ lowest bottle price £11

✪ Large and glossy Thai

The old Yum Yum was much as you would expect a neighbourhood Thai restaurant to be – cheap, cheerful and on Stoke Newington Church Street. Then the proprietors took over a large and imposing building on the High Street and after the usual planning angst and consequent delays opened the new Yum Yum – a 260-seater that is even busy off-peak. There's a courtyard and fountain (the outdoor tables will appeal as global warming does its stuff) and some really steep steps leading up to a huge modern dining room. For once the general rule (starters better than mains) seems less secure: familiar dishes like chicken satay; Thai spring rolls; and Thai fishcakes are sound – the fishcakes are good and suitably chewy, but everything comes with rather sweet bottled sauce. The rest of the menu has more to offer. The soups include tom khar – hot and sour with coconut; and tom yum – spicy hot and sour with lime leaves. The curries range from a rather good kang mussaman made with peanuts and pumpkin – bonus points for leaving the lamb on the bone, that does improve the gravy; to kang ped phed, which is a red curry made with duck. Noodle dishes like pad Thai are sound enough. Service is friendly, if sometimes a little confused. Drink Tiger beer, but not so much that you are in danger of falling down those vertiginous steps.

South

Battersea, Clapham and Wandsworth

1000 metres

Butcher & Grill

39–41 Parkgate Road, SW11 ■ 020 7924 3999 &

⊖ Clapham Junction/Queenstown Road BR

🍴 British/steak

🕐 Mon to Sat 12.00–15.30 & 18.00–23.00, Sun 12.00–16.30, breakfast daily 08.30–12.00;

🖰 www.thebutcherandgrill.com

🖥 all major credit cards ■ 12.5% optional service added

££ starters £4.95–£12.50 ■ mains £7.50–£25 ■ sides £2.75–£4 ■ desserts £5–£7.50 ■ kids' menu £5.25 ■ lowest bottle price £14.50

⭐ From chopping block to plate

This place is the brainchild of a butcher and a restaurateur and confronts our view of where meat comes from. On the one hand this is a good thing, as having to walk through a butcher's shop into the dining area does underline the craft skills linked to good-quality meat. On the other, anyone with latent veggie tendencies may be tipped over the edge by seeing their dinner laid out in the raw. Matters are exacerbated by the pictures around the dining room, which also feature carcasses. The food is agreeably straightforward and well sourced. Starters include Caesar salad; terrine with brioche toast; and H. Forman's excellent smoked salmon. The mains are divided up into mains – duck cassoulet; steak and kidney pie; fish of the day – and grills, which given the name over the door must be what you are here for. There's a burger – fine, but still a burger – and then on to the steaks: onglet, sirloin, rib eye, rump, fillet, t-bone and a magnificent rib of beef for two to share. The steaks are well matured and well cooked, and for genuine carnivores there is even a 'pick a larger steak from the counter' option. The accompaniments are sound and you can add Hollandaise sauce or onion gravy. Desserts range from chocolate fondant to rice pudding or profiteroles. Service is friendly and the wine list has scope for exploration. The tables outside get booked early during good weather.

→ For branch, see index or website

Chez Bruce

2 Bellevue Road, SW17 ■ 020 8672 0114

⬤ BR Wandsworth Common

🍴 French

🕐 Mon to Fri 12.00–14.00 & 18.30–22.30; Sat 12.30–14.00 &
18.30–22.30; Sun 12.00–15.00 & 19.00–22.00

🖱 www.chezbruce.co.uk

🖥 all major credit cards ■ 12.5% optional service added

££ lunch Mon to Fri £25.50 (3 courses), Sat £27.50, Sun £32.50
■ dinner Mon to Sun £37.50 (3 courses) ■ lowest bottle price £16.50

✪ A national treasure

Bruce Poole's comfortable little restaurant is the perfect example
of how to reach for a Michelin star and still keep your feet on
the ground. Chez Bruce stands for honest, unfussy, earthy, richly
flavoured food. The menu boasts old-fashioned dishes that never
pander to the latest gastro trend and make use of less fashionable
ingredients – like pig's trotters, rabbit or mackerel. Prix fixe three-
course menus and truly amazing cooking combine to make this place
bargain HQ. The menu changes from day to day. The kind of starters
you can expect are Jerusalem artichoke soup with chanterelles; gratin
of hare with spätzle chestnuts and melted Beaufort cheese; fillet of
red mullet with baby squid and aubergine purée. Or there might be
a classic lurking – perhaps vitello tonnato. Main course dishes are
deeply satisfying. You might find calf's tongue with Savoy cabbage
cocotte potatoes, crisp brains and Madeira; or fillet of Scottish Pollack
with buttered winter vegetables, beurre blanc and mussels. This is
one of the last strongholds of offal (perhaps the reason why this
restaurant is the favourite haunt of so many off-duty chefs?). Look
out for sweetbreads, or perhaps calf's liver. Interest from Michelin
has led to the wine list being extended and refined and it now wins
prizes of its own. The sweets here are well-executed classics: proper
crème brûlée, or rhubarb and champagne trifle. No wonder you have
to book one month ahead for a table at dinner. Go for lunch instead
– it'll make your day.

China Boulevard

1 The Boulevard, Riverside West, off Smugglers Way, SW18

■ 020 8874 9878

◉ Wandsworth Town BR

🍽 Chinese/dim sum

🕐 daily 12.00–23.00; dim sum 12.00–17.00

🔗 www.chinaboulevard.com

💳 all major credit cards ■ 12.5% optional service added

££ dim sum £2.50–£3.90 ■ starters £4.50–£9.80
　　■ meat dishes £6.80–£9.50 ■ fish dishes £8.80–£27
　　■ sides £1.80–£4.80 ■ menus £15–£30pp ■ lowest bottle price £16

⊙ Large, glam and sophisticated riverside Chinese

This big and glossy Chinese restaurant is striving to make a
go of it while marooned in the ground floor of a vast residential
development. It is a huge place offering wedding parties for 400
people (500 if you spill over into the terrace area), there is a focal
point bar and stairs sweep away to a second floor. In the private
rooms Karaoke is threatened. There is also a tank with live lobsters,
crabs and some magnificent turbot all waiting to be the centrepiece
of someone's gourmet dinner. The dim sum are very sound – all the
usual favourites: har gau (prawn dumplings); baked pork puffs; char
sui pau (the large doughy buns with a sweet and savoury middle);
steamed chive and prawn dumplings. The main menu is evenly
balanced between run-of-the-mill staples like crispy duck and some
more interesting dishes: steamed turbot; flash-fried lobster with
garlic crisp; yam and chicken hotpot; deep-fried black cod with spicy
sauce; and drunken chicken. There is also a rotisserie section and the
crispy belly pork is exemplary – meaty, crisp and surprisingly lean.
Service is attentive, and as well as seeming very fresh the food is well
presented. China Boulevard is indubitably hard to find, but as a friend
who lives locally observed, 'I do come down here quite often – the
local tip is next door!' Remember that customers get free parking for
four hours in the car park opposite the Holiday Inn Hotel.

The Fish Club

189 St John's Hill, SW11 ■ 020 7978 7115

⊖ BR Clapham Junction

🍴 Fish

🕐 Tues to Sat 12.00–22.00; Sun 12.00–21.00

🌐 www.thefishclub.com

🖫 all major credit cards ■ no service added

££ starters £2.95–£7.95 ■ mains £4.95–£11.95 ■ sides £1.50–£3.95
■ desserts £2.95–£3.95 ■ lowest bottle price £12.95

✪ The future of fish and chips

The Fish Club isn't a club, it's something much more intriguing.
Deoparting from the normal run of fish and chip shops, it is run by
chefs, not 'fryers'. As you walk in you'll spot a large chilled counter
playing host to plenty of spanking fresh fish; there's an open kitchen;
there is a fryer, but there is also a grill. The blackboard lists what is
on offer and everything is cooked to order. The fish and chips to go
is served up in a cardboard box (like an oversize pizza box), but if you
eat in you get real china and cutlery at the large refectory tables to
the rear. The menu always includes one classic battered fish – often
this fish is from a less fashionable species like coley; the proprietors
make every effort to wean their customers off endangered fish like
cod. Starters range from oysters to potted shrimps. For mains, if you
don't fancy battered fish with chips, how about a pair of small 'slip'
soles grilled with butter? Or a whole Royal Bream chargrilled? Or a
perfectly cooked wing of skate? And to go with your fish, choose
from chips (very good, crisp outside, fluffy within) or sweet potato
chips (as good as the chips, but with a caramelised sweetness). Even
the sauces are pukka – try the salsa verde or the tartare sauce. The
prices tend to be at restaurant levels rather than competing with the
chippies, but for fresh fish cooked carefully that seems just.

→ For branch, see index or website

Four O Nine

409 Clapham Road, SW9 ■ 020 7737 0722

⊖ Clapham North

🍴 French

🕐 Mon to Sun 18.00–22.30

🔗 www.fouronine.co.uk

🖥 all major credit cards ■ 12.5% optional service added

££ starters £6–£8.50 ■ mains £16–£18 ■ desserts £6–£7
   ■ lowest bottle price £15

⭐ Good cooking at fully fledged restaurant

As we look closer and closer at the credentials of gastropubs,
restaurants like Four O Nine come along to muddy the waters.
The dining room occupies the first floor of a pub, but crucially this
restaurant has its own door, its own stairs and even its own little roof
terrace to accommodate hapless nicotine addicts. The dining room
furniture looks gastropubby and there is a handsome — bar but this
is a restaurant. And one that serves very decent French food. If you
read the menu and spot a faint influence from Chez Bruce (see p.
332) pat yourself on the back, the chef here once worked there. Every
dish is seasonal and as a result the menu changes, but you could start
with Jerusalem artichoke velouté with fresh truffles; cassoulet with
crisp confit duck leg, ham hock and a garlic crust; or a Provençal fish
stew with red mullet, mussels and rouille. Mains range from daube
of beef with parsnip purée and buttered carrots to risotto of wild
mushrooms with parmesan cream and rocket salad, or crisp fillet of
sea bass with olive oil mash, grilled courgette and gremolata. Flavours
are pronounced and the presentation on the plate is blissfully
straightforward. Puds veer from poached English rhubarb with
champagne sorbet to hot chocolate pudding. Cheeses are from Neal's
Yard. Friendly service, reasonably priced wines, good cooking and
food that's sophisticated in its simplicity.

Gastro

67 Venn Street, SW4 ■ 020 7627 0222

⊖ Clapham Common

🍴 Very French

🕒 daily 08.00–24.00

🗔 all major cards except Amex ■ 12.5% optional service added

££ starters £3.50–£17.60 (½ lobster) ■ mains £13.75–£20.95
■ sides £2.95–£4.50 ■ desserts £4–£5 ■ menus: lunch Mon to Fri
£9.95 (2 courses); Sunday roast £12.95 ■ lowest bottle price £12

✪ French to the coeur

Gastro was a pathfinder as Cla'am scampered headlong towards
trendiness. And where once all was favouritism for regulars, and a
no-bookings policy, now you may need a reservation to get in. The
food is still unabashed about its Frenchness, but there are competing
eateries up and down Venn Street, and Gastro is no longer streets
ahead. The staff are French and the menu lists all the Gallic favourites,
which tend to be inexpensive and generously portioned. Think
yourself back to your last French holiday, make the same sort of
allowances for casual service and unprepossessing ambience, and
enjoy yourself. Under hors d'oeuvres you'll find a pukka soupe de
poissons with the classic trimmings – croute, cheese and garlic
jollop. Ordering seafood is straightforward: oysters are sold in sixes;
mussels arrive à la marinière; and Monsieur Le Tourteau is exactly that
– a whole Cornish crab and mayonnaise. No arguments there. The
mains will also cosset any Francophile tendencies you may have: selle
de chevreuil grillée; boudin noir Tatin au Calvados; or an authentic
entrecôte grillé, sauce Béarnaise, frites. And there is always decent
pommes purées. Fish dishes are well represented: try the roulade of
salmon with spinach and a saffron sauce. For puds think pâtisserie,
and good pâtisserie at that. The wine list has perked up of late, and
there are some specialist ciders on offer which are always welcome.

Gourmet Burger Kitchen

44 Northcote Road, SW11 ■ 020 7228 3309

⊖ BR Clapham Junction

🍽 Burgers

🕐 Mon to Fri 12.00–23.00; Sat 11.00–23.00; Sun 11.00–22.00

🍗 www.gbkinfo.co.uk

🗄 all major credit cards ■ no service added

££ burgers £3.95–£7.40 ■ sides £2.00–£5.95
   ■ lowest bottle price £10.50

✪ The acceptable face of the hamburger

On the face of it, the words 'gourmet burger kitchen' do not make
easy bedfellows. 'Gourmet' contradicts 'burger' and 'kitchen' has an
unnervingly homely ring to it. But taken as a whole phrase, you can
see the intention. Anyway, at GBK they seem to care about the future
of burgers and in 2007 even introduced a new organic buffalo burger
from the butcher's shop at Laverstoke Park. The room is cramped and
dominated by a large counter behind which there seem to be serried
ranks of waitresses and chefs. Everything is pretty casual – you go
up to the bar, order and pay, and then your meal is brought to the
table. The menu starts at the 'classic – 100 per cent Aberdeen Angus
Scotch beef, salad and relish'. It also offers the blue cheese burger,
which adds the tang of Stilton to the main event; the chilli burger;
the avocado and bacon burger; the pesterella – with fresh pesto and
mozzarella; lamb; venison; chicken, bacon and avocado; chorizo;
or for vegetarians there is even a 'burger' made from Portabella
mushroom; or aubergine and goat's cheese; or falafel. The fries are
good and the side salad is excellent, with fresh leaves and a perky
dressing. The Gourmet Burger Kitchen has a good feel to it, the food
is top quality and despite the dread word 'gourmet', prices are not
out of reach.

→ For branches, see index or website

Metro Garden Restaurant & Bar

9 Clapham Common South Side, SW4 ■ 020 7627 0632

⊖ Clapham Common

🍴 Modern British

🕐 Mon to Fri 18.00–23.00; Sat 12.00–23.00; Sun 12.00–22.30

🖥 www.metromotel.co.uk

🖬 all major credit cards except AmEx ■ 12.5% optional service added

££ starters £5.95–£6.95 ■ mains £11.50–£19.75 ■ sides £2.75–£3.75
■ desserts £4.25–£8.95 ■ set dinner £26.50 (3 courses)
■ lowest bottle price £13.25

✪ Your own secret garden

As you emerge from the southern exit of Clapham Common tube station, Metro is facing you – which is presumably how the place came by its name. Over the years the charming 'secret' garden has become such a widely known secret that the proprietors bit the bullet and changed the name to include it. As you'd expect of any establishment thoughtful enough to provide blankets for the dogs of Sunday brunchers lingering over the newspapers in the secluded garden, the Metro Garden Restaurant has become something of a neighbourhood favourite. The food is interesting, but mercifully simple. Start with an oven-baked pumpkin half moon with a brioche and gruyere crust; fresh crab and coriander croquettes on mixed leaves; a chicken liver and spiced rum parfait with home-made gingerbread; a grilled halloumi salad; or a pretty international Welsh rarebit made with grilled Portobello mushroom and pancetta. Main courses are very much in tune with the local customer – monkfish with creamy curried mussels on squid ink pasta; a kumquat marinated duck breast; a traditional risotto spiked with truffle and wild mushroom; or a rack of venison with creamed cabbage and bacon. Puds are mainstream: banoffee pie; apple tarte Tatin; or an over-indulgent chocolate nemesis – the chocoholic's dish of choice. The service is slick but friendly, the wine list sound rather than adventurous, which means that it delivers pretty much exactly what is wanted by the local clientele.

Ransome's Dock

35–36 Parkgate Road, SW11 ■ 020 7223 1611

BR Battersea Park

🍽 British

🕐 Mon to Fri 12.00–23.00; Sat 12.00–23.00; Sun 12.00–15.30

🖰 www.ransomesdock.co.uk

🖫 all major credit cards ■ 12.5% optional service added

££ starters £6.50–£8.95 ■ mains £13.00–£22.50 ■ sides £3.50–£5
■ desserts £5.50–£7.50 ■ set lunch £15.50 (2 courses)
■ lowest bottle price £13.50

⭐ A British restaurant with notable wine list

Ransome's Dock is a versatile restaurant, both formal enough
for those little celebrations or occasions with friends, and informal
enough to pop into for a single dish at the bar. The food is good,
seasonal and made with carefully sourced ingredients. Dishes are well
cooked, satisfying and unfussy; the wine list is encyclopaedic; and
service is friendly and efficient. All in all, Martin Lam and his team
have got it just right. Everything stems from the raw ingredients:
Ummera organic smoked salmon; Creedy Carver ducks; potted
shrimps from Morecambe Bay. The menu changes monthly, but the
philosophy behind it does not. There's an extensive brunch menu at
the weekend. Before rampaging off through the main menu, look
over the daily specials. If nothing tempts you, turn to the seven or
eight starters. If it's on, make a beeline for the warm Lincolnshire
smoked eel, with warm buckwheat pancake and crème fraîche. It's
very rich and very good. Or there may be Perroche goat's cheese
crostini with tapenade; or Morecambe Bay potted shrimps with
wholemeal toast. Main courses are well balanced: Dutch calf's liver
may come with red wine and bacon sauce and bubble and squeak. Or
there's 'Label Anglais', chicken breast with ricotta gnocchi, or there
may be a 'shorthorn' sirloin steak with big chips. Puddings run from
the complicated – a hot prune and Armagnac soufflé with Armagnac
custard, to the simple – rhubarb fool.

Tom Ilic

123 Queenstown Road, SW8 ■ 020 7622 0555   ♿

⊖ BR Queenstown Road

🍽 Modern British

🕐 Wed to Fri 12.00–14.30 & 18.00–22.30; Tues & Sat 18.00–22.30;
Sun 12.00–15.30

⌁ www.tomilic.com

🗠 all major credit cards ■ 12.5% optional service added

££ starters £4.75–£7.50 ■ mains £9.75–£13.50 ■ sides £2.50
■ desserts £4.50 ■ set menus Wed–Fri lunch £12.50 (2 courses)
& £14.95 (3 courses); Sun lunch £14.50 (2 courses) & £16.95 (3
courses) ■ lowest bottle price £13

✪ Accomplished cooking at neighbourhood prices

Towards the end of 2007 Tom Ilic took the latest step in his cheffy
odyssey – after several high-profile posts he returned to 123
Queenstown Road, where he had once a lowly job in the kitchens.
This time, however, Ilic has his name over the door and his savings
on the line. His cooking style has always been a joy, with its emphasis
on robust dishes and big flavours, plenty of pork and plenty of
offal. The dining room is modern and unfussy, with plain tables and
somewhat austere chairs. The menu evolves gradually, with dishes
being added and dropped, but you may be offered starters like seared
mackerel horseradish soufflé, watercress salad; or a crab and avocado
salad with a gazpacho vinaigrette; or honey-glazed pork belly with
black pudding, apples and a parsnip purée (if ever there was a main
course masquerading as a starter this is it – very rich, pork cooked
to melting and the silky parsnip purée standing in as sauce). Mains
range from slow-cooked beef with roast bone marrow – very
satisfying, the beef tender and the root vegetables caramelised; to a
roast saddle and braised neck of lamb; or baked fillet of sea bass with
parmesan gnocchi. The standard of cooking is high and the dishes
are complex and well thought through. Puds hit the spot: sticky
toffee pudding; lemon tarte; pear Tatin. This is a friendly place where
everyone cares, and the wine list is accessible and affordable. Enough
to make you wish you lived in SW8.

Trinity

4 The Polygon, SW4 ▪ 020 7622 1199

⊖ Clapham Common

🍴 Modern British

🕐 Mon 18.30–22.30; Tues to Sat 12.30–14.30 & 18.30–22.30;
Sun 12.30–15.00 & 19.30–22.30

🔗 www.trinityrestaurant.co.uk

💳 all major credit cards ▪ 12.5% optional service added

££ starters £7–£11 ▪ mains £17–£19 ▪ desserts £7–£10
▪ lunch £15 (2 courses) & £20 (3 courses)
▪ Sunday lunch £25 (3 courses) ▪ 5-course tasting menu £35
▪ lowest bottle price £16.50

✪ Local but sophisticated

Trinity's chef Adam Byatt did well at Clapham icon Thyme, left for
the West End, returned chastened, and opened Trinity. It bedded in
well and is now the top local resto. The dining room here is spacious
and airy, the wine list is thoughtful and the service is polished. The
food is ambitious, dishes are both seasonal and well presented.
The menu changes monthly so starters may range from Jerusalem
artichoke soup with artichoke crisps and thyme Chantilly to crab,
avocado and apple salad; pressed terrine of Middle White pork with
prunes and pistachios; ragout of razor clams, salted courgettes, chilli
with fregola; deep-fried duck egg on brioche with a sauté of duck
hearts, sauce ravigote; or lasagne of crisp sardines, basil pesto and
red pepper piperade. These are rich, well-seasoned, well-balanced
dishes. For mains there may be a ballotine of pollock and chorizo with
a ragout of baby octopus; caramelised breast of duck with celeriac
purée; glazed belly of middle White pork, with braised pig's head;
or sauté of red label guinea fowl with buttered wild mushrooms.
Desserts are elaborate – caramel poached pears with spiced
Madeleines; Valrhona chocolate hot pot with malted milk ice cream;
working up to a spiced plum tart Tatin. You get the feeling that Trinity
is moving smoothly from being the best resto in Clapham to one that
is worth driving to from anywhere in South London.

The Westbridge

74–76 Battersea Bridge Road, SW11 ■ 020 7228 6482

Clapham Junction/Queenstown Road BR

Gastropub/British

Mon to Fri 12.00–17.00 & 17.00–22.00; Sat & Sun 11.00–17.00 (brunch); 17.00–22.00

www.thewestbridge.co.uk

all major credit cards ■ 12.5% optional service added

££ starters £2.95–£10.50 ■ mains £8.50–£12.50 ■ sides £2.50 ■ desserts £4.75 ■ lowest bottle price £12.50

✪ Comfortable gastropub doesn't abandon the 'pub' bit

The Westbridge has a good line of form; one of its principals is also involved in Le Café Anglais (see p. 136) and in 2008 this site emerged from the doldrums refitted as a comfortable gastropub. Presumably, long ago in the mists of time, number 74 must originally have been a real pub. In recent memory, however, it has been various un-memorable bars. This is an agreeable place with good fundamentals, there is well-kept beer and a well-groomed wine list with price tags that do not frighten. The small terrace to the front is a bit close to the traffic for all but the most dedicated smoker, but there is a beer garden to the rear. The food is comfort-meets-pride-of-Britain. Start with a pint of prawns; pea and ham soup with crusty bread; roast butternut squash, chick pea and feta salad; or steamed mussels with a sauce made from Duvel, a fine Belgian beer. The mussels are exemplary, with plenty of dill. Mains include Gilthead bream with tomato fondue; a grilled pork chop with Dauphinoise potatoes; Welsh lamb rump with red chilli risotto; or crab and smoked haddock fishcakes – large and with an admirably crisp exterior. There is also a 'beef' section offering decent steaks and hamburgers, all made with Aberdeen Angus from Donald Russell. Service is chirpy and efficient and the puds are resolute – chocolate bread and butter pudding; apple crumble with custard.

Bermondsey and Borough

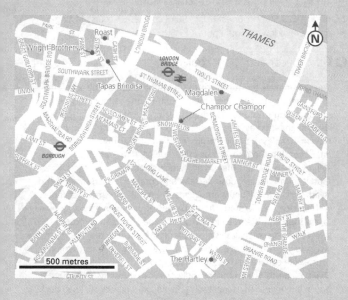

Champor Champor

62 Weston Street, SE1 ■ 020 7403 4600

⊖ London Bridge

🍽 Asian eclectic

🕐 Tues to Fri 12.00–14.30 & 18.15–22.15; Mon & Sat 18.15–22.15

🖰 www.champor-champor.com

🖶 all major credit cards ■ 15% optional service added

££ menus: £23.50 (2 courses) & £27.90 (3 courses); 7-course tasting menu £45 ■ lowest bottle price £13.50

✪ Glam décor and glam cooking

You are unlikely to stumble into Champor Champor by accident, as this brightly painted, genuinely eccentric little restaurant is marooned on the barren shores of Weston Street. The two proprietors describe the food as 'creative Malay-Asian' and the chef, Adu Amran Hassan, handles not only the presentation of the dishes but also the interior design. Despite various expansions and revamps the resto still only seats 40, but there is a 'members' lounge' downstairs. The food is tough to categorise, but the presentation is sophisticated and stylish and all the flavours are agreeably upfront. The menu changes with the seasons. To start, there may be baby squid in a South Indian rasam soup with steamed idli bread; steamed boneless chicken with sweet mango and chilli salsa; or Penang soft-shelled crab rojak with sweet spicy peanut gravy, which attracts a small supplement. Main courses are equally eclectic: roast fillet of ostrich, sweet and spicy soy, Thai basil pesto rice (another supplement); Balinese-style baked sea bream in banana leaf, fennel somtam, coconut rice; or stir-fried duck breast with chestnut holy basil and chilli herb rice salad. This is well-judged, adventurous cookery and makes a pleasant change. Even the desserts are suitably exotic – 'rich chocolate and cardamom pudding, avocado and sweet basil quenelle' touches several bases. The wine list is refined, but fairly priced, and there is a range of moody Asian beers.

The Hartley

64 Tower Bridge Road, SE1 ■ 020 7394 7023

⊖ Bermondsey

🍽 Modern British/gastropub

🕓 Mon to Fri 12.00–15.00 & 18.00–22.00; Sat 11.00–16.00 &
18.00–22.00; Sun 12.00–21.00

🖰 www.thehartley.com

🖥 all major credit cards ■ 12.5% optional service added

££ starters £4.50–£7.50 ■ mains £8–£13 ■ sides £2.50–£4.50
■ desserts £4.50–£7 ■ lowest bottle price £12

✪ Gastropub deserves to be jammed

Hartley, as in the famous jam maker. The Hartley company's old
jam factory is on the other side of Tower Bridge Road and has been
redeveloped into expensive loft apartments. So in this instance it's a
case of where once there was jam there's now plenty of bread. This
gastropub aims at the newer, richer locals, and although the menu
has been tamed somewhat since the early days, dishes now lie within
the comfort zone and prices are competitive. The kitchen knows its
stuff: with room for big flavours, sound combinations of ingredients,
unfussy dishes, and unpretentious eating. The blackboard features
the daily specials and the menu itself changes from time to time.
Setting aside the merits of 'pan-fried foie gras with home-made
brioche and Sauternes jelly', what about chicken and pancetta terrine
served with mango chutney; or carpaccio of tuna with guacamole,
sliced fennel and toast? These are interesting combinations. Mains
offer steady fare – there's a burger made from rump steak; a double
salmon and watercress fishcake; confit duck served with Jerusalem
artichoke mash; and snail and wild mushroom pie with puff pastry
and buttered curly kale. Puds appeal – hot chocolate tart with vanilla
ice cream. There is a brunch menu including a 'Full English Breakfast'
that includes a smoked Toulouse sausage – Oh! The shame of it! The
wine list is on a blackboard over the bar and offers sound bottles at
sensible prices. Service is informal and friendly.

Magdalen

152 Tooley Street, SE1 ■ 020 7403 1342

⊖ London Bridge

🍽 British

🕐 Mon 18.30–22.30; Tues to Sat 12.00–14.30 & 18.30–22.30

🌐 www.magdalenrestaurant.co.uk

🗗 all major credit cards ■ no service added

££ starters £6–£10.50 ■ mains £13.50–£19 ■ sides £3.50
　■ desserts £5–£7.50 ■ lowest bottle price £16

⭐ Honest British cooking

The ethos of this place is 'gastropub plus'. You can book a table in the dining room upstairs, but you cannot book for the downstairs room, where it is strictly first come, first served. The menu changes every session and dances to the tune of the seasons and the whim of the kitchens. The produce used here has basic and down-to-earth credentials aplenty – Longhorn beef; Middle White pork; Devon crab; wild sea bass. The place is comfortable and the prices do not scald. As wise guys are prone to say, 'What's not to like?' The chef partner here has a line of form back to The Anchor & Hope (see p. 186) and the styles of cooking are similar. Starters may include a duck sausage with lentil toast; or a splendid dish teaming smoked trout, chicory and sweet mustard; or hot foie gras, prunes and Armagnac. Main courses include at least one dish that is for two to share – a whole roast calf's kidney, shallots and sherry vinegar. Or there may be a confit rabbit leg with spring vegetables and aioli; baked turbot with melted leeks and red wine; or a roast Middle White loin, green bean vinaigrette. Puds are good – chocolate pot and preserved cherries; French toast and strawberry jam with vanilla ice cream; green apple sorbet. This is a friendly place with attentive but unintrusive service and it even has a friendly wine list with some lesser known and more interesting bottles.

Roast

The Floral Hall, Borough Market, SE1 ■ 020 7940 1300

London Bridge

British

Mon to Fri 07.00–10.00, 12.00–15.00, 17.30–23.00;
Sat 08.00–10.00, 12.00–16.00 (brunch), & 18.00–23.00;
Sun 12.00–16.00

www.roast-restaurant.com

all major credit cards ■ 12.5% optional service added

££ starters £6.50–£14 ■ mains £14.50–£25 ■ sides £3.80–£4.50
■ desserts £5.50–£8.50 ■ lowest bottle price £16

⊗ Stunningly beautiful space, resolutely British food

Borough Market provides an essential focus for all London foodies
and Roast is there to make sure that in this welter of gourmet activity,
British cooking gets a fair shout. As an objective this is so worthwhile,
so long awaited and so deserving of your support that you should
make a booking now without worrying about the fine detail like
food, service and ambience. Don't worry though – the dining room
is outstandingly beautiful, a glazed box 'hanging' over the busy food
market. By day the sunshine streams in (when there is any) and by
night your view may be of floodlit St Paul's in all its glory. The menu
at Roast changes weekly. Typical starters range from dressed Dorset
crab; to potted salt beef; Cullen skink; Neal's Yard goat's curd with
pickled beetroot and port; or Orkney haggis with celeriac and oxtail
sauce. The mains carry the theme forward – pot-roast organic
chicken thighs; poached smoked haddock; steamed game pudding;
parsnip hash; an organic rump steak from Laverstoke Park, and so
it goes on. The roast potatoes are cooked in dripping and there are
some fine grandstand dishes to share, such as the 'roast rib of beef'
– for four and with a three-figure price tag! At Roast the ingredients
are fresh and the cooking good. Puds are trad, service is charming
and the wine list has some Brit wines and a good many superb Brit
beers.

Tapas Brindisa

18–20 Southwark Street, SE1 ■ 020 7357 8880

⊖ London Bridge

🍴 Spanish/tapas

🕐 Mon to Thurs hot tapas & salads 12.00–15.00 & 17.30–23.00 (cold tapas all day); Fri & Sat 09.00–11.00 (breakfast) 12.00–16.00 (lunch), 17.00–23.00 (dinner), (cold tapas 12.00–23.00)

🖰 www.brindisa.com

🖯 all major credit cards ■ 12.5% optional service added

££ cold tapas £1–£20 ■ hot tapas £3.95–£12 ■ breads £2.60 ■ desserts £2.95–£5 ■ lowest bottle price £15.75

❂ Worth queuing for

London foodies owe a large debt of gratitude to Brindisa. This small food importer (which marked its twentieth birthday in 2008) was a genuine pioneer and introduced both chefs and public to lots of delicacies we now take for granted: fine Spanish cheeses; smoked paprika; huge and glorious anchovies; air-dried tuna and many other goodies. This is the Brindisa tapas bar and it is awesomely busy; on a warm summer's evening both the bar and the pavement are crowded with people waiting for a table. When you get lucky, start with an olive – it sounds pretty tame but the 'large Gordal olives with olive oil and orange' are amazing, with each monster olive stuffed with a piece of orange to give a great combination of flavours. The charcuterie is exemplary (which should not surprise, as Brindisa imports many of the hams proudly displayed in posher restaurants). Go for the regional selection plate. The chorizo is also good. The Spanish omelettes are large, solid and substantial, with a good flavour. The speciality cheeses are good. The croquettas are good. The fancier dishes also work well – pan-fried asparagus comes with a fried duck egg and Serrano ham; sautéed chicken livers come with capers and Fino sauce. Puds range from turrón mousse with Pedro Ximénez to Spanish rice pudding with citrus zest. Service is polished with dishes arriving briskly, and the wine list has some easy options.

Wright Brothers

11 Stoney Street, Borough Market, SE1 ■ 020 7403 9554

⊖ London Bridge

🍴 Fish/oysters

🕐 Mon to Fri 12.00–22.30; Sat 11.00–22.30 (no hot food 15.00–18.00)

🖱 www.wrightbros.eu.com

🗗 all major credit cards ■ no service added

££ oysters £7.10–£9.60 (6) ■ starters £6.50–£14.75
■ mains £6.75–£16.60 ■ sides/salads £3.50–£4.30
■ fruits de mer £25–£96.50 ■ lowest bottle price £15

✪ Oyster bar and Porter house

There are two Wright brothers: one is to be found at Borough Market, wheeling and dealing in oysters while overseeing this small and charming bar restaurant – and his name isn't even Wright! Meanwhile, the other is in a boat on the Helford river in Cornwall tending the oysters at the western end of the supply chain. These guys do know oysters, and if oysters are your thing this place is for you. Even when there isn't an 'r' in the month the oyster menu could read: Duchy of Cornwall, large; wild Colchester, large; Maldons; Carlingford Loch; Fines Claires, medium. All in perfect condition and just needing a slice or two of Irish head chef David Burke's rather good soda bread to set them off. There is also a blackboard with other temptations: oyster rarebit; potted shrimp; crab soup; razor clams marinière; crisp squid. If seafood appeals there is a splendid fruits de mer, and it can be turned into a seriously excessive experience by paying the steep ante and opting for the 'fruits de mer deluxe'. The dessert section has been pared down and the offer is either home-made Cointreau chocolate truffles or a serious British cheese plate, sourced from the nearby Neal's Yard cheese emporium. To drink there is porter; a crisp English cider; and there's a wine list with all the reasonably priced, crisp white wine you could wish for. This is a good place to play truant and while away an afternoon.

Brixton and Herne Hill

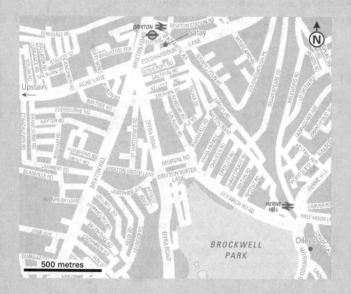

Olley's

67–69 Norwood Road, SE24 ■ 020 8671 8259   &

⊖ BR Herne Hill

🍽 Fish & chips

🕐 Mon 17.00–22.30; Tues to Sun 12.00–22.30

🖱 www.olleys.info

🖨 all major credit cards accepted ■ no service added

££ starters £4.25–£4.75 ■ mains £8.95–£20.70 ■ sides £2–£3
   ■ desserts £3–£5 ■ daily lunch special £6.50
   ■ lowest bottle price £13.50

✪ Prize-winning fish and chips

Olley's is single-minded: this is a famous fish and chip shop. It is famous because it has won various well-deserved awards. Just across the road from Brockwell Park, it has quietly but inexorably expanded, taking over one shop front after another until it now accommodates 90 diners on two floors. There is a separate area devoted to takeaways. The list of starters is to the point. You can opt for fresh grilled sardines; prawn cocktail; or battered calamari. On to more serious matters – the chips are good here. The proprietor, Harry Niazi, believes in pre-blanching, and when done well this technique guarantees chips that are fluffy inside and crisp outside. The mushy peas are commendable and so are the wallys, which non-Londoners will know better as gherkins. The fish is a triumph: fresh, white and flaky inside, crisp and golden outside – obviously the fryer knows his craft. Setting aside the matter of chips, the leader board reads as follows: cod, plaice, haddock, salmon, monkfish, swordfish, halibut and hake. You can also choose to have your fish grilled or steamed, the latter being the best way when it comes to sea bass or Dover sole. Desserts are steady, and there is a whole menu of liqueur coffees. If you have the temerity to ask for a fish and *large* chips, the plateful that arrives is so huge you can only assume the staff are taking the proverbial.

Satay

447 Coldharbour Lane, SW9 ■ 020 7326 5001

⊖ Brixton

🍴 Indonesian/Eclectic

🕐 Mon to Fri 12.00–17.00 & 18.00–23.00; Sat & Sun 14.00–17.00 & 18.00–23.00

🖱 www.sataybrixton.com

🖪 all major credit cards ■ 12.5% optional service added

££ starters £2.90–£4.20 ■ mains £3.50–£6 ■ sides £1.80–£3.60 ■ desserts £2.95–£3.80 ■ lunch special £4.95 ■ set dinner £13.95 ■ lowest bottle price £11.95

✪ Food to centre stage!

Tucked away behind the Ritzy cinema, this lively establishment dropped the word bar from its title and renamed itself as 'Satay' in February 2008. The proprietors felt that the food wasn't getting the recognition it deserved, with too much emphasis being on the bar, the music and the impromptu art gallery. The core dishes on the new menu are still mainly Indonesian but now there are some interlopers from Thailand, Vietnam, Japan, China and Malaysia. The new menu starts with a wave of satays – chicken, beef negril, king prawn, fiery lamb, ninja chicken! Then there are 'little dishes': spring rolls, chicken gyoza, duck wraps, crab cakes. Then curries: Thai green and red curries, lazy beef rendang, and a Penang curry all appeal; stir fries, ranging from ginger chicken to 'mean black bean' and king prawn sambal; and rice and noodle dishes – the subtly named 'big belly Pad Thai and old favourite Singapore noodles. Then come the 'classics': crispy snapper, gado gado, and Mr Wang's crispy beef. And finally salads: Thai beef salad, papaya salad. On the face of it this is an appealing menu with a welcome touch of 'something for everyone'. Dishes are marked out as being mild, medium or spicy. Those graded as 'spicy' carry on this resto's great tradition for serving some good and uncompromising hot food. Desserts range from a noir sticky rice cake to pandan cake and bananas in coconut milk. There is a very competitive set lunch available from Monday to Friday between 12.00 and 17.00 which costs under a fiver.

Upstairs

89b Acre Lane (entrance Branksome Road), SW2

■ 020 7733 8855

⊖ Brixton

¶⊙¶ French

🕒 Tues to Sat 18.30–22.30

⌂ www.upstairslondon.com

🖰 all major credit cards ■ 12.5% optional service added

££ two courses £21; three courses £25; four courses (to include cheese) £30 ■ lowest bottle price £14

✪ Tiny, but perfect

This is the kind of local restaurant we all wish we had at the bottom of our street. It's a French-run, French-inspired operation and the ultra-short menu offers three starters, three mains and three puds. Upstairs is spread over two floors above what was once a chemist's shop on the corner of Acre Lane and Branksome Road. On floor one there's a small bar and on floor two there's a 24-seater dining room. Décor is quirky-modern meets restaurant-functional. The shortness of the menu and the small size of the dining room mean that every dish ends up very fresh and very seasonal. The cooking is exemplary. To start you might have to choose between a smoked haddock fishcake; a well made chicken liver and foie gras parfait; and a chilled tomato consommé with mozzarella. On to mains – an elegant sea bass; a bavette with shallot purée and chips the size of railway sleepers (more like pont neuf potatoes); a risotto with spring vegetables; or the special, a chunk of halibut – perfectly cooked – with morels and asparagus. This is very good eating, and there's the exemplary plate of cheese or the blackberry and white chocolate trifle. The wine list is short and priced to please. Service is friendly as the staff squeeze through the crowded room. For food of this quality the prices are amazingly low. No wonder everyone's smiling.

Kennington, Vauxhall and Elephant & Castle

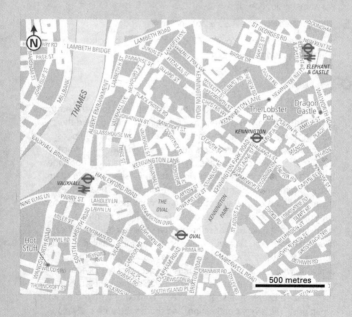

Dragon Castle

110 Walworth Road, SE17 ▪ 020 7277 3388

⊖ Elephant & Castle

|◉| Chinese/dim sum

🕐 Mon to Sat 12.00–23.00 (23.30 Fri & Sat); Sun 11.30–23.00

🖱 www.dragoncastle.eu

🖶 all major credit cards ▪ 10% optional service added

££ starters £4.80–£80 (abalone) ▪ mains £8.50–£22.80 ▪ desserts £3.80
▪ menus £13.80–£33.80pp ▪ lowest bottle price £11.80

⭐ Unlikely location for Chinese superstar

The regeneration of the Elephant & Castle is proving to be a
long drawn-out and pretty laborious process, and until you spot a
squadron of pigs barrel-rolling over the vast roundabout it's best
to step off the Walworth Road into the Dragon Castle – a really
excellent Chinese restaurant. You can tell that this place is good
from the moment you walk in; even early in the week it is heaving.
The room is huge, there is an imposing staircase, there is a stag's
head over the bar, and service is slicker than the Chinatown norm.
All the steady old favourites are listed and done well, but it's better
to stray off the beaten track. a starter of eel strips stir fried with
chilli is very good; crispy salt and pepper squid is freshly cooked and
tender. A dish of pork hock cooked in a pot with preserved plums
is a) enormous b) delicious and c) has a fabulous texture. Look out
for the steamed chicken with ginger sauce. The best dish is from the
Chef's Specials menu and is a whole crab braised in a pot with beer
and cellophane noodles. You wait while it is cooked but it's time well
spent – this dish is a classic and may be 'best ever' crab. The only
other essential is to cast your eye over the mix 'n' match vegetables
– water spinach with chilli and preserved bean curd is epic. Really
good food.

Hot Stuff

19 Wilcox Road, SW8 ■ 020 7720 1480

⊖ Vauxhall/Stockwell

🍴 Indian

🕐 Mon to Fri 12.00–22.00; Sat 15.00–22.00

🖱 www.eathotstuff.com

🗗 all major credit cards ■ no service added

££ starters £1.50–£6.50 mains £2.75–£8.50 ■ sides £2.75–£4
■ desserts £2.50–£4.50 ■ unlicensed, BYO (no corkage)

✪ Small, Indian and hot stuff

Run by the Dawood family, this tiny restaurant is something of an institution. Despite expansion and full use of the pavement in the summer, it has only a few seats and offers simple and startlingly cheap food to an enthusiastic local following. The food is just what you would expect to get at home – assuming you were part of Nairobi's Asian community. Trade is good and the dining room, though unprepossessing, is welcoming: all soft blues and orange with an array of different-coloured chairs. The starters are sound rather than glorious, so it's best to dive straight into the curries. There are various chicken curries and lamb curries, all keenly priced. It is hard to find any fault with such a cheap dinner. The most expensive option is in the fish section: king prawn biryani, which costs about the same as you would pay for a dish of curried spud in the West End. The portions aren't monster sized, and the spicing isn't subtle, but the welcome is genuine and the bill is tiny. Try the delights of the stuffed paratha – light and crispy with potato in the middle, they taste seriously delicious. Chickpea curry, the special daal and the mixed vegetable curry all hit the spot with vegetarians. For meat-eaters, the chicken Madras is hot and workmanlike, while the chicken bhuna is rich and very good. Beware: Hot Stuff closes prudently before the local pubs turn out.

The Lobster Pot

3 Kennington Lane, SE11 ■ 020 7582 5556

⊖ Kennington

🍴 Very French/fish

🕓 Tues to Sat 12.00–14.30 & 19.00–23.00

🖱 www.thelobsterpotrestaurant.co.uk

🖬 all major credit cards ■ 12.5% optional service added

££ starters £6.50–£13.50 ■ mains £16.50–£26.50
■ desserts £5.30–£7.50 ■ 'surprise' 8-course menu £39.50 (or £44.50 with lobster) ■ lowest bottle price £14.50

✪ Very French, very fishy

You have to feel for Nathalie Régent. What must it be like to be married to – and working alongside – a man whose love of the bizarre verges on the obsessional? Britain is famed for breeding dangerously potty chefs, but The Lobster Pot's chef patron, Hervé Régent, originally from Vannes in Brittany, is well ahead of the field. Walk down Kennington Lane towards the restaurant and it's even money as to whether you are struck first by the life-size painted plywood cut-out of Hervé dressed in oilskins, or the speakers relaying a soundtrack of seagulls and melancholy Breton foghorns. These clues all point towards fish. The fish here is pricey, but it is fresh and well chosen. Starters range from well-made, very thick, traditional fish soup to a really proper plateau de fruits de mer. The main course specials sometimes feature strange fish that Hervé has discovered at Billingsgate. As well as classics like l'aile de raie au beurre noisette (skate with brown butter), there are good spicy dishes, such as filet de thon à la Créole, which is tuna with a perky tomato sauce. Simpler, and as good in its way, is les crevettes grillées à l'ail, big prawns in garlic butter. The accompanying bread is notable, a soft, doughy pain rustique, and for once le plateau de fromage à la Française doesn't disappoint. Many customers are content to relax and leave everything to Hervé and the 'menu surprise' — eight courses and great value.

Putney

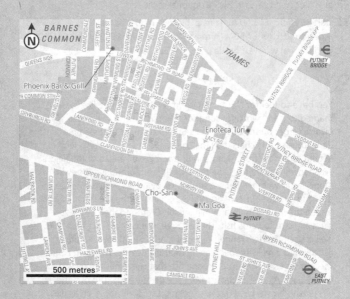

Cho-San

292 Upper Richmond Road, SW15 ■ 020 8788 9626

⊖ BR Putney

🍴 Japanese

🕐 Tues to Sun 12.00–14.30 & 18.30–22.30

🔖 Mastercard, Visa ■ 12.5% optional service added

££ sushi £3–£5.90 (for 2 pieces) ■ mains £7–£10 ■ desserts £2.60–£5
■ sashimi/sushi set £19.90 ■ lowest bottle price £16.90; sake £3.50

✪ Neighbourhood Japanese restaurant

Too many Japanese restaurants use extremely high prices and
ultra-swish West End premises to keep themselves to themselves. As
a European adventurer basking in the impeccably polite and attentive
service, it's hard not to feel a little anxious. What should you order?
How do you eat it? Will it taste nice? How much does it cost? If you
have ever been assailed by these worries you should pop along to
Cho-San in Putney. This is your chance to try all those dishes you have
never had, without wounding your pocket. The sushi is good. The
sashimi is good. And a giant boat of assorted sushi and sashimi, with
miso soup and dessert, is both good and good value. But why not
try some more obscure sushi? The price of even the fancier items is
reasonable here. Or, if you prefer your fish cooked, choose the perfect
tempura cuttlefish – a stunning achievement, its batter light enough
to levitate. And then there are always the kushiage dishes, where
something is put onto a skewer, gets an egg and breadcrumb jacket
and is treated to a turn around the deep-fryer. Ordering tori kushiage
gets you two skewers, chicken and a chunk of sweet onion. Delicious.
Or opt for tempura king prawn. Then there are the meat dishes, the
fish dishes, the rice dishes, the soba noodles, and the hot sakes, cold
sakes and beers. You could eat your way to a good understanding of
Japanese food here. Ask the charming, helpful staff and get stuck in.

Enoteca Turi

28 Putney High Street, SW15 ■ 020 8785 4449   ♿

⊖ Putney Bridge

🍴 Italian

🕐 Mon to Sat 12.00–14.30 & 19.00–23.00

🖰 www.enotecaturi.com

🖻 all major credit cards; no cheques ■ 12.5% optional service added

££ starters £7.50–£12.50 ■ mains £11.50–£20.50 ■ sides £3.50–£4.50
■ desserts £5.50–£6.50 ■ lunch £14.50 (2 courses) & £17.50 (3 courses) ■ lowest bottle price £14.50

✪ Italian wines, a long list and a strong list

If you like your Italian food a little more adventurous, then it is worth making the journey to Putney and Giuseppe Turi's pretty little restaurant. It offers a very genuine and personal version of Italian regional cooking – dishes from Veneto, Umbria, Liguria and Puglia. Enoteca takes its name from the Italian term for a smart wine shop and there's a monumental list of more than 90 specialist Italian wines and a separate by-the-glass menu, offering 11 regional wines – an excellent way to educate the palate. As for the food, at lunch there is a shortened version of the dinner menu and dishes are a couple of pounds cheaper. You'd do well to start with asparagus served with Parmesan-coated, deep-fried egg, or perhaps a plate of antipasto Pugliese – marinated, grilled vegetables served with a fava purée. Among pasta dishes may be ravioli di castagne e ricotta, or pappardelle con ragu d'anatra. Main courses may include stinco d'agnello con purée di patate e cipolline, which is lamb shank with spring onion and potato purée; or coniglio avvolto in speck con patate e prugne – rabbit wrapped in speck and served with potatoes and prunes. Desserts will test your mettle – go for the torta di cioccolata con nocciole, a blockbusting chocolate and hazelnut cake, or perhaps the particularly good, authentic tiramisù. Booking is essential, even in midweek. More of a wine bluff than a wine buff? Check out the wines recommended alongside each dish.

Ma Goa

244 Upper Richmond Road, SW15 ■ 020 8780 1767

⊖ BR Putney/East Putney

|O| Indian

🕒 Mon to Sat 18.30–23.00; Sun 13.00–16.00 & 18.00–22.00

🖰 www.ma-goa.com

🖫 all major credit cards ■ 12.5% optional service added

££ starters £3.75–£5 ■ thali £10.95 ■ mains £7.85–£13.50
　　■ sides £1–£4 ■ desserts £3.75–£4 ■ Sunday lunch buffet £10
　　■ Early Bird (pre-20.00, not Sun) £10 & £13 ■ lowest bottle price £10.95

✪ Goan home cooking

It seems that every year sees a further expansion of this family-run business, but despite the stylish décor, the café-style chairs and tables, and the computer system to handle bills and orders, the overwhelming impression you are left with when you visit Ma Goa is of home cooking. This place is as far as you can possibly get from the chuck-it-in-a-frying-pan-and-heat-it-through school of curry cookery. The food is deceptively simple, slow-cooked and awesomely tasty. The menu is fairly compact: half a dozen starters are followed by a dozen mains, while a blackboard adds a couple of dishes of the day. Shrimp balchao is a starter made from shrimps cooked in pickling spices and curry leaves. Sorpotel is made from lamb's liver, kidney and pork in a sauce rich with roast spices, lime and coriander. The Ma Goa chorizo is rich, too, with palm vinegar, cinnamon and green chillies. Main courses are amazing. The spices are properly cooked out by slow cooking, which makes lifting the lids of the heavy clay serving pots a voyage of discovery. Porco vindaloo, sharp with palm vinegar, is enriched with lumps of pork complete with rind. Ma's fish caldin is a kind of fish stew with large chunks of fish in a coconut-based sauce. Vegetarians are equally well served. Bund gobi is stir-fried, shredded cabbage with carrots, ginger and cumin, while beringella is an aubergine dish made with pickling spices. The rice here is excellent.

→ For branch, see index or website

Phoenix Bar & Grill

162–164 Lower Richmond Road, SW15 ■ 020 8780 3131 ♿

⊖ BR Putney

🍴 Italian

🕐 Mon to Thurs 12.30–14.30 & 19.00–23.00; Fri & Sat 12.30–14.30 & 19.00–23.30; Sun 12.30–15.00 & 19.00–22.00

🖰 www.sonnys.co.uk

🗄 all major credit cards ■ 12.5% optional service added

££ starters £5.50–£9.50 ■ mains £9.50–£17.50 ■ sides £2.50–£3.00 ■ desserts £4.50–£9.50 ■ menus: lunch Mon to Sat £9.50 (1 course), £13.50 (2 courses) & £15.50 (3 courses); dinner Sun to Thurs £10.50 (1 course), £15.50 (2 courses) & £17.50 (3 courses) ■ lowest bottle price £11.95

✪ Adding tone to the neighbourhood

This restaurant is a member of London's leading family of neighbourhood restaurants and is related to Sonny's (see p. 385). All these restaurants are just trendy enough, the service is just slick enough and the cooking is marginally better than you would expect – with competitive pricing. There's a large, white-painted room inside and a large, white-painted courtyard out front where you can eat alfresco. Starters may include Dorset crab with guacamole and tomato vinaigrette; artichoke, pear and crunchy Pecorino salad; chicken liver and foie gras parfait with mixed leaves. The famous vincisgrassi maceratesi – an epic eighteenth-century truffled lasagne – is on the menu and is a 'must-have' indulgence. Mains range from risotto with red wine and Italian sausages; through grilled wild halibut; slow-roast pork belly with roast beetroot and chicory; to roast loin of venison with red cabbage and polenta; or sea bass 'al cartoccio', with braised fennel, prawn and tomato. There's a flexible and good-value set menu – how does tomato and buffalo mozzarella salad, followed by pan-fried salmon with escarole, and apple crumble with custard sound? Among the puds are chocolate cake with toasted almond ice cream; spumone Amaretto; and pannettone bread and butter pudding with vanilla ice cream. Service is friendly and the wine list has bottles for most circumstances.

Tooting, Balham and Wimbledon

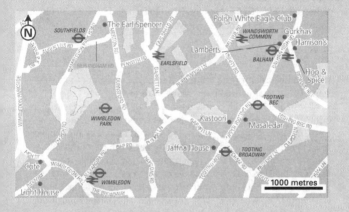

Côte

8 High Street, Wimbledon, SW19 ■ 020 8947 7100 &

⊖ Wimbledon

🍽 French

🕐 Mon to Thurs 08.00–23.00; Fri & Sat 08.00–01.00; Sun 08.00–22.30

🗃 all major credit cards ■ 12.5% optional service added

££ starters £4.50–£6.50 ■ mains £7.95–£15.95 ■ sides £2.75–£2.95
■ desserts £3.95–£5.95 ■ prix fixe (Mon to Fri until 19.00) £9.95 (2
courses) & £11.95 (3 courses) ■ lowest bottle price £12.95

✪ Brasserie woos Wimbledon

It would be easier if restaurants that so obviously set out to be the
start of a successful mega-chain were always awful. We're fond of
small restaurants, we like family businesses, we like low-key French
dishes. Côte is large, corporate and serves sound Brasserie fare in
clean, modern, slick surroundings. The second link in the Côte chain is
to be found on Wardour Street and from then on the sky's the limit.
This is a very considered venture, it offers a highly accessible menu
featuring the kind of French food we all like to eat, so it is no surprise
that this resto is very busy — one mid-week lunch time the back room
was home to 40 women and one token male. The starters range from
a well-made terrine; to soup; and some surprisingly good salads —
chicory, Roquefort and walnuts; or rocket, baby gem, roast tomato
and soft egg. Then there are some light dishes such as salmon
hollandaise or a green risotto. The mains range from steak haché and
hachis Parmentier to moules frites. As is often the case, dishes get
better as they get simpler, such as the roast chickens from the Landes
and the good steaks. The frites are very French. Puds are sensibly
chococentric with mousse; or chocolate sauce over vanilla ice cream;
and a chocolate pot. The wine list is unaggressive with enough class
for the SW19ers. A happy place, doing a decent job.

→ For branch, see index

Gurkhas

1 The Boulevard, Balham High Road, SW17

■ 020 8675 1188

 Balham

¡●¡ Indian

🕙 Tues to Sat 18.00–23.30 Sun 12.00–22.30

🖻 all major credit cards ■ 10% optional service added

££ starters £3.50–£4.50 ■ mains £6.50–£13.25 ■ sides £3.75–£4.50
　■ desserts £3–£4 ■ lowest bottle price £12.50

✪ Nepali dishes at unpretentious resto

This place has a growing reputation and in spring 2008 was listed
as one of Michel Roux junior's (see Le Gavroche, p. 89) favourite
eating places. The light and spacious room has a parquet floor and
this is a restaurant where your napkin comes in a stylish napkin ring
and there are over-size wine glasses. Great efforts have also been
made with the presentation of the dishes on the plate and there's
a good deal of 'arranging' and 'sauce drizzling' going on, which is
largely superfluous given the interesting and well-cooked food. From
the starters dayalu is a simple potato cake made with lentils, and
served with a fine-grained, spicy, sesame sauce. The nakasee is also
good – a bamboo skewer of chicken with another delicious sauce.
Or there's bhutuwa, which is a stir-fry made with chunks of highly
seasoned chicken liver. Main courses include a series of dishes made
in the 'chuli', a charcoal-fuelled beehive oven. Gurkhali chicken is
very good, with a green marinade and strong flavours. Khasi tang is
a large lamb shank served on the bone with rich gravy, while 'sherpa
hot' is a dish that looks as if it has come from Lancashire – lamb curry
is topped with discs of potato, giving a new credibility to the term
hotpot. Vegetable dishes are also attractive; rato farsi is a mild curry
made with pumpkin. Gurkhas deserves your support for daring to do
something different, and for the genuine smiley welcome.

Harrison's

15–19 Bedford Hill, SW12 ▪ 020 8675 6900

⊖ Balham

🍴 Modern British

🕐 daily 09.00–22.30 (no hot food 15.00–18.00 Mon to Fri & 16.00–18.30 Sat & Sun)

🖰 www.harrisonsbalham.co.uk

🖻 all major credit cards ▪ 12.5% optional service added

££ starters £4.50–£8.50 ▪ mains £9.50–£17.50 ▪ sides £3
▪ desserts £3.59–£6.50 ▪ lowest bottle price £13

⊗ In the comfort zone

Sam Harrison is the agreeable fellow who set up Sam's Brasserie in Chiswick (see p. 426). Expansion was always an integral part of his strategy so when this Bedford Hill site (formerly known as the Balham Bar and Grill) came on the market he stepped in. The locals do not seem to mind the re-branding, and why should they, this place is admirably focussed on delivering what they want. By day Harrison's holds what may be the largest baby buggy rally in Balham and there are serried ranks of high chairs plus attendant ladies who croissant; ladies who latte; and even ladies who lunch. In the evening the bar comes into its own while the dining area fills with couples who don't wish to cook their own evening meal. The food is sound rather than gastronomic and the regularly changing menu makes a virtue out of comfort food. Starters may include deep-fried squid, with a very good spicy anchovy mayonnaise; Coln Valley smoked salmon on a potato rosti; or a salad of marinated beetroot with parsley and feta. Mains range from a straightforward onglet and chips; to a butternut squash risotto; or pan-fried monkfish and king prawns with (a slightly less successful) green curry sauce. Puds are led by ice cream and sticky toffee pudding. Service is efficient and there is no time wasting. The wine list is well spread and runs from cheap to extravagant.

→ For branch, see index or website

Hop & Spice

53 Bedford Hill, SW12 ■ 020 8675 3121 ♿

 Balham

 Sri Lankan

🕐 Mon & Tues 18.00–22.30; Wed–Sat 18.00–23.00; Sun 18.00–22.00

🔗 www.hopandspice.com

🗔 all major credit cards ■ 10% optional service added

££ starters £3.75–£5.95 ■ thali dishes £3.15–£4.95 ■ sides £1.25–£2.95
■ desserts £3.45–£4.95 ■ lowest bottle price £11.95

⭐ Beer & curry

It is always laudable when someone takes a long hard look at a
tried-and-tested formula and goes on to upgrade and improve it. Hop
& Spice opened in November 2006 with the promise that we would
get beer and curry reflected in the name. The curry was represented
by a range of Sri Lankan dishes and the beer by a list that stretched
from Lion – a Sri Lankan lager – to Youngs Double Chocolate Stout
(by way of Paulaner Bavarian Wheatbeer). This is a pleasant modern
restaurant that has a real buzz to it, the dishes come as small
portions; you order about four per person and they arrive on a thali.
The food is good and fresh, although the kitchen has eased back on
the chilli (should you want hot Sri Lankan food, try Jaffna House –
see p. 368). The daily specials are worth a look, otherwise the Jaffna
coconut lamb, the fried spiced chicken, the Batticaloan king prawn,
and the Ceylon calamari are all very sound. Hidden away at the end
of the menu are a few main courses – lamb kottu roti is a trad dish
made from a combination of noodle-like strips of roti stir-fried with
lamb, chilli and egg: not authentically hot, but great comfort food.
This is a jolly place, although the bill can creep up if you succumb to
greed and over-order an extravagance of the little dishes.

Jaffna House

90 Tooting High Street, SW17 ■ 020 8672 7786

⊖ Tooting Broadway

🍽 Sri Lankan

🕐 daily 12.00–24.00

🖰 www.jaffnahouse.co.uk

🖃 all major credit cards ■ no service added

££ starters 40p–£1.50 ■ mains £3.50–£9 ■ sides £1.25–£3.50
■ desserts £1.25–£1.50 ■ lunch menu £4 (vegetarian) & £4.75 (non-vegetarian) ■ lowest bottle price £6.50

✪ Glorious food, glorious prices

Jaffna House is a charming, simple, scruffy place. The food is Sri Lankan, very good, often very spicy and implausibly cheap. At the front there is a basic café and takeaway area, while at the back (the entrance is actually on Coverton Road) you'll find the dining room, which is not that much smarter than the café. Service is friendly, but there is one trap: in the 'smart' bit there are two menus, one for starters and one for main courses – it is easy to get carried away and order your whole meal from the starters menu. The starters are good, even if there is an emphasis on frying (but thankfully the fried food is well done, dry and crisp). Vadai are small patties of mixed lentils, fried. Mutton rolls are delicious – filled pancakes, breadcrumbed and deep-fried. Vaaipan are hand-grenade sized balls sweetened with mashed banana and fried. Fish cutlets are similarly shaped, subtly spiced fishcakes. Bridging the gap to the main courses are the 'devilled' dishes – mutton or beef. These are strongly flavoured, dry curries and they are hot. Among the curry leaves and onions there are enough green chillies to make the lips sting. Then the menu romps on through hoppers to various kotthu, which are made with chopped-up rotis; plus a strange Sri Lankan speciality called pittu, a kind of rice flour stodge; dosas and a few curry house staples. Best to stick with the Sri Lankan dishes and drink cold Lion beer.

Kastoori

188 Upper Tooting Road, SW17 ■ 020 8767 7027

⊖ Tooting Broadway

🍴 Indian/vegetarian

🕐 Mon & Tues 18.00–22.30; Wed to Sun 12.30–14.30 & 18.00–22.30

🔲 Mastercard, Visa ■ no service added

££ starters £3–£4.50 ■ mains £5–£6.50 ■ sides £2.50–£3
   ■ desserts £3.50–£3.75 ■ lowest bottle price £10.95

✪ Veggie food with real class

Anyone who is genuinely puzzled that people can cope with and indeed enjoy a diet of vegetables alone should try eating at Kastoori. Located in a rather unpromising-looking bit of town, Kastoori is a Gujarati 'Pure Vegetarian Restaurant'. The food they serve is leavened with East African influences, and the large and cavernous restaurant is run by the admirably helpful Thanki family – do be sure to ask their advice, and act on it. First onto the waiter's pad (and indeed first into the mouth, as they go soggy and collapse if made to wait) must be dahi puri – tiny, crispy flying saucers filled with a sweet-and-sour yogurty sauce, potatoes, onions, chickpeas and so forth. You pop them in whole; the marriage of taste and texture is a revelation. Samosas are excellent and the onion bhajia are also very impressive – bite-sized and delicious, a far cry from the ball-of-knitting served in most high street curry emporia. Then make sure that someone orders the vegetable curry of the day, and others the outstanding cauliflower with cream curry and special tomato curry – a hot and spicy classic hailing from Katia Wahd. Leave room for the chilli banana – bananas stuffed with mild chillies (an East African recipe), and mop everything up with generous helpings of puris and chapatis. The smart move is to ask what's in season, as the menu is littered with oddities that come and go. For example, there's a 'beans curry' subtitled 'Chef's Choice'.

Lamberts

Station Parade, Balham High Road, SW12 ■ 020 8675 2233

⊖ Balham

🍽 Modern British

🕐 Mon to Fri 19.00–22.30; Sat 12.00–15.00 & 19.00–22.30;
Sun 12.00–21.00 (roasts)

🖰 www.lambertsrestaurant.com

🖶 all major credit cards except AmEx ■ 12.5% optional service added

££ starters £6.50–£8.50 ■ mains £15–£17 ■ sides £2–£3.50
■ desserts £5.50 ■ midweek set menu £15 (2 courses) & £18 (3
courses) ■ lowest bottle price £14.50

✪ Suave and ambitious local resto

There is something appealing about the naked ambition on display
at Lamberts. When a restaurant in downtown Balham refuses the
safe Brasserie-local-hero option, and aims for complex presentation,
better ingredients, and more sophisticated dishes you have to wonder
whether the public will respond favourably. Obviously the SW12'ers
have hidden depths, as Lamberts seems busy enough despite little
foibles like charging for bread – a practice that makes the hackles
rise wherever it is encountered. The best way to describe the food
here is complex. Sourcing is given full credit on the menu – Farmer
Sharp's Herdwick mutton; fish from Ben's fish on Mersea Island; Red
Poll steak and kidney pudding. From the starters a wild rabbit and
mushroom terrine is well made and served with a hazelnut brioche;
three scallops are presented on dollops of white bean purée with
a piece of braised pig's cheek sitting in a shell; or there's a simpler
offering like dressed Isle of Wight cock crab. Mains range from British
saddleback – loin, belly and trotter with kale mash and apple; to
guinea fowl with roast Jerusalem artichokes; or yet another triptych
featuring mutton, wether and lamb. There is a great deal of emphasis
on presentation here but the cooking is technically adept with careful
balancing of flavours and textures. Puds are glossy, such as rhubarb
tart yoghurt and honey ice cream, while the wine list has something
for everyone.

Light House

75–77 The Ridgeway, SW19 ■ 020 8944 6338

⊖ Wimbledon

🍽 Modern European

🕐 Mon to Sat 12.00–14.30 & 18.00–22.30; Sun 12.00–15.00

🖰 www.lighthousewimbledon.com

🖰 all major credit cards ■ 12.5% optional service added

££ starters £5.50–£11 ■ mains £11.50–£16.50 ■ sides £3–£3.50
   ■ desserts £5.50–£7.50 ■ lunch menu Mon to Sat £14 (1 course)
   & £16.50 (2 course) ■ early evening (Mon to Thurs 18.00–19.30)
   £14.50 (1 course) & £18.50 ■ Sun lunch £18 & £23
   ■ lowest bottle price £13

⭐ Sophisticated local resto

Light House is a strange restaurant to find marooned in leafy
suburbia – you would think that its modern, eclectic menu and
clean style would be more at home in a city centre than in a smart,
quiet, respectable neighbourhood. Nevertheless, it continues to do
well. First impressions always count, and a light, bright interior plus
genuinely friendly staff make both arriving and eating at Light House
a pleasure. At first glance, the menu seems to lean towards Italy, but
there are also North African, Spanish and British influences. Starters
may range from tuna nori roll with wasabi mayonnaise; to leek and
potato soup with crème fraîche; Longhorn beef koftas, raita and
lemon; or seared scallops with Jerusalem artichoke purée. It would
be very easy to get this sort of 'shopping list' cooking wrong, but in
fact Light House puts together some very successful combinations
of taste and texture. From the mains, baked sea bass is served with
steamed broccoli, green beans anchoiade and Parmesan; confit duck
leg comes with red lentil dhal; grilled rib eye steak with sweet potato
mash; and roast cod with baked swede, samphire and herb-baked
Portobello mushrooms. Puddings are solid rather than fancy but
can still delight – hot chocolate mousse with cherry ice cream; sticky
ginger cake with poached pear; and lemon curd cheese cake with
poached rhubarb. The wine list features twenty each of whites and
reds, and crosses as many frontiers as possible.

Masaledar

121 Upper Tooting Road, SW17 ■ 020 8767 7676

⊖ Tooting Bec/Tooting Broadway

🍴 Indian

🕐 daily 12.00–24.00

🔲 Mastercard, Visa ■ no service added

££ starters £1.95–£3.25 ■ mains £5.25–£8.95 ■ sides £3.50–£3.95
■ desserts £1.50–£2.95 ■ lunch special (12.00 to 18.00) £3.95
■ unlicensed (BYO)

✪ Good food, great value

**What can you say about a place that has two huge standard
lamps,** each made from an upturned, highly ornate Victorian
drainpipe, topped with a large karahi? When it comes to interior
design, Masaledar provides plenty of surprises, and a feeling of
spaciousness. This is a busy and friendly place that is obviously a
mainstay for many locals both for eating in and takeaways. The food
is fresh, well spiced and cheap – vegetable curries and meat curries
are sound and at bargain prices. Stick to the simple home-style dishes
here and your reward will be well-balanced comfort food. For starters
there are samosas – meat or vegetable. Or try the chicken wings from
the tandoor, or the delicious lamb chops. You might move on to a
rich chicken or lamb biryani, or try a classic dish like methi gosht –
this is strongly flavoured and delicious, guaranteed to leave you with
fenugreek seeping from your pores for days to come. Then there's the
rich and satisfying lamb Masaledar, which is disarmingly described
as 'our house dish cooked to tantalise your taste buds'. The freshly
made breads are terrific, especially the thin rotis. Although there is
no alcohol sold here, the proprietors allow BYO without making a
charge, so take some quenchers with you. Look out for the various
deals that range from 'all-day lunch platter' to 'birthdays, parties,
conferences – private parties of up to 120'.

Polish White Eagle Club

211 Balham High Road, SW17 ■ 020 8672 1723

⊖ Balham

🍽 Polish

🕒 Sun to Fri 12.00–15.00 & 18.00–23.00; Sat 12.00–22.30

🕸 www.whiteeagleclub.co.uk

🖪 all major credit cards except AmEx ■ 10% service added for parties over 5

££ starters £2.75–£4.95 ■ mains £5.95–£14.95 ■ sides £1.95–£3.15 ■ desserts £1.50–£3.75 ■ set lunch £7 (soup & main) set dinner £9.90 (soup & main) ■ lowest bottle price £11

✪ Hearty Polish food, charming people

The White Eagle Club is a large and imposing building on Balham High Road. Tacked onto one side is the Balham Spiritualist Church and, as you climb the steps, you may pass a sandwich board advertising salsa classes. Ignore both attractions – you are here to dine. Ferret your way through the bar to the surprisingly spacious dining room. Sit down and give yourself time to take in the décor; it is implausible but they have managed to include every paintwork technique, and nearly all of the design excesses from three series of *Changing Rooms*. Design students should come here for blinis and a good stare. Starters include four different soups; platters of herrings; Polish smoked meats; a giant portion of blini with smoked salmon and caviar – no frills, no fripperies. Crack open a bottle of one of the five different Polish beers and tuck in. Main courses are formidable 'bigos my lwski z ziemniakmi puree' is the famous hunter's stew – sausage, sauerkraut and onions combining to make a real rib sticker. Or go for roast duck with wild mushroom sauce and dumplings; a Vienna schnitzel with a fried egg; a huge knuckle of pork; or a plate-sized potato pancake folded around a dollop of goulash. Puds are pretty cakey – an obdurate cheesecake; apple cake; and the alluringly named 'fancy cake'. This is a very charming place, hearty food, strong drinks, modest bills and a warm welcome.

The Earl Spencer

, 260 Merton Road, SW18 ■ 020 8870 9244

⊖ Southfields

🍽 Modern British/gastropub

🕐 Mon to Sat 12.30–15.00 & 19.00–22.30; Sun 12.30–15.30 & 19.00–22.00

🖱 www.theearlspencer.co.uk

🖬 Mastercard, Visa ■ no service added

££ starters £5–£7.50 ■ mains £7.00–£11.50 ■ sides £2.50–£3.50 ■ desserts £4.50–£6.50 ■ lowest bottle price £11

✪ Good pub, good gastro

The Earl Spencer is an old-style gastropub and it is no surprise that it is a past winner of Pub of the Year. There are few design fripperies, the room is plain, large and bare. The bar serves decent beer. Service is friendly, and the wine list offers sound value. The menu is an ever-changing one: things run out, dishes are seasonal, but the standard of cooking remains pretty high. As you read the menu dishes merge from starters to mains but you could start with half a pint of home-smoked shell-on prawns, with aioli and lemon; a seasonal soup like winter minestrone with pesto and Borlotti beans; or a home-made pork and chicken liver terrine served with piccalilli. Then move on to the bowl of steamed mussels with white wine and tarragon; the warm tart of melted onion, Cheddar and tomato; a whole baked plaice, new potatoes, broccoli and parsley sauce; meatballs with spaghetti – an oldie but a goodie – or a chargrilled pork loin chop with a ham and potato gratin. There's no pretentious presentation, no towering mounds or artful squiggles. You get good, fresh, well-cooked food. Puds range from the straightforward: sticky ginger pudding, toffee sauce; to the downright self-indulgent – black velvet sorbet (which is made with Guinness and blackcurrant), or an apricot and almond tart served with crème Anglaise. There is also an ambitious plate of fine cheeses. This is how gastropub food should be.

Tower Bridge

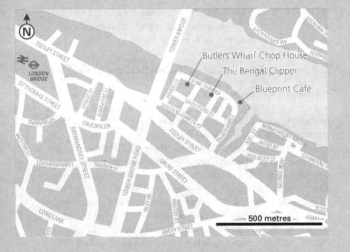

The Bengal Clipper

Shad Thames, SE1 ■ 020 7357 9001

⊖ Tower Hill

🍽 Indian

🕐 Mon to Sat 12.00–14.30 & 18.00–23.30, Sun 12.00 –16.00 (buffet)

🖰 www.bengalclipper.co.uk

🖻 all major credit cards ■ 12.5% optional service added

££ starters £4.75–£7.95 ■ mains £9.50–£18 ■ sides £2.25–£4.95
■ desserts £3.15–£5.95 ■ banquet £25 per person (4 people or
multiples of 4) ■ lowest bottle price £14.95

❂ Large and glossy, but still a curry house

The red jacketed waiters swarm around this 130-seat restaurant
while the pianist improvises energetically on the grand piano which
has been squeezed in between the front door and the gents. Rather
charmingly, the Bengal Clipper takes a pride in both its décor and its
service (which is very smooth indeed). The customer base, however, is
more interested in a good curry, often after they have already taken
on board a good deal of refreshment. The menu descriptions may be
a tad florid but the curries are old fashioned – there's a good deal of
food colouring used; and the predominant flavour is sweet followed
closely by hot, chilli hot. Stick to the familiar High Street dishes and
you will not be disappointed. Starters include chicken 65; a Goan fish
masala; plus crab cakes and kebabs; crisp fried okra; and everything
up to and including 'The Bengal Clipper's version of the onion bhaji'.
The long list of main course sings from the same hymn sheet: there's
butter chicken; rogan josh; chicken tikka shashlik; several prawn
dishes including gold chingri pardnashin – large prawns served in a
coconut shell; or gosht dalcha, which is rich and heavy with spices.
The vegetable dishes include some hidden gems, such as the simple
combination of yellow lentils and spinach. It's best to use the Bengal
Clipper in exactly the same way as the other customers – a handy
place for a decent curry.

Blueprint Café

Design Museum, Shad Thames, SE1 ■ 020 7378 7031

 Tower Hill

 British

🕐 Mon to Sat 12.00–15.00 & 18.00–23.00; Sun 12.00–16.00

🖱 www.danddlondon.com

🗄 all major credit cards ■ 12.5% optional service added

££ starters £5–£8 ■ mains £10–£18 ■ sides £2.50–£3
■ desserts £5–£7.50 ■ set meal Sun £17.50 (3 courses)
■ lowest bottle price £15

⭐ Seriously good cooking, splendid view

The Blueprint Café is one of those restaurants that has been quietly going about its business for so long that it has merged imperceptibly into the background. If the Blueprint had opened in the last year or so it would be attracting rave reviews and people would be mobbing the place. Consider just two points: there's a great-value set menu, and a secondary wine list that offers twenty decent wines at knockdown prices. The dining room is modern but unthreatening, and occupies a glass-fronted box jutting out towards the river – the views of Tower Bridge are amazing. The food is very good indeed. The menu changes every day and is market driven. How about nettle and celery soup? Or beetroot, soft-boiled egg and horseradish? Or there might be preserved garlic, tapenade and goat's cheese – light and lemony goat's cheese on toast, with coarsely chopped olive tapenade, and a whole head of garlic softened and sweetened by slow cooking. Or maybe a warm smoked eel sandwich with red onion pickle appeals? The mains carry on the theme with fresh seasonal dishes: halibut with parsley and anchovy sauce; a tart made with Durrus cheese, potatoes and rosemary; beef and parsley pie – slow-cooked beef in gravy rich with parsley butter. What a good pie! Poached turbot with morels successfully teams a huge chunk of plain steamed fish with a cream sauce. Puds range from almond tart to crème brûlée, by way of a very rich choco-laden gâteau, the St Emilion.

Butlers Wharf Chop House

36e Shad Thames, SE1 ▪ 020 7403 3403

 Tower Hill

🍽 British

🕐 Mon to Sat 12.00–15.00 & 18.00–23.00; Sun 12.00–15.00

🖱 www.danddlondon.com

▤ all major credit cards ▪ 12.5% optional service added

££ starters £6–£24 ▪ mains £14–£26 ▪ sides £1.95–£4.50
▪ desserts £5.59–£8.50 ▪ lunch menu £22 & £26
▪ lowest bottle price £17.50

✪ Flying the flag for Brit producers

Butlers Wharf Chop House really deserves everyone's support, for this is a restaurant that makes a genuine attempt to showcase the best of British produce. There's superb British meat, splendid fish, and simply epic British and Irish cheeses. What's more, the Chop House wisely caters for all, whether you want a simple dish at the bar, a well-priced set lunch, or an extravagant dinner. You'll also find whimsical seasonal specials; in May there may be 'braised grey squirrel and Guinness stew with horseradish dumplings' – very rich and delicious. The dining room is spacious and bright, and the view of Tower Bridge a delight, especially from a terrace table on a warm summer's evening. The menu changes regularly, but tends to feature starters such as potted Morecambe Bay shrimps; goats' cheese and caramelised red onion tart; or Loch Fyne smoked salmon. Mains will include dishes like fish and chips with mushy peas; steak and kidney pudding; and roast wild boar with spring greens; as well as the house specialities such as a flawless roast beef with suitable trimmings. After that you just might be able to find room for a pud like rhubarb crumble tart with vanilla ice cream, even if the sticky toffee pudding is a dish too far. Dinner follows the same principles, but is priced à la carte. Service is friendly even when things are busy (which they usually are).

West

Barnes, Sheen and Kew

The Brown Dog

28 Cross Street, SW13 ■ 020 8392 2200

⊖ Barnes Bridge BR

📶 Modern British/gastropub

🕐 Mon to Fri 12.00–15.00 & 19.00–22.00; Sat 12.00–15.30 & 19.00–22.00; Sun 12.00–15.30 & 19.00–21.00

🖰 www.thebrowndog.co.uk

🖃 all major credit cards ■ 12.5% optional service added for parties of 6 or more

££ starters £4–£8.50 ■ mains £12.50–£16.50 ■ desserts £5–£5.50 ■ lowest bottle price £14.50

✪ Restaurant cooking at restaurant prices

The Brown Dog is the latest incarnation of this strange ex-Watneys pub that is hidden away in the houses behind the school. It's unlikely that anyone would ever happen upon it by accident. The Dog is an elder sibling to the Wellington (see p. 45) and its proprietors have a good grasp of what makes a good gastropub great. The standard of cooking here would be the envy of many larger, posher, restaurants. It may be seen as pricey, but the locals pack the place – no doubt grateful for good food, simple presentation and an informal atmosphere. The menu changes daily and starters range from chargrilled lemon thyme sardines to a belting smoked ham hock terrine with celeriac remoulade, confit prunes and a leaf salad (everything about this dish is right, good remoulade, well-seasoned terrine, nice little salad, good toast, simple presentation). Mains offer pan-fried pollack with samphire; 48-day aged rump steak from the 'Ginger Pig Butchery'; or a rack of Welsh lamb (perfectly cooked) on a bed of petit pois à la Francaise with some new potatoes and a little salad of mixed leaves with slivers of poached lamb's tongue. This is a very good dish, seasonal and satisfying. Desserts veer from a good cheese option to raspberry and chocolate Eton mess. You'll also find well-kept real ales, an unaggressively priced wine list, and cheerful service. Your only problem is finding the place.

The Glasshouse

14 Station Parade, Kew Gardens, Surrey ■ 020 8940 6777

⊖ Kew Gardens

🍴 Modern British

🕐 Mon to Fri 12.00–14.30 & 18.30–22.30; Sat 12.00–14.30 &
18.30–22.30; Sun 12.30–15.00 & 19.30–22.00

🖰 www.glasshouserestaurant.co.uk

🗗 all major credit cards ■ 12.5% optional service added

££ lunch £23.50 (3 courses) ■ dinner £35 (3 courses) ■ tasting menu
(Mon-Fri) £50 ■ lowest bottle price £16

✪ Elegant restaurant, elegant cooking

The Glasshouse has settled into its dual role, part local hero and
part Michelin-starred destination restaurant. Chef Anthony Boyd
honed his craft at the much-decorated Square (see p. 105) and
Chez Bruce (see p. 332). At The Glasshouse he has developed a style
of his own. The interior has a clean-cut, modern feel to it and the
comfortable chairs are worthy of a special mention. The food is good.
Very good. After a slight blip when the menu briefly went à la carte
normal service was resumed with two very competitive fixed-price
offers, while for the full Michelin experience there's a multi-course
tasting menu. The imaginative and straightforward cooking owes
much to French cuisine. Starters range from foie gras, confit hare and
artichoke terrine; to celeriac soup with braised oxtail and horseradish
Chantilly; or a warm salad of wood pigeon with balsamic vinegar and
deep-fried truffled egg. Mains may include steamed sea bass with
rice noodles, crab, chilli and garlic; roast duck breast and pastilla of
leg with Jerusalem artichoke purée; or braised shank of venison with
carrot, swede and potato mash. Puddings have a deft touch and
include favourites like Pedro Ximenez sherry trifle; prune and Calvados
ice cream with shortbread; or a hot chocolate mousse with milk
chocolate sorbet. The wine list is short and thoughtfully drawn up,
with one or two unusual selections.

Mango and Silk

199 Upper Richmond Road West, SW14 ■ 020 8876 6220

⊖ BR Mortlake

🍴 Indian

🕐 Tues to Fri 18.00–22.00; Sat & Sun 12.00–15.00 & 18.00–22.30

🖱 www.mangoandsilk.co.uk

🖶 all major credit cards ■ no service added

££ starters £3.95–£5.50 ■ mains £6.95–£8.25 ■ sides £1–£2.95
■ lowest bottle price £10.50

⭐ Famous chef cooks local

Udit Sarkhel has had a glittering career. After several glory years in
the kitchens at the Bombay Brasserie, he set up his own restaurant in
SW18 and went on to win a hatful of awards. So it was somewhat
disappointing when Sarkhel's shut and Udit moved to Brighton,
deciding to channel his creativity into painting. The good news is that
he's back in the kitchen. Mango & Silk opened towards the end of
2007 and the short menu features many of Udit's signature dishes.
This place is a local hero – sophisticated cooking and spicing, friendly
service, modern décor and gentle prices! Just about everything you
need from the perfect local restaurant. Starters include the famous
chicken 'sixers' from Hyderabad – meaty chicken wings given the
hot and sharp treatment; also splendid lamb samosas accompanied
by chickpeas; and Goan prawn balchao – large prawns and a rich
sauce served with bread. What impresses most about these dishes is
the integrity of the spicing; they are not dumbed down in any way
and the 'hot' dishes are gratifyingly hot. Mains continue the theme,
with jardaloo ma gosht – a Parsee dish of lamb and apricots; a
wonderful prawn patia – king prawns in rich gravy with chunks of
aubergine and red pumpkin; kozhi vartha kosambu – a South Indian
chicken curry made with coconut. The breads are particularly fresh
and praiseworthy. Great food and reasonable prices. Welcome back
Mr Sarkhel.

Riva

169 Church Road, SW13 ■ 020 8748 0434   ♿

⊖ BR Barnes Bridge

🍴 Italian

🕐 Mon to Fri 12.00–14.30 & 19.00–23.00; Sat 19.00–23.30;
Sun 12.00–14.30 & 19.00–21.30

🗄 all major credit cards ■ 12.5% optional service added

££ starters £8–£12.50 ■ mains £13.50–£23 ■ sides £2.50–£3.50
■ desserts £6.50–£7 ■ lowest bottle price £15

✪ Authentic Italian food

Andrea Riva has always been something of a darling of the media
and his sophisticated little restaurant exerts a powerful pull, strong
enough to convince even fashionable folk to make the dangerous
journey to the south bank of the Thames. When they get there they
find a rather conservative-looking restaurant, with a narrow dining
room decorated in dull greens and faded parchment, and chairs that
have clearly seen service in church. As far as the cuisine goes, Riva
provides the genuine article, so most customers are either delighted
or disappointed, depending on how well they know their Italian food.
The menu changes regularly with the seasons. Starters are good. The
frittelle is a tempura-like dish of deep-fried Mediterranean prawn,
salt cod cakes, calamari, sage and basil, with a balsamic dip. Serious
Italian food fans, however, will find it hard to resist the pasta and
risotti – papardelle con fave e guanciale teams broad beans and pigs'
cheeks. Among the main courses, branzino al rucola stands out – a
fillet of sea bass with a rocket and tomato sauce served with baked
fennel and broccoli. Fegato burro con salvia is a classic – calf's liver
served with sage butter, mashed potato and red onions. There is a
long dessert list ranging from tiramisù and panna cotta to crespelle di
prugne con mirtilli. The house wines are all priced at a very accessible
level.

Sonny's

94 Church Road, SW13 ■ 020 8748 0393

⊖ BR Barnes Bridge

ⅉ◐ Modern British

🕐 Mon to Sat 12.30–14.30 & 19.30–23.00; Sun 12.30–15.00

🕙 www.sonnys.co.uk

🖥 all major credit cards ■ 12.5% optional service added

££ starters £4.75–£9.50 ■ mains £10.50–£18.50 ■ sides £2.50–£3
■ desserts £5.50–£7.50 ■ menus: set lunch Mon to Sat £13.50 &
£16.50 ■ set dinner Mon to Thurs £17.50 & £19.50
■ Sunday lunch £21.50 ■ lowest bottle price £12.50

✪ The outlook is sunny

Perceptive Barnes-ites have been supporting Sonny's since Modern
British cuisine was just a twinkle in a telly chef's eye. The interior of
the resto is modern but gratifyingly unthreatening and there is a busy,
casual feel about the place. Sonny's shop next door sells a good many
of those little delicacies that you would otherwise have to journey to
the West End to secure. But do not be deceived into thinking that the
cooking here is suburban. The menu changes to reflect the seasons,
so you might find starters like duck liver parfait Cadillac raisins; or
a classic steak tartare with pain Poilaine; or pan-fried gnocchi with
truffle oil. Main courses may include stalwarts like confit pork belly,
pommes purée, spinach and Madeira jus. But there is room for a
splendid veggie option like a double-baked cheese soufflé; and a
good fish dish like poached halibut in lobster broth; or steamed
scallops with cauliflower purée and caviar velouté. The service is
welcoming and the wine list provides some sound bottles at sound
prices. Puddings are comfortable: tarte Tatin is served with Calvados
ice cream; or choose crème brulée or sticky toffee pudding. There's
also a decent set dinner Monday to Thursday. Sonny's is the kind of
restaurant we would all like to have at the end of the road; friendly,
serving good food, and comfortable.

→ For branches, see index

Chelsea and Fulham

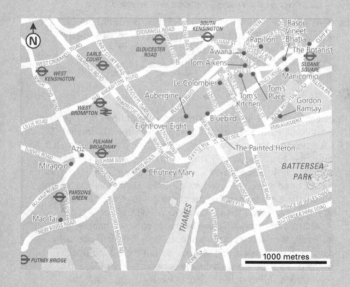

Aubergine

11 Park Walk, SW10 ■ 020 7352 3449

South Kensington

French

Mon to Fri 12.00–14.30 & 19.00–23.00; Sat 19.00–23.00

www.auberginerestaurant.co.uk

all major credit cards ■ 12.5% optional service added

££ lunch £29 (3 courses, £34 with wine) ■ dinner £68 (3 courses)
■ gourmand £78 (7 courses, £132 with wine)
■ lowest bottle price £22

⭐ Good cooking based on quality ingredients

It's hard to imagine it, but a decade or so ago this neck of the woods was a bleakish place to eat out – Aubergine changed all that, and it merits the accolade 'old-established'. Now it is both familiar enough, and light and airy enough, for even the most discerning of ladies who lunch. The best of everything in season and a talented kitchen make for a busy place, so booking is a must. William Drabble is a very skilful chef. A £34 lunch that comprises a nage of brill with soft herbs, followed by ballotine of guinea fowl with creamed chanterelles and then pistachio soufflé chocolate sauce, plus all the pomp and ceremony of a serious restaurant and half a bottle of decent wine, is an undeniable bargain. Even at full throttle the main dinner menu is still priced reasonably for cooking of this calibre. Starters may include ravioli of oxtail, caramelised onions and foie gras; or pan-fried red mullet with braised Jerusalem artichokes. Main courses include dishes such as fillet of John Dory with salsify; and best end of lamb with garlic purée. These are well-conceived and well-executed dishes, beautifully presented. Desserts are equally accomplished – white chocolate bavarois with bottled cherries; confit pineapple with coconut ice cream. The service is accomplished and unobtrusive, and the wine list can test the bravest wallet.

Awana

85 Sloane Avenue, SW3 ■ 020 7584 8880   ♿

⊖ Knightsbridge/Sloane Square

🍴 Malaysian

🕐 Mon to Wed 12.00–15.00 & 18.00–23.00; Thurs to Sat 12.00–15.00
  & 18.00–23.30; Sun 12.00–15.00 & 18.00–22.30

🖰 www.awana.co.uk

🖽 all major credit cards ■ 12.5% optional service added

££ starters £6.50–£10.50 ■ satay bar from £5 ■ mains £9.50–£25
  ■ sides £2–£3.50 ■ desserts £6–£7.50 ■ 10-course tasting menu £36
  ■ lowest bottle price £19

✪ Full-on Malaysian opulence

There is more highly polished hardwood here than even the
trendiest of restaurant designers could have dreamt of. Awana is a
London representative of an international restaurant group and we
are talking slick and Ritzy rather than cheap and cheerful. Which
makes a change, as most of London's Malaysian restaurants fall into
the latter category. The 'Satay Bar' dishes up a gently spicy peanut
sauce with a broad array of little skewers – salt water tiger prawns,
scallops, corn-fed chicken, fillet of lamb; there's even a veggie option:
'tofu and tomato'. In the main, the satay is well done. Other notable
starters are rusuk kambing panggang – grilled lamb ribs; and the
rojak buah, which is a Malaysian sour fruit salad. Then there are
traditional soups – sup kambing is a thick lamb soup not dissimilar
to a Welsh cawl, but with the flavour sharpened by Malay herbs. The
classic curries such as kari ikan, red snapper in coconut curry, are well
handled. And there are also various stir-fries and rice dishes – the ikan
bawal putih is a whole pomfret fried with a ginger crust. Service is
very friendly and this restaurant is unusual in that it is a Malay resto
with a sommelier and a lengthy wine list. Desserts include those
famously bizarre Malay concoctions that team cooked beans with
shaved ice, but the home-made ice creams are the best option – jack
fruit, tamarind.

Aziz
24–32 Vanston Place, SW6 ■ 020 7386 0086   ♿

⊖ Fulham Broadway

🍽 Middle Eastern

🕐 Mon to Sat 12.00–24.30; Sun 10.00–24.00

🖰 www.delaziz.co.uk   smokers – seating outside

🗄 all major credit cards ■ 12.5% optional service added

££ mezze £3–£7.50 ■ mains £7.50–£18 ■ desserts £5–£5.50
   ■ menus: lunch £12.50 (2 courses); dinner £18 (3 courses)
   ■ lowest bottle price £12.50

✪ Comfortable Middle Eastern eating

Aziz has a very large and dominant site on Vanston Place, partly because it is neighbour to del'Aziz, which is a shop and deli (and, it must be admitted, virtually another restaurant) – they are all part of the same operation. Proximity to counters laden with good things benefits the vibe, which is helpful, as the restaurant known formally as Aziz looks very posh. There is no hint of Middle Eastern scruffiness here: all is modern, and all is elegant. Flavours are upfront, and prices are not that fierce. The menu splits into a number of sections – you'll find hot and cold mezze, then main course dishes. From the mezze, trad dishes like houmous and marinated baby aubergine with sumac and chilli are done well. 'Hot mezze' such as the spicy beef sausage stew in pomegranate syrup or the minced lamb and apricot keftas borek are elegant and delicious, though they blur the line with main courses. These are divided up in complex fashion. There are grills – merguez, kebabs, and platters. Then 'from the hob and oven' – tagines, roast meats. And finally 'catch of the day' – red mullet, sea bass, sole … as available. Desserts are particularly fine: warm fruit katafi with yoghurt and honey, Middle Eastern pastries. The wine list has a good spread and gentle prices. At Christmas del'Aziz does a good trade in cooked turkeys to carry home. Scrooge would be pleased.

→ For branches, see index or website

Bluebird

350 King's Road, SW10 ■ 020 7559 1000

● Sloane Square

🍽 Modern British

🕐 Mon to Fri 12.00–15.00 & 18.00–23.00; Sat 12.00–16.00 &
18.00–23.00; Sun 12.00–16.00 & 18.00–22.00

🖰 www.bluebird-restaurant.com

🖬 all major credit cards ■ 12.5% optional service added

££ starters £5.50–£13.50 ■ mains £7.50–£30 ■ sides £3.75–£5.50
■ desserts £6–£8.50 ■ set menus (Mon to Fri 12.00–15.00 and Mon
to Sun 18.00–19.00): £12.95 (2 courses) & £15.95 (3 courses);
■ lowest bottle price £18

✪ Honest food, ingredient-driven menu

In the spring of 2007 Bluebird celebrated its tenth birthday with
a rigorous makeover. The new bar and dining areas seem to flow
into one another and there's a more homely feel to the place. The
dining chairs are comfortable and the service manages to be both
slick and friendly at the same time. The menu here has morphed
a good deal since the last edition of this guide. The emphasis on
regional produce is still there but it has been tamed somewhat and
dishes are simpler. Starters range from a Montgomery cheddar and
spinach tart; to potted crab and Morecambe Bay shrimps; or Loch
Fyne smoked salmon. Then there are old favourites like Caesar salad;
shellfish minestrone; macaroni cheese; and steak and ale pie. It's as
if the kitchen has been told to rein things in a little. The mains are
simple, salt-marsh lamb comes with lentils, ceps and bacon; there's
a rib-eye steak from Dedham and it comes chargrilled with chips and
red-wine butter; and there's a salmon fishcake with sauce gribiche.
Puds continue to stress quality ingredients so you could enjoy warm
Ambrosia rice pudding with Agen prunes. Despite being a large
restaurant (together the bar and dining room seat 200), things seem
to run pretty smoothly. The wine list ranges from middleweights to
heavyweights, but there seems to be something to suit most Chelsea
pockets.

The Botanist

7 Sloane Square, SW1 ■ 020 7730 0077

⊖ Sloane Square

🍴 Modern British/gastropub

🕐 Breakfast: Mon to Fri 08.00–12.00; Sat & Sun 09.00–12.00. Lunch: Mon to Fri 12.00–15.30; Sat (brunch) 12.00–16.30; Sun (lunch) 12.00–16.30. Tea: Mon to Sat 15.30–18.00. Dinner daily 18.00–22.30

🖱 www.thebotanistsloanesquare.com

🖻 all major credit cards excluding AmEx ■ 12.5% optional service added

££ starters £5–£14 ■ mains £12–£24 ■ sides £3.50–£4 ■ desserts £5–£6
■ lowest bottle price £15

⭐ Gastropub meets Brasserie

As you will have gathered from the complicated, what's served-when entries under 'opening times' above, the Botanist is trying hard to be an all-day, all-singing Brasserie. It opened in June 2008 and superficially has much in common with the team of gastropubs built up by the Martin brothers (see the Gun, p. 234, and the White Swan, p. 229, to name but two). It fits seamlessly into its surroundings – in this instance Sloane Square – and offers the kind of food that the locals want to eat. The breakfast menu ranges from granola to kipper by way of scrambled eggs; the afternoon tea provides cakes and scones; and the bar menu acts as 'sweeper' and dishes up a decent fishcake or steak tartare to take care of any gap between mealtimes. The main menu features starters such as pan-fried scallops, curried apple and potato purée, golden raisin and caper beurre noisette; Cornish crab and avocado ravioli; or a warm Stilton and white onion tart served with a roast pear and rocket salad. Mains include the seriously complicated 'Botanist seasonal salad' – green and white asparagus, baby spinach, baby gem, radicchio, sun blush tomatoes, fresh peas, broad beans, goats' cheese, and Jersey Royal potatoes all dressed with a lemon vinaigrette; or lemon sole meunière; roast lamb neck; or braised shoulder and haricot bean cassoulet. The Botanist is a busy place, but thankfully the service is slick enough to keep pace.

Chutney Mary

535 King's Road, SW10 ■ 020 7351 3113

⊖ Fulham Broadway

⑩ Indian

🕐 Mon to Fri 18.30–23.00; Sat 12.30–14.30 & 18.30–23.00;
Sun 12.30–15.00 & 18.30–22.30

🖰 www.realindianfood.com

🖥 all major credit cards ■ 12.5% optional service added

££ starters £6.75–£12.50 ■ mains £15.50–£21 ■ sides £1.75–£7.50
■ desserts £5.50 ■ menus: Sat & Sun brunch £22 (3 courses)
■ lowest bottle price £17.50

✪ Elite Indian restaurant

Chutney Mary is an elegant place to eat and the dramatic look
of the dining room owes a good deal to an able theatrical lighting
designer. But the men in the kitchen know their job and turn out
refined Indian food. This is not a cheap restaurant, but the quality
of cooking is such that it comes under the heading of 'justifiable
extravagance'. Start with the murgh nahari shorba – a light chicken
broth with aromatic spices. Delicious. Or there's the tokri chaat,
which is an edible basket filled with various street-food treats and
topped with yogurt and chutney. Or the crispy shrimp; or the duck
galouti – very tender kebabs served with blueberry chutney. Mains
are equally impressive. Mangalore jheenga are giant prawns, chilli-hot
and tamarind-tangy. There's a Goan green chicken curry; lamb nalli
korma (a kind of slow-cooked, mild-spiced, osso buco) or Keralan
pepper roast duck with a cinnamon coconut sauce. Side dishes are
good and there's a Punjabi vegetarian thali that combines kadai
paneer, tadka dal, aloo ghobi, bhuna palak and wadi pulao. Breads
are good here – try lacchi paratha. The dessert menu is also inspired
– there is a garam masala brûlée, or a dark chocolate fondant served
with orange blossom lassi. Service is attentive and there is a book-
sized wine list backed by a wine cellar that would put many French
establishments to shame.

Le Colombier

145 Dovehouse Street, SW3 ■ 020 7351 1155

⊖ South Kensington

🍴 Very French

🕐 Mon to Sat 12.00–15.00 & 18.30–22.30; Sun 12.00–15.30 &
18.30–22.00

🖰 www.lecolombier-sw3.co.uk

🗗 all major credit cards ■ 12.5% optional service added

££ starters £5.80–£13.20 ■ mains £13.50–£25.80 ■ sides £2.50
■ desserts £5.80 ■ set menu £16.50 (2 courses)
■ lowest bottle price £14.90

✪ The Parisian quartier of Chelsea

Viewed from the pavement outside on Dovehouse Street you can
see that Le Colombier was once a classic, English, street-corner pub.
But now it's a pub that has a small, glassed-in area in front, covered
with tables and chairs. How very Parisian, you might think, and you
would be right. This is a French place. It is run by Monsieur Garnier,
who has spent most of his career in the slicker reaches of London's
restaurant business. With his own place he has reverted to type and
everything is very, very French. The menu is French, the cooking is
French, the service is French and the décor is French. The cooking is
about as good as you would have found in a smart Routiers in rural
France during the 1970s. Starters include such bistro classics as oeufs
pochés en meurette; soupe de poisson; and feuilleté d'escargots à la
crème d'ail. And there are oysters; goat's cheese salad; and duck liver
terrine. Listed under 'les poissons' there is sole de Douvres meunière
and coquilles St Jacques with a truffled cauliflower purée. Under 'les
viandes' there is steak tartare with pommes frites; filet de boeuf au
poivre; and fricassée de rognons de veau à la Dijonnaise. Under 'les
grillades' are the steaks and chops. Puddings include crêpes Suzette.
Both the service and the approach to wine are as French as the menu.

Eight over Eight

392 King's Road, SW3 ▪ 020 7349 9934

⊖ Sloane Square

🍴 Asian eclectic

🕐 Mon to Fri 12.00–15.00 & 18.00–23.00; Sat 12.00–16.00 & 18.00–23.00; Sun 18.00–22.30

🖰 www.rickerrestaurants.com

🖼 all major credit cards ▪ 12.5% optional service added

££ starters £3.50–£6.50 ▪ mains £9–£21.50 ▪ sides £3–£4.50
    ▪ desserts £5–£6.50 ▪ lunch Mon to Sat £15 (2 courses + wine)
    ▪ lowest bottle price £14

✪ Chelsea but inscrutable

The name Eight over Eight derives from some obscure tenet of Oriental numerology – the East seems to have taken the art of 'lucky numbers' to another level. This establishment is part of Will Ricker's expanding empire that also includes E&O and XO (see pp. 114 & 288). The front part of Eight over Eight is dedicated to a large and busy bar where chic cocktails predominate, while the rear is the dining room and is edged with booths. The cuisine is described as 'Pan Asian', so dim sum jostles with futo maki rolls, tempura, sashimi and curries, before the menu leads on to salads, then barbecued and roasted meats. It is an eclectic selection and there is something on the menu to whet any appetite. Start with old favourites like chilli-salt squid; or pork spare ribs; or prawn and chive dumplings, none of which are cheap, but all of which are presented very elegantly. The sashimi and roll sushi is fresh and good. The curries are well spiced, and the salads most interesting – how does duck, watermelon and cashew salad appeal? Or maybe warm chicken and coconut salad? Service is slick and drinks range from cocktails to cold beer by way of a serious wine list. But do beware, picking lots of dishes can mean ending up with lots of middling price tags and a rather grown-up bill.

→ For branches, see index or website

Gordon Ramsay

68–69 Royal Hospital Road, SW3 ■ 020 7352 4441 &

⊖ Sloane Square

◉ French

⏱ Mon to Fri 12.00–14.00 & 18.30–23.00

⊕ www.gordonramsay.com

⊟ all major credit cards ■ 12.5% optional service added

££ set lunch £40 (3 courses) ■ à la carte £85 (3 courses) & £110 (7 courses) ■ lowest bottle price £20

⭐ Temple to gastronomy

The Gordon Ramsay empire continues to expand around the world, but even with the increasing television workload and the seemingly clockwork addition of yet more restaurants, head office in Chelsea continues to be packed. As ever, the set lunch is a bargain for such Michelin-endorsed, three-star gastronomy – as long as you can get a booking. The menu here evolves gently. On the main menu, look out for a ravioli of lobster, langoustine and salmon poached in a bisque and served with a lemongrass and chervil velouté; or sautéed foie gras with roast lamb sweetbreads, Cabernet Sauvignon vinegar and almond velouté; or slow-braised pied de cochon pressed then pan fried with poached quail's egg – as robust and delicious as you could wish for. And those are just starters! Mains intrigue: chargrilled monkfish tail with confit duck, layered aubergine and red wine sauce; oven-roast Bresse pigeon with grilled polenta and crisp lardons, golden beetroot and date sauce. Even the desserts show novel combinations – Granny Smith parfait with honeycomb, bitter chocolate and Champagne foam. To order successfully here, just pick a dish or an ingredient you like and see how it arrives; you won't be disappointed. The system is that reservations can only be made two months in advance, so there is the usual phone scrum – or you could try for a cancellation at the last minute.

Manicomio

85 Duke of York Square, SW3 ■ 020 7730 3366 &

⊖ Sloane Square

🍽 Italian

🕐 Mon to Fri 12.00–15.00 & 18.30–22.30; Sat 12.00–17.00 (brunch) &
18.30–22.30; Sun 12.00–16.00 (brunch) & 18.30–22.00

🖰 www.manicomio.co.uk

🖯 all major credit cards ■ 12.5% optional service added

££ starters £8.50–£10.75 ■ mains £9.50–£24 ■ sides £4–£5
■ desserts £6.50–£9 ■ lowest bottle price £14.50

✪ Comfortable, neighbourhood Italian

Manicomio is an easy-going restaurant that manages to bring
off a difficult trick. Despite being a relatively new project, it gives
the impression of being long established, due to genuine brickwork
and middle-of-the-road décor. The dining room was carved out of
one end of the Duke of York barracks. There are some seats outside,
which is great if the weather is clement, dodgy when relying on the
space heaters. Service is slick and Italian, which description accurately
sums up most of the wine list as well. The cooking is good and the
menu broadly seasonal. Manicomio is not a place to look for gentle,
peasant Italian fare, as there is an edge of chic to even the simplest
dishes here – but this is Sloane Square after all. Starters such as
the classic combination of Parma ham, pears and Ubriaco cheese
are done well; or buffalo mozzarella with roast peppers and grilled
aubergines. Also a risotto made with radicchio and red wine. The
pasta dishes are sophisticated: linguine with crab chilli and garlic; or
garganelli with grey mullet. Main courses are modern variations on
old favourites: pot-roast shoulder of veal with lentils and dragoncello;
tiger prawns with scallops and borlotti beans; or chargrilled Label
Anglais chicken. Puds are trad: Giandula chocolate mousse, or
semifreddo al Torrone. The brunch menu served at weekends is a cut-
down version of the à la carte.

Mao Tai

58 New King's Road, SW6 ■ 020 7731 2520

⊖ Parsons Green

🍽 Chinese

🕐 Mon to Sat 18.15–23.30; Sun 12.00–15.00 & 18.15–22.00

🖱 www.maotai.co.uk

🖯 all major credit cards ■ 12.5% optional service added

££ dim sum £4.50–£7.50 (18.15 to 20.00) ■ starters £3.50–£12.50
■ mains £9.50–£26.50 ■ sides £5.50–£12.50 ■ desserts £5–£7.50
■ lowest bottle price £14.50

✪ Polished local Chinese resto

Mao Tai is much more Chelsea than Chinatown, both in
appearance and in the kind of food it serves. It's a pretty restaurant,
cleverly lit, well decorated and with brisk, efficient service. The menu
has evolved over the years and the ground has shifted away from the
fiery Sichuan influences to something more suave that touches base
in Japan, Thailand and all points east. Such surroundings – and, to
be fair, such food – do not come cheap. Still, you'll leave well fed and
well looked-after, as both the cooking and service are slick and chic.
Start with something seafoody from the appetisers menu – razor
clams; scallop ceviche; salt and pepper prawns. Dumplings feature:
try pork and radish; prawn and chive; mushroom and spinach;
prawn and bamboo shoots (served until 20.00). There are also
serious restaurant dishes at serious prices – caramelised black cod,
miso marinade; tenderloin tataki; red snapper with ponzu shoyu;
seafood tobanyaki. Or perhaps black pepper sirloin appeals? Onwards
to sautéed chicken with almonds and yellow bean; or rabbit with
lemongrass and garlic; and even sweet and sour pork with fresh
pineapple. In the vegetable section there's asparagus lily bud and
lotus root; French beans with pork mince and chilli; and an aubergine
lychee curry. In the face of all these rather exalted dishes and rather
exalted prices, the Mao Tai boast may make sense: 'Mao Tai does not
use MSG'.

Miraggio
510 Fulham Road, SW6 ■ 020 7384 9774

⊖ Fulham Broadway

🍽 Italian

🕐 daily 12.30–15.00 & 18.00–23.00

🖱 www.miraggio.co.uk

🖅 all major credit cards ■ 10% optional service added

££ starters £2.50–£11 ■ mains £6.50–£19.50 ■ sides £2.95–£5.50
■ desserts £2.95 –£4.25 ■ lowest bottle price £9.50 (BYO downstairs
– corkage £3.50 a bottle)

✪ Friendly, no-fuss neighbourhood Italian

A bright café-style atmosphere and a simple rustic air belie the
quality behind this family-run establishment. The menu is wide
ranging and comes from the kitchen of 'Mamma Maria'. Your first
sign of this is the appetising choice of antipasti. There are mouth-
watering, wafer-thin strips of chargrilled courgette and aubergine;
nutty little boiled potatoes with virgin olive oil and roughly chopped
flat-leaf parsley; strips of grilled peppers; small and large mushrooms;
and a trad Parmigiano, aubergine and tomato bake with tiny melted
mozzarella cheeses. It's enough to stop even the most jaded foodie
in their tracks. For starters, choose the antipasto Miraggio and you'll
get the best the next door deli has to offer. Otherwise, try beef
carpaccio with rocket and Parmesan, or melanzana alla Parmigiano,
baked aubergine rich with cheese. Pastas include the usual suspects:
fettucine alla Bolognese, and linguine with fresh seafood in tomato
sauce. There are plenty of meat and fish choices too, including
spigola alla griglia, grilled sea bass; calamari alla griglia, a dish
of perfectly cooked squid; and vitello alla Milanese; calves' liver
Veneziana; or lamb fillet wrapped in puff pastry. Puddings include
what is claimed to be the best tiramisù in the area; champagne or
fruits of the forest sorbets; and zoccolette, a home-made profiterole
with a Nutella filling. Service is efficient but friendly and the kitchen is
to the rear, which is good if you like watching cooks at work.

The Painted Heron

112 Cheyne Walk, SW10 ■ 020 7351 5232

⊖ Fulham Broadway

🍴 Indian

🕐 Mon to Fri 12.00–14.30 & 18.00–23.00; Sat 18.00–23.00;
Sun 12.00–14.30 & 18.00–21.30

🖰 www.thepaintedheron.co.uk

🖯 all major credit cards ■ 12.5% optional service added

££ starters £5–£10 ■ mains £11–£18 ■ sides £2.50–£5 ■ desserts £3–£4
■ Sunday lunch set menu £22.50 (3 courses) Sunday lunch platter
£11 & £16 ■ lowest bottle price £15

✪ Sophisticated restaurant, sophisticated flavours

The Painted Heron has got the balance between authenticity and
modernist reinvention about right. The food here is honest, well
spiced, and not too fussily presented. The room is cool and elegant,
no flock wallpaper, nothing over the top. Service is sound and, as in
so many modern Indian establishments, a lot of effort has gone into
the wine list. The standard of cooking is high and it is no wonder
that the Heron has skewered a very long list of awards. Lunches are
quiet, but in the evening this is a busy place, so you should book. The
à la carte menu changes gradually as dishes come and go. Among
the starters may be soft-shell crabs fried in sesame and chilli butter;
tandoori lamb chops with nutmeg; or paneer cheese tikka with spiced
aubergine and pineapple. Mains are well conceived. The spicing is
upfront and enjoyable, and although they are Indian dishes, they are
described in European terms – duck breast in a puréed spinach and
mint curry; wild Alaskan black cod in samphire marinade; guinea fowl
roast with cottage cheese and green chilli paste; diced mutton leg dry
roast with bhuna spices. The vegetable sides will double up as veggie
mains – spicy chick pea and mushroom curry; or spinach and baby
corn with cumin and garlic. There are delicious European-style puds –
apple pie with rose syrup.

Papillon

96 Draycott Avenue, SW3 ▪ 020 7225 2555

⊖ Sloane Square/South Kensington

🍴 French

🕐 Mon to Fri 12.00–15.00 & 18.00–24.00; Sat 12.00–16.00 & 18.00–24.00, Sun 12.00–18.00 & 19.00–22.30

🖑 www.papillonchelsea.co.uk

🖬 all major credit cards ▪ 12.5% optional service added

££ starters £5.75–£16.50 ▪ mains £14.50–£30 ▪ salads £8–£18.50 ▪ desserts £6–£9 ▪ menu du marché £14.50 (2 courses) & £16.50 (3 courses) ▪ lowest bottle price £18

✪ South of France docks in Chelsea

Somehow Papillon sits in its own little bubble of Frenchness. That's not the rough and tumble French peasant kind of Frenchness, but rather the mythical suave and well-heeled part of France towards the South where style is all. The service is Gallic and slick – having somewhere highly civilised and open for breakfast, lunch and dinner must be very handy for Sloanes and Sloaney mummies alike. The room is comfortable and the menu scores a bull's eye with its intended constituency of lunching ladies. There are salads, which are reasonably priced and box the compass from Nord (salad with snails and lardons) all the way to Sud (salad leaves, wild mushrooms, ham and poached egg). The starters range from various soups (including a trad fish soup) to scallops with a parsnip purée and beurre blanc; snails baked in garlic butter; or trad steak tartare. Mains carry on the French-bourgeois-but-smarter feel – sea bream in salt-crust pastry; Dover sole Meunière with steamed potatoes and French beans; braised lamb shank with a ragout of coco beans; Chateaubriand Rossini; roast turbot 'Grand Mère'; and côte de veau rôti with aligot potato (for two). Puds put a modern spin on classic dishes – you could try a coconut and tapioca blancmange with mandarin sorbet! The wine list is well balanced, ranging from the sensible to the sublime with prices to match.

Rasoi Vineet Bhatia

10 Lincoln Street, SW3 ■ 020 7225 1881

⊖ Sloane Square

🍴 Indian

🕐 Mon to Fri 12.00–14.15 & 18.00–23.00; Sat 18.00–23.00

🖰 www.vineetbhatia.com

🗇 all major credit cards ■ 12.5% optional service added

££ starters £10–£18 ■ mains £14–£38 ■ sides £4–£7 ■ desserts £8–£9
■ menus: lunch £21 (2 courses) & £26 (3 courses); gourmand £75 (7
courses, £124 with wine); veg gourmand £69 (7 courses); dégustation
lunch £36 (5 courses, £85 with wine) ■ lowest bottle price £20

⊗ Indian superstar

This restaurant belongs to Vineet Bhatia and his wife. It is small
(eight tables at the back and half a dozen in front), it is classy, and
'this time it's personal'. The food is Michelin two star level (if only we
could rely on their Francophile inspectors agreeing!). This is Indian
food at its finest – simple, intensely flavoured, well-spiced dishes with
inspired combinations of colour and texture. Service is friendly (this is
a family business) and there is a buzz of excitement about the place.
The menu gourmand is a long multi-course affair, full of surprises,
delicious and wholly satisfying. Starters may include a crab platter
comprised of a south Indian crab cake, crab chutney and a crab and
corn samosa. Or wild mushroom khichdi, mini papad and makhani
ice cream; or tandoori quail and potato tikki. From the carte there's
an amazing lobster dish – grilled ginger and chilli lobster, spiced
lobster jus, curry leaf and broccoli khichdi … and then the plate is
dusted at the table with sour spices and cocoa. The lobster is perfectly
cooked and the khichdi is like a spicy risotto, and there's the added
perfume of cocoa. Other mains include tandoori lamb chops, and
a crusted seafood biryani served with raita; or slow-cooked pepper
duck served in a coconut korma sauce with walnut and potato tikki.
The wine list is Chelsea and zips up towards the Château Latour.
There's a pudoholics dessert platter.

→ For branch, see index

Tom Aikens

43 Elystan Street, SW3 ■ 020 7584 2003

⊖ South Kensington

🍽 Modern British

🕒 Mon to Fri 12.00–14.30 & 18.45–23.00

🖱 www.tomaikens.co.uk

🖯 all major credit cards ■ 12.5% optional service added

££ set lunch £29 ■ 3-course à la carte £65 ■ 7-course tasting menu £80
■ 'classic' menu £100 ■ lowest bottle price £20

✪ Fine dining, top cooking

The Tom Aikens restaurant empire continues to grow. As well the
Michelin-spangled Chelsea head office, there's the nearby Tom's
Kitchen (see next page) and his new fish and chip shop Tom's Place
(see the page after that!). As befits fine dining, service here is silky
and the food is sophisticated and considered. A very rewarding place
to eat. Setting aside (and you shouldn't) the set lunch, there's an à
la carte option and the full tasting menu – seven courses and coffee.
All dishes are imaginative, well presented and with good assertive
flavours. From the starters crayfish tails and claws are poached and
served with coco bean purée and mousse and Jabugo ham; while
pickled artichokes are teamed with artichoke mousse and both pink
fir apple and charlotte potatoes; or there's poached ray wing with
apple tapioca, parsley oil, celeriac and apple rémoulade. For mains
Dover sole is poached in red wine; or there's a roast veal sweetbread
with veal shin, polenta and truffle; or salt-marsh lamb served
with a sheep's cheese tart. Puds are also complex and rewarding
– fresh pomegranate with poached quince, pistachio nougat and
pomegranate mousse, or coffee parfait with hazelnut cake, coffee
mousse and coffee crème Anglaise. The wine list is extensive, but
advice is to hand. You should eat here soon: you're worth it!

Tom's Kitchen

27 Cale Street, SW3 ■ 020 7349 0202 &

⊖ South Kensington

|O| Modern British

🕐 Mon to Fri 07.00–10.00 (breakfast) 12.00–15.00 (lunch) & 18.00–22.45 (dinner); Sat 10.00–15.00 (brunch) & 18.00–23.00; Sun 11.00–15.00 (brunch) & 18.00–22.00

🖰 www.tomskitchen.co.uk

🗗 all major credit cards ■ 12.5% optional service added

££ starters £5.50 to £12.50 ■ mains £10.50 to £21 ■ sides £3.50 ■ desserts £6 ■ lowest bottle price £14

✪ A very Chelsea sort of local

Tom Aikens is taking over the neighbourhood, the eponymous H.Q. is just a chef's trot away on the preceding page, and then there's the fish and chipper (see next page). There is a Parisian concept of the 'bistro en face': Tom's Kitchen is not very 'en face', but it certainly feels bistro-like, and is certainly very busy. The high ceilings and bare-looking décor work well, giving an almost refectory feel. The kitchen operates to the side of the dining room and has a 'modesty screen' formed by the high-level pass. The menu bends over backwards to offer normal, straightforward, honest, salt-of-the-earth dishes, but seen from a rather Chelsea viewpoint and with rather Chelsea price tags. Starters may include celeriac remoulade with Bayonne ham and toasted sour dough – good ham, good bread, rather tame remoulade; and beetroot cured salmon; or a red wine risotto with caramelised shallots. Mains range from roast chicken (free range, of course) with Cabernet Sauvignon vinegar and Dijon mustard; to slow-roast pork loin with buttered lentils. Desserts may include chocolate fondant with pecan ice cream; a lemon thyme panna cotta; or home-made vanilla yoghurt with churros. The service is sharp at Tom's Kitchen, which is a good job as the restaurant is a local favourite. The wine list starts steady and then offers scope all the way up to the extravagance zone.

Tom's Place

1a Cale Street, SW3 ■ 020 7351 1806 &

⊖ South Kensington

🍽 Fish & chips

🕐 daily 11.00–23.00

🖱 www.tomsplace.org

🖫 all major credit cards ■ 12.5% optional service added

££ fried fish £8 to £11 ■ bowl food £11.50 to £18 ■ grilled fish £7.50 to £17.50 ■ sides £1 to £3 ■ ice cream £3 ■ lowest bottle price £16

✪ Le patron pêche ici

Why, you are wondering, are there three consecutive pages in this guide featuring restos on the same patch, and run by the same chap? The answer lies in our mission to offer a good spread of restaurants in every part of town. These three diverse restos – a top-end, fine-dining venue; a local brasserie; and a chip shop – are all representatives of good eating in Chelsea. Each fulfils a different need and the fish and chip shop provides well-cooked, sustainable fish and top-class chips plus a chance to burnish your green credentials. There is a slightly embarrassing video loop of the proprietor on a fishing boat wrestling with monsters from the deep, but then you get to eat them. The fried fish is well done, good batter that ends up crisp so that the fish is steamed within it. If you have never tried gurnard you're in for a surprise and a delicious treat; or there's pollack, line-caught cod, Megrim sole or squid. The chips are large, suitably crisp outside, suitably fluffy within. If you are not after classic fish and chips there are bowl meals – moules, bouillabaisse, spaghetti vongole – and grilled fish options, such as Cornish sardines and sea bass. The décor is modern, service is slick, and the place is packed. Two tiny chip shop niggles: there are no wallies (gherkins) and the home-made tomato ketchup is on the sweet side.

Ealing and Acton

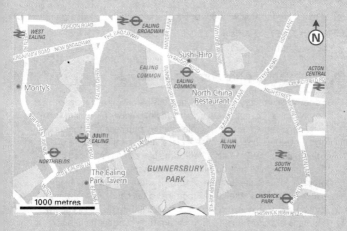

The Ealing Park Tavern

222 South Ealing Road, W5 ■ 020 8758 1879

⊖ South Eailing

🍴 Modern British/gastropub

🕐 Mon 18.00–22.15; Tues to Sat 12.00–15.00 & 18.00–22.15;
Sun 12.00–16.00 & 18.00–21.00

🖰 www.ealingparktavern.co.uk

🖰 all major credit cards ■ 12.5% optional service added

££ starters £5–£7.50 ■ mains £9.50–£15 ■ desserts £5–£7.50
■ lowest bottle price £12.50

✪ Comfortable neighbourhood gastropub

It doesn't seem very long ago when this place was a lager and
football hovel. Then it reverted to its original name, The Ealing Park
Tavern, and settled into a new role as a tidy pub serving rather good
food as it slowly but surely won a place in the local repertoire of
eating places. The Tavern is a handsome place and is founded on
the simple premise that hospitality is important. The bar has two or
three decent real ales and the wine list is short, but gives a fair choice
at accessible prices. The dining room has a tall counter separating it
from an open kitchen and the menu is chalked up on a blackboard.
The menu is a short one, but it is thoughtfully written, it changes
daily and there is something for everybody. Starters may include a
mushroom soup with white truffle oil; wood pigeon Wellington,
bubble and squeak; blue cheese and beetroot tart; or 'nose to tail
suckling pig and foie gras terrine, toast and chutney' – all sound
stuff with dishes making good use of British produce to deliver big
flavours. Main courses are well presented, substantial and seem
pretty good value. There may be roast salmon, mashed potato and
purple sprouting broccoli; beef and ale pie, mash and green beans;
or roast lamb rump, minted chickpeas and babaganoush. Puds are
comforting and comfortable – apple and sultana crumble; chocolate
brownie with vanilla ice cream; or sticky toffee pudding.

Monty's

Ealing Broadway Shopping Centre, 11 High Street, W5

■ 020 8579 4646

⊖ Ealing Broadway

🍽 Indian

🕐 daily 12.00–14.30 & 18.00–23.30

🗐 all major credit cards ■ no service added

££ starters £2.50–£5.95 ■ mains £6–£13.75 ■ sides £3.90
■ desserts £2–£3.50 ■ set meal £15.95 ■ lowest bottle price £12.80

⊗ Iconic Nepalese restaurant

It's a family affair! Bishnu Karki oversees Monty's on Northfield Avenue, while his son Dipendra runs the High Street Monty's. The third family restaurant is called the Usha (named after Dipendra's Mum) and is on the Uxbridge Road. All three are recommended and the menu doesn't vary too much from site to site. The High Street branch is a brisk and busy restaurant characterised by interesting dishes that come in huge portions. The room is bright and modern – no flock wallpaper here – and there's a small mezzanine floor up a flight of stairs. Everything is very fresh, from the poppadoms and chutneys to the platter of salads that arrives while you wait. The menu touches on all the old curry house favourites but the big sellers are the Nepalese dishes. The cooking is top notch, curries are rich and distinctively spiced, and each one is more fascinating than the last. Try the fried lamb tikka – dry and well spiced, or the chilli chicken – complete with plenty of wicked green chilli. At Monty's they are not afraid to give a dish plenty of oomph. Other stand-outs include the Kathmandu dal chicken – the rich sauce is thickened with lentils, a very attractive texture. Even the simplest dishes like the Kathmandu aloo follow the formula – a large portion, well-spiced and very delicious. Leave room for the excellent breads.

→ For branch, see index or website

North China Restaurant

305 Uxbridge Road, W3 ▪ 020 8992 9183

⊖ Ealing Common

🍴 Chinese

🕐 Mon to Thurs & Sun 12.00–14.30 & 18.00–23.30; Fri & Sat
12.00–14.30 & 18.00–24.00

⌁ www.northchina.co.uk

🖻 all major credit cards ▪ 10% optional service added

££ starters £4.50–£6.50 ▪ mains £5.50–£12.50 ▪ sides £2.20–£4.50
▪ desserts £3.80–£6.80 ▪ set dinners £14.50–£20.50
▪ lowest bottle price £12.80

✪ Duck from Peking arrives in Acton

The special Peking duck, which always used to require 24 hours'
advance notice, is now so popular that the restaurant cooks a few
ducks every day regardless. So you don't always have to pre-order.
But then you do, because it is so popular that they cannot guarantee
you'll get one unless you order it. The North China has a 24-carat
local reputation; it is the kind of place people refer to as 'being as
good as Chinatown', which in this case is spot-on, and the star turn
on the menu doesn't disappoint. Unlike most other – upstart, deep-
fried – crispy ducks, the Peking duck here comes as three separate
courses. First there is the skin and breast meat, served with pancakes,
shreds of cucumber and spring onion, and hoisin sauce. Then a fresh
stir-fry of the duck meat with bean sprouts, and finally the meal ends
with a giant tureen of rich duck soup with lumps of the carcass to
pick at. It is awesome. So what goes well with duck? At the North
China familiar dishes are well cooked and well presented. You might
start with barbecued pork spare ribs, or the lettuce wraps, made with
prawn and chicken. For a supplementary main course, prawns in chilli
sauce, although not very chilli, is teamed with fresh water chestnuts
and tastes very good. Singapore fried noodles are powered by curry
powder rather than fresh chilli, but fill a gap.

Sushi-Hiro

1 Station Parade, Uxbridge Road, W5 ▪ 020 8896 3175

⊖ Ealing Common

🍽 Japanese

🕐 Tues to Sun 11.00–13.30 & 16.30–21.00

🗗 cash only ▪ no service added

££ sushi 60p £12 ▪ sashimi platter £40 ▪ sake & beer £2.20

✪ Best-ever sushi

Sushi-Hiro is a very self-effacing sort of restaurant. The sign outside says 'Sushi-Hiro, Japanese Gourmet Foods' and it is absolutely true. When you push open the door you find that half the room is given over to a waiting area for takeaway customers, there's a sushi counter with stools, a handful of tables and that's about it. The menu offers sushi in various guises. You are given a miniature clipboard with a small form to fill in your order and that's when it all gets tricky, as there are 50 or so boxes to tick. The best strategy is to start with the chef's selection of superior nigiri, which brings ten pieces of sushi – tuna, salmon, herring roe, turbot, bass, red clam, scallop, salmon roe, red bream and sweet shrimp. Try them all and then repeat the ones you like the most. The sushi here is very good: the rice is soft and almost warm, the balance between the amount of rice and amount of topping is just about perfect, and the fish is squeakily fresh and very delicious. Or try a piece of eel – very rich, or mackerel – a revelation: it's light and not oily at all. Alternatively, go for pickled plum roll. This is made with rice, pickled plum and shiso leaves, which have an addictive flavour. Or try salmon roe – salty and sticky. Then round things off with a small bowl of rather splendid miso soup, which comes with a couple of little clams lurking in the depths.

Earls Court and
South Kensington

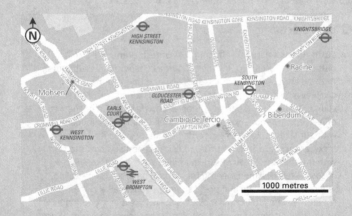

Bibendum

Michelin House, 81 Fulham Road SW3 ■ 020 7581 5817 ♿

⊖ South Kensington

🍴 French

🕐 Mon to Fri 12.00–14.30 & 19.00–23.00; Sat 12.30–15.00 &
19.00–23.30; Sun 12.30–15.00 & 19.00–22.30

🖰 www.bibendum.co.uk

🖶 all major credit cards ■ 12.5% optional service added

££ lunch £25 (2 courses) & £29.50 (3 courses) ■ dinner: starters
£9.50–£19.50 ■ mains £17–£29 ■ sides £3.75–£4.75
■ desserts £8.50–£10 ■ lowest bottle price £17.95

⭐ Comfort food for the comfortably off

This is the restaurant where Simon Hopkinson first made a
big impression and the kitchens are now in the capable hands of
Matthew Harris. When Bibendum opened some decades ago they
used to change the colourway of all the soft furnishings four times a
year to keep pace with the seasons, but now it is just the continually
changing menu that dances to that rhythm. So depending on
when you visit, starters may include omelette Arnold Bennett; black
truffle, leek and Taleggio tarte fine; or Middle White brawn with
eggs au verte. The main course dishes are an alluring combination
of classics and old favourites – 'deep-fried haddock with chips and
tartare sauce' is fish and chips with a serious price tag, but if you are
in the mood what could be nicer than really good fish and chips?
Or how about a whole roast Anjou pigeon with glazed apple and
celeriac? Or calves' tongue and boudin noir with braised cabbage
and grain mustard? Or a grilled veal chop with Roquefort butter?
Puds are in the same vein – a baked chocolate and ginger mousse
cake; caramelised poached pear; or tarte fine aux pommes. The wine
list has something to daunt even the bravest wallet. Service is silky
smooth. Bibendum is a charming, perfectionist, expensive sort of
restaurant.

Cambio de Tercio

163 Old Brompton Road, SW5 ■ 020 7244 8970

⊖ Gloucester Road

🍴 Spanish

🕐 Mon to Fri 12.30–14.30 & 19.00–23.30; Sat 12.00–15.00 &
19.00–23.30; Sun 12.00–15.00 & 19.00–23.00

🖱 www.cambiodetercio.co.uk

🖫 all major credit cards ■ no service added

££ starters £6.25–£14 ■ mains £13.90–£15.50 ■ sides £3.50–£5
■ desserts £4.75–£7 ■ lowest bottle price £17

✪ Exceptional Spanish cooking

One of the big surprises of the past decade has been the rise and
rise of Spain as a gastronomic force. Spanish restaurants were always
known for obsessively hunting down the very best ingredients, but
recently they have somehow added flair, excitement and invention
to the mix and it is very welcome. Cambio de Tercio manages to
showcase all these virtues at once. The cooking is very good here.
You can start with a plate of 'Joselita Gran Reserva' – 100g of Iberico
ham made from the famous pata negra acorn-fed pig, a very princely
and pricey porker indeed. Or there's a red tuna tartare that comes
with pistachio mustard and salmon caviar – delicious and with several
complementary textures; or sardines marinated in cider vinegar; or
Serrano ham croquetas – crisp outside, melting within. Or how about
a new take on the famous Galician dish: at Cambio the octopus
comes with sweet paprika, olive oil and potato cream, and it's very
good indeed. Main courses are also inspired and inspiring, including
slow-roasted leg of baby lamb with confit potatoes; fillets of red
mullet Ronda style; or a dish of oxtail cooked slowly and gently until
the juices caramelise. The wine list is a monster – take your pick
of sixteen fine wines from the Ribera del Duero, or explore other
lesser-known Spanish regions. Service is formal and helpful, and the
restaurant buzzes along until late – very much as it would in Spain.

→ For branch, see index or website

Mohsen

152 Warwick Road, W14 ■ 020 7602 9888

⊖ Earls Court

🍽 Iranian

🕐 daily 12.00–24.00

🖻 cash or cheque only ■ no service added

££ starters £2.50–£3.50 ■ mains £7–£11 ■ desserts £2.50–£3
   ■ dish of the day £7 ■ unlicensed, BYO (no corkage)

✪ Griller thriller, the Iranian way

Just suppose that you are visiting Homebase on the Warwick Road.
Across the road between the two pubs you will see Mohsen, a small,
busy Iranian restaurant. This place looks un-prepossessing but the
food is very honest and delicious. In the window is the oven, where
the bread man works to keep everyone supplied with fresh-from-the-
oven sheets of bread. The bread is terrific and the waiters conspire
to see that it arrives in relays and never has a chance to get cold. The
starters list is largely made up of things to go with the bread. You
must have sabzi, a basket containing fresh green herbs – tarragon,
flat parsley and mint – plus a chunk of feta. Eat it with your bread.
Or there's maast o mouseer, which is a dish of yogurt and shallots.
Or chicken livers cooked with mushrooms. The main courses tend to
revolve around grilled meat – joojeh kabab, for example, is a poussin
which is jointed, marinated, grilled and served on rice. Then there is
chello kabab-e-barg, which is outstanding – a tender fillet of lamb,
flattened and grilled. It's traditionally accompanied by an egg yolk
and is probably Iran's National dish, as it says on the menu 'We only
use the finest baby lamb fillet'. Look out for the dish of the day;
on Wednesday it is kharesh badenjan, a stonking stew of lamb and
aubergines. Drink aromatic Iranian tea from tiny, gilded glasses.

Racine

229 Brompton Road, SW3 ■ 020 7584 4477

⊖ Knightsbridge/South Kensington

🍽 French

🕐 Mon to Fri 12.00–15.00 & 18.00–22.30; Sat 12.00–15.30 & 18.30–22.30; Sun 12.00–15.00 & 18.00–22.00

🗗 all major credit cards ■ 14.5% service added

££ starters £5.75–£13.25 ■ mains £13.25–£21.50 ■ sides £3.25–£5.95 ■ desserts £6–£7.50 ■ set lunch & dinner £16.50 (2 courses) & £18.50 (3 courses) ■ lowest bottle price £15.50

⭐ Homage to traditional French food

Racine goes from strength to strength. It fields something of a foodie 'dream team' – chef Henry Harris and front-of-house Eric Garnier – and the food is French. Not just any old French, but familiar, delicious, nostalgic dishes from the glory days of French cooking. The dining room at Racine is dark brown and comfortable. The service is friendly and Gallic. The prices are reasonable, and haven't crept up too much year on year. It's no surprise that this place is busy enough to make booking an imperative. Henry Harris is a very good cook and his menus are invariably skilfully written. Everything tempts, everything is priced reasonably, and he takes a great deal of trouble to source and buy top-quality seasonal ingredients. To start with, expect simple but glorious combinations such as jambon de Bayonne with celeriac rémoulade; pâté de foie de volaille et fines herbes; melted Raclette, beetroot and caper relish; or a truly wonderful warm garlic and saffron mousse with mussels – light and airy, with a triumphant texture and a delicate taste. Mains continue the 'classical' theme: roast skate with Bordelaise sauce; tête de veau with a well-made sauce ravigote; plus chicken, chops, steak and fish. The dessert menu deals in classics: petit pot au chocolat; strawberries in Beaujolais; and Mont Blanc, which is a rich chestnut purée with meringue and chocolate sauce. The wine list is Francocentric, but merciful – even the smart bottles seem reasonably priced.

Hammersmith and Chiswick

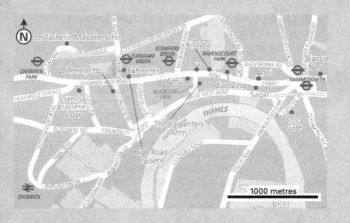

Agni

160 King Street, W6 ■ 020 8846 9191

⊖ Hammersmith/Ravenscourt Park

⦿ Indian

🕐 daily 17.00–23.00

🖰 www.agnirestaurant.com

🗗 all major credit cards ■ 10% optional service

££ starters £3.25–£5.95 ■ mains £6.50–£12.95 ■ sides £2–£4.75
■ desserts £3–£4.50 ■ thalis £10.95–£14.95
■ lowest bottle price £12.50

✪ Ambitious Indian wins awards

King Street Hammersmith has always played host to a number of decent Indian restaurants and, as is the nature of such things, there is a continual turnover, but Agni looks set for a good run. The head chef won his spurs in big-name kitchens like Zaika and Veeraswamy, and the Michelin people have given Agni a 'bib gourmand'. The dining room is bright and modern while the service standards are high. The restaurant's claim is that you can 'discover India through its culinary heritage' and the menu includes a broad spread of regional dishes. Starters are split into vegetarian and non-vegetarian and include some well-made street food delights: Mumbai bhel – puffed rice and Bombay mix; chicken 65 from Hyderabad – chilli-hot chicken wings. Mains include four Hyderabadi biryanis, some of which are 'sealed pot' variety. There is a good selection of vegetarian meals ranging from an indulgent vegetable makhni to okra masala. The 'curry and rice plates' also appeal – Kolhapuri chicken is a rich curry with ginger garlic and red chilli; or there's a seafood moilee from Kerala that teams fish, prawns, squid, mussels and coconut. It's worth trying the thalis, which are large 'build-it-yourself' complete meals. Ordering a Royal thali gets you three appetisers, any of the curry and rice selections, two vegetable dishes, dal and raita, poppadoms, pudina paratha, salad and rice. Agni is a bright place serving above-average regional dishes at accessible prices.

Azou

375 King Street, W6 ■ 020 8563 7266 ♿

⊖ Stamford Brook/Ravenscourt Park

🍴 North African

🕐 Mon to Fri 12.00–14.30 & 18.00–23.00; Sat & Sun 18.00–23.00

🖱 www.azou.co.uk

🗄 all major credit cards ■ 12.5% optional service

££ starters £3.50–£5.95 ■ mains £6.95–£16.50 ■ sides £2.30–£3.95
■ desserts £3.50–£3.95 ■ lowest bottle price £10.50

⭐ North African food, warm welcome

Azou is a small, comfortable, informal North African restaurant
where you can enter into the spirit of things and end up sitting on
the floor on a cushion. It is run by husband-and-wife team Chris
and Chris Benarab, who are most hospitable. The kitchen knows its
business, and the classics – tagines, couscous and brochettes – are
presented with some panache. The menu gets down to business. First
there is a list of kemia, by way of starters. These are the North African
equivalent of tapas and include all the favourites, from dips such
as hummus to various salads hot and cold, and 'briks' from Tunisia,
which are deep-fried filo parcels of potato, tuna and egg. The many
main courses meander on from dishes like mechoui – lamb shank
– to a volley of different tagines served with couscous by way of an
accompaniment. The 'Berber' teams vegetables and chickpeas while
'Fish' combines fish, shellfish and prawns with a gently sour sauce.
The 'Constantine' is made from lamb but has a bit more chilli kick
to it. Or there's the tagine el ain, which is lamb shank with prunes,
apricots and almonds. Onwards to several couscous dishes; you
can have your stodge with merguez, fish or various other options,
all the way up to Couscous Royale, which seems to include almost
everything! Puds are traditional – North African cakes or fruit salad
with ice cream. To drink, there's a sound Moroccan wine and an
interesting beer from Casablanca.

Bianco Nero

206 Hammersmith Road, W6 ■ 020 8748 0212 &

⊖ Hammersmith

🍴 Italian

🕐 Mon to Fri 12.00–15.00 & 18.00–22.00; Sat 18.00–23.00

🖰 www.bianconerorestaurants.com

🖰 all major credit cards ■ 12.5% optional service added

££ antipasti £6.50–£10 ■ salads £5.50–£10.50 ■ pasta £6.50–£11.50
■ mains £16–£18 ■ sides £3.50 ■ desserts £6–£9.50 ■ set meals
(lunch, and dinner between 18.00 and 19.00) £14.50 (2 courses)
£18.50 (3 courses) ■ lowest bottle price £12.50

✪ Italian and aspirational

Since opening in the autumn of 2007 this small, starkly elegant
black and white Italian restaurant has gone from strength to
strength, partly on the back of some good reviews, but mostly
because it offers the local businesses a decent lunch spot. The appeal
is a simple one: this is a neighbourhood Italian but with better
than average cooking, a certain sleek style and Taittinger as house
champagne. The head chef here served time at Al Duca (see p. 128)
and the same sort of tidy regional dishes prevail here. Start with a
warm poached egg with a Parmesan tuille and crisp bacon, spinach
salad. Or how about calamari fritti with a hot and sour red pepper
sorbet, which sounds like a bridge too far but is really good – crisp
squid rings and a tangy-tasty sorbet-salsa. There's a ribollita, which
is a section of salads including pear and walnut with blue cheese. Or
several dual-sized pasta dishes ranging from a chunky number which
teams conchigliette, broccoli and Italian sausage to black and white
tagliatelle with mussels, clams and plenty of garlic. Mains are quite
pricey but done properly. Choose from osso buco on a well-made
saffron risotto; calves liver Veneziana; or grilled tuna with sautéed
spinach. The wine list is short and ungrasping while the puddings
range from the omnipresent tiramisù to warm apple cake. A jolly, and
welcome, new arrival.

The Carpenters Arms

91 Black Lion Lane, W6 ■ 020 8741 8386

🚇 Stamford Brook

🍽 Modern British/gastropub

🕐 Mon to Sat 12.30–15.00 & 19.00–22.00; Sun 12.00 –16.00 & 19.30–21.30

🖵 all major credit cards ■ 12.5% optional service added

££ starters £4–£9 ■ mains £10.25–£15 ■ sides £2.50–£3 ■ desserts £5 ■ lowest bottle price £14.50

⭐ An even-tempered gastropub

Somewhere along the line gastropubs started to believe their own publicity, they morphed into restaurants and their pricing nudged ever upwards. The Carpenters Arms seems to buck that trend and is closer to the true spirit of Gastropubbery than many other new arrivals. The cooking here is accomplished, with a good balance to the dishes, simple presentation and a tolerable price tag. The dining area is small, the kitchen is tucked away and the staff are friendly. The menu offers eight starters and half a dozen mains. It is admirably seasonal and changes from day to day. You may end up choosing between chickpea soup with dandelion; a beetroot, squash, goats' cheese and walnut combination; rock oysters; or crab, Savoy cabbage, red onion, soft-boiled egg and toast – sparkling fresh crab, the brown meat spread on toast. Or go for a very respectable plate of Spanish cured meats. Mains range from a well-made tomato risotto; a couple of chunky wild boar chops with kale; or a pair of roast quail served with chips. Grilled calves' liver, hispi cabbage and cauliflower is a simple dish done well. A large slab of pollock comes with potted shrimps and lentils and is very delicious. Puds are modernist but appealing – affogato al caffe or a bitter chocolate tart. The wine list has a good selection of bottles in the key sub-£30 area. The Carpenters is an asset to the locality – friendly, fairly priced food and wine and good cooking.

Fishworks

6 Turnham Green Terrace, W4 ■ 020 8994 0086

⊖ Turnham Green

🍴 Fish

🕐 Mon to Fri 12.00–14.30 & 18.00–22.30; Sat 12.00–15.00 & 18.00–22.30; Sun 12.00–15.00

🖰 www.fishworks.co.uk

🖬 all major credit cards ■ no service added

££ starters £4.95–£14 ■ mains £9.50–£26 ■ sides £1.95–£2.95
   ■ desserts £4.90–£6.90 ■ fruits de mer £19.95–£24pp
   ■ children's menu £4–£5 ■ lowest bottle price £15.95

✪ Fresh fish and wet fish

There's something spooky about this part of Chiswick – the last few years have seen it turn from middle-class respectable to restaurant gulch. Fishworks is one of the London links in a growing chain and the vibe is right. Inside is a pretty, modern dining room with a gardeny bit at the rear. There's a longish menu and a very long list of specials on a blackboard. From the starters, perhaps the fish soup with traditional accompaniments appeals? Or there may be a dressed Dartmouth crab. Or how about south Devon mussels steamed with white wine, garlic and parsley? Or smoked haddock fishcakes with spinach and Hollandaise sauce? Alternatively, try the 'skate with black butter and capers'. There is a serious fruits de mer menu. And there are 'whole fish – for the table', such as a wild sea bass for two, which can be roast with garlic or baked in a salt crust. Vegetables are simple and good. The bread is good. This is a comfortable place where the fish are both skilfully chosen and skilfully cooked. The wine list is eclectic and there are some interesting bottles at accessible prices. Start with some cold Bayeux cider and look out for the unusual Picpoul de Pinet from the Languedoc – bone dry, white and zingy. Service is friendly and attentive. All in all, a very satisfying place.

→ For branches, see index or website

The Gate

51 Queen Caroline Street, W6 ■ 020 8748 6932

⊖ Hammersmith

🍴 Vegetarian

🕐 Mon to Fri 12.00–14.45 & 18.00–22.45; Sat 18.00–23.00

🖰 www.thegate.tv

🖥 all major credit cards ■ 12.5% optional service added

££ starters £4.50–£6 ■ mains £8.50–£13.75 ■ sides £2.95
   ■ desserts £4.50–£5.50 ■ lowest bottle price £13

✪ Indulgent, senior veggie restaurant

The extraordinary thing about The Gate (which is tucked away
behind the Hammersmith Apollo) is that you hardly notice that it's a
vegetarian restaurant. This is enjoyable dining without the meat. It's
not whole food, it's not even healthy; indeed, it's as rich, colourful,
calorific and naughty as anywhere in town. The clientele is a quiet
and appreciative bunch of locals and pilgrims – it's unlikely that
anyone could just stumble across this hidden-away, former artists'
studio. The airy décor and the high ceiling give it a serene, lofty
feel, which may be The Gate's only nod to veggie solemnities. The
short menu changes regularly, but starters are always well balanced
and attractive. There's usually a tart, like the three-onion tart. Also
excellent are the plantain and sweet potato fritters, which are served
with a sweet chilli sauce. Portions are hearty, so it's a good idea to
share starters in order to pace yourself and sample all the courses.
The mains are generally well executed. Parsnip risotto made with
Arborio rice and finished with Dolcelatte and Parmesan; an aubergine
schnitzel; a trompette and root vegetable ragu; or potato gnocchi
topped with Stilton and served on a bed of Portobello mushrooms.
Puddings range from a splendid prune and Armagnac chocolate
fondant to an apple frangipan, or a steamed date pudding. Those
without a sweet tooth should go for the cheese plate. The drinks list
is extensive, and the wine selection has something for everyone.

High Road Brasserie

162 Chiswick High Road, W14 ■ 020 8742 1717 &

⊖ Turnham Green

🍴 Modern European

🕒 Mon to Fri breakfast 07.00–12.00, lunch & dinner 12.00–23.00; Sat & Sun breakfast 08.00–12.00; brunch & dinner 12.00–23.00; (24.00 on Sat)

🕯 www.highroadhouse.co.uk

🖰 all major credit cards ■ 12.5% optional service added

££ breakfast £3–£8 ■ starters £4.50–£9.50 ■ mains £12–£28 ■ sides £3.50 ■ desserts £6 ■ prix fixe lunch £13 (2 courses) & £16 (3 courses) ■ lowest bottle price £12

✪ Busy, buzzy, brassy Brasserie

When the High Road Brasserie opened its doors for the first time the staff were driven backwards by a wave of customers eager to push their way in. The Chiswickians were waiting impatiently for this place, perhaps because it's part of the Soho House group which has successful operations in Soho, New York – and Shoreditch! Upstairs there is a private member's club and some elite bedrooms, all is chic and all is smart – what's not to like? The Brasserie is a fine example of what a Brasserie should be, a comfortable room dominated by a traditional bar, with brisk but friendly service, a long menu and accessible food. Starters range from simple soups, to omelette Arnold Bennett, eggs Benedict or steak tartare. Under the heading 'salads and sandwiches' you'll find temptations like a smoked eel, ventreche, watercress and horseradish – there's something about the food offering that makes you feel the Brasserie has tried to list everything you might conceivably want. There's a seafood section that goes from oysters to dressed Dorset crab and a whole lobster and chips. There are grills – rib steak, rack of lamb, veal kidneys, rare grilled tuna. Then there are the mains – a whole roast duck, shepherd's pie, or veal Milanese. The cooking is good, presentation is unfussy, there's a long wine list and prices are not excessive. The customer is not infallible, but in this case the happy locals are right to be smug.

Indian Zing

236 King Street, W6 ■ 020 8748 5959   &

⊖ Ravenscourt Park

🍴 Indian

🕐 Mon to Sat 12.00–15.00 & 18.00–23.00, Sun 13.00–16.00 & 18.00–22.30

🖰 www.indianzing.co.uk

🖰 all major credit cards ■ 12.5% optional service added

££ starters £3–£7 ■ mains £7.80–£13.50 ■ sides £2–£5.50
   ■ thalis £13 & £18 ■ desserts £4–£5 ■ lowest bottle price £13

⭐ A modern Indian with vibrant spicing

It is hard to live up to a name like Indian Zing, but chef-proprietor Manoj Vasaikar manages it. Vasaikar (who was well reviewed for his previous restaurant) is not only a good cook, but also a thoughtful one, blending India's regional recipes and traditional ingredients with modern techniques and presentation. Starters include dahi kachori – little pastries filled with a spicy mixture and topped with sprouted beans and yogurt. Or nawabi lamb salli – made from lean minced lamb with fenugreek. The patrani macchi is a real star, a fillet of fish cooked with green herbs and coconut and rolled in a banana leaf. There is even green peppercorn malai tikka, an upmarket chicken tikka, the chicken pieces marinated with green peppercorns and cheese. The main courses are also well done, and for once there is a splendid vegetarian dish: 'tandoori artichoke and paneer in mahi khaliyaa sauce', which is a skewer from the tandoor that features chunks of paneer cheese with a decent chilli rub, baby artichokes and onions. The gravy is heavy with cashew nuts and tomatoes. There's a Malabar chicken curry billed as chilli hot, but coming to table medium, with plenty of coconut milk, mustard seed and curry leaves. The dhansaak is made with dill, pumpkin and lentils and has a good depth of flavour. The kitchen gets the spicing just about perfect in every dish – Indian Zing is what it's called and Indian zing is what you get.

Knaypa

268 King Street, W6 ■ 020 8563 2887

⊖ Ravenscourt Park

🍴 Polish

🕐 Mon to Wed 12.00–15.00 & 18.00–23.00, Thurs to Sun 12.00–15.00 & 18.00–24.00

🌐 www.theknaypa.co.uk

🗄 all major credit cards ■ no service added

££ starters £4.10–£6.95 ■ mains £7.15–£17.90 ■ sides £3
　 ■ desserts £3.50–£3.85 ■ set lunch £5.99 (2 courses)
　 ■ lowest bottle price £10.50

⊗ Lightly polished Polish

Knaypa (Polish for pub) has a foot in both camps. On the one hand there are the old-fashioned, solid, hearty, filling dishes that are traditional in Polish restaurants, while on the other the owners have tried for a more modern and less institutional atmosphere. The result is a friendly, unpretentious ground-floor restaurant with a blond wood floor (somewhat bizarrely studded with red lights) and comfortable red leather chairs. The downstairs dining room is a little more trad and little darker. This isn't a pub as we know it, but the mood is lifted by young and enthusiastic Polish waitresses. As an 'amuse' you get a couple of slices of decent rye bread and a small pot of smalec – this is a lard-heavy pork rillettes and is surprisingly delicious. The starters range from the ubiquitous pickled herrings; to an interesting smoked sheeps' milk cheese; soured rye flour soup with sausage; and borscht – the borscht is well done with a good balance of sweet and savoury and some commendably light veal ravioli. Mains are sterner stuff. There is bigos – hunter's stew with sauerkraut; pierogi – dumplings; stuffed cabbage leaves; and a formidable golonka – an enormous pork shank that comes with a decent mustard sauce and mash. The food is wholesome and good, with a little bit more attention paid to presentation than in many trad Polish restaurants. The range of strong beers is magnificent.

Sagar

157 King Street, W6 ■ 020 8741 8563

⊖ Hammersmith

🍴 Indian/vegetarian

🕒 Mon to Thurs 12.00–14.45 & 17.30–22.45; Fri 12.00–14.45 &
17.30–23.30; Sat 12.00–23.30; Sun 12.00–22.45

🖱 www.gonumber.com/sagar

🖫 all major credit cards ■ no service added

££ starters £2–£3.50 ■ mains £3.75–£6.75 ■ sides £1.50–£4.95 desserts
£2.25–£2.75 ■ lunch special £4.95 (3 courses)
■ thalis £9.95–£12.45 ■ lowest bottle price £10.95

⊙ Clever cooking, stunning vegetarian food

A cheerful restaurant with charming and attentive waiters,
modernist wood-panelled walls, and menu copy boasting that
the chef hails from Udipi in Karnataka, somewhere that has great
resonance in the pantheon of Indian vegetarian cooking. What is
more remarkable is the sheer cleverness of the dishes. This is food
created in what we would see as impossible circumstances, because
the ingredient list seems remarkably short – potatoes, rice and rice
flour, lentils, onions, spinach, cabbage, cheese, ghee – plus the
elements that bring it all together, the magnificent South Indian
spices. You can enjoy a succession of full-flavoured dishes where each
texture and combination of textures is wildly different. Start with
some street food bits and pieces, such as dahi potato puri with the
welcome tang of tamarind – those crisp little puri that you pop into
your mouth whole so that they burst; excellent samosas – well spiced
and with plenty of filling; or try the rasam – a very rich, chilli hot,
lentil soup. From the mains the paper masala dosa is worth ordering
for the spectacle alone: it is huge, paper thin, very crisp, and comes
with a dish of curried potato. The lemon rice is very delicious. The
sag paneer has lumps of cheese in a rich spinach goo. The suki bhaji
is cabbage and onion cooked with coconut. All these dishes have
an astonishing depth of flavour and inspired spicing – it is easy to
overeat here. Very clever cooking indeed.

→ For branches, see index or website

Sam's Brasserie & Bar

11 Barley Mow Passage, W4 ■ 020 8987 0555 &

⊖ Turnham Green/Chiswick Park

🍽 Modern European

🕐 Mon to Fri breakfast/brunch 09.00–12.00; lunch 12.00–15.00;
dinner 18.30–22.30; Sat & Sun breakfast/brunch 09.00–16.00;
dinner 18.30–22.30 (Sun 22.00)

🖰 www.samsbrasserie.co.uk

🖰 all major credit cards ■ 12.5% 'optional' service added

££ starters £4.75–£7.50 ■ mains £9.50–£16.50 ■ desserts £6–£7
■ set lunch Mon to Fri £11.50 (2 courses) & £15 (3 courses)
■ set dinner (18.30–19.30) £13.50 (2 courses) & £17.50 (3 courses)
■ lowest bottle price £13

⭐ Beware the bloody Mary

This Brasserie opened just before the 'High Road' (see p. 422) and
where the latter is chic, Sam's is comfortable; it's a bit cheaper; it's a
bit less flash. Since opening, Sam's has settled comfortably into its own
niche. Sam was formerly manager at Rick Stein's Seafood Restaurant in
Padstow and he has obviously learned a thing or two about matching
the ambience to the customers. So much so that there is already a
second Brasserie in the chain (see page 366). The Barley Mow centre
is the new name for an old paper factory and the large spaces lend
themselves to this modern, comfortable, informal Brasserie. There is
a small gallery that seats 25, which does duty as a private room, and
the dining room proper has a window to the kitchen. The head chef is
Rufus Wickham and his menu manages to combine comfortable with
interesting. A fish soup comes with classic trimmings and is rich and
smooth. There's a Belgian endive, pear and walnut salad. Or linguine
with cherry tomatoes and confit garlic. Main courses range from grilled
Cornish sardines with rocket and gremolata to rump of lamb with
gratin Dauphinoise. The puds are sound – lemon tart; apple crumble;
vanilla pannacotta. Service makes light of the large numbers and is
informal without being slack. The wine list ambles through the familiar
regions with plenty to drink at reasonable prices.

→ For branch, see index

Tosa

332 King Street, W6 ■ 020 8748 0002

⊖ Stamford Brook

🍴 Japanese

🕘 daily 12.30–14.30 & 18.00–23.00, (Sun 22.30)

🖺 all major credit cards except Amex ■ 10% optional service added

££ starters £1.30–£12 ■ mains £5.50–£12 ■ desserts £1.90
■ lowest bottle price £11.50

✪ Friendly people, delicious food

Tosa is a small but very busy Japanese restaurant. Forget that
leisurely seat at the sushi bar: sometimes it seems as if there are
more front-of-house staff than customers and they whirl about with
elegant little platefuls. The whole show is orchestrated by the 'bing
bong' of the lift from the kitchen which gives the place the feel of a
madcap airport lounge in the holiday season. The menu is a long one
and you are encouraged to pillage all sections. This grazing approach
works really well with Japanese food. No more worrying about the
correct etiquette and which dish follows which; just get stuck in.
From the starters try the agedashi tofu – chunks of deep-fried tofu in
a rich soya broth. Or the specials list might yield up something like a
deep-fried soft shell crab. Then there are the soups. And the noodle
dishes. Then there are crisply dry tempura. For me, the stars of the
show come from the robata grill, small skewers each seemingly more
delicious than the last – ox tongue with salt and lemon; crisp chicken
skin; kamonegi (duck breast); and the fabulous shisomaki which
teams shiso leaves with pork tenderloin. Fill out any odd corners with
some sashimi or nigiri sushi. Or perhaps some of the vegetable dishes
like French beans with black sesame sauce to provide a good change
of pace. The food here is delicious. The service is both attentive and
friendly. And whenever you need one, a cold Asahi beer appears as if
by magic.

La Trompette

5–7 Devonshire Road, W4 ■ 020 8747 1836 &

 Turnham Green

🍽 French

🕑 Mon to Sat 12.00–14.30 & 18.30–22.30; Sun 12.30–15.00 & 19.00–22.00

🖰 www.latrompette.co.uk

🖶 all major credit cards ■ 12.5% optional service added

££ lunch Mon to Fri £23.50 (3 courses); Sat £25; Sun £29.50
■ dinner £35.50 (3 courses) & £45 (3 courses plus cheese)
■ lowest bottle price £19.50

✪ Seriously good cooking

La Trompette has put down roots and become something of a local hero, even impressing the Michelin men enough to gain a star in 2008. This state of affairs isn't a great surprise as Trompette is a thoroughbred from the same stable as Chez Bruce (see p. 332), The Glasshouse (see p. 382) and The Square (see p. 105). The dining room is comfortable with a good deal of light oak and chocolate leather on show. The kitchen knows its stuff, so the food is very good, the wine list is comprehensive, the pricing is restrained and the service is on the ball. The prix fixe arrangements are straightforward – it is always comforting to know what kind of bill you are in for as you set off; just about the only supplement is when you add an extra cheese course, something that is well worth your while. The menu changes daily. Presentation is simple, but elegant. Starters may include such delights as tartare of Cornish mackerel with quails' eggs; boudin blanc with Madeira sauce; or seared loin of tuna with a salad of radish coriander, soy and sesame. Mains are rich and satisfying. In the appropriate season you might be offered Royal bream with beurre noisette and mashed potatoes; duck magret with braised Savoy cabbage; roast fillet of beef with shallot purée and oxtail ragout; or breast and leg of poulet noir with potato gnocchi. Puds range from classics such as Valrhona chocolate mousse to coconut sorbet. Enjoy!

Le Vacherin Malcolm John

76–77 South Parade, W4 ■ 020 8742 2121

Chiswick Park

French

Mon 18.00–22.30; Tues to Thurs 12.00–15.00 & 18.00–22.30; Fri & Sat 12.00–15.00 & 18.00–23.00; Sun 12.00–15.00 & 18.00–22.00

www.levacherin.co.uk

all major credit cards ■ 12.5% optional service added

££ starters £6.25–£9 ■ mains £14.50–£21 ■ desserts £4.95–£7 ■ lowest bottle price £14.50

⊗ Francophile English chef does excellent job

It's hard to know how to pigeonhole Le Vacherin. Despite having an English chef (who after some years has at last incorporated his name with that of the restaurant), this is a defiantly French establishment and the menu is littered with nostalgic, rustic dishes – very Elizabeth David. The cooking is good here – well-balanced dishes, intense flavours, good seasoning and a healthy dollop of real passion. The dining room décor is something of a French cliché – it certainly looks the part. And perhaps there's some lingering memory of 1970s fondue, but the starter of a whole baked Vacherin is immensely popular and the kitchen gets through 40 to 50 a week. Apart from the Vacherin itself (served as starter for two, baked with an almond crust), various other opening moves appeal: old-style Burgundy snails with pungent garlic butter; a warm salad of scallops, black pudding and Alsace bacon; or a Gruyère cheese tart. There are a dozen main courses: côte de boeuf sauce Béarnaise; confit Old Spot pork belly and lentils; a whole grilled lemon sole; or shin of veal with saffron risotto. The wine list has some sensibly priced, straightforward bottles – note those from the South West of France. If you get to the dessert course still unswayed by the merits of molten cheese, then opt for one of the classics – fondant au chocolat; île flottante; crème brûlée; or prune and Armagnac tart.

Richmond and Twickenham

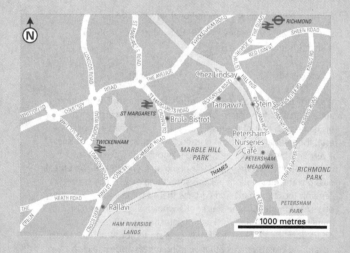

Brula Bistrot

43 Crown Road, Twickenham, Middx ■ 020 8892 0602

⊖ BR St Margaret's

🍴 French

🕐 daily breakfast 08.00–12.00; lunch 12.00–15.00; dinner 18.00–22.00

🖰 www.brula.co.uk

🖶 Mastercard, Visa ■ no service added

££ starters £4.50–£10 ■ mains £10–£22.50 ■ sides £3–£3.50
■ desserts £4.75–£7.75 ■ menus: prix fixe lunch £12.75 (2 courses)
& £14.50 (three courses); prix fixe dinner £17 (3 courses Fri & Sat
18.00–19.00); Sun lunch £15.75 (3 courses)
■ lowest bottle price £12.75

✪ The French quarter of St Margaret's

At the turn of the century, two friends chose St Margaret's as a
locale and, as they were called Bruce Duckett and Lawrence Hartley,
opened a restaurant called Brula. Pretty soon the business had
become so successful that they had to move across Crown Road
into larger premises. Now the Brula Bistrot (the name was enlarged,
in keeping with the new premises) is no longer a cramped affair.
There are large windows with a profusion of rather elegant stained
glass. Thankfully, the food and philosophy have endured – well-
cooked French bistro food, limited choice, low, low prices. Lunch is a
particular bargain. The menu changes weekly, so you might choose
between dishes such as potage du jour; goat's cheese salad; or
terrine de campagne. Then on to fish of the day with mussels and
beurre blanc; a leek and Roquefort quiche; or steak frites. Finally,
you get to decide between tarte du jour, marquise au chocolat, or a
French cheeseboard. All very French. Running alongside is the Bistrot
list, informal à la carte – celeriac remoulade with Bayonne ham; crab
salad; coquilles St Jacques; venison sauce poivrade; or a cassoulet
Touloussiene. The Frenchness even extends to the apéritifs – it's time
for kir, or kir royale. And, should you spurn these blandishments, the
wine list is short and agreeably priced with a good showing at the
cheaper end.

→ For branch, see index or website

Chez Lindsay

11 Hill Rise, Richmond, Surrey ■ 020 8948 7473

⊖ Richmond

🍴 Very French/pancakes

🕐 Mon to Sat 12.00–23.00; Sun 12.00–22.00

🗗 Mastercard, Visa ■ 12.5% optional service added

££ starters £4.25–£10.75 ■ mains £12.70–£27.50 ■ sides £2.75–££3.50 ■ desserts £3.50–£5.50 ■ menu du midi £9.75 ■ set lunch £14.50 (2 courses) & £17.50 (3 courses) ■ set dinner £16.50 (2 courses) & £19.50 (3 courses) ■ lowest bottle price £9.50 cider, £13.75 wine

✪ Breton through and through

At first glance, Chez Lindsay looks rather like Chicago in the 1920s – all around you people are drinking alcohol out of large earthenware teacups. The cups are, in fact, traditional Breton drinking vessels known as bolées, the drink is cider, and Chez Lindsay lists a trio of them, ranging from Breton brut traditionnel to Norman cidre bouché. Most people are attracted to this small, bright restaurant by the galettes and crêpes, though the menu also includes a regularly changing list of hearty Breton dishes – especially fish. It's a place for Francophiles; both the kitchen and the front of house seem to be staffed entirely by Gauls, which in this instance means good service and tasty food. Start with the moules à la St Malo, which are cooked with shallots, cream and thyme. Then you must decide between the galettes or more formal main courses. The galettes are huge buckwheat pancakes, large and lacy, thin but satisfying. They come with an array of fillings: egg and ham; scallops and leeks; Roquefort cheese, celery and walnuts; and 'Chez Lindsay', which is cheese, ham and spinach. The other half of the menu features a good steak frites and lots of fish and shellfish. The 'choucroute de mer' is an interesting dish, containing smoked haddock, salmon and king prawn and served with new potatoes. Or there's the bar grillé – a whole grilled sea bass with salad and new potatoes. Real pud enthusiasts will save themselves for the chocolate and banana crêpe.

Pallavi

1st Floor, 3 Cross Deep Court, Heath Road, Twickenham, Middx
■ 020 8892 2345

⊖ BR Twickenham

🍽 Indian

🕐 Mon to Sun 12.00–15.00 & 18.00–23.00 (24.00 Sat & Sun)

🖰 www.mcdosa.co.uk

🖶 all major credit cards ■ 10% optional service added

££ starters £2.50–£5.95 ■ dosai £3.95–£5.95 ■ mains £4.50–£7.95
■ sides £2.50 ■ desserts £2 £3.50 ■ lowest bottle price £10.95

✪ The soul of Kerala in the heart of Twickenham

This is a small outpost of an extensive Indian restaurant empire.
Pallavi is one of the simplest and the cheapest, and started its days
as a large takeaway counter with just a few seats, then moved over
the road from the original site to smarter premises. The cooking
has travelled well, and still deserves the ultimate compliment – it is
genuinely home-style, with unpretentious dishes and unpretentious
prices. True to its South Indian roots, there is an impressive list of
vegetarian specialities, but the menu features just enough meat and
fish dishes to woo any kind of diner. Start with that South Indian
veggie favourite, the Malabar masala dosa. This huge, crisp pancake
is made with a mixture of ground rice and lentil flour, and is a
perfect match for the savoury potato mixture and chutney. Or try the
delightfully named iddly, a steamed rice cake made with black gram,
which is eaten as a breakfast dish in India. The main dishes are simple
and tasty, and are served without fuss. For unrepentant carnivores,
chicken Malabar or keema methi both hit the spot. But there are
also some interesting fish dishes, including the fish moilee. Veggies
are good, too: try parippu curry – split lentils with cumin, turmeric,
garlic, chillies and onions; or the cabbage thoran – sliced cabbage
with carrots, green chillies and curry leaves. The pilau rice, lemon rice
and coconut rice are tasty, and the parathas are even better – try the
green chilli or the sweet coconut variety.

Petersham Nurseries Café

Church Lane, off Petersham Road, Richmond, Surrey

■ 020 8605 3627 ⟨accessibility symbol⟩

⟨tube⟩ Richmond

⟨food⟩ Modern British

⟨clock⟩ Tues to Sat lunch 12.30–14.30 (Teahouse 09.00–17.00) Sun: lunch 12.30–14.30 (Teahouse 11.00–17.00)

⟨web⟩ www.pertershamnurseries.com

⟨cards⟩ all major credit cards ■ 12.5% optional service added

££ starters £11.50–£14.50 ■ mains £17–£26 ■ desserts £7
■ lowest bottle price £14.50

✪ Heaven for ladies who lunch

Let's get the baggage out of the way first. Yes, this place is hell to find. Yes, the parking is a nightmare. Yes, the expense makes you wince. There…feel better? Now consider the plus points, eating in an elegant greenhouse is delightful (they should get a prize for best ever table display – a jam jar full of blue cornflowers). The short menu (five starters, five mains) is a work of art, enormous care has been taken to source the finest ingredients and then they have been handled with due respect. The standard of cooking is very good. A starter of bresaola is teamed with sheeps' milk ricotta and crushed peas with a mint dressing – the beef is perky and the pea concoction good enough to eat on its own. Or how about a carpaccio of smoked haddock with slivered raw courgettes, crème fraîche and purple basil? Salty, smoky and unctuous all at once. The main courses also deliver plenty of flavour and often it is the accompaniments that stand out, such as a perfectly roast quail comes on a delicious sweet potato mash with spinach. This is adroitly seasoned and very good indeed. A veal chop (again perfectly cooked) comes with a creamy dish of courgettes and some splendid rosemary aioli. Puds are sublime – note the exceptionally good chocolate mousse. Service can be leisurely and thankfully the wine is not priced quite as mercilessly as the menu.

Stein's

The Tow Path, rear of 55 Petersham Road, Richmond, Surrey

■ 020 8948 8189

⊖ BR Richmond

🍴 German

🕐 May–mid-October (depending on weather): daily 12.00–22.00 (opening at 10.00 in high summer); rest of year: Sat & Sun 12.00–22.00

🖥 www.stein-s.com

🗄 all major credit cards except AmEx ■ no service added

££ starters £2.75–£6 ■ mains £7–£8 ■ desserts £3–£4$ ■ lowest bottle price £13.50

⭐ Bavarian beer garden on Thames towpath

This must be the only restaurant in London that has no indoor seating of any kind. In front of the hut that lies 'to the rear of no. 55 Petersham Road' there are enough tables and benches to seat 200. The idea is that Stein's is open until 22.00, with lunch served between noon and 15.00; and breakfast, dinner, or just coffee and cake all fitting into the day as relevant. This place has a restaurant licence so you can only drink alcohol when you order food and then it is limited to beer and wine. The two main draught beers are Paulaner Helles (the golden lager-style one) and Erdinger Weissbier (the cloudy wheat beer one) and are very good. The 'Bavarian specialities' on the menu revolve around sausages, and very good they are, too. The Nuernberger wurst are small and well-spiced cousins to our own chipolatas. The Thuringer bratwurst is a larger, meaty, porkier number. There is kassler – a smoked pork chop; and there's tageseintopf mit semmel – a bargain bowl of stew. The curious will want to try 'currywurst' – either the Theuringer or Polnische sausage with home-made spicy curried sauce. The sausages come with decent sauerkraut and mash. And some dishes can be teamed with bratkartoffeln, which translates as chunky sauté potatoes with attitude. Stein's is an eccentric, jolly sort of place to eat and seems popular with students at the nearby London German School.

Tangawizi

406 Richmond Road, Richmond Bridge, Middlesex

■ 020 8891 3737

BR Richmond

Indian

Mon to Sat 18.30–23.00

all major credit cards ■ no service added

££ starters £4.50–£9.95 ■ mains £6.95–£12.95 ■ sides £3.95
■ desserts £3.25–£4.95 ■ lowest bottle price £11.95

⊕ Modernist Indian restaurant, modernist prices

Tangawizi is the Swahili word for ginger, but despite East African ownership, this restaurant seems conservative menu-wise. You won't find any of the great East African-Asian dishes on a list that in the main confines itself to North Indian favourites. The décor is certainly modern enough, with low lights and mauve walls, angular tables and comfortable chairs. Service is friendly and there is live music on Friday nights. Starters range from chowk ki tikki, potato cakes served with chutneys, to chicken tikka or jhinge coco, large prawns marinated with coconut and ginger before being cooked in the tandoor. Alternatively there are plenty of old favourites like seekh kebab. Portions are large, but perhaps not quite large enough to compensate for prices that would be more at home in the West End than Richmond. Main courses are sound and the spicing is well balanced, although there is an occasional lack of seasoning. Methi wala chicken is a grand dish, rich and simple. Tanghai lamb comes to table in a hollowed-out coconut, the sauce made from curry leaves and coconut (a South Indian excursion). The breads – notably the onion kulcha and the mint paratha – are well done. Tangawizi is an ambitious Indian restaurant, determined to stand out from the late-night curry houses. The food is good, but you do wish that they would throw caution to the wind and add some more interesting East African dishes to the menu.

Shepherd's Bush and Olympia

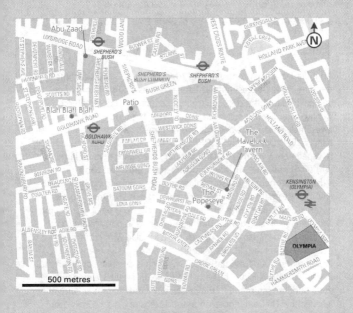

Abu Zaad

29 Uxbridge Road, W12 ▪ 020 8749 5107

⊖ Shepherd's Bush

🍴 Syrian

🕒 daily 12.00–23.00

🖰 www.abuzaad.co.uk

🖨 all major credit cards except AmEx ▪ no service added

££ starters £2–£3 ▪ mains £4–£11 ▪ desserts £2 ▪ no alcohol

⭐ Damascus in W12

Abu Zaad is a busy, popular and friendly place, but it bears the trappings of its success lightly. It still serves as a pit stop for coffee and pastries and the cooking arrangements are still dominated by a charcoal grill and a full-sized bread oven. The food is good and awesomely cheap. The décor teams rich greens with decorative metal panels – very Damascene. This may be the cheapest place in London to experiment with meze. Here, a trifling sum will get you a large portion of makanic – meaty, chipolata-sized sausages; baba ganouj – delicious aubergine mush; foul mesdames – boiled fava beans with chickpeas, tomato and lemon juice; or hummus. A stunning haystack of tabbouleh comes with spankingly fresh chopped parsley and mint. Ordering a dish called falafi brings four crisp and nutty falafel. You must try the fattoush, a fresh, well-dressed salad with croûtons of deep-fried flatbread. In fact, all meze you order will arrive with a basket of delicious fresh flatbread. The food is described on the menu as 'Damascene Cuisine', but most of these dishes are claimed by every Middle Eastern chef. Drink a glass of carrot and apple juice and feel healthy. The menu goes on to list dozens of main courses, from rich casseroles to charcoal grills, and they are all reasonably priced. There's a good case for not bothering with a main course here – simply order seven or eight meze between two.

Blah Blah Blah

78 Goldhawk Road, W12 ■ 020 8746 1337

⊖ Goldhawk Road

🍽 Vegetarian

🕐 Mon to Sat 12.00–14.30 & 18.30–22.30 (Fri & Sat 22.45)

🖰 www.gonumber.com/2524

🗗 cash or cheque only ■ no service added

££ starters £4.95–£5.45 ■ mains £9.95–£11.95 ■ desserts £5.45
■ unlicensed, BYO (£1.45 corkage pp)

✪ Very sound veggie resto

Blah Blah Blah is an old-time veggie haven, and has décor to
match. The floors, tables and chairs are wooden, there are blinds
rather than curtains, and the only decorations of note are driftwood
and old iron lamps. Add wallpaper music and the echoing noise
levels become formidable. Legend has it that an old chap called Paul
McCartney was overheard here asking for the music to be turned
down. The menu casts its net widely and you can expect dishes
with all manner of influences, but all of them reasonably priced
and generously portioned. Among the starters might be cream of
asparagus soup; plum tomato and mozzarella gallette; a Greek
salad; and a spicy Indian potato cake filled with curried cauliflower,
carrots and peas. Dodging over to the Windies, there may be plantain
fritters made with raisins, ginger and sweet potato and served with a
tomato, chilli and pineapple sauce. Main courses are similarly eclectic.
Choose from mixed wild mushroom risotto; yam chimichanga (a stew
rolled in a multigrain tortilla); 'roast vegetables gougere', which is
choux pastry pieces containing roast butternut squash, broccoli and
Emmental cheese; or a Middle Eastern pie filled with new potato,
chilli and tomatoes. Puds are rewarding: glazed lemon tart; rhubarb
and apple charlotte; banana toffee and pecan crumble; and the
'wicked' chocolate truffle tart.

The Havelock Tavern

57 Masbro Road, W14 ■ 020 7603 5374

Kensington Olympia

Gastropub

Mon to Sat 12.00–14.30 & 19.00–22.00; Sun 12.00–15.00 & 19.00–21.30

www.thehavelocktavern.co.uk

all major credit cards except AmEx ■ no service added

££ starters £4.50–£8 ■ mains £8.50–£13 ■ desserts £4.50
   ■ lowest bottle price £12.10

Honest gastropub

The Havelock is a pub that is at ease with itself and thoroughly at home in the midst of a sea of jolly expensive houses. If you want to go out for a smart meal in W14 you have probably got the wherewithal to hail a taxi and head for any restaurant in Central London — ergo a neighbourhood eatery here needs to be well grounded. The Havelock Tavern has a large bar and an outdoor area to the rear. The tables and chairs are mis-matched, the seating is crowded and everything is refreshingly normal. There's decent beer to be had — both bitters and lagers — and the wine list is surprisingly eclectic. The food is good, with an emphasis on fresh-looking platefuls with big flavours. The menu changes from service to service as dishes are added or run out. This translates as good, seasonal cooking. Starters might include a chilled gazpacho; deep-fried whitebait with aioli and lemon; or a beltingly good bruschetta of duck livers, bacon, rocket and green beans — great flavours and textures, one large toast sodden with the juices from the livers. The starters merge into the mains, which includee salad of grilled asparagus, marinated peppers and goats' cheese; Toulouse sausages, Borlotti beans, bacon, tomato and spinach; or crispy lamb shoulder with flatbread plus a cucumber and coriander salad — great contrasting textures. Puds are sound — chocolate Nemesis; lemon and blueberry panna cotta.

Patio

5 Goldhawk Road, W12 ■ 020 8743 5194

⊖ Goldhawk Road

|O| Polish

🕑 Mon to Fri 12.00–15.00 & 18.00–23.30; Sat & Sun 18.00–24.00

🗗 all major credit cards ■ no service added

££ starters £3.50–£6.80 ■ mains £8.50–£14.90 ■ desserts £3.50
■ set menus: lunch & dinner £15.99 ■ lowest bottle price £11.50

✪ Polish hospitality writ large

A former opera singer, the ebullient Eva Michalik and her husband
Kaz have been running this restaurant for more than a decade and
little changes from year to year. At Patio you get good, solid Polish
food in a friendly, comfortable atmosphere and for a relatively small
amount of money. And this little restaurant is a people-pleaser –
you can just as easily come here for an intimate tête-à-tête as for
a raucous birthday dinner. There are two floors; downstairs feels a
little cosier and more secluded. The set menu (available at lunch and
dinner) is Patio's trump card. For a surprisingly small sum, you get a
starter, main course, dessert, petits fours – and a complimentary shot
of vodka. Starters may include plump and tasty blinis with smoked
salmon; wild mushroom soup; Polish ham; or herrings with soured
cream. Everything is fresh and carefully prepared. For mains, there's
a good selection of meat, fish and chicken dishes – the scallops in
dill sauce, when available, are outstanding. Or you might try one of
the traditional mains like chicken Walewska; beef goulash; bigos –
hunter's stew; or lemon sole. Be prepared, too, for high-octane puds,
such as the Polish pancakes with cheese, vanilla and rum – the fumes
alone are enough to send you reeling. Also good is the hot apple
charlotka with cream. For those after more variety, the à la carte
offers further choice, and for not a great deal more money.

The Popeseye

108 Blythe Road, W14 ▪ 020 7610 4578

⊖ Hammersmith

🍴 Steak

🕐 Mon to Sat 19.00–22.30

🖰 www.popeseye.com

🗗 cash or cheque only ▪ 12.5% optional service added

££ steaks £10.95–£47.45 ▪ sides £3.95 ▪ desserts £4.95 –£5.75
▪ lowest bottle price £11.50

✪ Steak eaters – red in tooth and claw

Just suppose you fancy a steak – a good steak, and perhaps a glass (or bottle) of decent red wine to go with it. You're interested enough to want the best, probably Aberdeen Angus, and you want it cooked simply. The Popeseye is for you. All the meat here is 100% grass-fed Aberdeen Angus and the restaurant is a member of the Aberdeen Angus Society. The dining room is small, and things tend to get chaotic. As to the food, there is no choice: just various kinds of steak and good chips, with home-made puddings to follow. Oh, and the menu starts with the wine list. You choose what you want to drink, and only when that's settled do you choose your steak – specifying, of course, the cut and the size (and they come very big here), and how you want it cooked. Now, about these steaks. Popeseye comes in 6oz, 8oz, 12oz, 20oz and 30oz, as does sirloin, and fillet. You get excellent chips whichever steak you order and you can add a side salad to assist your vitamin intake. The puddings come from the home-made school of patisserie – such delights as apple crumble; sticky toffee pudding; and lemon tart. The wine list is an ever-changing reflection of what can be picked up at the sales and represents good value. There are fine clarets and Burgundies, plus the best of the Rhône, Australia, Argentina, Chile and Spain – and there are also two white wines on offer for people who have lost the plot.

→ For branch, see index or website

Southall

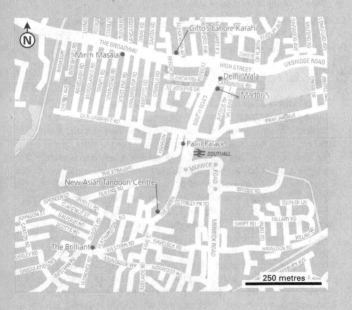

The Brilliant

72–76 Western Road, Southall, Middx ■ 020 8574 1928 ♿

⊖ BR Southall

|●| Indian

🕐 Tues to Fri 12.00–14.30 & 18.00–24.00; Sat & Sun 18.00–23.30

🖱 www.brilliantrestaurant.com

🖫 all major credit cards ■ no service added

££ starters £2–£16 ■ mains £4.50–£14 ■ sides 50p–£4.50
   ■ desserts £3–£4.50 ■ 4-course set menus (for parties of 10 or more)
   £17.40pp ■ lowest bottle price £9

✪ Splendid East African-Asian dishes

The Brilliant is a Southall institution. For more than thirty years the Anand family business has been a non-stop success and it is now a bustling 250-seater over two floors that is continually updated to make it, in the words of the proprietors, 'More like the West End'. The food at The Brilliant is East African-Asian, and very good indeed, richly flavoured and well balanced. To start with, you must try the butter chicken. A half-portion will do for two people as a starter. This dish is an enigma: somehow it manages to taste more buttery than butter itself – really delicious. There's also jeera chicken, rich with cumin and black pepper. And chilli chicken, which is hot, but not quite as hot as it used to be. If you're in a party, move on to the special meal section – these come in two portion sizes, suggested for three people and five people. Methi lamb, masaladar lamb, and palak chicken are all winners. Or there's the wonderfully good keema peas – a very rich curried mince with peas. Honest food. Alternatively, choose among the single-portion curries, which include masala fish, a curry of unimaginable richness with good firm chunks of boneless fish. As well as good rotis, the bread list hides a secret weapon, the kulcha. Hot from the kitchen, they are amazing – it's best to order a succession so that they don't go cold. Some dishes have been reformulated to make them healthier, but it's better to indulge yourself in the butter chicken and kulchas.

Delhi Wala

11 King Street, Southall, Middx ■ 020 8574 0873   ♿

⊖ BR Southall

🍽 Indian/vegetarian

🕐 daily 08.00–22.00

🗗 all major credit cards except AmEx ■ no service added

££ starters 75p–£4.50 ■ mains £2.50–£5 ■ sides 60p–£4.50
   ■ desserts £1–£3.50 ■ no alcohol

✪ Bright and bustling Veggie with sweetshop

What is it about the lighting in these Indian quick food places?
The myriad light bulbs make eating here like sitting in the beam of
a searchlight. Delhi Wala is a very practical kind of place, utilitarian
tables and chairs, tiling (bright), polished floor (bright) and cheap,
fresh veggie dishes that come to table briskly from the kitchen at
the back. From the 'snacks freshly prepared' try the samosas —
plump and spicy; the onion bhajis   savoury and crisp; the bhel
puri — something of a star of many different textures, all brought
together with a sweet and sour tang; or the paneer tikka, chunks
of cheese with a savoury twist and that familiar red outside. For
'specials' read main courses. There's a substantial dish of Bombay
aloo, which is nicely spiced, or a chana bhatura, which is a rich dish
of chickpeas with that most self-indulgent of Indian fried breads.
Simple breads like the stuffed paratha are also well done here. If
there is a dish you would like that is not on the menu, it is worth
asking the helpful waiters; such an enquiry brought very good stuffed
bitter gourds (karela). There should also be a portion of vegetable
biryani underpinning your order — this is a very good dish, rich and
well flavoured. At the end of the meal brave souls with an ultra
sweet tooth will turn their attentions to the sweets, which occupy
the display running down the left-hand side of the room. A friendly
restaurant serving good, cheap vegetarian food.

Gifto's Lahore Karahi

162–164 The Broadway, Southall, Middx ■ 020 8813 8669 &

🚇 BR Southall

🍴 Indian

🕐 Mon to Thurs 12.00–23.30; Fri to Sun 12.00–24.00

🗄 all major credit cards ■ no service added

££ starters 90p–£4.90 ■ mains £4.90–£9 ■ sides £1–£2.50
　■ desserts £1–£3.30 ■ unlicensed, BYO (no corkage)

✪ Magnificent Indian food factory

There is no more competitive place for an Indian restaurant than Southall, which makes it all the more remarkable that Gifto has not only been busy for so many years, but continues to expand and add yet more covers. Downstairs is a barn of a room with the open kitchen running along one side and serried ranks of tables on the other. There's a newer room upstairs, but both are busy and there is often a queue at the door on Saturday or Sunday. Gifto's Lahore Karahi specialises in freshly grilled, well-spiced meats and simple curries. The food is good, cheap and takes a minimal time to get from chef to diner. Whatever you add to fill out your order, you should start with bread. The stuffed paratha is good – thin and almost flaky, and both the plain naan and the Peshwari naan are delicious. Accompany them with an order of chicken tikka, seekh kebab or the splendid tilapia fish – whole, marinated and cooked in the tandoor. The curries are served in a karahi here and taste very fresh and vibrant. The saag gosht is exemplary, the spinach melting down to make a rich sauce. Also good are the butter chicken, and the karela gosht – lamb and chunks of bitter melon in an intensely flavoured sauce. Either drink the various freshly squeezed juices or bring your own supplies of alcohol. Service is quick and efficient.

Madhu's

39 South Road, Southall, Middx ■ 020 8574 1897   &

⊖ BR Southall

⦿ Indian

🕐 Mon & Wed to Fri 12.30–15.00 & 18.00–23.30; Sat 18.00–24.00 &
Sun 18.00–23.30

🗃 all major credit cards ■ no service added

££ starters £5–£16 ■ mains £9–£10 ■ sides £1.50–£10
■ desserts £3.50–£5.50 ■ menu: 4-course lunch & dinner £20
■ lowest bottle price £9

✪ Very plush resto, very good food

Both Sanjay Anand and his restaurant Madhu's have collected a
hatful of awards. In 2007, however, these were all eclipsed by a well-
deserved MBE, and there is a new spring in the step of the waiters
at this slick establishment with its proud red M. The food here is very
good and the whole operation is polished, from the smart white
asymmetric china to the serried ranks of gleaming cutlery. There is
even Louis Roederer Cristal on the wine list. Take heart: the cooking
has not lost its way. The food here is predominantly East African-
Asian, and is well spiced with good, full-on flavours – thank goodness
nothing has been toned down. Starters are pricey, but portions are
good. Try the famous butter chicken: very tender, very delicious.
Or there are the lamb chops – well spiced and juicy. Main courses
also come in large portions. Masala fish is a hunk of tilapia in a rich
tomatoey sauce. The simple dishes are well made – sag gosht is a
good choice, lamb cooked with fresh spinach and agreeably spicy.
The vegetable section hides some treasures: bhune karele, a bitter
gourd stuffed and then oven-roasted, is a particularly fine and vibrant
dish. Breads are good, particularly the bhatura, which is a fluffy cross
between chapati and doughnut. If you can avoid the allure of the
Roederer Cristal, you'll find Tusker and Whitecap beer. Make sure that
they are cold.

Mirch Masala

171–173 The Broadway, Southall, Middx ■ 020 8867 9222 ♿

⊖ BR Southall

🍴 Indian

🕐 daily 12.00–24.00

🗐 all major credit cards ■ no service added

££ starters £2–£8 ■ mains £6–£14 ■ sides 70p–£6.50
■ desserts £1.50–£3.50 ■ unlicensed

✪ Modern restaurant, modern Pakistani food

The original Mirch Masala is still plying its trade in Norbury, South London, and the second branch is busy in Tooting, but this imposing restaurant in Southall has taken pride of place as the flagship. The other branches were the kind of establishments where customers raved about 'food so good' that they could forgive any amount of scruffiness. But this resto is a smart affair: new chairs, stone floor, big windows, smart open kitchen. Prices have gone up a little, but the menu is the same and the cooking still tastes fresh and feisty. Be careful to specify how hot you want your dishes to be. As you sit down you get a pappadum and a plate of cucumber and raw onion. From the starters the best choice is to stick to the 'non-vegetarian warmers'. Seek kebabs, chicken tikka and fish tikka are good. The lamb chops are very good – good crispy bits and plenty of fresh bread stuffed with onions. The vegetarian dishes are also strong here – look out for the karahi butter beans methi. There is a new range of 'deigi' dishes, which is a kind of steam-roasting, but the simple karahi curries cooked to order are too good to miss. Very fresh, with plenty of fresh herbs and clean flavours, they include karahi ginger chicken, karahi methi gosht and, best of all, karella gosht, which is lamb with bitter melon. The breads are good and the rice dishes sound. Cheap, fresh food, served quickly and without fuss.

→ For branches, see index or website

New Asian Tandoori Centre

114–118 The Green, Southall, Middx ■ 020 8574 2597

⊖ BR Southall

🍽 Indian

🕓 Mon to Thurs 09.00–23.00; Fri to Sun 09.00–23.30

🗗 cash or cheque only ■ no service added

££ starters £3.50–£5.50 ■ mains £4–£8 ■ sides £1.50–£3.50
   ■ desserts £1–£3 ■ lowest bottle price £10

✪ Cheap and cheerful Indian food palace

The New Asian Tandoori Centre is enough to puzzle the most
exalted branding consultant. In 2006 it was called the New Asian
Tandoori Centre, (but with 'Roxy Restaurant' etched onto the
windows). Now the menu is headed Roxy Restaurant and the NATC
bit is a mere strapline. No matter, of the three dining areas (posh,
ordinary and takeaway, from left to right) pick the middle way.
Service is friendly and, except for the tandoori dishes, the food arrives
briskly. The menu offers the kind of strongly flavoured food you
would expect in a Punjabi café. Start with good jeera chicken, rich
with cumin, or simple savoury kebabs: chicken or lamb. Or there's
a vegetable pakora. The boneless fish tikka is stunning. With the
rather good breads in support (chapattis, bhaturas, naans), a few
starters and grilled meats could easily make a meal. But it would be
a pity to miss out on the main course dishes. The menu is split into
two halves: vegetarian and non-vegetarian. In the veggie section try
a good bhindi dish of fine soggy aubergines; Bombay aloo; chana
dal, a delicious rich yellow chickpea sludge; dal makhani; or a curry
made with karela, bitter melon (the latter two only at the weekend).
Meat-eaters will enjoy the butter chicken; the bhuna chicken; the
economically named lamb curry; and the bhuna lamb that is served
only on Saturday and Sunday.

Palm Palace

80 South Road, Southall, Middx ■ 020 8574 9209

⊖ BR Southall

🍴 Sri Lankan

🕐 daily 12.00–15.00 & 18.00–23.30

🖯 all major credit cards ■ no service added

££ starters £2.50 ■ mains £5.50 ■ sides £4.50 ■ desserts £2.50–£4.50
■ lowest bottle price £10

✪ Sri Lankan better-than-café

The Palm Palace may be short on palms, and it is not palatial by
any manner of means, but the food is great. This is the only Sri
Lankan restaurant among the restaurant turmoil that is Southall,
and the menu features a great many delicious and interesting dishes.
As is so often the case with Sri Lankan food, the 'drier' dishes are
particularly appealing, and there is a good deal of uncompromising
chilli heat. The dining room is plain but comfortable, service is friendly
and attentive. For a starter, try the mutton rolls – long pancake rolls
filled with meat and potatoes. Or the fish cutlets, which are in fact
spherical fishcakes very much in the same style as those you find in
smart West End eateries, but better spiced and a tenth of the price.
Move on to a 'devilled' dish: mutton, chicken or, best of all, squid
– these dishes combine spices with richness very well. There was a
time when every curry house in the land featured Ceylon chicken, but
here you'll find a short list of real 'Ceylon' curries, including mutton:
they're good, if straightforward. Try the chicken 65. The name is said
to refer to the age of the chicken in days; any younger and it would
fall apart during cooking; any older and it would be too tough. The
hoppers (Sri Lankan pancakes) are good fun: string hopper, egg
hopper, milk hopper. Try a simple vegetable dish as well. Sag aloo
brings fresh spinach and thoughtfully seasoned, well-cooked potato.

→ For branch, see index or website

Index of branches

Cây Tre 243

Vietnamese
Branch at:
Viet Grill, 58 Kingsland Road, E2
  tel 020 7739 6686

Club Gascon 218

French
Branches at:
Cellar Gascon, 59 West Smithfield,
  EC1
  tel 020 7600 7561
Le Cercle, 1 Wilbrahim Place, SW1
  tel 020 7901 9999
Comptoir Gascon, 61–63
  Charterhouse Street, EC1
  tel 020 7608 0851

Côte 364

French
Branch at:
123 Wardour Street, W1
  tel 020 7287 9280

Dehesa 158

Spanish
Branch at:
Salt Yard, 54 Goodge Street, W1
  tel 020 7637 0657

E & O 114

Asian eclectic
Branches at:
Eight over Eight, 392 King's Road,
  SW3
  tel 020 7349 9934
XO, 29 Belsize Lane, NW3
  tel 020 7994 3474

Eight over Eight 394

Asian eclectic
Branches at:
E & O, 14 Blenheim Crescent, W11
  tel 020 7229 5454
XO, 29 Belsize Lane, NW3
  tel 020 7994 3474

The Fish Club 334

Fish
Branch at:
57 Clapham High Street, SW4
  tel 020 7720 5853

Fishworks 420

Fish
Branches at:
177 New Kings Road, SW6
  tel 020 7384 1009
134 Upper Street, N1
  tel 020 7354 1279
89 Marylebone High Street, W1
  tel 020 7935 9796
54 Northcote Road, SW11
  tel 020 7228 7893
57 Regents Park Road, NW1
  tel 020 7586 9760
188 Westbourne Grove, W11
  tel 020 7229 3366
13/19 The Square, Richmond, TW9
  tel 020 8948 5965

Gourmet Burger Kitchen
337

Burgers
Branches at:
331 West End Lane, NW6
  tel 020 7794 5455
333 Putney Bridge Road, SW15
  tel 020 8789 1199

131 Chiswick High Road, W4
  tel 020 8995 4548
49 Fulham Broadway, SW6
  tel 020 7381 4242
15–17 Hill Rise, Richmond
  tel 020 8940 5440
50 Westbourne Grove, W2
  tel 020 7243 4344
200 Haverstock Hill, NW3
  tel 020 7443 5335
88 The Broadway, Wimbledon,
  SW19
  tel 020 8540 3300
15 Frith Street, W1
  tel 020 7494 9533
84 Clapham High Street, SW4
  tel 020 7627 5367
35 Haven Green, Ealing, W5
  tel 020 8998 0392
121 Lordship Lane, East Dulwich,
  SE22
  tel 020 8693 9307
Unit 4, Condor House, St Paul's
  Church Yard, EC4
  tel 020 7248 9199
163–165 Earls Court Road, SW5
  tel 020 7373 3184
13–14 Maiden Lane, WC2
  tel 020 7240 9617
107 Old Brompton Road, SW7
  tel 020 7581 8942
45 Greenwich Church Street, SE10
  tel 020 8858 3920
44/46 The Brunswick Centre, WC1
  tel 020 7278 7168
Unit 24, Jubilee Place, Canary
  wharf, E14
  tel 020 7719 6408
45 Topsfield Parade, Tottenham
  Lane, N8
  tel 020 8347 5241
160 Portobello Road, W11
  tel 020 7243 6597

Unit 2a, Tower Place, EC3
  tel 020 7929 2222

Hache 264

Hamburger
Branch at:
329–331 Fulham Road, SW10
  tel 020 7823 3515

Hamburger Union 25

Burgers
Branches at:
4–6 Garrick Street, WC2
  tel 020 7279 0412
25 Dean Street, W1
  tel 020 7437 6004
341 Upper Street, N1
  tel 020 7539 4436
1 South End Road, NW3
  tel 020 7794 7070
64 Tottenham Court Road, W1
  tel 020 7636 0011
325 Charing Cross Road, WC2
  tel 020 7839 8100

Harrison's 366

Modern British
Branch at:
Sam's Brasserie, 11 Barley Mow
  Passage, W4
  tel 020 8987 0555

Istanbul Iskembecisi 250

Turkish
Branches at:
Zara, 11 South End Road, NW3
  tel 020 7794 5498
Kazan, 34–36 Houndsditch, EC3
  tel 020 7626 2222
93–94 Wilton Road, SW1
  tel 020 7233 7100

Index of restaurants by cuisine

Modern European

Modern French

Index of restaurants by name

Nobu 99

Japanese
19 Old Park Lane, W1
tel 020 7447 4747

The Norfolk Arms 54

Gastropub/tapas
28 Leigh Street, WC1
tel 020 7388 3937

**North China
Restaurant** 408

Chinese
305 Uxbridge Road,
W3
tel 020 8992 9183

Northbank 208

Modern British
Millennium Bridge, One
St Paul's Walk, EC4
tel 020 7329 9299

Number 12 55

Modern Italian
12 Upper Woburn
Place, WC1
tel 020 7693 5429

Nyonya 120

Malaysian/Chinese
2a Kensington Park
Road, W11
tel 020 7243 1800

O

Odette's 269

Modern European
130 Regent's Park
Road, NW1
tel 020 7586 8569

Olley's 351

Fish & chips
67–69 Norwood Road,
SE24
tel 020 8671 8259

One O One 66

French/fish
Sheraton Park Tower,
101 William Street,
SW1
tel 020 7290 7101

O's Thai Café 277

Thai
10 Topsfield Parade, N8
tel 020 8348 6898

P

The Painted Heron
399

Indian
112 Cheyne Walk,
SW10
tel 020 7351 5232

Palki 121

Indian
44 Golborne Road,
W10
tel 020 8968
8764/0393

Pallavi 433

Indian
1st Floor, 3 Cross Deep
Court, Heath Road,
Twickenham, Middx
tel 020 8892 2345

Palm Palace 450

Sri Lankan
80 South Road,
Southall, Middx
tel 020 8574 9209

Papillon 400

French
96 Draycott Avenue,
SW3
tel 020 7225 2555

**Paradise – by way
of Kensal Green** 314

*Modern British/
gastropub*
19 Kilburn Lane, W10
tel 020 8969 0098

El Parador 270

Spanish/tapas
245 Eversholt Street,
NW1
tel 020 7387 2789

good food tastes better with TIO PEPE

TIO PEPE

JEREZ
XERES SHERRY

Fino Muy Seco

PALOMINO
FINO

www.gonzalezbyass.es

'One useful tip as you work your way through the many restaurants in this, the largest ever, edition of the Guide: there is no better precursor to a good meal than a glass of chilled Tio Pepe – a drink that could have been designed specifically for sharpening the appetite and fine tuning the taste buds. Cheers!'

Charles R Campion